RACISM
AND SOCIAL INEQUALITY
IN CANADA
Concepts, Controversies and Strategies of Resistance

Vic Satzewich, Editor
McMaster University

THOMPSON EDUCATIONAL PUBLISHING, INC.
Toronto

Copyright © 1998. Thompson Educational Publishing, Inc.
14 Ripley Avenue, Suite 104
Toronto, Ontario, Canada M6S 3N9
Tel (416) 766–2763 / Fax (416) 766–0398
email: thompson@canadabooks.ingenia.com

We acknowledge the financial support of the Government of Canada through the Book Publishing Industry Development Program for our publishing activities.

Canadian Cataloguing in Publication Data

Main entry under title:

Racism and social inequality in Canada

Includes bibliographical references.
ISBN 1-55077-100-0

1. Racism — Canada. 2. Canada — Race relations. 3. Equality — Canada.
I. Satzewich, Victor Nicholas, 1961-   .

FC104.R355   1998   305.8'00971   C98-931222-4
F1035.A1R32 1998

Copyedited by Elizabeth Phinney.
Cover painting by Karolina Malek, 1998.

Printed and bound in Canada on acid-free paper.
1 2 3 4   04 03 02 01 00 99 98

Contents

List of Contributors

Anton Allahar is Professor of Sociology at the University of Western Ontario. He has written a number of books, including *Class, Politics and Sugar in Colonial Cuba* (1990); *Generation on Hold: Coming of Age in the Late 20th Century* (1994); *Sociology and the Periphery* (1995); *Richer and Poorer: Social Inequality in Canada* (1998).

Raymond Breton is Professor Emeritus of Sociology at the University of Toronto and a Fellow of the Royal Society of Canada. Among his recent publications are *The Illusion of Difference: Realities of Ethnicity in Canada and the United States* (C.D. Howe Institute, 1994, with Jeffrey Reitz) and *Why Meech Failed: Lessons for Canadian Constitutionmaking* (C.D. Howe Institute, 1992).

Tania Das Gupta is Associate Professor in the Sociology Department of Atkinson College at York University. She is the author of *Racism and Paid Work* (1996) and *Learning from Our History: Community Development by Immigrant Women in Ontario* (1986). Her current research is on homework in the South Asian community and on poisoned work environments.

Scott Davies is Associate Professor of Sociology at McMaster University. His main research interest is in the sociology of education, focusing on educational stratification, transitions from education to employment, and school politics. He has published in many international journals and is a member of the editorial board of *Sociology of Education*. Also, with Neil Guppy, he has written *The Schooled Society: Changes and Challenges in Canadian Education* (Statistics Canada/Nelson).

George J. Sefa Dei is Associate Professor in the Department of Sociology in Education and Equity Studies at the Ontario Institute for Studies in Education of the University of Toronto and is currently the Head of the Centre for Intergrative Anti-Racism Studies. He is currently completing a major research project on best/exemplary practices of inclusive schooling in Ontario public schools.

Thomas Dunk is Associate Professor of Sociology at Lakehead University. He is the author of *It's A Working Man's Town* (McGill-Queen's University Press, 1991). His current research examines the relationships between class, race and environment in identity.

Neil Guppy is Professor of Sociology and Associate Dean of Arts at the University of British Columbia. His research interests focus on education, especially social choice and educational attainment. Along with Scott Davies, he has just written *The Schooled Society: Changes and Challenges in Canadian Education* (Statistics Canada/Nelson).

Carl E. James teaches in the Faculty of Education at York University. His research and teaching interests examine issues related to urbanization, youth, class, gender, and racism. He is the author of *Seeing Ourselves: Exploring Race, Ethnicity and Culture* (Thompson Educational, 1995).

Della Kirkham is a Doctoral candidate at Carleton University in Sociology. Her area of interest is political sociology and her current research is on the role of the federal state in the formation and reformation of Canadian national identity.

Peter S. Li is Professor of Sociology at the University of Saskatchewan. He is also in charge of the Economic Domain in the Prairie Centre of Excellence for Research on Immigration and Integration. He is author of many articles and books. His most recent books are *The Chinese in Canada,* Second Edition (1998) and *The Making of Post-war Canada* (1996).

Edite Noivo teaches in the Department of Sociology, Université de Montreal. Author of *Inside Ethnic Families: Three Generations of Portuguese-Canadians* (McGill-Queens' University Press, 1997). She is a minority-group scholar whose research interests include racism, ethnic identities, immigrant families, and inter-racial couples.

J. Rick Ponting is Professor of Sociology at the University of Calgary. He is the co-author (with Roger Gibbins) of *Out of Irrelevance* (1980) and his most recent book is *First Nations in Canada: Perspectives on Opportunity, Empowerment, and Self-Determination.*

Jeffrey G. Reitz is Professor of Sociology and Research Associate at the Centre for Industrial Relations at the University of Toronto. His most recent book is *Warmth of the Welcome: The Social Causes of Economic Success for Immigrants in Different Nations and Cities* (Boulder, CO: Westview Press, 1998). Currently, he is completing a comparative study of the economic status of immigrants in Canada and foreigners in Germany.

Vic Satzewich is Associate Professor in the Sociology Department at McMaster University. He is the author of *Racism and the Incorporation of Foreign Labour* (Routledge, 1991) and *First Nations: Race, Class and Gender Relations* (Nelson, 1993, with Terry Wotherspoon). His current research is on the Ukrainian diaspora.

Alan Simmons is Associate Professor of Sociology and a Fellow of the Centre for Research on Latin America and the Caribbean at York University. His research concerns international migration in the Americas, immigration to Canada from less-developed countries, and Canadian immigration policy. His most recent book is *International Migration, Refugee Flows and Human Rights in North America: The Impact of Trade and Restructuring* (Center for Migration Studies, Staten Island, 1996).

Steven Small teaches in the Department of African-American Studies at the University of California at Berkeley. He is currently writing a book on Blacks of mixed African and European origins in Jamaica and Georgia during slavery. His most recent book is *Racialized Barriers: The Black Experience in the United States and England during the 1980s* (Routledge, 1994).

Acknowledgments

This book, which started out as a good idea for a "quick" project, has had an extraordinarily long history. It has followed me around for six years, through my work at four universities in three different provinces. Some day I will write a book about this book. In the meantime, though, I would like to thank each of the contributors for the time, effort and thought they put into their chapters and for sticking with this project for so long. It has been nothing short of a privilege for me to work with a group of such fine and decent colleagues. I would also like to thank Keith Thompson of Thompson Educational Publishing for his professionalism, his suggestions for improving the coverage of topics and for his interest in publishing this book. Linda Mahood, who trained as a sociologist but is now a historian and master military strategist, lets me win at *Risk: The Game of World Domination* once in a while in order to protect my fragile male ego from getting too bruised. She has lived with this project for as long as I have. She managed to restore my sense of humour during some hectic times even though she was burdened with her own research commitments. My two kids, Jack Satzewich and Lucy Satzewich, kept bugging and distracting me for the whole time that this book has been in preparation, so any errors, mistakes, oversights, faults, contradictions, silences, omissions or other problems can be blamed on them. Still, I hope they don't grow up too fast.

For B. Singh Bolaria, Peter Li and Bob Miles,
in partial repayment of outstanding debts.

Introduction

This book is about race, racism and social inequality in contemporary Canada. The study of racism is now firmly entrenched within academic research agendas in the social sciences and humanities (Henry et al., 1995). Scholarly funding agencies, such as Heritage Canada's Canadian Ethnic Studies Program and the Canadian Race Relations Foundation, have begun to display an increased willingness to fund research on various aspects of racism. The term *racism* is also used routinely in public debate. It is now common to read a newspaper or hear a newscast in which an individual, an idea, an institution or a social practice has been called racist. In the House of Commons, for example, Prime Minister Chrétien called Reform Party Member of Parliament Robert Ringma a racist for his comment that an employer should have the freedom to fire a black or gay person if their presence was turning away customers. Statistics Canada was called racist for its collection of data on the racial makeup of the Canadian population for the 1996 census. A proposed change to Canadian immigration policy that would require all future immigrants to speak either English or French has been called racist because it is claimed that this measure will surreptitiously limit the abilities of non-Europeans to enter the country. In 1993, the Toronto producers of the musical *Show Boat* were condemned as racist because of their intention to put on a production that contained a range of early twentieth-century negative stereotypes about African Americans. The *Into the Heart of Africa* exhibit at the Royal Ontario Museum in 1990-91 was called racist for what critics felt was its distorted interpretation of colonialism and its failure to present an African perspective on colonialism (Henry et al., 1995).

The ease with which racism is now invoked to label and describe a whole range of individuals, events, ideas or social institutions is, in many ways, a positive development. Historically, many Canadians have been reluctant to admit that they, their ideas and their behaviours have contributed to the social marginalization, denigration and inferiorization of others based on the negative evaluation of "race" difference. Furthermore, one of our most enduring national myths is that there is less racism here than in the United States. A close examination of the historical record (Bolaria and Li, 1988), and a recent comparative study (Reitz and Breton, 1994), suggests that Canadians do not have anything to be smug about. Racism was an important part of the process of state formation in this country (Ng, 1988), and the dichotomy between a supposedly multicultural Canada and an American melting pot appears to be significantly overdrawn. In such a context, admitting that racism is a problem in society can lead to greater self-understanding and to positive change. This is particularly so if allegations and accusations of racism are accompanied by sober and non-defensive reflection, analysis and debate about how well certain ideas, behaviours and institutional practices fit with the values of freedom, equality, respect and fairness that most Canadians cherish. In other words, to be able to engage in social debate about the meaning of race and racism, and the impact of racism on individuals and institutions, is a sign not only of a healthy democracy but also of individual and societal maturity.

One of the troubles, however, with the term *racism* is that it is both a sociological concept and a political epithet. Few words in the English language carry the same negative connotations. Ironically, even those individuals and organizations who by any objective definition espouse racist ideas tend to deny that they are racist. A study conducted in the United States in the late 1980s, for example, showed that even public supporters of the Ku Klux Klan denied that they were racist (cited in Reitz and Breton, 1994). Hard core racists often distance themselves from the label and few wear "racist" as a badge of honour (Barrett, 1987:331). There is, moreover, perhaps no better way to publicly discredit someone than to call them a racist. To be called a racist is to be labelled as outside the pale of civilized society and debate, as someone whose ideas are not worthy of serious consideration (Miles, 1993). Using the term racism in public and political life is, therefore, not always intended to be the beginning of a consciousness-raising exercise that will ultimately lead to greater understanding; rather it is a way of silencing individuals and groups, and a way of closing off public debate surrounding complex, controversial or unpopular ideas, policies or practices.

Racism cannot always, nor should it always, be discussed dispassionately. At the same time, though, despite the increased ease with which an individual or institution is labelled as racist, the term tends to be used without much precision or rigour by the general public, the media, or politicians. This ambiguity means there is a danger associated with the way that racism is sometimes cavalierly hurled as an epithet of abuse. If racism is a label that is applied indiscriminately (no pun intended), and without precise meaning and supporting evidence, its power as both a political category and a sociological concept may become undermined.

One of the more difficult social and sociological challenges that arises in this context is to be able to develop an approach that is able to analyze the complex and multifaceted manifestations of racism in Canada without using the term racism in such a broad fashion that it looses all specificity and meaning. People advocate or oppose certain ideas, policies and practices for many different reasons. Some of those reasons may genuinely reflect explicitly stated, or implicitly held, racist attitudes, but some may also reflect certain political and philosophical differences about the way that society should operate. Small "l" liberalism, small "c" conservatism, small "s" socialism or any other political ideology, all carry different ideals about how societies should operate, the nature and legitimacy of social inequality, and what, if anything, should be done about social problems. Each of these ideologies may moreover make certain implicit and explicit assumptions about the nature of race and the position of minority groups in society. In this context, it is vitally important to know why and how certain groups of people articulate certain kinds of ideas and whether those ideas genuinely stem from racism or whether they stem from different philosophical assumptions about the world.

Similarly, social institutions emerge and operate on the basis of a combination of explicitly stated goals and more informal sets of ideas and practices. The way that social institutions work also reflects complex power relations, where groups of people with more power, whether they are social classes, genders or races, are better able to impose their will on those institutions than others. In other words, some social structures and ideas can legitimately be termed racist and analyzed as such, but it also has to be possible, at least conceptually, to make a distinction between a racist and a non-racist social institution or idea. Conceptual clarity, definitions and empirical evidence are therefore vitally important to academics, and they should be as important to others as well. At the risk of appearing pedantic, it seems to me that if a claim is made that someone or something is racist then that claim needs to be demonstrated through a combination of theoretical and empirical analysis rather than simply *asserted* as a fact in and of itself.

Let me say from the outset that my caution about the use of the term *racism*, and my wider interest in conceptual clarity, is not meant to devalue anyone's experience of racism, nor the wider significance of racism in Canadian society. I am convinced that racism is an everyday reality for many Canadians, that racist ideas and practices affect individuals and groups in very real ways and that racism is something that is not only a part of Canada's history, but an important aspect of current circumstances.

This book is not primarily about race and racism in Canadian history. The emphasis here is on current realities, concerns and debates. For readers interested in the analysis of historical manifestations of racism in Canada, there is a solid body of work to which one can refer (see Bolaria and Li, 1988; Roy, 1989; Winks, 1971; Anderson, 1991; Avery, 1995; Titley, 1986; Walker, 1980; Shaffir and Levitt, 1987). At the same time, however, some historical context is important.

Until the 1960s, racism was a fairly blatant and obvious aspect of Canadian society. Racism played a role in shaping individual attitudes, state policies and institutional arrangements in the economy, the political system and civil society.

Historically, the two policy fields that contained the most visible manifestations of racism were immigration and Indian affairs.

The history of Canadian immigration is, in part, a history of particular forms of inclusion and exclusion (Avery, 1995). Race, along with class, gender, sexual preference, political orientation and health status formed a basis for the selection and rejection of potential immigrants. As John Porter put it in his 1965 classic *The Vertical Mosaic*, one of the prerogatives of the dominant English and French charter groups in Canada was to decide "what other groups ... [were] to be let in and what they ... [would] be permitted to do" (Porter, 1965:62). The groups who were let into the country, as well as the groups who were barred and/or discouraged from entering, were both subject to racialized evaluations of their cultural, political and economic capacities. The racist hierarchy of desirability that was part of Canadian immigration policy until the 1960s ranked the capacities of potential immigrants, and was responsible for assigning groups to particular niches in the economic order of Canada.

Racist exclusions in immigration policy were, therefore, quite common. Until the 1960s different groups were subject to various forms of exclusion. In the case of people from China, the head tax (which was first introduced in 1885 and pegged at fifty dollars per person and subsequently raised to one hundred dollars in 1900 and five hundred dollars in 1903) and the Chinese Immigration Act of 1923 were based explicitly on the idea that Chinese people were racially inferior and that they caused problems wherever they settled (Li, 1988). Sometimes racist exclusions were masked for diplomatic reasons. The Continuous Passages Regulation implemented in 1908 was aimed at stopping the flow of immigration from India. While the regulation was couched in non-racist language and therefore made no mention of the alleged racial inferiority of people from India, the intention was nevertheless to bar Indians from emigrating to Canada. In a seemingly innocuous fashion, the regulation stated that anyone wishing to come to Canada had to do so via one continuous sea journey. India, however, did not have direct steamship connections to Canada at the time, and so travellers from India had to take two separate sea journeys. Non-racist language was used in this context, in part because Canadian officials were concerned that an explicitly racist immigration regulation which barred people from India would have negative consequences for "our" British cousins in India. After all, British colonial policy was accompanied by the rhetoric of a "free and equal" empire. Since both Canada and India were parts of this empire, an explicitly racist immigration regulation in Canada had the potential of undermining British authority in India (Bolaria and Li, 1988).

Racialized evaluations also determined who was let into the country, and figured in defining what was suitable work for different immigrant groups. The term *race* was applied to a wide range of European groups who would not now be considered to be "racially" different from the two dominant charter groups (Woodsworth, 1972). Such beliefs, though, had a real impact on the placement of immigrants into Canadian society. For example, while Ukrainian immigrants were generally regarded as racially and culturally inferior to immigrants from northern and western Europe, at the turn of the century government officials such as Clifford Sifton nevertheless felt that they did have a place in an expanding society. Sifton's comment in 1923 that "I think a stalwart peasant in a sheepskin coat, born on the soil, whose forefathers have been farmers for ten generations, with a stout wife and half a dozen children is good quality" (cited in Lehr, 1991:38) suggested that Ukrainian men and women were racially suited to the heavy, backbreaking work involved with pioneering in the Canadian west. Similar kinds of evaluations characterized immigration officials' views of the labour market capacities and capabilities of Italians, Portuguese, Poles and other European groups well into the 1950s (Iacovetta, 1992).

The federal government's dealings with status Indians during the last half of the nineteenth and first half of the twentieth centuries is the other policy field that contained unabashedly racist assumptions and practices. Nineteenth century legislation governing Indians and land reserved for Indians was replete with racist assumptions and stereotypes concerning the cultural, if not biological inferiority, of Indians. Two of the precursors of the *Indian Act* of 1876 were the 1857 *Act for the Gradual Civilization of the Indian Tribes* and the 1859 *Civilization and Enfranchisement Act*. The titles of these pieces of legislation clearly suggest, in a racist fashion, that Aboriginal people were viewed as uncivilized human beings whose cultures were decidedly inferior to British culture, and who required considerable coaching and guidance before they could be brought up to the level of Europeans (Satzewich and Wotherspoon, 1993).

Racism was, though, not only confined to the titles of government legislation. Cultural and religious practices of Aboriginals were regarded as retrograde, and in need of not only transformation but complete elimination (Pettipas, 1995). The residential school system established in the late nineteenth century was based on the racist assumption that Aboriginal childrens' family and community life was culturally bankrupt. The best way to re-socialize the children, so it was thought, was to separate them from the corrupting influence of family and community and place them in boarding schools some distance from their homes. Aside from being taught about the salutary effects of hard manual labour, boys and girls in these schools were also taught to despise their appearance, language, culture, religion, family and community (Miller, 1996).

Indian people were also denied various kinds of civil, economic and political rights that other Canadians took for granted. Status Indians could not vote in federal elections until 1960. They were granted provincial voting rights in different provinces throughout the 1950s and 1960s; the last province to allow Indians the right to vote was Quebec in 1969, a time frame which is well within the living memory of many Indian people. Indian people were also required by law to seek permission from the federal government to sell any crops or commodities that were produced on reserve land. While the rationales underlying these various policies and practices were complex, they were, in part, based on the racist assumption that Aboriginal people had a child-like nature and needed the help and protection of benevolent government officials who had their best interests at heart. While many of the more blatantly racist elements of the Indian Act have now been eliminated, it remains a highly paternalist document that continues to disempower Indian people and communities.

Finally, it is important to remember that racism in Canadian history was not confined to the level of state policy. In Canada, there was also a significant level of what Essed (1991) calls "everyday racism": put-downs, degradations and denials of human dignity that groups of people were subjected to in their everyday lives. Examples of everyday racism are legion. There were signs posted outside of restaurants and public parks in Toronto in the 1930s saying, "No Jews or Dogs Allowed" (Levitt and Shaffir, 1987). Jews were not allowed to play at certain public golf courses and were known to be kicked off courses when clubhouse officials were alerted to their presence. Black people were denied service in certain restaurants in Canada until the 1960s, and restrictive covenants in wills and real estate transactions meant that in some neighbourhoods home owners could not sell their property to Jews and/or Blacks (Henry et al., 1995). Since racial discrimination was not illegal in Canada at that time, groups subject to racist practices could do little to change the situation.

Canada in the late 1990s is in many ways a very different place from the Canada that existed in the 1920s, or even the 1950s and 1960s. It is possible to empirically trace the slow abandonment of official racism in government policy in the 1960s and 1970s, the growth in importance of human rights codes and legislation and the changing attitudes of Canadians towards various ethnic and racial groups. Racial discrimination was prohibited by the Canadian Bill of Rights in 1960. Canada officially abandoned racial criteria for the selection of new immigrants in the mid-1960s, when the points system was introduced. The official discourse of Canadian Indian policy shifted in the 1950s away from the language of assimilation and towards more politically neutral terms like integration, which arguably had fewer racist connotations. The 1982 Charter of Rights and Freedoms prohibits discrimination on the grounds of "race, national or ethnic origin, colour [or] religion" (among other factors), provides for equality before and under the law and establishes the constitutional legality of affirmative action and equity programs in order to address problems of discrimination.

It is clear that when considering state policy, Canada is a fundamentally different place now than it was half a century ago. However, certain troubling questions remain. For example, how far have these policy changes permeated other aspects of Canadian society? Have the changes in legislation necessarily translated into changes in both individual and institutional behaviour? And to what extent have these policies been successful in curbing discrimination and racism?

Surveys that try to measure the nature and extent of racist attitudes are inconclusive on these questions, in part because of the lack of a clear definition of what constitutes racism, and in part because of the variety of ways in which racism is operationalized by researchers. Certainly, few Canadians now admit to believing in the biological inferiority and superiority of groups of people. A 1990 survey conducted by Decima Research Ltd. found, for example, that 90 percent of Canadians agreed that "all races are created equal." Some portion of the remaining 10 percent could legitimately be termed racist, because they disagreed with the statement. Others however, did not know (which also probably qualifies as a form of racism), or did not answer the question (cited in Reitz and Breton, 1994:67-68).

Other sociologically informed public opinion surveys point to a variety of opinions about minority groups and minority relations in Canada. Some of the attitudes of Canadians could certainly be described as racist, although it is unclear whether the attitudes are based on a belief in inherent biological inferiority of certain groups or on the negative evaluation of cultural difference. In the early 1980s, a Gallup poll asked a sample of Canadians to respond to a wide range of statements about various racial issues. In the survey, 19 percent of respondents agreed that "riots and violence increase when non-whites are let into a country"; 21 percent disagreed with the statement that "non-white immigration has made Canada a culturally richer country"; 14 percent agreed that "racial mixing violates the teachings of the Bible"; 12 percent agreed that "I would cut off all non-white immigration to Canada"; 28 percent agreed with the statement "I don"t mind non-whites but I'd rather see them back in their own country"; and 31 percent claimed that they "would support organizations that worked towards preserving Canada for whites only." When the results of the survey were released at the Race Relations and the Law Conference in Vancouver in 1982, many felt that the results showed cause for concern about increasing racial intolerance in Canada.

Social distance studies also suggest that Canadians display varying levels of "comfort" when it comes to interacting with members of different ethno-cultural and religious groups. A 1991 study conducted by The Angus Reid Group showed, for example, that Canadian-born respondents indicated greater levels of "comfort" when interacting with Canadians of British, Italian, French, Ukrainian, German and Jewish origin. Respondents reported significantly less "comfort" when interacting with Canadians of West Indian Black, Moslem, Arab,

Indo-Pakistani, and Sikh origin or religion (Angus Reid Group, Inc. 1991:51). These findings are consistent with research on the prestige rankings of various ethno-religious groups, which also place Europeans at the top of prestige scales and various "non-white" and non-Christian groups near the bottom.

If the survey results are somewhat inconclusive about the extent and prevalence of racist attitudes and discrimination in Canada, the biographies and autobiographies of Black, Aboriginal and other minority Canadians paint a less ambiguous picture of the nature and significance of racism in contemporary Canada. Clifton Ruggles in *Outsider Blues* offers a poignant description of the subtle and not-so-subtle slights, attitudes, looks and practices which constantly remind him that for many people he is not a true "Canadian" even though his ancestors came to Canada over three hundred years ago because of their loyalty to Britain. Cecil Foster's (1996) account of the meaning of being Black in Canada is a biting condemnation of the way that racist exclusions, stereotypes and practices have an impact on all Black people in Canada. He argues that regardless of class background and gender, and whether they are first, second or third generation or the descendants of Loyalists, Black people face a certain set of common experiences of racism that help to bind them together. Patricia Monture-Angus (1995) in *Thunder in My Soul: A Mohawk Woman Speaks* describes the pain associated with the everyday experiences of racism, the repeated assaults on her identity from not only the media but also from the halls of academe, and the way that the understanding of Aboriginal peoples' position in Canada is often laden with ethnocentric and racist assumptions.

The recognition that racism is a fundamental aspect of our history, that a certain portion of Canadians do hold racist attitudes and beliefs and that many people believe that racism is a fundamental aspect of the way that Canadian society is organized, gives rise to at least two important, and difficult, sociological questions. Does racism continue to inform and structure how our institutions operate, and what does racism mean in contemporary Canadian society? In different ways, the chapters in this book try to provide answers to these questions. They also try to provide the reader with some conceptual tools and empirical evidence that can be used as a basis for discussion and debate about the meaning and significance of race, racism, racialization and social inequality in contemporary Canada. The chapters do not simply recount examples of racist ideas and racist practices, but also seek to sociologically analyze those ideas and practices. Collectively, the chapters in this volume analyze the social and structural conditions which give rise to various forms of racism, the extent to which racism permeates the way that certain social institutions operate, how groups of people have organized against racism and the ways that racism is linked to class, gender and ethnicity in Canada.

The reader should, however, be forewarned. This book will no doubt be a disappointment for those looking for simple answers to these complex questions and for those who are looking for the final word on whether Canada is indeed "a racist society." The authors in this collection do not agree on the significance of race and racism in contemporary Canada. Some see race and racism as a fundamental organizing principle of our society and of certain institutional spheres; others see racism as more situational, subtle and muted in its forms and consequences; others point to the significance of the racialization of certain aspects of Canadian society, but do not necessarily see the racialization of social life to being equivalent to racism; and yet others argue that allegations of racism in certain institutional spheres tend to be overplayed at the expense of class differences, and that Canadian society is much more open and equal than is often thought.

Some of the referees who evaluated this manuscript before publication were particularly troubled by the latter arguments. They found them to be "offensive" and to reflect "neo-conservative" thinking. This kind of political abuse meted out to scholars who venture to say, in effect, that the emperor may not be wearing any clothes, is a troubling development in academic life. I think it is far more useful to think of these disagreements as reflecting differing approaches to the definition of racism, its measurement and analysis. The reader will find in the chapters in this volume a mix of quantitative, qualitative, textual and theoretical analysis; detailed case studies and statistical analysis of nation-wide Census and other data. Based on these differing styles of sociological research, the authors sometimes arrive at quite different conclusions about the meaning and significance of race and racism in contemporary Canada. This is not a sign of poor scholarship, bad faith, or I might add, a weak editorial hand on my part. Rather it is a sign of healthy debate in which race and racism are subject to various kinds of sociological analysis. If you find the chapters in this book raise more questions than they answer, if they make you mad enough (or "offend" you enough) to go out and seek more information and research on racism in Canada, and if they contribute to further thought and debate about the meaning and significance of race and racism, then I will consider the time reading them well spent.

The first three chapters in this volume try to set a conceptual and comparative context for the discussions of the meaning and significance of racism in contemporary Canada. In chapter 1, I critically evaluate some of the key concepts that appear in later chapters. I analyze the various ways that the concepts of race, racism and racialization have been defined and analyzed within sociology, and discuss some of the ways that sociologists have conceptualized the links between racism, class and gender relations. In chapter 2, Jeffrey Reitz and Raymond Breton tackle head-on the issue of whether racism in Canada carries less social significance than it does in the United States. In this chapter, Reitz and Breton are interested in developing an empirically rigorous and truly comparative approach to understanding racism in Canada. They argue that Canadians and Americans are, on balance, more similar than they are different when it comes to attitudes and behaviour towards racial minorities. This is not a comforting conclusion given the way that we tend to think of ourselves as being so different from Americans.

Chapter 3 is written by Steven Small, a sociologist at the University of California in Berkeley. Small is one of the leading analysts of race and racism in the United States and Britain, and makes a consistently strong case for the use of "the racialization problematic" as a way of studying race, racism and discrimination. This is a conceptual framework derived from a combination of symbolic interactionism and political economy. His chapter deals with the issues of race, racialization and racism in the United States and is included in this book because much of the imagery about race and racism in Canada is derived from interpretations of the American situation. There is also a spill-over effect into Canada of some of the American cultural politics of race. Canadians were seemingly as well versed about the politics of the O.J. Simpson trial as many Americans; there were "riots" in Toronto in April of 1992 after the Rodney King verdict was reached in the United States; and Aboriginal youth gangs in Winnipeg have incorporated some of the symbols, argot and mannerisms of American inner-city street gangs (Roberts, 1996). Small negotiates through a variety of conceptual and empirical issues, not only to assist in clarifying the meaning of race and racism and help us to understand the way that American society operates, but also to shed light on what is, and what is not, particular about the meaning and significance of racism in Canada.

The next five chapters are concerned with the analysis of race and racism within certain institutional settings in Canada. Emphasis in this section is placed on unravelling the links between race and racism and wider sets of class and gender relations within Canadian immigration policy and administration, the labour market, the education system and the justice system. As some of the chapters in this section note, it does not make sense to talk about institutional racism without at the same time recognizing that institutions in Canada also operate on the basis of, and allocate resources and rewards to people based on, gender attributes and class background.

Chapter 4, "Racism and Immigration Policy" by Alan Simmons, carefully delineates the kind of evidence that is required to support the argument that racism continues to characterize Canadian immigration policy. As he notes, 1962 was a benchmark year in Canadian immigration history insofar as the Canadian government officially abandoned country of origin—which was the main signifier of race—as a basis for immigrant selection. Questions remain, however, about the extent to which racial biases still exist within Canadian immigration policy, control, selection and administration. After a careful review of the available evidence, he characterizes Canadian immigration policy as neither blatantly and obviously racist nor anti-racist. Instead, Simmons argues that, while economic objectives have clearly taken priority during the past thirty years, there is still a space for what he calls neo-racism to play a role in the formulation and implementation of immigration policy.

Chapter 5, by Peter Li, is an analysis of the social and market value of race. The Canadian economy is widely recognized to be characterized by inequalities of class and gender, but more contested is the claim that it differentially evaluates people on the basis of the colour of their skin. Li uses 1991 Census data to argue that the Canadian economy places a market value on skin colour, such that those defined as non-White suffer an income penalty while most White Canadians receive an income premium.

Chapter 6, "Race and Canadian Education" by Scott Davies and Neil Guppy, contains an expression of caution over what they see as an overplaying of the extent of racism in Canadian schooling, both historically and at present. They suggest that current educational attainments of Canadians are shaped by a complex of factors stemming from the wider context of race relations, economic prospects and cultural identity of groups of people. They argue that the empirical evidence for the existence of institutional racism in Canadian schools is in fact limited. While they recognize that students in schools may be subject to racist slurs and attitudes in both the classroom and the playground, they question whether racism has the widespread negative consequences for student achievement with which it is often attributed. Using contemporary debates about multicultural schooling and school choice, they also raise hard questions about the recent racialization of Canadian education and the wisdom of adopting race-conscious approaches to teaching and learning in Canada.

Chapter 7, "'Up to no Good': Black on the Streets and Encountering Police" by Carl James, explores the relationship between Black youth and police in southern Ontario. His chapter is particularly concerned with analyzing how Black youth have come to understand and interpret the way that police stop, question and search them in public places such as streets and shopping malls. He shows how various racialized stereotypes inform the nature and extent of police discretion, and how stereotypes that Black youth are "up to no good" become a self-fulfilling prophecy. James also presents a fresh analysis how "the street" is differently understood and experienced by youth and by police, how their different understandings of what should go on in the street result in conflict and friction and how the street is becoming a site of contestation between police and Black youth.

Chapter 8, "Racism in Justice: Perceptions," is a selection from the Commission on Systemic Racism in the Ontario Justice System. The chapter deals with perceptions that Ontarians have of racism in the justice system. In particular, the chapter presents the results of specially commissioned opinion surveys that examine whether the residents of what was formerly Metro Toronto believe that judges treat all people fairly, and whether members of the legal profession expressed concerns over the issue of racism in the justice system. The Commission found, among other things, that there was a widespread perception on the part of Black, Chinese and White Torontonians that judges do not treat people fairly and that they discriminate on the basis of race; that there is substantial variation among justice professionals in their perceptions of racial discrimination in Ontario's courts; and that there exists strong resistance by some judges and lawyers to any suggestion of racial discrimination in criminal courts in the province.

The next four chapters analyze the expressions of racism by selected social groups. As Stuart Hall and others note, racism is not a static ideology or set of social practices but rather takes on specific meaning in different circumstances. The forms, expressions and meanings of racism vary on the basis of those who articulate and put into practice racist ideas, as well as on the basis of those who are the particular targets of those ideas and practices. These chapters emphasize that what exists in Canada is not so much *racism*, but rather a range of socially and historically specific *racisms*. Thus, the expressions of racism need to be analyzed in their historical and social specificity, which in turn takes into account variables such as class, ethnicity and political interests.

Chapter 9, by Tom Dunk, is entitled "Racism, Ethnic Prejudice, Whiteness and the Working Class." His chapter is concerned with one of the central, yet in Canada underresearched, problems in the sociology of race and racism; namely the meaning and significance of working-class racism. Dunk argues that while there can be no doubt that racism and ethnic prejudice are important elements of working-class culture, the same essentialist thinking that underpins race and ethnic prejudice is operative in the way that members of the working class are often portrayed. He presents a comprehensive and critical review of various theoretical approaches that have tried to analyze working-class racism. For Dunk, the difficult conceptual task is to explain racism within the working class without simply reproducing negative stereotypes about working-class culture. Edite Noivo, in "Neither 'Ethnic Heroes' nor 'Racial Villains': Inter-Minority Group Racism" (chapter 10) is concerned with the equally complex question of why minority groups who have been racialized in the past now themselves help reproduce racist understandings of newer immigrant groups. In particular, Noivo's interest is in explaining the paradox associated with the articulation of racism and the practice of discrimination on the part of those "White ethnics" who themselves were subject to racism and discrimination after their arrival in Canada. Using data collected among Greek and Italian immigrants in Montreal, she cautions against simplistic dichotomies between "racists" and "racialized," and suggests that they are often the same people. She concludes with an analysis of why it is so difficult for racialized minorities to form common identities and strategies as a way of combatting racism.

Chapter 11 is entitled "The Reform Party of Canada: A Discourse on Race, Ethnicity and Equality" and is authored by Della Kirkham. Kirkham focuses her attention on the Reform Party as one of the relatively new voices on the Canadian political landscape. While certain individual members of the Reform Party have articulated blatantly racist (and homophobic) sentiments over the past several years, Kirkham focuses on the more difficult question of the extent to which racialized and racist discourses inform Reform Party policies on multiculturalism and immigration. She argues that, like the new right in the United States, the Reform Party has successfully re-articulated racial-ethnic discourse by using what appear to be neutral "code words" to describe various kinds of problems and policies, but which in fact carry racialized meanings. In chapter 12, Rick Ponting provides systematic empirical data on the stereotypes that non-Aboriginal Canadians have of Aboriginal peoples, the impact of those stereotypes on Aboriginal peoples, and the complex nature of Canadian public opinion regarding the issues of self-government and Aboriginal rights. He shows, among other things, that over the years there has been a deterioration in public support for Aboriginal concerns, and cautions that public opinion should not be discounted when it comes to understanding the ways that governments respond to Aboriginal issues.

The final three chapters of this volume are concerned with conceptual, empirical and philosophical issues related to anti-racism strategies and practices. Chapter 13, "The Politics of Educational Change: Taking Anti-Racism Education Seriously" by George Dei, makes a strong case for linking educational with wider social change. He argues that in a pluralistic society, the challenge of establishing inter- and intra-group sociability cannot be confined to simply "teaching" people to live together peacefully, but must also involve the sharing of power, wealth and social resources. For Dei, the key to the success of any anti-racism initiative is to not get bogged down by questions of interpretation and meaning, but rather to find ways to transform social and political structures that are involved in the distribution of valued goods in society. Chapter 14, "Anti-Racism and the Organized Labour Movement" by Tania Das Gupta, reviews some of the main dimensions of racism in the organized labour movement, and some of the problems and issues encountered with anti-racism in unions and organizing around employment equity. Based on interviews with union activists, she argues that work on anti-racism and employment equity is fraught with contradictions. While the organized labour movement has taken a key leadership role in publicly supporting various kinds of human rights and equity issues, there remain systemic obstacles within unions that hinder the effective implementation of anti-racism initiatives. The final chapter is by Anton Allahar and is entitled "Race and Racism: Strategies of Resistance." Allahar begins by examining why ethno-racial identity markers have remained salient despite predictions by sociologists from a variety of theoretical traditions about their imminent demise. He then goes on to critically analyze three strategies of resistance to racism: multiculturalism and accommodation; assimilation; and violent, physical engagement of the racist aggressor. He concludes with a discussion of the ways in which strategies of resistance are conceptualized within neo-Marxist debates about the relative importance of race versus class in political consciousness and opposition in capitalist society.

References

Anderson, K. 1991. *Vancouver's Chinatown: Racial Discourse in Canada, 1875-1980*. Montreal and Kingston: McGill-Queen's University Press.

Angus Reid Group. 1991. *Multiculturalism and Canadians: Attitude Study 1991. National Survey Report*. Submitted to Multiculturalism and Citizenship Canada.

Avery, D. 1995. *Reluctant Host: Canada's Response to Immigrant Workers*. Toronto: McLelland and Stewart.

Banton, M. 1970. "The concept of racism." In S. Zubaida, ed. *Race and Racialism*. London: Tavistock.

Barrett, S. 1987. *Is God a Racist?: The Right Wing in Canada*. Toronto: University of Toronto Press.

Bolaria, S. and P. Li. 1988. *Racial Oppression in Canada*. Toronto: Garamond Press.

Essed, P. 1991. *Understanding Everyday Racism: An Interdisciplinary Theory*. Newbury Park: Sage.

Foster, C. 1996. *A Place Called Heaven*. Toronto: Harper-Collins.

Henry, F. et al. 1995. *The Colour of Democracy: Racism in Canada*. Toronto: Harcourt Brace.

Iacovetta, F. 1992. *Such Hardworking People*. Toronto: McGill-Queen's University Press.

Lehr, J. "Peopling the prairies with Ukrainians." In Lubomyr Luciuk and Stella Hryniuk, eds. *Canada's Ukrainians: Negotiating an Identity*. Toronto: University of Toronto Press.

Li, P. 1988. *The Chinese in Canada*. Toronto: Oxford University Press.

Ng, R. 1988. "Racism, sexism and Canadian nationalism." In Society for Socialist Studies, eds. *Race, Class and Gender: Bonds and Barriers*. Toronto: Between the Lines Press.

Miles, Robert. 1993. *Racism After "Race Relations."* London: Routledge.

Miller, J. 1996. *Shingwauk's Vision. A History of Native Residential Schools*. Toronto: University of Toronto Press.

Monture-Angus, P. 1995. *Thunder in My Soul: A Mohawk Woman Speaks*. Halifax: Fernwood.

Pettipas, K. 1995. *Severing the Ties That Bind*. Winnipeg: University of Manitoba Press.

Porter, J. 1965. *The Vertical Mosaic*. Toronto: University of Toronto Press.

Reitz, J. 1988. "Less racial discrimination in Canada, or simply less racial conflict? Implications of comparisons with Britain." *Canadian Public Policy* 14(4):424-441.

_____ and R. Breton. 1994. *Illusion of Difference: Realities of Ethnicity in Canada and the United States*. Toronto: C.D. Howe Institute

Roberts, D. 1996. "The street gangs of Winnipeg." *Globe and Mail*. May 18, 1996, D5.

Roy, P. 1989. *A White Man's Province: British Columbia's Politicians and the Fear of Asians*. Vancouver: University of British Columbia Press.

Ruggles, C. 1996. *Outsider Blues*. Halifax: Fernwood.

Satzewich, V. and T. Wotherspoon. 1993. *First Nations: Race, Class and Gender Relations*. Toronto: Nelson.

Shaffir, W. and C. Levitt. 1987. *The Riot at Christie Pits*. Toronto: Lester and Orpen Dennys.

Titley, B. 1986. *A Narrow Vision: Duncan Campbell Scott and the Administration of Indian Affairs in Canada*. Vancouver: University of British Columbia Press.

Winks, R. 1971. *The Blacks in Canada: A History*. Montreal: McGill-Queen's University Press.

Woodsworth, J.S. 1972. *Strangers Within Our Gates*. Toronto: University of Toronto Press.

1

Race, Racism and Racialization: Contested Concepts

Vic Satzewich

Writing in 1970, Michael Banton argued that "as a biological doctrine, racism is dead" (1970:28). He argued that after World War II, a concerted effort on the part of both natural and social scientists led to the debunking of theories which posited the existence of biologically superior and inferior groups of people. Horrified by the Nazi's mass murder of six million Jews for the sake of the preservation of supposed German racial purity and superiority, the newly formed United Nations lent its weight to challenging biologically grounded racial theories. It did this by having the United Nations Educational, Scientific and Cultural Organization (UNESCO) organize a series of four conferences (held in 1950, 1951, 1964, and 1967) on race and racism. A stated goal of these conferences was to scientifically discredit racist doctrines which asserted, among other things, that the population of the world was divided into different races and that these races could be ranked in a hierarchy of biological superiority and inferiority (Montagu, 1972:x). According to both Banton and Ashley Montagu (1972), these conferences, coupled with wider developments in science, were successful in helping to undermine the validity of Nazi biological doctrines. This in turn led to a wider de-racialization of the world and the public rejection of racist ideas and practices (see also Barkan, 1992).

In 1978, sociologist William Julius Wilson suggested that there was a "declining significance of race" in the United States (1978). Wilson argued that there were three stages to the history of Black-White relations there. The first stage, the pre-industrial, was characterized by blatant and obvious racism where African Americans were exploited as slaves on plantations and subject to racial-caste oppression. The second stage, the industrial, lasted from emancipation in the last quarter of the nineteenth century to the New Deal in the 1930s. It was characterized by industrial expansion and a combination of class conflict and racial oppression. The third, and current, stage began after the Second World War. This involved a transition from racial to class-based inequality. In this stage, racial discrimination was made illegal, and various affirmative action programs were put in place. These provisions have allowed African Americans with educational credentials to move into the middle class. African Americans who do not have access to education and training, and whom Wilson terms "the black underclass," continue to occupy subordinate positions within society (Wilson, 1987). However, their current economic subordination is not due to racist exclusionary practices but rather to inner-city capital flight (Wilson, 1978:2-3). While admitting that "racial conflicts" have not disappeared from America, he argues that the basis for these conflicts has shifted from the economic to the socio-political order and "therefore do not play as great a role in determining the life chances of individual black Americans as in the previous periods of overt racial discrimination" (Wilson, 1978:23).

From the vantage point of the late 1990s, Banton's argument that racism is dead and Wilson's argument about the declining significance of race seem to be overly optimistic. Even though race is a hollow biological concept, race and racism remain socially, politically and scientifically significant in a variety of different contexts. Lawyers, journalists and members of various publics in a number of countries continue to debate the significance of the so-called "race card" in the O.J. Simpson civil and criminal trials. Affirmative action programs in the United States and employment equity programs in Canada have come under attack, in part, because they are said to be "reverse racism" (Fleras and Elliot, 1995). The police and justice systems in a variety of countries are routinely accused of racism when it comes to the policing of minority communities (Cashmore and McLaughlin, 1991; Baker, 1994). The Dominion Bureau of Statistics abandoned its use of race as a category describing the makeup of Canada in 1951 in favour of the more neutral concept of origin, but after a forty-five year hiatus Statistics Canada is once again collecting data on the racial makeup of Canada. Universities in North America are being denounced for offering students, not only a Eurocentric, but also a racist curriculum that does not reflect the lived experiences, world views and concerns of all members of the campus community (Schuman and Olfus, 1995). And some academics in both Canada and the United States have tried to rekindle scientific debates about the relationship between genetics, social behaviour and intelligence (Rushton, 1994; Herrnstein and Murray, 1994).

Clearly, race and racism continue to be important aspects of social reality in a variety of countries. But even if we agree with Cornell West (1993) that "race matters," there is no agreement about what race refers to; how race came to matter historically; how, why and to whom race continues to matter; what makes an idea, behaviour or institution racist; what should be done about race and racism; and what are the links between racism and class and gender relations. This chapter cannot address all of these questions. Instead, it has three more modest objectives. First, its delineates some of the main lines of academic debate about the concepts of race, racism and racialization. Second, it contexualizes and anticipates some of the issues and debates that are addressed in later chapters of this book. And third, it aims to spur further thought and debate that will further the analysis of race and racism in Canada.

There are four sections to this chapter. First, I consider the concept of race and how it has been defined in both scientific and public discourse. Second, I make a case for the sociological study of the process of racialization. Third, I critically analyze sociological definitions of racism, including a discussion of new racism and the concept of institutional racism. Finally, I conclude with a review of various approaches that have been taken to understand the links between race, and class and gender.

The Concept of "Race": From Lineage, to Biological Reality, to Social Construct

The word *race* has been around for a long time in written English. Michael Banton (1987:1) traces its origin in the English language to a poem written by William Dunbar in 1508, which was entitled "The Dance of the Sevin Deidly Sins." Since then, the term *race* has been used to refer to a lineage, to biologically distinct groups of people, and most recently, to a socially constructed label used to describe certain patterns of physical and genetic difference. In this section, I want to provide a brief account of the different ways that race has been defined.

Banton argues that before the late eighteenth century, the term race referred only to a class or category of people or things. These classes or categories were not seen as biologically distinct, nor were they seen as situated in a hierarchy of superiority and inferiority. When the term was applied to human beings, it was used to refer to a lineage or line of descent where particular groups of people were attributed with a common history (Banton, 1987:xi). In seventeenth century England, for example, some thinkers used the idea of race to try to explain the historical origins of English people. Some thought that the English were the descendants of a German (Saxon) race that had settled in England in A.D. 449, and that the Norman invasion of the eleventh century led to the domination of that Saxon race by an "alien Norman race" (Banton, 1987:12-13). While there was an interest in the analysis of the conflicts between these so-called races, there was not much interest in why they differed beyond their lineage.

Collette Guillaumin comes to a similar conclusion in the case of France (1995). She argues that before the French Revolution, the term race was used in a legal sense to describe people with a common lineage. Race was a self-defined category used by the French aristocracy to define themselves, their ancestors and their descendants. Aristocratic families defined themselves as a race, and saw themselves as racially distinct from others in France by virtue of their common blood and descent.

Guillaumin and Banton agree that there was a shift in the meaning of race in the late eighteenth and early nineteenth centuries as it increasingly took on biological connotations. According to Banton, by the late eighteenth century, politicians, scientists, philosophers and other thinkers started to use the term race to refer to groups of people who were believed to be inherently and biologically different. There was in Banton's terms a "racialization of the world"; the race concept was increasingly used to define and explain human physical, social and intellectual variation by reference to biology (1977). They differ, though, in their explanations of why the meaning of race changed. For Banton, the racialization of the world was the result of a particular moment in the history of science. Racial theories that made increasing reference to biology were born out of European scientists' honest attempts to explain the physical and cultural diversity that had been exposed through European colonialism and overseas expansion. In other words, increased awareness of human differences begat scientific theories of those differences.

Guillaumin, on the other hand, offers a more materialist explanation (1995). She argues that the change in the meaning of race in France was not simply the result of a scientific error, but rather was rooted in the changing class structure and configuration of power relations after the 1789 Revolution. In the late eighteenth century, the social objects of the term race changed: race became less of a self-defined label that persons adopted to describe themselves and their lineage. It instead became a category that was applied to various kinds of "others." Rather than being used as a category to define the "self," it was now used as a way to define "others," be they "Arabs," "Asiatics," "Jews," "Negroes" or "Blacks." But in addition to changes in to whom the concept of race referred, there were also changes in its meaning. Categorizing certain groups as races became linked with the negative evaluation of the "other's" social and biological capacities.

Guillaumin suggests that the transition from race as an self-defining characteristic to an externally imposed label to describe genetically distinct subgroups of the human population was rooted in the rise to power of the bourgeoisie (1995). The ascendant French bourgeoisie did not have access to the ideology of the aristocratic ruling class in which privilege was justified in terms of lineage, divine right or royal assent. In place of a racial ideology which justified domination on these grounds, race was used by the bourgeoisie as a way of describing and designating a variety of "others" who did not have the biological, social and intellectual wherewithal to themselves achieve positions of economic and political power.

Guillaumin puts it in the following terms:

> Torn between the nobility to which they did not yet belong and the populace which they had left behind, this aristocracy in function but not in name set about laying the foundations of a new elite which is still with us today. In the absence of coats of arms, titles and great houses, they therefore invented ability, aptitude, merit…. They also needed to define a common herd of their own, and they found it ready and waiting at the gates. At

the gates of the cities, into which the peasants moved to swell the ranks of industrial workers. At the gates of the nation, where conquered peoples came to pay tribute to their victors. At the gates of a strengthened and newly prominent religion. Workers, Negroes, Asiatics, Jews ... plebeians, primitives, foreigners ... Others. The guarantors of the legitimacy of the bourgeoisie's conquest of power (1995:54).

Race was therefore a label that was not only applied to non-French others, but was also applied to the French manual working class and peasantry. Put differently, subordinate social classes were also racialized and inferiorized, giving rise to what Balibar (1991) calls "class racism," and Miles (1993) "racisms of the interior."

Since the late eighteenth century, there have been two general criteria by which scientists have attempted to define and categorize the people of the world into a particular race. One strategy has been to try to divide humanity into particular races based on phenotypic, or physical characteristics that people display. A second has been to focus on genotype, or genetic differences. By the middle of the nineteenth century in Europe, there were many variations in the belief that inherent biological differences determined physical, social and intellectual abilities. In Britain in 1848, Charles Hamilton Smith published the *Natural History of the Human Species*. In it he argued that there were three relatively permanent and discrete "races": "Negro," "Mongolian" and "Caucasian." He argued that the "Negro" race possessed a relatively low cranial capacity and that this was responsible for their subordinate position in the American social structure. Others, like Robert Knox in *The Races of Men* (1850) also argued for a threefold racial classification of the world, suggested that physical differences determined cultural practices, and that race was the major determinant of different levels of cultural development.

These attempts to define racial categories and correlate them with social and cultural abilities are fraught with difficulties. Within population biology and branches of physical anthropology, racial classifications have no scientific validity (Rose, Kamin and Lewontin, 1984). In fact, the weight of scientific evidence is clearly tipped in favour of seeing race not as a basic characteristic that naturally divides the human species, but rather as a rather arbitrary *label* that has been used to describe and explain certain patterns of physical and/or genetic variation. Things like skin pigmentation certainly vary, and there may very well be differences in the geographical frequency distribution of certain genes. In other words, physical and genetic differences between individuals exist, but these are not race differences. Race is simply the label that has been used to describe certain kinds of human difference.

Within sociology, biologically grounded definitions of race have tended to be rejected in favour of definitions that focus on race as a socially constructed label (Anthias and Yuval Davis, 1992). This has led some social scientists to call for its abandonment as an analytical concept. At the same time, though, the social constructionist approach to race has been inconsistently incorporated into socio-logical analysis. While most sociologists recognize the socially constructed na-ture of race, some continue to use the term in ways that imply that it is a biological fact. Leo Driedger in *The Ethnic Factor: Identity in Diversity* recog-nizes that ""race" today is ... an arbitrary biological grouping of people on the basis of physical characteristics" (1989:295), but at the same time uses the term race in a way that suggests that it is a biological sub-division of the human species. In commenting on the nature of "socio-economic racial differentiation in Canada," he argues that "white Caucasians, largely of European origin, tend to rank high, while aboriginals, Blacks and some Asians of coloured or Negroid and Mongoloid racial origins rank low" (Driedger, 1989:156). Driedger's use of late nineteenth century racial categories to describe human beings seems to suggest that race is more than a label; people have a racial origin that they are born with, and this origin has certain social consequences.

Others, moreover, express ambivalence over the political implications of ana-lyzing race as a socially constructed label and abandoning it as an analytical concept. Some theorists have argued that sociologists who emphasize the so-cially constructed nature of race, and who advocate its rejection as an analytical category are unwittingly fuelling a conservative political agenda (Omi and Wi-nant, 1993:5). Critics of the social constructionist approach to race have argued that in defining race as a label with no analytical utility, social scientists end up denying the reality of racism and are thereby undermining the anti-racist strug-gle. They also argue that the refusal to employ race as an analytical concept is the same as saying, as some thinkers do, that "race does not matter in our society; we live in a colour-blind society that treats everyone equally." The maxim developed several years ago by W.I. Thomas, which says that if people define situations as real, they are real in their consequences, is often invoked by critics to justify the continued use of race as an analytical concept (Driedger, 1989; Fleras and Elliot, 1995). Critics argue that since many people think that races of people exist, and since in some cases they base their actions on the belief in race difference, then sociologists must continue to use race as an analytical concept even if does not have a valid basis in biology.

In defense of rejecting race as an analytical category, the political implications of using race in a way that reinforces the idea that it is biologically real are arguably far worse than the implications associated with its rejection. Think of the atrocities (slavery and the extermination of Jews, for example) that have been justified in the name of race and racial inferiority. Why would anyone want to defend the use of a scientifically discredited concept that has been used to justify such immense suffering? Goldberg puts the matter even more forcefully:

> The discourse promoting resistance to racism must not prompt identification with and in
> terms of categories fundamental to the discourse of oppression. Resistance must break
> not only with *practices* of oppression, although its first task is to do that. Resistance

must oppose also the *language* of oppression, including the categories in terms of which the oppressor (or racist) represents the forms in which resistance is expressed (1990:313-14).

Furthermore, no theoretical position can claim a monopoly over what is the most progressive anti-racist stance. Any anti-racist stance can be twisted, re-interpreted and re-defined by right-wing ideologues to further their own political objectives. Phillipe Rushton, the University of Western Ontario psychologist who has become the bad boy of Canadian academe, believes that there is something biologically real about race, that races have different sized brains and genitalia, and that these biological differences have important social and behavioural consequences (1994). One can easily imagine how Professor Rushton could seek legitimacy for his theory among academics and advocacy groups who uncritically defend the concept of race as a useful analytical category and as a way of describing groups of people.

Moreover, W.I Thomas' dictum can be interpreted in another way. Many people no doubt think that races exist in a biological sense. Such beliefs have certain consequences in terms of how they live their lives, whom they want their children to marry, whom they seek out as personal friends, how they interact with others, and how some peoples' abilities and characters are evaluated. But just because many people hold to the idea of race as part of their common sense, and even though the belief has social consequences, this does not mean that sociologists need a *concept* of race to be able to analyze those ideas and consequences. Some anti-government groups in the United States, such as the Posse Comitatus and the Freemen, believe that the United States government is under the control of a complex network of individuals and organizations that include Jews, Communists and the United Nations (Ridgeway, 1995). This belief has real consequences for how members of these groups live, how they view the American government and how they interact with law enforcement officials. If critics of the social constructionist approach to race are correct, then sociologists who analyze these organizations should employ as an *analytical* concept the "Jewish/Communist/United Nations conspiracy." Advocating the employment of the conspiracy as a sociological concept because some people believe in the conspiracy and because those beliefs have real consequences contributes to its reification. In other words, an idea becomes elevated to the status of a thing. "The problem" is not defined as anti-Semitism, which is a form of racism; instead it comes to be defined as "the conspiracy."

Since racism is grounded, in part, in a belief about the real and natural sub-division of the human population into discrete races, any sociological approach to understanding racism, as well as any anti-racist strategy, should proceed from a critique of that initial assumption. It is precisely for this reason that some sociologists insist on putting "race" in quotation marks to indicate that it is a problematic concept. In short, if race is a concept of questionable scientific status, and indeed, if biological and physical criteria are of little validity as a basis for sub-dividing the people of the world, then care needs to be taken in how the concept of race is incorporated into sociological analysis. The study of the causes and consequences of the belief in race is an issue different from the study of the effects of race on occupational status and income. Indeed, the former constitutes the essence of one of the central problems in the contemporary sociology of race and racism: how and why did the race label come to be applied to groups of people, and how and why does the race label continue to be reproduced, even in the context of the general scientific discrediting of the concept of race? The study of these kinds of questions is what Steven Small refers to as "the racialization problematic" (1995).

The Racialization Problematic

Scholars from a variety of academic disciplines have become interested in the concept of racialization. While there are subtle differences in the way that the term is defined, the most comprehensive definition has been developed by Miles. For Miles, racialization refers to "those instances where social relations between people have been structured by the signification of human biological characteristics in such a way as to define and construct differentiated social collectivities" (1989:75). The crucial element to the process of racialization is the delineation of group boundaries and identities by reference to physical and/or genetic criteria or by reference to the term race. There are two implications of this definition. First, a process of racialization can occur even in the specific absence of the term race. When American commentators assert that "Black/White relations in the United States are at the breaking point," they are constructing collectivities on the basis of physical characteristics, and hence defining a relationship between groups in a racialized fashion. Even though the discourse may not contain references to the term race, there is nevertheless a process of signification of physical difference that counts as racialization. Second, a process of racialization can occur when the term race is present to define particular groups and their relationships, even though these groups may not necessarily be defined as possessing distinctive physical or genetic characteristics. André Siegfried's *The Race Question in Canada* tried to provide an analysis of French-English relations in Canada at the turn of the century (1907). Siegfried suggested that Canada had a race problem, but nowhere in his book did he argue that English and French were biologically distinct. He instead focused on cultural and religious characteristics as the basis of race difference. So while particular groups may be labelled as races it sometimes happens that these groups and their inter-relations are defined culturally rather than biologically. This would continue to warrant consideration as an instance of racialization.

The contemporary significance of the term racialization can be illustrated by two recent controversies. The first is the Writer's Union of Canada's "Writing Thru Race" conference held in Vancouver in 1994, and Neil Bissoondath's subsequent criticism of the conference in *Selling Illusions: The Cult of Multiculturalism in Canada* (1994). The aim of the conference was to allow Aboriginal people and visible minorities the opportunity to "address the issue of 'race' and racism in contemporary writing in Canada." This was to be achieved through personal discussions by First Nations' writers and writers of colour. Only certain literary events were open to the public. Bissoondath argued that the organizers were engaging in "a kind of racism" when they limited registration for the discussions to people of colour and First Nations. He equated this with the kind of "racial approach that produced *Mein Kampf* and apartheid" (Bissoondath, 1994:163-64). Others condemned the racial exclusiveness of the conference and suggested that the use of racial categorizations as boundary-maintaining mechanisms was inherently *racist*.

Defenders of the conference, including Myrna Kostash, the chair of the Writer's Union, and Art Miki, the chair of the Union's Racial Minority Writers' Committee, argued that while the conference did reflect a wider *racialization* of Canadian society, this was not necessarily racist. Miki admitted that "some writers, particularly those not racialized as 'of colour,' may be tempted to critique this policy as exclusionary and separatist." His defense of the conference, though, was that First Nations' writers and writers of colour needed a chance to discuss their experiences of racism and marginalization from the mainstream literary world in a way that did not have to take account the potential defensiveness of "White" participants.

A similar debate took place in 1995 at the University of Guelph, where a group of students wanted to establish a lounge that was for the use of students of colour. Their aim also was to create a space where they could discuss among themselves their experiences of racism and discrimination. Following the announcement of the intention to establish the lounge, other students complained that the lounge was racist because it would exclude White students. In turn, supporters of the lounge called the critics racist for their opposition.

Are racial categorizations necessarily racist? Is the desire to create and sustain group boundaries on the basis of certain physical characteristics, or by reference to a common race, racist? Does racial categorization necessarily lead to the formation of hierarchies? These questions are, of course, not new (Porter, 1987:121). The Writing Thru Race conference and the issue of a lounge for students of colour are not cases of racism, but rather are instances of racialization. In both cases, groups attached social significance to, and group boundaries were formed around, physical differences. In this way, Art Miki was right. To adopt an identity, whether externally imposed or self-defined, that revolves around certain characteristics such as skin colour reflects a process of racialization but is not necessarily racist. Many people in Canada use the category of race and/or physical differences such as skin colour to define both themselves and others (James, 1994; Jhappan, 1996), but this is not the same as Adolph Hitler calling Jews a menace to civilization as we know it. The latter claim was based on the Nazi's negative evaluation of racialized "others," while attempts to form group boundaries on the basis of race by groups themselves usually involve efforts to project positive collective images (Appiah, 1990). Bissoondath may dislike racial identities and may prefer defining himself in individualistic terms, but he misunderstands the difference between racism and racialization.

In sum, there are a whole range of identities, relations and boundaries in Canada and elsewhere that are instances of racialization. But if these racialized identities, relations and boundaries are not necessarily racist, what is the difference between racialization and racism?

The Debate about Racism

In questioning the analytical utility of the concept of race, and in its place advancing the concept of racialization, we have yet to say anything about the concept of racism. We should not conclude that racism is also a concept with little analytical utility. Even though races of people do not exist in a real, biological sense, people admittedly think and act as if they do, and they hold certain beliefs about groups defined as racially different. How can an idea, behaviour or social practice be defined as racist? Put differently, what makes a racialized discourse or practice turn into a racist discourse or practice?

Racism, as noted in the introduction, is both a sociological concept used to describe certain aspects of social reality and an epithet used in public discourse as a means of politically discrediting certain actions, beliefs or policies. Even though it is central to public discourse and academic analysis, there is no consensus on how the term should be defined. This section critically evaluates a number of competing approaches to the definition of racism.

In *The Idea of Race*, Michael Banton argues that the term *racism* should refer to a very specific kind of idea (1977). For Banton, racism is a historically limited concept, developed in the realm of science, and consists of the "doctrine of racial typology." Banton creates a Weberian ideal type of "doctrine of racial typology" out of the variety of scientific ideas about race prevalent in Europe in the late nineteenth and early twentieth centuries. He suggests that the "doctrine of racial typology" consisted of a relatively systematic set of ideas which claimed that much of human history and culture could be explained by reference to innate biological differences between groups, and that such races could be arranged in a hierarchy of superiority and inferiority. This doctrine consisted of five inter-related suppositions:

1. there exist distinct and permanent types of Homo Sapiens;

2. the physical appearance and behaviour of individuals is an expression of a discrete biological type which is permanent;

3. cultural variation is determined by differences in biological type;

4. biological variation is the origin of conflict between both individuals and nations;

5. races are differentially endowed, such that some are inherently superior to others.

Banton argues that the concept of racism needs to be limited to describe this particular combination of beliefs that were prevalent in the world of science until the middle of this century. Since these ideas are now scientifically discredited, "racism is dead." Banton argues that most of the current negative evaluations of "otherness" are better described as forms of ethnocentrism.

Banton's definition of racism was initially criticized by John Rex (1983). Rex argued that Banton's definition was too narrow for what it excluded from consideration as racism. Rex suggested that expressions of hostility and the justification of unequal treatment may not necessarily take the form of explicit, logical and scientific theories, but rather can also take the form of stereotypes, proverbs, symbols and folklore. Thus, the definition of racism should not be confined to those ideas which were held by scientists up until the early 1950s, but should be broadened to include "commonsense" ideas. For Rex, racism should not only refer to scientific ideas about the supposed relationship between biology and cultural, social and intellectual ability, but also to their "functional equivalents." In his view what defines ideas as racist is that

> they see the connection between membership of a particular group and of the genetically related sub-groups (i.e. families and lineage's) of which that group is composed and the possession of evaluated qualities as completely deterministic. It doesn't really matter whether this is because of men's [sic.] genes, because of the history to which their ancestors have been exposed, because of the nature of their culture or because of divine decree (Rex, 1983: 159).

Thus, folk ideas about cultural or historical determination constitute functional equivalents to biologically based theories of race.

Rex's approach to defining racism, which sees racism as the negative evaluation of any biologically defined collectivity, is also developed by British philosopher Martin Barker. Like Rex, Barker insists that in the late 1970s a "new racism" emerged in Britain (1981). Barker felt that in the 1970s certain British Members of Parliament developed a new strategy when it came to speaking out against British immigration policy. Since the 1940s, that policy had permitted people from former colonies in Asia, Africa, and the Caribbean relatively unrestricted entry into the country. In the 1970s, the policy was criticized by many British conservatives who felt that it was undermining the "British way of life."

Margaret Thatcher's infamous "swamped" speech in January 1978 became the quintessential expression of British anxieties about immigration from India, the Caribbean and Pakistan. In her speech, she stated the following:

> If we went on as we are, then by the end of the century there would be 4 million people of the New Commonwealth or Pakistan here. Now that is an awful lot and I think it means that people are really rather afraid that this country might be swamped by people with a different culture. And, you know, the British character has done so much for democracy, for law, and done so much throughout the world, that if there is a fear that it might be swamped, people are going to react and be rather hostile to those coming in (cited in Barker, 1981:15).

Mrs. Thatcher's speech made no references to British biological superiority and Indian, Pakistani or Black biological inferiority. Instead, immigrants from these areas were identified as culturally different from British people, and that was the source of problems in British society. According to both Barker and Rex, this kind of cultural argument was as racist as saying that "Black people are genetically inferior to Whites and should therefore not be allowed to enter Britain as immigrants." According to Barker, then, the "new racism" consists of the belief that "human nature is such that it is natural to form a bounded community, a nation, aware of its differences from other nations. They are not better or worse. But feelings of antagonism will be aroused if outsiders are admitted" (Barker, 1981:21). Thus, the new racism is the belief that there are naturally occurring sub-divisions of the human population ("races" of people) who normally constitute themselves into nations, and that these nations prefer to maintain exclusive group boundaries. In this context, the new racism does not make reference to biological and cultural *inferiority* but rather to inherent cultural, "racial," and national *difference*. Such differences are defined by new racists as the source of social antagonisms and are then used as grounds for various kinds of social exclusions. Biological versions of racism may very well be "dead," but other forms of racism have emerged in their place.

In Canada, Henry, Tator, Mattis and Rees in *The Colour of Democracy: Racism in Canada* take up Baker's more broad conceptualization, and combine it with the concept of aversive racism to advance the concept of democratic racism. For Henry et al., democratic racism refers to a peculiarly Canadian form of racism that reflects an effort to reconcile two fundamentally conflicting sets of values. They argue that many Canadians take pride in their commitment to democratic principles such as justice, equality and fairness, but at the same time hold negative attitudes about, and discriminate against, minority groups. Democratic racism is seen as an ideology that tries to reconcile these two sets of conflicting values and processes. Henry et al. then go on to catalogue a list of specific beliefs and arguments that in Canada constitute democratic racism: "Racism cannot exist within a democratic society"; "discrimination is a problem faced by everyone from time to time"; "racism is a result of immigration"; "racial conflict occurs because of racial diversity in society"; "minority groups refuse to fit in and adapt to Canadian society"; "minority groups cannot fit into Canadian society"; "people of colour have cultural problems, race is not the issue"; "non-Whites lack the skills and motivation to succeed"; "multicultural policies are sufficient, racism comes from ignorance"; "racism is a problem for non-Whites to solve"; "all we need to do is treat everybody equally"; "although racism exists, individuals have the right to freedom of speech"; and "anti-racism initiatives are racism in reverse" (Henry et al., 1995:19-21).

Rex's, Barker's and Henry et al.'s approaches to the definition of racism are improvements over Banton's, insofar as each is broad enough to include beliefs that are not necessarily grounded in a scientific discourse. However, their breadth is also their shortcoming. Let us take Henry et al.'s definition of democratic racism as an example of the problem associated with broad definitions of racism. While some of the ideas and arguments they list as manifestations of democratic racism can legitimately be termed racist, their definition is so broad that any idea that denies, negates, questions or contextualizes the significance of racism directed against Black people is seen to be automatically racist.

For example, Henry et al.'s list of instances of democratic racism includes the belief that "White European immigrants also experienced discrimination (1995)." They argue that "equating racial disadvantage and discrimination against White European immigrants ignores the importance of the history of colonization, subjugation and oppression of people of colour by Canadians of European origin" (Henry et al., 1995:22) and is therefore a form of democratic racism. Prejudice and discrimination directed against central, eastern and southern European immigrants to Canada is well documented by historians and social scientists. As J.S. Woodsworth's (1972) *Strangers Within Our Gates* clearly demonstrates, immigrants from these areas were regarded as racially different from, and inferior to, British and northern European races during the early part of the twentieth century. At that time, there was no consensus on whether these immigrants were in fact "White." Even though these immigrants were later defined by the dominant British elite as falling within the boundaries of "White Canada," during the early years of this century, they were nevertheless racialized others who were seen to be of dubious value to Canada. Many historians and social scientists genuinely believe that European immigrants, who are now defined as White, experienced racial discrimination in Canada. It may have been a relatively short-lived set of experiences confined to the immigrant generation, but it was nevertheless experienced as racism, and it did have certain social consequences. Recognizing the reality of the racialization of certain European immigrants to Canada during the late nineteenth and early twentieth centuries should not necessarily be seen as a way of invalidating or underplaying the racism experienced by people of colour.

Similarly, it is difficult to see why critics of employment equity and support-ers of the federal government's policy of multiculturalism should both necessar-ily be labelled as democratic racists. According to Henry et al. (1995), the many Canadians who believe that, through their support of multicultural policy and through their active involvement in multicultural festivals and programs, many of Canada's racial problems will be solved are actually democratic racists. The belief that multiculturalism can solve all racial problems may be politically naive and sociologically simplistic (in the sense that it assumes that racism is a cultural problem rather than a problem of power relations). However, naive and simplistic solutions to the problem of racism do not necessarily mean that they are racist solutions.

Furthermore, people oppose employment equity policies on a number of grounds. Some of the opponents of employment equity are certainly motivated by negative beliefs about minority groups ("minorities have too much power in society today"). However, others oppose the policy because they misunderstand its intent or believe that its implementation has undermined the principle of merit. Others support the general goals of employment equity but disagree with its current form and with how the concept of visible minority is defined (Synott and Howes, 1996:156). Yet others genuinely believe that racial discrimination is not a major problem in our society (or at least to the extent that it limits opportu-nities), and so see employment equity programs as unnecessary. Opposition may also reflect different political philosophies about the role of the state in attending to past discrimination and question whether the new generation of labour market entrants should be the ones to pay for the so-called "sins of our fathers (and mothers)." Opposition to employment equity is multifaceted and not all of the opposition is necessarily grounded in the negative evaluation of racialized groups.

In sum, Henry et al. seem to label as racist all those ideas and arguments that do not conform to their particular vision of social reality and of social, economic and political change. This is precisely the danger associated with broadening the definition of racism that Michael Banton recognized nearly thirty years ago. He was concerned that there was a tendency to "label some views and movements as 'racist,' as if by doing so they were proving that they did not need to be studied seriously" (Banton, 1970:32; see also Amit-Talai, 1996:92).

My own view is that Miles offers a sociological definition of racism that is broad enough to encompass the many forms and expressions of racism, but narrow enough to be able to clearly distinguish racism from non-racism. Racism, he argues, refers to ideas that delineate group boundaries by reference to race or to real or alleged biological characteristics, and which attribute groups so racial-ized with other negatively evaluated characteristics. There are four important implications associated with this definition. First, racism presupposes a process of racialization; there has to be a sense in which groups of people are seen to be biologically, physically or racially different from some "other." Second, some type of implicit or explicit negative evaluation of race or biological difference needs to be present before an idea can be labelled as racist. Alternatively, "the other" must be seen as having inducing some type of negative consequence for "the self." Thus, the idea that "race mixing reduces the genetic fitness of the White population" is racist, but so too is the idea that "Black people from the Caribbean, because of their unique history and culture, are unable to adapt to Canadian society and therefore cause problems in this country." Third, racism can take the form of a relatively coherent theory developed in the realm of science, or it can consist of less coherent stereotypes, folklore and common sense. Fourth, racism is practically adequate insofar as it is not a false ideology that is imposed on people, but rather is seen as part of an explanation of how the world works. Collectively, these observations about the concept of racism mean that what exists is not so much racism, but rather a range of *racisms*. The expressions, forms and targets of racism vary on the basis of historical, social and economic conditions (Miles, 1989:77-84). Part of the task of sociology, then, is to analyze the varied meanings, expressions and significance of racism.

Institutional Racism

Joe Feagin and Hernan Vera argue that, in the United States, "black racism does not exist," because racism "is more than a matter of individual prejudice and scattered episodes of discrimination." In their view, "there is no black racism because there is no centuries-old system of racialized subordination and dis-crimination designed by African Americans to exclude white Americans from full participation in the rights, privileges and benefits of this society" (Feagin and Vera, 1995:ix).

While I disagree with Feagin and Vera's assertion that racism is the sole preserve of White people, they are correct in their view that racism can and does involve more than a matter of individual or group prejudice. They recognize that racist ideas often inform the way that social institutions work. Racism, in other words, is also about power and the unequal distribution of scarce resources. The concept of institutional racism refers to circumstances in which social practices and institutions are guided by racist ideas. There are at least three possible forms that institutional racism can take.

First, there are circumstances where certain exclusionary practices are derived from a set of racist ideas, but where those practices are no longer guided by those ideas. An example of this form of institutional racism would be the Caribbean Seasonal Agricultural Workers Program in Canada. This program enables work-ers from the Caribbean to enter Canada on a seasonal, contractual basis in order to work in the southwestern Ontario fruit and vegetable industry. When the program began in 1966, the Canadian government admitted just under three hundred workers on a trail basis. In the mid-1960s, this migrant labour stream was justified, in part, on the grounds that Black workers from the Caribbean were racially suited to long days of strenuous labour under the hot southern Ontario sun, but racially unsuitable as permanent immigrants. Canadian government officials feared that, because of their supposed racial inferiority, if they were admitted as immigrants, they would cause certain race problems to emerge. This migration stream still operates (now over twelve thousand workers from the Caribbean and Mexico enter Canada each year to work on southern Ontario farms), but the racist ideas are no longer used in its continued justification. Even though racist ideas do not form part of the present justification of the program, the system did have its origins in explicitly racist ideas and therefore continues to warrant being considered a form of institutional racism (see Satzewich, 1991).

Second, there are circumstances where a racist discourse is modified in such a way that the explicitly racist content is eliminated, but the new words carry the original meaning. For example, the transformation of an explicitly racist into an apparently non-racist discourse occurred when the Canadian federal government modified the Immigration Act in 1953. In the 1953 Act, the federal government had the power to limit or prohibit the entry of immigrants for any of the following reasons:

(i) nationality, citizenship, ethnic group, occupation, class or geographical area of origin;

(ii) peculiar customs, habits, modes of life or methods of holding property;

(iii) unsuitability having regard to the climatic, economic, social, industrial, educational, labour, or other conditions, or requirements existing, temporarily or otherwise;

(iv) probable inability to become readily assimilated or to assume the duties and responsibilities of Canadian citizenship within a reasonable time after their admission (quoted in Rawlyk, 1962:292-93).

There are no explicit references in this list to race as a possible basis for excluding groups of potential immigrants from Canada. The government had earlier publicly abandoned race as a basis for exclusion, in part because of post-War diplomatic concerns. The explicit use of race as a basis for exclusion of immigrants to Canada was little different from the assumptions underlying Nazi Germany's efforts to maintain racial purity via the mass murder and deportation of Jews and other inferior races. Canadian officials were therefore reluctant to keep race on the immigration books out of fear over the international censure that would have inevitably come their way. Post-War Canadian immigration legislation therefore contains a gamut of what Omi and Winant call "code words": words, phrases and symbols that indirectly refer to racial themes but which do not refer directly to race or biology (1986:120). The references to "geographical area of origin," "peculiar customs, habits, modes of life or methods of holding property," "unsuitability having regard to climatic ... conditions" were euphemisms that gave immigration officials the power to exclude immi-grants because of their presumed racial inferiority without actually using terms like colour, race or biology.

Third, there are circumstances where institutional practices are based on ap-parently universalistic and non-racist rules, standards and procedures, but where those standards may in turn have negative effects for certain minority groups. This is sometimes also referred to as systemic discrimination. Height and weight requirements for jobs did not necessarily have their origin in racist ideas, but these requirements meant, for example, that for may years certain Asian groups, who were on average shorter that Europeans, found it difficult to obtain employ-ment with police forces and fire departments. Word-of-mouth recruiting and inflated educational requirements for non-technical jobs are also identified as forms of institutional racism that unintentionally put certain groups at a disad-vantage when it comes to the distribution of scarce resources.

Race, Class and Gender

"Race, class and gender" has become the new mantra among Canadian schol-ars (Agnew, 1996:3). Researchers from a variety of disciplines, theoretical tradi-tions and substantive areas advocate with varying degrees of commitment and consistency the need to take into account race, class and gender. As we have seen, there is no consensus in academic literature on the definition of the con-cepts of race, racialization and racism. There are also equally contentious debates about the definition and significance of the concepts of "class" and "gender." It should therefore come as no surprise that there is also no consensus about the meaning of the "race, gender, class" trio, how to conceptualize their inter-rela-tionship or which takes precedence in shaping the social position, experiences and identities of groups within Canadian society (Daly, 1994). There are class approaches to race and gender, gender approaches to race and class, and race approaches to class and gender (see Solomos, 1986; Stasiulis, 1989; Bonacich, 1980; Agnew, 1996; and Jhappan, 1996, for summaries of this literature).

At the risk of oversimplification, there are two ways in which race, class and gender are analyzed in the social sciences. The first is to see the trio as providing the basis for experience and position in society. Put in empiricist terms, they are considered as independent variables that have various kinds of determinant and historically specific effects. Thus, the most usual way that the trio is treated within sociology is to use them as discrete variables that alone or in combination have an effect on a group's identity, experiences or socio-economic position. These variables are analyzed in terms of their effects on a variety of institutions and social processes. Based on interviews, Helen Ralston, for example, con-cludes that "race, class and language interact as significant variables to determine the actualities of everyday life [for immigrant women]. Above all, they contribute to the differential work experience among white and non-white immigrant women" (Ralston, 1991:131). Monica Boyd's work on earnings inequality analyzes the way that these variables, among a range of others, have an impact on the wages and salaries of Canadian men and women (1992). Vijay Agnew is interested in the women's movement in Canada and tends to see the relationship between the three variables as additive: "race, class and gender intersect in the lives of women who have immigrated to Canada from Asia, Africa and the Caribbean" (1996:4). Agnew analyzes the ways that these variables interact to shape women's experiences in Canada, how they have provided the basis for political mobilization and how they have been dealt with by feminist organizations in Canada.

Critics of this approach to race, class and gender suggest that it is not good enough to say that gender, race and class interact. Instead, they suggest that it is necessary to identify the variable or variables that have the greatest impact on a group's identity, position and experiences. According to Stasiulis, Black feminists "have reached near unanimity in agreeing that race, rather than gender, has been the primary source of their oppression" (1987:5). While all Black feminists do not speak with one voice, many argue that their social position and experiences in Canada are primarily rooted in racist ideas and practices of employers, governments, police forces and service agencies. Since the reigns of power are still held by White men, and increasingly by White women, they argue that all women are not equally oppressed. Others argue that gender oppression precedes racial oppression. They argue that, historically, "sexism has preceded racism; that all women share some experiences (such as motherhood); that regardless of cultural variations, women are still constructed as women; and that most legal systems still justify sex discrimination but not race discrimination" (Jhappan, 1996:25).

The search for the most fundamental basis of oppression is not simply an academic problem that will be resolved through the development of better regression techniques or interview methods. It is also a central concern within the feminist movement in Canada and elsewhere when it comes to the development of political strategies (Jagger and Rothenberg, 1993). Some argue, though, that it is politically divisive and has tended to polarize the women's movement (Agnew, 1996). Others argue that it is also an inaccurate way of trying to understand the complexity of social reality. For Daly the search for the fundamental basis of oppression characteristic of some additive approaches to race, class and gender is fundamentally misplaced (1994). Jhappan argues that "the interaction of gender and race [and class?] produces a distinct result not captured by analyzing race and gender [and class?] separately" (1996). In other words, she suggests that it is not only impossible to decide when one is being discriminated against or otherwise oppressed because of one factor over another, but the factors compound one another to produce a unique phenomenon. Jhappan's understanding of the multiple layers of individual and collective identity, and the complex and contradictory ways in which advantages and disadvantages stemming from race, gender and class are played out in the labour market and other social sites, is important because it challenges simplistic accounts of the nature of identity and inequality in capitalist societies. However, it is also an attempt to theorize race, class and gender in a way that provides the basis for a more united feminist movement.

The second take on the way that race, class and gender trio are treated in Canadian academic literature is less common than the first, but has started to gain influence. In this approach, race, class and gender are understood as factors that help analyze the multiple meanings and expressions of racism. In addition to being interested in how these relations mediate the experiences of racism, it is concerned with how peoples' experiences stemming from their structural location in class, gender and racial hierarchies play a role in the expression and articulation of racist ideas. This approach is derived from some of Stuart Hall's insights about race, made in the late 1970s. According to Hall, racist ideas are

> not a set of false pleas which swim around in the head. They're not a set of mistaken perceptions. They have their basis in real material conditions of existence. They arise because of the concrete problems of different classes and groups in society. Racism represents the attempt ideologically to construct those conditions, contradictions and problems in such a way that they can be dealt with and deflected at the same moment (1978:35).

For Hall, it is necessary to understand the meaning of racism from the perspective of those who articulate racist ideas and engage in racist practices. It is not abstract individuals who express racist ideas or who engage in racist practices, but rather individuals who are located in specific class sites, who are of a particular gender and who define themselves as members of a particular race or ethnicity (Dunk, 1991). The conceptual and empirical problem for sociologists is being able to analyze and understand how the contradictions, stresses and problems that class, gendered and racialized actors face in their everyday lives leave them vulnerable and receptive to racist explanations of their circumstances and surroundings. The challenge is to do this in such as way as to not simply label, and hence dismiss, a certain set of ideas or practices as racist, but rather to understand the conditions that give rise to certain social actors' expressions of racism. This means that sociologically, the significance and consequences of racism depend not only on the race, class and gender of the objects of racist discourse, but also on the race, class and gender of those who articulate racist ideas (Warburton, 1992).

Conclusion

This chapter introduced the reader to some of the theoretical and conceptual debates about the meaning of the categories of race, racialization and racism. It also contextualized some of the theoretical concerns and issues that are developed more fully in the remaining chapters. In particular, this chapter was concerned with elaborating on conceptual tools that are useful in helping to analyze certain ideas, events or institutions as instances of racism. Insofar as there has been a tendency in Canada to use the term racism as both a sociological category and a epithet, it is imperative that social scientists be clear about the definition and meaning of terms and concepts. The chapter argued for the rejection of race as an analytical category, but the retention of the concepts of racialization and racism. Three forms of institutional racism were identified, and a brief overview of some of the debates about race, gender and class was offered. Again, many of the themes that were introduced in this chapter will be developed and explored more fully in the remaining chapters of this book.

REFERENCES

Agnew, V. 1996. *Resisting Discrimination: Women from Asia, Africa, and the Caribbean and the Women's Movement in Canada*. Toronto: University of Toronto Press.

Amit-Tali, V. 1996. "The minority circuit: Identity politics and the professionalization of ethnic activism." In V. Amit-Talai and C. Knowles, eds. *Re-Situating Identities: The Politics of Race, Ethnicity and Culture*. Peterborough: Broadview Press.

Anthias, F. and N. Yuval Davis. 1992. *Racialized Boundaries: Race, Nation, Gender, Colour and Class and the Anti-racist Struggle*. London: Routledge.

Baker, D. 1994. *Reading Racism and the Justice System*. Toronto: Canadian Scholars Press.

Balibar, E. 1991. "Class racism." In E. Balibar and I. Wallerstein. *Race, Nation, and Class: Ambiguous Identities*. London: Verso.

Banton, M. 1970. "The concept of racism." In S. Zubaida, ed. *Race and Racialism*. London: Tavistock.

_____. 1977. *The Idea of Race*. London: Tavistock.

_____. 1987. *Racial Theories*. London: Cambridge University Press.

Barkan, E. 1992. *The Retreat of Scientific Racism*. Cambridge: Cambridge University Press.

Barker, M. 1981. *The New Racism*. London: Junction Books.

Bissoondath, N. 1994. *Selling Illusions: The Cult of Multiculturalism in Canada*. Toronto: Penguin.

Bonacich, E. 1980. "Class approaches to ethnicity and race." *Insurgent Sociologist* 10:2.

Boyd, M. 1992. "Gender, Visible Minority and Immigrant Earnings Inequality: Reassessing an Employment Equity Premise." In V. Satzewich, ed. *Deconstructing A Nation: Immigration, Multiculturalism and Racism in '90s Canada*. Halifax: Fernwood.

Cashmore, E. and E. McLaughlin. 1991. *Out of Order: Policing Black People*. London: Routledge.

Daly, K. 1994. "Class-race-gender: Sloganeering in search of meaning." *Social Justice* 20:56-71.

Driedger, L. 1989. *The Ethnic Factor: Identity in Diversity*. Toronto: McGraw-Hill Ryerson.

Feagin, J. and H. Vera. 1995. *White Racism*. New York: Routledge.

Fleras, A. and J. Elliot. 1995. *Unequal Relations: An Introduction to Race, Ethnic and Aboriginal Dynamics in Canada*. Toronto: Prentice Hall.

Goldberg, D. 1990. "The social formation of racist discourse." In D. Goldberg, ed. *Anatomy of Racism*. Minneapolis: University of Minnesota Press.

Guillaumin, C. 1995. *Racism, Sexism, Power and Ideology*. London: Routledge.

Hall, S. 1978. "Racism and reaction." In *Five Views of Multi-Racial Britain*. London: Commission for Racial Equality.

Henry, F., C. Tator, W. Mattis and T. Rees. 1995. *The Colour of Democracy: Racism in Canadian Society*. Toronto: Harcourt Brace.

Herrnstein, R. and C. Murray. 1994. *The Bell Curve: Intelligence and the Class Structure in American Life*. New York: The Free Press.

Jaggar, A. and P. Rothenberg, eds. 1993. *Feminist Frameworks*, 3rd edition. New York: McGraw-Hill.

James, C. 1994. *Seeing Ourselves: Exploring Race, Ethnicity and Culture*. Toronto: Thompson Educational.

Jhappan, R. 1996. "Post-modern race and gender essentialism or a post-mortem of scholarship," *Studies in Political Economy*, 51:15-64.

Knox, R. 1850. *The Races of Men: A Fragment*. London: Renshaw.

Mason, D. 1986. "Controversies and continuities in race and ethnic relations theory." In D. Mason and J. Rex, eds. *Theories of Race and Ethnic Relations*. Cambridge: Cambridge University Press.

Miles, R. 1989. *Racism*. London: Tavistock.

_____. 1993. *Racism After "Race Relations."* London: Routledge.

Montagu, A. 1972. *Statement on Race*. New York: Oxford University Press.

Omi, M. and H. Winant. 1986. *Racial Formation in the United States*. London: Routledge.

_____. 1993. "On the theoretical status of the concept of race." In C. McCarthy and W. Critchlow, eds. *Race: Identity and Representation in Education*. London: Routledge.

Porter, J. 1987. *The Measure of Canadian Society: Education, Equality and Opportunity*. Ottawa: Carleton University Press.

Ralston, H. 1991. "Race, class, gender and work experience of South Asian immigrant women in Atlantic Canada." *Canadian Ethnic Studies* 23:129-139.

Rawlyk, J. 1962. "Canada's immigration policy, 1945-1962." *The Dalhousie Review* 42:287-300.

Rex, J. 1983. *Race Relations in Sociological Theory*. London: Routledge and Kegan Paul.

Ridgeway, J. 1995. *Blood in the Face: the Ku Klux Klan, Aryan Nations, Nazi Skinheads, and the Rise of a New White Culture*. New York: Thunder's Mouth Press.

Rose, S., L. Kamin and R. Lewontin. 1984. *Not in Our Genes: Biology, Ideology and Human Nature*. Harmondsworth: Penguin.

Rushton, P. 1994. *Race, Evolution and Behaviour: A Lifestyle Perspective*. New Brunswick, N.J.: Transaction Publishers.

Satzewich, V. 1991. *Racism and the Incorporation of Foreign Labour: Farm Labour Migration to Canada Since 1945*. London: Routledge.

Schuman, D. and D. Olfus. 1995. *Diversity on Campus*. Toronto: Allyn and Bacon.

Siegfried, A. 1907. *The Race Question in Canada*. London: E. Nash.

Small, S. 1995. *Racialized Barriers: The Black Experience in the United States and England in the 1980s*. London: Routledge.

Smith, C.H. 1848. *The Natural History of the Human Species*. Edinburgh: Lizars.

Solomos, J. 1986. "Varieties of marxist conceptions of 'race,' class and the state: A critical analysis." In D. Mason and J. Rex, eds. *Theories of Race and Ethnic Relations*. Cambridge: Cambridge University Press.

Stasiulis, D. 1987. "Rainbow feminism: Perspectives on minority women in Canada." *Resources for Feminist Research* 16: 3-9.

_____. 1989. "Theorizing connections: Gender, race, ethnicity, and class." In P. Li. *Race and Ethnic Relations in Canada*. Toronto: Oxford University Press.

Synnott, A. and D. Howes. 1996. "Canada's visible minorities: Identity and representation." In V. Amit-Talai and C. Knowles, eds. *Re-Situating Identities: The Politics of Race, Ethnicity and Culture*. Peterborough: Broadview Press.

Warburton, R. 1992. "Neglected aspects of the political economy of Asian racialization in British Columbia." In V. Satzewich, ed. *Deconstructing A Nation: Immigration, Multiculturalism and Racism in '90s Canada*. Halifax: Fernwood.

West, C. 1993. *Race Matters*. New York: Vintage Books.

Wilson, W.J. 1978. *The Declining Significance of Race*, 2nd edition. Chicago: University of Chicago Press.

_____. 1987. *The Truly Disadvantaged: The Inner City, the Underclass, and Public Policy*. Chicago: University of Chicago Press.

Woodsworth, J.S. 1972. *Strangers Within Our Gates*. Toronto: University of Toronto Press.

2

Prejudice and Discrimination in Canada and the United States: A Comparison

Jeffrey G. Reitz and Raymond Breton

How do Canadians and Americans compare in terms of racial and ethnic prejudice and discrimination? In this chapter, we shall attempt to answer this question, using not only measures of overt prejudice but also measures of the extent to which people in the two countries uphold negative stereotypes of minorities, seek to maintain "social distance" between themselves and members of other groups (in this context, our analysis will consider attitudes toward immigration, minorities as neighbors, and intermarriage), and withhold support from government's taking action against discrimination. We shall also examine evidence, derived from "field trials," of direct discrimination in employment.

Prejudice is a matter of attitudes, discrimination is a matter of behavior. Both things are difficult to measure. Racial and ethnic prejudice has become much less socially acceptable than it once was. Discrimination in employment or housing is not only less socially acceptable, it is illegal. Many observers argue, however, that prejudice and discrimination persist in concealed form. People hide their real attitudes, discriminate in a covert manner, and tolerate discriminatory institutions. It is not easy to turn these attitudes and this behavior out into the daylight, as writers from Gordon Allport (1954) to Studs Terkel (1992) have found.

Our purpose here is not to resolve the problems of measurement. Rather, it is to see whether the standard indicators of prejudice and discrimination, which are perhaps flawed, suggest in any way that there is a difference between the level of prejudice and discrimination in Canada and the level in the United States. The familiar Canadian assumption that the level in Canada is lower can, we believe, be meaningfully addressed in this way.

This chapter comprises Chapter 4 of *The Illusion of Difference: Realities of Ethnicity in Canada and the United States* by Jeffrey G. Reitz and Raymond Breton (Toronto: C.D. Howe Institute, 1994). The material is reproduced here by permission of the authors and the publisher.

Trends within Each Country

In both Canada and the United States, a range of indicators of racial attitudes show certain positive trends. The National Academy of Sciences report, *A Common Destiny: Blacks and American Society* (Jaynes and Williams, 1989), gleaned data from dozens of national opinion polls conducted between 1942 and 1983. These polls, the results of which are summarized in Table 2-1, show growing and now virtually universal verbal commitment to the principle of racial equality. White preferences for "social distance" from Blacks in various settings have declined significantly. Although popular support for government policies and programs to assist Blacks remains low and has shown no consistent trend over time, there has been no major White "backlash."

In Canada, race is less salient, and there is less research.[1] Without doubt the climate in Canada too has improved since the Second World War, when racially exclusionary immigration policies were still in effect. For its study, *The Economic and Social Impact of Immigration*, the Economic Council of Canada assembled data from existing surveys of intolerance (Swan, 1991:111-113). The council reported a positive trend among anglophones on an index of "tolerance." However, the study did not present specific quantitative results, and the index included items on gender as well as race. Henry's finding that one Torontonian in six expresses "very racist" views (Henry, 1978:1) is similarly difficult to compare with other studies, since the index of racism is a combination of 29 correlated items that address a complex range of perceptions and attitudes.

These parallel attempts at trend analysis invite several observations. First, data on racial attitudes in Canada are so much less plentiful than data on attitudes in the United States that clear comparisons are difficult. Second, the existence of positive trends in racial attitudes in both countries may be a point of similarity between them, even if in some ways these changes prove superficial. Definitive comparison must focus on specific key areas, an approach that, as we shall show, yields interesting results. And third, the comparative data are very time-sensitive. One cannot meaningfully compare U.S. data from the 1960s with Canadian data from the 1970s or 1980s. In fact, our goal here is really to measure the trajectory of change in the two countries. One might say that what is at issue is not the extent of cross-national differences, but the approximate number of years (if any) that one country may be ahead of the other in terms of changes in racial attitudes.

Overt Racism and Negative Racial Stereotypes

U.S. survey research clearly shows that overt racism, by which we mean the explicit assertion of innate White superiority, is now expressed only by a small

---

[1] For a review of the Canadian research, see Henry, 1986.

Table 2-1: Trends in Racial Attitudes among Whites in the United States

Type of Question	Question	First and Last Year Asked	Percent Change from First to Last Year	Percent Positive Last Time Asked
Principle	Same schools	1942/1982	+58	90
	Equal jobs	1944/1972	+52	97
	Same transportation	1942/1970	+42	88
	Residential choice (NORC)[a]	1963/1982	+32	71
	Residential choice (ISR)	1964/1976	+23	88
	Same accommodations	1963/1970	+15	88
	Black candidate (Gallup)	1958/1983	+44	81
	Black candidate (NORC)	1972/1983	+12	85
	Against intermarriage laws	1963/1982	+28	66
	Intermarriage	1958/1983	+36	40
	General segregation[b]	1964/1978	+8	35
Implementation	Federal job intervention	1964/1974	-2	36
	Open housing	1973/1983	+12	46
	Federal school intervention	1964/1978	-17	25
	Busing (ISR)	1972/1980	0	9
	Busing (NORC)	1972/1983	+6	21
	Accommodations intervention	1964/1974	+22	66
	Spending on blacks	1973/1983	-1	26
	Aid to minorities	1970/1982	-4	18
Social distance	Few (Gallup)	1958/1980	+20	95
	Few (NORC)	1972/1983	+2	95
	Half (Gallup)	1958/1980	+26	76
	Half (NORC)	1972/1983	0	76
	Most (Gallup)	1958/1980	+9	42
	Most (NORC)	1972/1983	-6	37
	Next door	1958/1978	+30	86
	Great numbers	1958/1978	+26	46
	Same block	1942/1972	+49	85
	Black dinner guest	1963/1982	+26	78
Miscellaneous	Thermometer rating[c] of blacks	1964/1982	+1	61
	Ku Klux Klan rating[d]	1965/1979	-13	71
	Intelligence	1942/1968	+30	77
	Civil rights push	1964/1980	+6	9
	Black push	1963/1982	+18	39

Note: NORC is the National Opinion Research Center; IRS is the Institute for Social Research.

[a] This item uses a Likert scale response format. The percentages reported involve a combination of "disagree slightly" and "disagree strongly" responses.

[b] The trend for this item is probably affected by a contextual linkage to the federal school intervention implementation item.

[c] The feeling thermometer is a standard question used in the National Election Study. It calls for respondents to rank groups or individuals on a 100 point scale, where 0 indicates very cold feelings, 50 indicates neutral feelings, and 100 indicates very warm feelings.

[d] The rating scale runs from -5 to +5. The figures reported indicate the percentages or people giving "highly unfavourable" ratings of the Ku Klux Klan (scores or -4 or -5).

Source: The table is from Jaynes and Williams 1989, 122-123. It is based on data from Schoman et al. 1985; and Bobo, 1987.

minority. Schuman, Steeh and Bobo (1985:125) show that, as recently as the 1940s, only 50 to 60 percent of Americans outside the South—and even fewer in the South—endorsed the innate equality of Blacks, agreeing that "Negroes are as intelligent as White people" and can "learn things just as well if they are given the same education and training." Since the 1950s, the proportion has been at least 90 percent.[2]

A survey conducted in 1990 by Decima Research Ltd. permits a comparison of the two countries. The Canadians in the survey were, overall, slightly less overtly racist than the Americans, but only slightly: 90 percent of the Canadians and 86 percent of the Americans agreed that "all races are created equal" (*Maclean's*, 1990). This difference is insubstantial. Large majorities in both countries deny overt racism.

The denial of overt racism in both countries is also reflected in the fact that few people support organizations with explicitly racist philosophies. The 1989 National Academy of Sciences study (Jaynes and Williams, 1989) found that, in the United States, support for the Ku Klux Klan had increased somewhat during the late 1960s and 1970s but was still marginal. KKK groups in Canada and indigenous organizations with racist messages, such as the Western Guard or the Heritage Front, also have few members (Barrett, 1987; Sher, 1983; and see Schoenfeld, 1991). Actually, many supporters of groups such as the KKK deny that they are racists. One-third of the respondents in a survey conducted in and near Chattanooga, Tennessee, had favourable views of the KKK. Many of them cited the KKK as a "charitable" organization and as one that supported law and order; they may have been dissembling their knowledge of its racial views (Seltzer and Lopes, 1986:95). In both countries, some mainstream politicians, too, have been accused of appealing to hidden racial feelings, though as a rule they deny this intention.

How widespread are hidden racist attitudes? Is there more hidden racism in one country than the other? When racism is discussed in public debate, the reference is often really not to overt racism but rather to hidden racism, or to negative racial stereotyping. To what extent do people hold views that might reflect an unexpressed belief in White superiority?

U.S. attitude surveys show that some of those who deny racism in fact have racist views that are easily brought to the surface For example, when Americans are asked to explain why so many Blacks are poor, many of them refer to innate racial inferiority. The General Social Surveys (GSS) for 1988 and 1989 asked the following question:

2
    According to a poll conducted in 1989 by the *Los Angeles Times*, 90 percent of the population of Los Angeles said that "Blacks are as intelligent as White people—that is, Blacks learn just as well if they are given the same education." The percentage among "WASPs" was 92 percent.

On the average Blacks have worse jobs, income, and housing than White people. Do you think that these differences are ... (a) mainly due to discrimination, (b) because most Blacks have less in-born ability to learn, (c) because most Blacks don't have the chance for education that it takes to rise out of poverty, and (d) because most Blacks just don't have the motivation or will power to pull themselves out of poverty? (Kluegel, 1990:514)

The proportion of respondents who chose the explanation "Blacks have less in-born ability," either alone or in combination with other explanations, was 20.8 percent (Kluegel, 1990:517). Thus, although few Whites explicitly challenge the proposition (put forward in the 1990 Decima survey, for example) that all races are created equal, a significantly larger proportion refer to inherent racial inferiority when asked to explain Black poverty. Some people explain Black disadvantage as "God's plan" (Kluegel and Smith, 1986:188).

Many Americans, in shifting away from overt racist views, have embraced what Kluegel calls "individualistic" explanations for Black-White inequality (Kluegel, 1990:515) They say that Blacks lack motivation or have an inferior culture. They deny "structuralist" explanations—that Blacks lack educational and employment opportunity or experience discrimination. In the 1977 GSS, the proportion of respondents who explained Black poverty by reference to innate Black inferiority was 26 percent (Kluegel and Smith, 1986:188; see also Sniderman and Hagen, 1985:30). In 1988-89, as we have shown, it was about 21 percent. Throughout this period, most endorsed individualist explanations, and only about 25 to 30 percent believed that Blacks experienced any significant discrimination. In fact, the 1977 GSS showed that the same proportion felt that Blacks were given preference—that there was discrimination against Whites (Kluegel, 1985:768). "Young and old Americans alike appear to believe that discrimination in the work force *currently* does not function to limit opportunity for Black workers to any substantial degree" (Kluegel, 1985:771).

Does the belief that Blacks bring disadvantage on themselves reflect racial prejudice? In many cases perhaps not, but Kluegel (1990:516) shows that the two things are related empirically. In the United States, overt racists—those who say that Blacks are disadvantaged because they are inferior—are the group most likely to believe that Whites have the right to Whites-only neighborhoods and to favour laws against intermarriage. Kluegel calls these matters "traditional indicators of prejudice," since they reflect a desire to exclude people on the basis of race.[3] However, although those who say that Blacks bring disadvantage on themselves are less likely than the overt racists to have these traditional prejudices, they are more likely to have them than are those who cite discrimination to explain why Blacks are disadvantaged. So those who cite Black motivation are more likely than are those who cite discrimination to believe that Black exclusion is justified.

---

[3] See our discussion of "social distance" below.

What are the comparable Canadian attitudes? Canadian explanations for mi-nority-group disadvantage are not, of course, strictly comparable with American explanations. Asking Canadians about minorities in Canada is obviously not necessarily the same as asking Americans about minorities in the United States. Nevertheless, in the 1987 Canadian Charter Study about 70 percent of the re-spondents agreed that "immigrants often bring discrimination upon themselves by their own personal attitudes and habits," 25 percent disagreed, and the re-maining 5 percent gave various qualified responses or "don't know" (Sniderman et al., 1991).[4] The proportion of those who cited an "individualistic" explana-tion—70 percent—is about the same as the proportion in the United States. Thus, Canadians, like Americans, frequently deny that the minorities in their respective countries are the victims of racial discrimination. Of course, it is arguable what is in fact the case in each country We examine data relevant to the actual compara-tive extent of discrimination below. For now, we simply note that Canadians and Americans seem to be alike in tending to prefer individualistic explanations of minority disadvantage to explanations that cite discrimination.

Some interesting comparative data are available on racial jokes. In the 1990 Decima survey, more Americans than Canadians—46 percent versus 38 per-cent—said they never told racial jokes.[5] Americans may be more on guard against giving racial offense than Canadians are, perhaps because of the greater salience of racial conflict in the United States.

Anti-Semitism

In both countries, the Jewish group is long-established and largely urban, accounts for 1 to 2 percent of the population, and has high average levels of educational and occupational attainment and earnings (Lieberson and Waters, 1988; Li, 1988; Reitz, 1990). Because of this similarity, comparisons of negative attitudes and behavior toward Jews provide a particularly good indication of relative predisposition toward ethnic tolerance. For Jews, unlike Blacks, the issue of relations with the other groups arises in a very similar way in the two coun-tries.

Studies that measure the prevalence of negative stereotypes of Jews have produced remarkably similar aggregate results in the United States and Canada. We compare results from the Charter Study in Canada in 1987 (Sniderman et al., 1992; 1993) with those from a U.S. survey reported by Martire and Clark (1982:17) in 1981. In three of the four comparisons, as Table 2-2 shows, about one Canadian in five and one American in five gave a response that described the

---

[4]
    We would like to thank Joseph Fletcher for providing us with access to this information about the Charter Study.

[5]
    Maclean's, June 25, 1990, p.52. The proportions of Americans who rarely, sometimes, or often told ethnic or racial jokes were 25, 25, and 4 percent, respectively; the corresponding figures for Canadians were 28, 26, and 7 percent.

Table 2-2: Attitudes toward Jews in Canada and the United States

	United States (1981)		Canada (1987)
1.	"Jews don't care what happens to anyone but their own kind." Probably true: 16% Probably false: 59% Not sure: 25%		"Most Jews don't care what happens to people who aren't Jewish." Agree: 19% Disagree; 68% Don't know: 12%
2.	"Jews today are trying to push in where they are not wanted." Probably true: 16 Probably false: 70 Not sure: 14		"Most Jews are pushy." Agree: 34 Disagree: 55 Don't know: 11
3.	"Jews have contributed much to the cultural life of America." Probably false: 14 Probably true: 53 Not sure: 33		"Jews have made an important contribution to the cultural life of Canada." Disagree: 21 Agree: 63 Don't know: 15
4.	"Jews are more willing to use shady practices." Probably true: 23 Probably false: 46 Not sure: 31		"Jews are more willing than others to use shady practices to get ahead." Agree: 23 Disagree: 61 Don't know: 14

Sources: The Canadian data are from the Charter Study (see Sniderman et al., 1991). Data were collected by the York University Institute of Behavioural Research in 1987 (2,080 in sample); the questions used here are numbers i15-i19. We thank Joseph Fletcher for providing access to these data. The US data were collected by Yankelovich, Skelly and White, Inc. in 1981 (1,072 in sample) and reported by Martire and Clark, 1982:17.

Jewish group in a negative way. Canadians were more likely than Americans, however, to agree that Jews are "pushy."

There are positive stereotypes of the Jewish group as well as negative ones. Smith (1990:9), using GSS data, found that, in the United States, the general population rates Jews above "Whites" in relation to the descriptive tags "rich," "hard-working," "not violent," "intelligent," and "self-supporting."

In both countries, anti-Semitic stereotypes have their greatest currency within certain other minority groups. The frictions between Jews and these other minorities are secondary ethnic conflicts, derived from broader patterns of ethnic disadvantage. In Canada, French-Canadian attitudes toward Jews are more negative than those of any other group (Sniderman et al., 1991). However, French-Canadian attitudes toward other minorities are also more negative. At the same time, there is greater pressure toward conformity—including ethnic assimilation—in Quebec than there is in the rest of the country. These are classic patterns in group conflict: suspicion of outsiders and closing of ranks among insiders.

In the United States, there is a roughly parallel tension between Jews and Blacks. This tension is at least in part the result of a reactive response among Blacks, rather than an indication that Blacks have a greater predisposition to anti-Semitism than other groups. The position of Blacks in the United States has also led to tensions between Blacks and other minorities, including Asians and Hispanics (Oliver and Johnson, 1984; Johnson and Oliver, 1989; Rose, 1989).

One can compare anti-Semitic behavior in the United States and Canada by using the "audit of anti-Semitic incidents" that B'nai Brith, the Jewish service organization, publishes in each country. The Anti-Defamation League of B'nai Brith in the United States reports 1,879 incidents in 1991 (ADLBB, 1991:29). In Canada, the equivalent organization is the League for Human Rights of B'nai Brith, whose more positive-sounding name suggests a less conflictful or more tolerant setting. Nevertheless, the number of incidents reported in Canada in 1991 was 251 (LHRBB Canada, 1991:4), more than might be expected given the roughly 10-to-1 U.S.-Canadian population ratio. The totals for 1982 to 1992, however, uphold the ratio—there were 12,665 incidents in the United States and 1,191 in Canada. The year-to-year figures fluctuate not quite in lock step, responding similarly to events such as the Persian Gulf War, which seemed to provoke increases in anti-Semitic incidents—and anti-Muslim incidents as well—in both countries.[6]

Thus, attitudes and behavior reflect very similar patterns of anti-Semitism in the two countries. This case, free from some of the methodological complexities that affect other comparisons, does not support the hypothesis that Canadians are more tolerant than Americans.

Social Distance

Social distance is a measure of dominant-group tolerance for social relations with members of a given minority. For a given minority, social distance is greater when the majority is unwilling to tolerate not only close relations such as marriage and family membership but also more distant relations. Thus, the majority may be unwilling to tolerate members of the minority as neighbors, as co-workers, or even as immigrants.

U.S. data show that social distances from the dominant English-origin group are greatest for Blacks and other racial minorities, less for southern Europeans, and least for northern Europeans (Bogardus, 1958; 1967). Surveys of university social science students conducted since the 1920s have shown that social distance for a variety of minority groups has declined over the years but that the

---

6
    Incident classification indicates that vandalism is more prevalent in the U.S. reports, harassment in the Canadian. Shefman (1987:6) states that the difference "may, in part, be attributed to the different legal and social traditions in Canada which demand action against prejudice and bigotry prior to action being taken." However, this *ad hoc* explanation does not account for the higher rates of harassment in Canada. Perhaps the reporting criteria vary.

rank-order of racial groups has remained fairly stable (see Owen, Eisner and McFaul, 1981; and Sinha and Barry, 1991). Table 2-3 shows how racial and ethnic groups in the United States have been ranked in various years. Sinha and Berry (1991), who have applied the concept of social distance to groups such as intravenous drug users, AIDS victims, people who have attempted suicide, and homosexuals, find that ethnic and racial groups are now less socially distant from the dominant groups than are these other groups. They suggest that race and ethnicity are becoming less important than behavior as a basis for discrimination.

Comparative Canadian data are available for national samples as well as student populations. The national data describe the "social standing" of ethnic and racial groups, which is presumably akin to social distance or group prestige. In a national survey on ethnic social standing, English- and French-Canadian respondents placed names in ranked categories. The results in Table 2-4 show a rank-order similar to the rank-order for U.S. minorities in Table 2-3. Racial minorities, including Blacks and Asians, are at the bottom, southern Europeans rank higher, and northern Europeans higher still (Berry, Kalin and Taylor, 1977; Pineo, 1977; and Angus Reid Group Inc., 1991). Driedger and Mezoff (1981) derive similar results from data on Manitoba university students (see also Dion, 1985).

Calculations of social distance index values on the basis of student samples yield similar results for the two countries. The 1977 figure for Blacks in the United States was 2.03 and a comparable figure for Blacks in Canada was 2.12; for West Indians it was 2.46 (Driedger and Mezoff, 1981).[7] For Chinese, the 1977 U.S. figure was 2.29, and the 1981 Canadian figure was 2.33. For Mexicans, the U.S. and Canadian figures were, respectively, 2.40 and 2.38; for Japanese, they were 2.38 and 2.40. There is one major discrepancy: the index value for American Indians in 1977 was 1.84, whereas the value for Native Indians in Canada, or at least in Manitoba, was substantially higher, 2.70.

No one has calculated precise index values for social distance between Whites and specific minorities in both countries on the basis of national or even general-population data, let alone data collected at comparable points in time. As Table 2-1 has shown, Jaynes and Williams (1989:122-123) summarized U.S. national survey data to demonstrate that White social distances from Blacks have declined. These and other potentially comparable data address specific components of social distance, such as acceptance of minorities as neighbors, or as family members through intermarriage, rather than social distance generally. The following subsections consider four of these specific components.

---

[7] A 1976 Toronto survey of the general population showed an index for Blacks of 1.95. For East Indians, the index was 2.04; for Pakistanis, 2.22; and for Italians, 1.34 (Henry, 1978:83).

**Table 2-3: Mean Social Distances of Ethnic and Racial Groups
in the United States, 1926-90
(as measured on the Bogardus social distance scale)**

	1926	1946	1956	1966	1977	1990
Groups included in the Bogardus scale						
Americans (US white)	1.10	1.04	1.08	1.07	1.25	1.13
English	1.06	1.13	1.23	1.14	1.39	1.15
Canadians	1.13	1.11	1.16	1.15	1.42	1.19
Italians	1.94	2.28	1.89	1.51	1.65	1.36
French	1.32	1.31	1.47	1.36	1.58	1.37
Germans	1.46	1.59	1.61	1.54	1.87	1.39
Americans Indians	2.38	2.45	2.35	2.18	1.84	1.59
Poles	2.01	1.84	2.07	1.98	2.11	1.68
Jews	2.39	2.32	2.15	1.97	2.01	1.71
Blacks	3.28	3.60	2.74	2.56	2.03	1.73
Chinese	3.36	2.50	2.68	2.34	2.29	1.76
Japanese	2.80	3.61	2.70	2.41	2.38	1.86
Russians	1.88	1.83	2.56	2.38	2.57	1.93
Koreans	3.60	3.05	2.83	2.51	2.63	1.94
Mexicans	2.69	2.89	2.79	2.56	2.40	2.00
Groups not included in the Bogardus scale						
Israelis	--	--	--	--	--	2.63
Palestinians	--	--	--	--	--	2.78
Iranians	--	--	--	--	--	3.03
Spread	2.54	2.57	1.75	1.49	1.38	1.90
Change in spread		+0.03	-0.82	-0.26	-0.11	+0.52

Note: The Borgadus social distance scale ranges from a low of 1.00 to a high of 7.00. The figures are based on mean ratings of the degree of distance that respondents would prefer to maintain between themselves and members of each group. The available responses are: acceptance "into my family through marriage or cohabitation" (1.00), acceptance "as close friends or room mate" (2.00), acceptance "in my dorm" (3.00), acceptance "as a co-worker or class mate" (4.00), acceptance "as speaking acquaintance only" (5.00), acceptance "as visitor only to my country" (6.00), and "would not accept into my country" (7.00).

Source: Sinha and Berry, 1991:7.

Immigration

One component of social distance is attitudes toward specific groups as immigrants. Canadians favour immigration more than Americans do, despite the fact that racial-minority immigration is currently greater in Canada. In the 1990 Decima survey, 58 percent of Americans wanted less immigration and only 6 percent wanted more (*Maclean's*, 1990:52). By contrast, 39 percent of Canadians wanted less immigration and 18 percent wanted more. Whether these more positive Canadian attitudes apply to "new" racial-minority immigrants is not clear. Nevertheless, in a 1976, Gallup poll, 63 percent of Canadians opposed racial

**Table 2-4: Social Standing of Minority Groups in English
and French Canada**

Minority Group	Social Standing as Ranked by:	
	English Canada	**French Canada**
Own group	83.1	77.6
English	82.4	77.6
Italians	43.1	51.3
French	60.1	72.4
Germans	48.7	40.5
Canadian Indians	28.3	32.5
Poles	42.0	38.0
Jews	46.1	43.1
Blacks	25.4	23.5
Chinese	33.1	24.9
Japanese	34.7	27.8
Russians	35.8	33.2

Note: The categories are placed in order of the comparable groups in Table 2-3; some groups are not included.
Source: Pineo, 1977:154.

restrictions and only 27 percent favoured them. In 1981, only 10 percent supported "cutting off all non-White immigration to Canada."[8]

American attitudes toward immigration appear to have turned negative as immigration increased after the 1960s. In a series of comparable polls, the proportion of Americans who wanted less immigration increased from 33 percent in 1965 to 61 percent in 1993.[9] There appears to be a nearly comparable trend in Canada. Angus Reid Group Inc. (1989:4-5) reports that the proportion of Canadians who think too many immigrants are coming to Canada increased from 30 percent in May 1988 to 31 percent in February 1989 and 43 percent in August 1989. An Ekos Research Associates Inc. poll showed that this proportion had risen to 53 percent by February 1994 (*Globe and Mail* [Toronto], March 10, 1994, p.A1). On the other hand, Environics polls conducted in 1986 and 1989 showed a decline in agreement with the statement that "there is too much immigration to Canada," from 66 percent to 57 percent (Angus Reid Group Ltd. 1989:5).[10]

Canadians' somewhat more positive attitudes may reflect their country's different historical and institutional context, rather than cultural predisposition.

8

The Gallup Omnibus survey for the Minister of State for Multiculturalism in November 1981 showed 43 percent in complete agreement with "open immigration" and 56 percent at least partly in agreement.

9

New York Times, June 27, 1993, 1 and 16. The polls were conducted by Gallup and the *New York Times* in collaboration with CBS News.

10

The greater opposition to immigration in the Environics polls may result from a positive-response bias. The Angus Reid question allowed respondents to say whether the numbers of immigrants were too many, about right, or too few.

Postwar Canadian immigration, mostly European in origin, has been a major element of economic and social development policy. Reimers and Troper (1992) argue that, in the United States, immigration has ceased to be a development policy and is now perceived as social welfare, and that public support has declined accordingly. Like Americans, and perhaps for similar reasons, Britons support racial minority immigration less than Canadians do. British immigration has been an obligation to former colonial territories in the Commonwealth, rather than a program of national development (see Reitz, 1988a; 1988b).

At the same time, there are signs that growing unease with immigration among White Canadians as well as among White Americans is, in fact, related to race, not just to numbers or to immigration goals. In a 1979 survey in Toronto (Breton et al., 1990:204), 63 percent of "majority Canadians" agreed that "present immigration laws make it too easy for certain groups to come to Canada." In identifying these "certain groups," respondents mentioned racial minorities three times more often than they mentioned other immigrant groups. European origin immigrants shared these concerns. In the United States, a recent *Newsweek* poll asked a comparable question in a national sample: "Should it be easier or more difficult for people from the following places to immigrate to the U.S.?" About half of the respondents said that it should be more difficult for people from China or other Asian countries to immigrate to the United States, and 61 percent said it should be more difficult for people from the Middle East to immigrate to the United States.[11] These results from the two countries seem to be roughly parallel.

Community and Neighborhood Residence

There has long been a significant cross-national difference in responses to racial minorities as neighbors. Comparative Gallup data assembled by Michalos (1982:169, 206) indicate that in 1963 only 3 percent of Canadians said that they would definitely move "if coloured people came to live next door" and 91 percent said that they would stay put. In the United States at that time, 20 percent said that they would move and only 55 percent said that they would stay

Things have changed since the 1960s, of course. Although racial preferences for neighbors are still significant and strong in the United States, feelings have relaxed noticeably over time. In the late 1960s, U.S. movers declined to 12 percent and stayers rose to 65 percent. In 1978, only 10 percent would move if a Black moved next door (Schuman, Steeh, and Bobo, 1985:106-108). As late as 1981, however, a majority of northerners preferred a mostly White neighborhood and one in four preferred an all-White neighborhood (Schuman, Steeh and Bobo, 1985:67). In the South, two-thirds preferred a mostly White neighborhood and the preference for an all-White neighborhood varied between 38 and 51 per-

---

11
Newsweek, August 9, 1993, p.25.

cent.[12] Openness to Black neighbors varies with the numbers of Blacks mentioned in the question. Figures in Table 2-1, above, show that whereas only 46 percent of White Americans said they would not move if Blacks came into their neighborhood in "great numbers," about 85 percent said they would not move if Blacks moved in "next door" or onto the "same block."

Canadian attitudes may not be markedly different, but in recent available surveys the same questions have not been asked. Replies to the most closely comparable questions do not suggest extreme cross-national differences. In the 1978-79 Ethnic Pluralism Survey in Toronto, two-thirds of the respondents said that they were willing to have a West Indian as a next-door neighbor "if you were completely free to decide yourself" (Breton et al., 1990:200). The proportion that responded positively to having Chinese, Italian, or Portuguese neighbors was about 85 percent.

Acceptance into Social Clubs

A willingness to accept racial minorities into private clubs would seem to indicate an even greater tolerance than does a willingness to accept them into neighborhoods. Yet the data for both countries show more support for open membership than for open neighborhoods. In a 1987 Gallup poll, only 15 percent of Americans and 12 percent of Canadians thought private clubs should have the right to exclude prospective members on the basis of race. The exclusion of minorities from social clubs may be regarded as a symbol of overt racism and may therefore be rejected even if there is a desire to exclude.

Intermarriage

Both Canadians and Americans have become more tolerant of racial intermarriage in recent decades, but Canadians continue to lead Americans in this regard. In Canada, disapproval of Black-White marriages declined from 52 percent in 1968 to 35 percent in 1973 (Michalos, 1982:205), and those who disapprove are now only a small minority—16 percent, according to a 1988 Gallup National Omnibus Newspaper poll. In 1988, according to the same poll, 72.5 percent of Canadians approved of Black-White marriages. Lambert and Curtis (1984) show that English-Canadian disapproval declined from 60 percent in 1968 to 24 percent in 1983; there was less disapproval in Quebec.

In the United States, disapproval of Black-White marriages declined from 72 percent in 1968 to 60 percent in 1972 (Michalos, 1982:205). Yet, in 1983, only 40 percent of Americans approved of marriages between Whites and any non-Whites (Schuman, Steeh and Bobo, 1985:74-76). The 1988 GSS showed that 25 percent of Americans think Black-White marriages should actually be outlawed

---

12
    The higher figure resulted from face-to-face interviews—in which, the authors suggest, the respondents could be sure that the interviewer was not Black.

(Niemi, Mueller and Smith, 1989:170). This figure represents a decline from earlier decades, but clearly the social climate in the United States is different from the social climate in Canada. The 1989 Decima poll confirms the difference: 32 percent of the American respondents, but only 13 percent of the Canadians said that they would be unhappy if one of their children "married someone from a different racial background." Only 15 percent of the Americans, but 25 percent of the Canadians, said that they would be "happy" (*Maclean's,* 1989).

To put the differences in the context of change, attitudes in the United States today are like those in Canada of a decade or more ago. The Canadian data cited above show a change of about 2 percentage points per year.[13] The U.S. data in Jaynes and Williams (1989:122) show a change of 1.5 points per year.[14] In the matter of opposition to intermarriage, two of the data sources cited above indicate a difference between the two countries of about 20 points.[15] Given a rate of 1.5 or 2 points per year, therefore, Canada may be ten or a dozen years ahead of the United States in the trend toward acceptance of interracial marriages.

Employment Discrimination

How much ethnic or racial discrimination actually occurs in each of the two countries? We shift here from attitudes to behavior. Racial or ethnic discrimination in employment is defined as the commission of acts that put people at a disadvantage in the search for work or in the workplace solely because of their racial or ethnic origins. Our focus here is on discrimination against racial minorities. In both Canada and the United States, as we shall show, most of the evidence suggests that discrimination against ethnic groups of European origin is not a major concern.

Discrimination is a complex phenomenon, and there are many different forms and sources of discrimination. Discrimination may be direct or indirect. Direct discrimination is a result of the unequal application of hiring criteria. It may be either overt or covert and, since overt discrimination is illegal, the research challenge is to identify covert discrimination. It may be either intentional or unintentional—a distinction of declining legal significance. And it may be motivated by any one or more of the following: negative attitudes toward racial

---

13
   This is based on a rough average from three sources: a decline of 37 points (from 53 to 16 percent opposed) in the Canada-wide data over the 20 year period 1968 through 1988 (1.85 points per year), a decline of 36 points (from 60 to 24 percent opposed) in the English-Canadian data over the 15-year period 1968 through 1983 (2.4 points per year), and a decline of 27 points (from 38 to 11 percent opposed) in the French-Canadian data over the same 15-year period (1.8 points per year).

14
   The Jaynes and Williams data show a positive change of 36 points in attitudes toward intermarriage over a period of 25 years (1.4 points per year) and a positive change of 28 points in attitudes toward intermarriage laws over a period of 19 years (1.5 points per year).

15
   The two sources are the 1968 Michalos data on Black-White intermarriage (72 percent opposition in the United States, 52 percent in Canada) and the 1989 Decima data on unhappiness about interracial marriage by one's own children (32 percent in the United States, 13 percent in Canada).

minorities and a desire to exclude them, which human capital economists call a "taste" for discrimination; negative stereotypes about the work potential of racial minorities, which are discriminatory when they are applied to an individual (whether or not the employer believes they are accurate for the group as a whole); economic incentives, which are a major topic of debate in economic and sociological discussions of labor markets; and social conventions or group pressures, such as when employee groups prefer, or are perceived to prefer, not to work with minorities.

Discrimination may also be indirect; that is, it may arise not from the unequal application of hiring criteria but from the discriminatory nature of the hiring criteria themselves. For example, discrimination may result indirectly from the established practice of "credentialism," or the use in hiring of educational criteria that are not actually related to the requirements of the job.[16]

One way to measure employment discrimination is to consider whether the occupations or earnings of racial minorities are commensurate with their job qualifications. We shall take up this question in Chapter 5 [*editor's note*—see Chapter 5 of *The Illusion of Difference: Realitites of Ethnicity in Canada and the United States*], which examines the overall social and economic incorporation of minorities. Although there are risks in drawing conclusions about discrimination from analyses of this kind, we shall argue that a comparison of Canada and the United States on this basis is nonetheless relevant to an assessment of discrimination in the two countries.

Complaints of discrimination to human rights commissions offer another potential measure of employment discrimination, but such data almost certainly reflect only a very small proportion of all discriminatory acts. What is more important, the data are not comparable, since the procedures used by human rights commissions vary widely from one jurisdiction to another.

Here we shall consider findings from racial discrimination "field trials," which have been conducted in comparable ways in Canada and the United States. In these exercises, actors from different racial groups apply for the same jobs and present identical qualifications. Any differences in the employers' responses may reasonably be taken as evidence of direct discrimination.

In Toronto, field trials conducted in 1984 by Henry and Ginsberg (1985) found that Whites received three times as many job offers as Blacks. Blacks were five times more likely than Whites to be told that a job had been filled when a subsequent White applicant was invited for an interview. The study provided strong evidence that racial discrimination significantly reduced the labor-market opportunities of Blacks in Toronto, and it received wide coverage in the media.

16

The terms "institutional discrimination" and "systemic discrimination" are in frequent use. Institutional or systemic discrimination is discrimination that occurs for reasons other than the racial attitudes of individual employers. This form of discrimination may be direct or indirect.

Henry (1989) conducted a replication of the 1984 field trials (Henry and Ginsberg, 1985) in 1989. The Economic Council of Canada argued that the new study showed "dramatic change," in that "there was now no racial discrimination in job offers based on face-to-face interviews" (Swan et al., 1991:118). However, the demand for labor in Toronto was much greater in 1989 than it had been in 1984, and heavy labor demand often temporarily improves the opportunities for disadvantaged groups.. The Economic Council maintained that "the tight labor market in Toronto cannot account in any obvious direct way for the 1989 results: the employers who were tested had the possibility of choosing between equally qualified Blacks and Whites" (ibid.). Thus, "employers have gradually become more tolerant, just like the rest of Canadians" (ibid.). This argument is not convincing. The research procedure specified that the Black applicants approach the employers first. In a tight labor market, employers are likely to hire the first qualified applicant who comes along. In nearly half of the 1989 field-trial cases in which a Black was hired, the offer was made "on the spot," before the White had a chance to apply (Henry, 1989:19-20). When these cases are removed from the analysis (to eliminate the effect of the strong labor demand), the results show that more job offers were made to Whites than to Blacks, and that no statistically significant change had occurred since 1984.[17] The research procedure appears to have given the Black applicant an advantage in 1989 that may have offset employer bias (see Reitz, 1993; 1994) Nevertheless, like the 1984 study, the 1989 study found many indications of discriminatory treatment (Henry, 1989:24-29).

Field trials in Washington, DC, and Chicago (Turner, Fix and Struyk, 1991) showed levels of discrimination comparable to those that Henry and Ginsberg found in Toronto in 1984. The study was undertaken to evaluate what its conductors describe as a belief—used as a basis for judicial and administrative decision making—that, because of American progress in combating discrimination, the country is "well on the way to becoming a colour-blind society" (Turner, Fix and Struyk, 1991:1). They refer to "some scholars who claim that most overt discrimination has been eliminated and … others who argue that the residual is not worthy of elimination by state coercion" (ibid.). In the U.S. study, Whites received three times as many job offers as Blacks (Turner, Fix and Struyk, 1991:19). They were also three times as likely to be invited for a job interview. "If equally qualified Black and White candidates are in competition for a job, when differential treatment occurs, it is three times more likely to favour the White applicant over the Black" (Turner, Fix and Struyk, 1991:32) Differential treatment was somewhat greater in the Washington trials than in those conducted in Chicago.

17
   The results showed less racial difference in 1989 than in 1984, but because of the small size of the two studies the evidence of change over time might be attributable to chance (with a probability greater than one in twenty).

The similarity between the results of the 1984 Henry and Ginsberg study and those of the Turner, Fix, and Struyk study suggests that discriminatory practices are not widely different in the two countries. The Economic Council of Canada's view that a form of racial discrimination of comparable importance in the two countries disappeared—in one country but not in the other—in a few years should not be accepted without a clear explanation of how it happened in such a short time.

Collective and Government Action against Discrimination

Americans have at times regarded race relations as one of their country's leading problems, a perception that has led to pressure for government action. A poll conducted in 1963, after a decade of growing racial unrest, showed that 52 percent of the U.S. population considered racial problems to be the most important problem facing the country; only 25 percent gave priority to the threat of war with the Soviet Union. Later, the prominence of the race issue receded, but it continues to be more significant in the United States than it has ever been in Canada (Michalos, 1982:189-201).

In the context of race, accordingly, Americans have been more likely than Canadians to favour government action. In 1970, 25 percent of Americans, but only 11 percent of Canadians, put "reducing racial discrimination" among the top three government priorities for the future (Michalos, 1982:202). And, of course, the U.S. government has indeed taken more action (Jain and Sloane, 1981; Jain, 1989). The Canadian federal government has avoided U.S.-style legislation to mandate equal employment on the ground that the problem is less serious in Canada (Reitz, 1988b).

The higher priority that Americans have placed on racial discrimination is attributable in part to the higher level of racial conflict in the United States; it does not necessarily indicate a greater underlying predisposition to favour government action against discrimination. Indeed, as racial conflict has declined, Americans' willingness to invoke government action against discrimination seems to have declined somewhat as well, even though racial tolerance has increased. Table 2-1 shows that, even as racial attitudes and social-distance scores improved in the 1970s and 1980s, Whites became more supportive of policies to assist Blacks only in the area of housing and accommodations, and less supportive of such policies in other areas, including schools.

Kluegel (1990) uses GSS data for 1986, 1988, and 1989 to probe Americans' attitudes toward assisting Blacks to achieve equality. The GSS respondents were asked the following:

> Some people think that Blacks have been discriminated against for so long that the government has a special obligation to help improve their living standards. Others believe that the government should not be giving special treatment to Blacks .... Where would you place yourself on this scale, or haven't you made up your mind on this?

Pooling the surveys, Kluegel finds that only 13.8 percent agreed that the government was obligated to help Blacks; 59.3 percent stated that the government had no such obligation, and 26.9 percent took a position in between. Pooled analysis of these surveys, plus others conducted in 1977 and 1985, showed that the U.S. population was evenly split between those who thought the government was doing too much—26.8 percent—and those who thought it was doing too little—24.7 percent.[18] Kluegel makes this point:

> The only substantial change between 1977 and the late 1980s in how Whites view the Black-White socio-economic gap is a decline in the attribution of that gap to inborn ability differences. This decline parallels the trend of declining traditional prejudice .... The abatement of perhaps the most invidious explanation for the Black-White status gap has not been accompanied by any noteworthy increase in attributions that favour efforts to provide equal opportunity for Black Americans. (Kluegel, 1990:523)

Smith's (1990:7) analysis of the 1990 GSS data shows that negative images of Blacks in the context of work and welfare have had a direct effect on support for affirmative action for Blacks Thus, although the explanations that Americans give for racial disadvantages have changed, there is a persistent reluctance to identify discrimination as a major cause of these disadvantages, and hence resistance to policies intended to offset discrimination, Bobo (1988:109) offers a group-conflict interpretation of this resistance, suggesting that Whites oppose "change that might impose substantial burdens on Whites."

In Canada, no survey has asked if the government has an obligation to secure equal opportunity for Blacks. The 1987 Charter Study,[19] however, did ask respondents if the government has an obligation to ensure equal opportunity in general. The statement "while equal opportunity to succeed is important for all Canadians, it's not really the government's job to guarantee it" elicited agreement from 63.3 percent of the respondents and disagreement from 33.7 percent By contrast, as we noted above, only 13.8 percent of Americans approved of government intervention to assist Blacks. Of course, Canadian opinions might be different if racial minorities were targeted as beneficiaries. Support for government action to ensure equal opportunity might not translate into support for government action to assist a particular group.

Sniderman and Hagen (1985) show that American rejection of government intervention is linked to "individualism," and suggest that individualist values militate against collective solutions. If this is true, then Canadians, who are less committed to individualism than Americans are, may be more willing to support government intervention. However, the causal relation between values and policy may work the other way: opposition to government assistance to Blacks may

---

18
  The overall results reported here are recalculated from Kluegel's (1990:521, Table 5).

19
  A survey of attitudes to the Canadian Charter of Rights and Freedoms is described in Sniderman et al., 1991. We are grateful to Joseph Fletcher for providing data from this survey reported below.

reinforce individualism, which, in turn, may be invoked to legitimate racial inequality.

Thus, although discrimination has been a bigger political issue in the United States than it has been in Canada, and although more government intervention has occurred in the United States, Americans are not more likely than Canadians to favour collective responses to discrimination. Given their greater individualism, they may be less likely. Earlier, we showed that Canadians and Americans seem to be equally uncomfortable with the idea that discrimination is an explanation for inequality. The fact that social distances are less great in Canada may not mean that Canadians are more open to government intervention to ensure racial equality.

Summary

The findings reviewed here suggest that, despite the historical differences between race relations in Canada and race relations in the United States, Canadians and Americans are roughly similar in their attitudes and behavior toward racial minorities. In both countries, Blatant racism is marginal and the social distance between racial minorities and other groups is diminishing. The incidence of anti-Semitic attitudes and behavior is about the same in each country, and so is the incidence of discrimination in employment. A majority of both Canadians and Americans feel that minorities are responsible for their own inequality, that discrimination is not a major cause of inequality and that government should not intervene to ensure equality

Although the social distance between the majority and the racial minorities has declined in both countries, it has consistently been smaller in Canada, especially in relation to intermarriage. Depending on the dimension of social distance in question, Canadian attitudes may be either comparable to American attitudes or a decade or more ahead of them.

One likely reason the social distance between the races is greater in the United States is that economic distance is greater as well—a point we shall discuss in Chapter 5 [*editor's note*—see Chapter 5 of *The Illusion of Difference: Realitites of Ethnicity in Canada and the United States*]. Another likely reason is that racial minorities constitute a much larger proportion of the total population in the United States than they do in Canada. Thus there may be a sense among White Americans that exclusion is necessary to maintain a degree of racial homogeneity that White Canadians take for granted.

The cross-national differences in social distance do not seem to produce significant differences between the two countries in regard to racial stereotyping, racial discrimination in employment and other important areas, the perception of discrimination as a cause of inequality, or willingness to support government intervention to oppose discrimination. Nor does the decline in social distance over time in both countries seem to have produced much change in any of these other matters. More research is needed on the impact of social values on attitudes and behavior toward racial minorities. Individualism in the United States may work against the adoption of public policies such as affirmative action. But Canadians, too, have been extremely reluctant to adopt such policies and, in fact, have adopted fewer of them. To the extent that Americans differ from Canadians by emphasizing equality of opportunity over equality of result, and to the extent that Canadians exhibit less religious traditionalism than Americans do, there may be greater tolerance of social diversity in Canada. However, the impact of these factors on the treatment of racial minorities in areas such as employment or government policy has yet to be demonstrated.

REFERENCES

Allport, Gordon W. 1954. *The Nature of Prejudice*. Cambridge, Mass.: Addison-Wesley Publishing Co.

Angus Reid Group Inc. 1989. Immigration to Canada: Aspects of Public Opinion. Report prepared for Employment and Immigration Canada. Winnipeg: Angus Reid Group Inc.

_____. 1991. Multiculturalism and Canadians: Attitude Study 1991 (National Survey Report). Report submitted to Multiculturalism and Citizenship Canada.

Anti-Defamation League of B'nai Brith. 1991. *1991 Audit of Anti-Semitic Incidents*. New York: Anti-Defamation League of B'nai Brith.

Barrett, Stanley R. 1987. *Is God a Racist? The Right Wing in Canada*. Toronto: University of Toronto Press.

Berry, John W., R. Kalin and D.M. Taylor. 1977. *Multiculturalism and Ethnic Attitudes in Canada*. Ottawa: Supply and Services Canada.

Bobo, Lawrence. 1987. "Racial Attitudes and the Status of Black Americans: A Social Psychological View of Change since the 1940s." Paper prepared for the Committee on the Status of Black Americans, National Research Council, Washington, DC.

_____. 1988. "Group Conflict, Prejudice, and the Paradox of Contemporary Racial Attitudes." In Phyllis A. Katz and Dalmas A. Taylor, eds. *Eliminating Racism: Means and Controversies*, pp.85-114. New York: Plenum.

Bogardus, Emory S. 1958. "Racial Distance Changes in the United States During the Past Thirty Years." *Sociology and Social Research* 43:127-135.

_____. 1967. *A Forty-Year Racial Distance Study*. Los Angeles: University of Southern California Press.

Breton, Raymond, et al. 1990. *Ethnic Identity and Inequality: Varieties of Experience in a Canadian City*. Toronto: University of Toronto Press.

Dion, Kenneth L. 1985. "Social Distance Norms in Canada: Effects of Stimulus Characteristics and Dogmatism." *International Journal of Psychology* 20:743-749.

Driedger, Leo and Richard Mezoff. 1981. "Ethnic Prejudice and Discrimination in Winnipeg High Schools." *Canadian Journal of Sociology* 6:1-17.

Henry, Frances. 1978. "The Dynamics of Racism in Toronto." Toronto: York University, Department of Anthropology. Mimeographed.

_____. 1986. "Race Relations Research in Canada Today: A 'State of the Art' Review." Paper presented at the Canadian Human Rights Commission Colloquium on Racial Discrimination, Ottawa, September 25.

_____. 1989. "Who Gets the Work in 1989?" Background paper. Ottawa: Economic Council of Canada.

_____ and Effie Ginsberg. 1985. *Who Gets the Work: A Test of Racial Discrimination in Employment*. Toronto: The Urban Alliance on Race Relations and the Social Planning Council of Metropolitan Toronto.

Jain, Harish. 1989. "Racial Minorities and Affirmative Action/Employment Equity Legislation in Canada." *Industrial Relations* 44(3):593-613.

_____ and P.J. Sloane. 1981. *Equal Employment Issues: Race and Sex Discrimination in the United States, Canada, and Britain*. New York: Praeger.

Jaynes, Gerald David and Robin M. Williams, Jr. 1989. *A Common Destiny: Blacks and American Society*. Washington, DC: National Academy Press.

Johnson, James H. and Melvin L. Oliver. 1989. "Interethnic Minority Conflict in Urban America: The Effects of Economic and Social Dislocations." *Urban Geography* 10(5):449-463.

Kluegel, James R. 1985. "If There Isn't a Problem, You Don't Need a Solution': The Bases of Contemporary Affirmative Action Attitudes." *American Behavioral Scientist* 28:761-84.

_____. 1990. "Trends in Whites' Explanations of the Black-White Gap in Socioeconomic Status, 1977-1989." *American Sociological Review* 55(4):512-525.

_____ and Eliot R. Smith. 1986. *Beliefs about Inequality: Americans' Views of What Is and What Ought to Be.* New York: Aldine de Gruyter.

Lambert, Ronald and James Curtis. 1984. "Quebecois and English Canadian Opposition to Racial and Religious Intermarriage, 1968-1983." *Canadian Ethnic Studies* 16(2):30-46.

League for Human Rights of B'Nai Brith Canada. 1991. *1991 Audit of Anti-Semitic Incidents.* Downsview, Ont.: The League.

Maclean's. 1989. "Portrait of Two Nations: The Dreams and Ideals of Canadians and Americans." July 3, 23-82.

_____. 1990. "Portrait of Two Nations: Should the Two Countries Become One?" June 25, 37-52.

Michalos, Alex C. 1982. *North American Social Report: A Comparative Study of the Quality of Life in Canada and the USA from 1964 to 1974,* Vol. 5., Economics, Religion and Morality. Dordrecht, Netherlands: D. Reidel.

Niemi, Richard G., John Mueller and Tom W. Smith. 1989. *Trends in Public Opinion: A Compendium of Survey Data.* New York: Greenwood Press.

Oliver, Melvin L. and James H. Johnson, Jr. 1984. "Inter-Ethnic Conflict in an Urban Ghetto: The Case of Blacks and Latinos in Los Angeles." *Research in Social Movements, Conflict and Change* 6:57-94.

Owen, Carolyn, Howard C. Eisner and Thomas R. McFaul. 1981. "A Half-Century of Social Distance Research: National Replication of the Bogardus' Studies." *Sociology and Social Research* 66(1):80-98.

Pineo, F. 1977. "The Social Standing of Ethnic and Racial Groupings." *Canadian Review of Sociology and Anthropology* 14:147-57.

Reimers, David M. and Harold Troper. 1992. "Canadian and American Immigration Policy since 1945." In Barry R. Chiswick, ed. *Immigration, Language and Ethnicity: Canada and the United States,* pp.15-54. Washington, DC: AEI Press.

Reitz, Jeffrey G. 1988a. "The Institutional Structure of Immigration as a Determinant of Inter-Racial Competition: A Comparison of Britain and Canada." *International Migration Review* 22(1):117-146.

_____. 1988b. "Less Racial Discrimination in Canada, or Simply Less Racial Conflict? Implications of Comparisons with Britain." *Canadian Public Policy* 14(4):424-441.

_____. 1990. "Ethnic Concentrations in Labor Markets and Their Implications for Ethnic Inequality." In Raymond Breton, Wsevolod Isajiw, Warren E. Kalbach and Jeffrey G. Reitz, *Ethnic Identity and Inequality: Varieties of Experience in a Canadian City,* pp.135-195. Toronto: University of Toronto Press.

_____. 1993. "Statistics on Racial Discrimination in Canada." *Policy Options* 14(2):32-36.

_____. 1994. "A Comment on de Silva and Palmer." *Policy Options* 15(2):7-9.

Rose, Harold M. 1989. "Blacks and Cubans in Metropolitan Miami's Changing Economy." *Urban Geography* 10(5):464-486.

Schoenfeld, Stuart. 1991. "Hate Groups, Hate Propaganda and Racial Conflict." Unpublished manuscript.

Schuman, Howard, Charlotte Steeh and Lawrence Bobo. 1985. *Racial Attitudes in America: Trends and Interpretations.* Cambridge, Mass.: Harvard University Press.

Seltzer, Rick and Grace M. Lopes. 1986. "The Ku Klux Klan: Reasons for Support or Opposition Among White Respondents." *Journal of Black Studies* 17(1):91-109.

Shefman, Alan. 1987. "Manifestations of Anti-Semitism in Canada: The 1987 Survey." In Frank Chalk, ed. *The Review of Anti-Semitism in Canada,* pp.3-7. Downsview, Ont.: League for Human Rights of B'nai Brith Canada.

Sher, Julian. 1983. *White Hoods: Canada's Klu Klux Klan.* Vancouver: New Star Books.

Simon, Julian L. 1989. *The Economic Consequences of Immigration.* Oxford; New York: Basil Blackwell.

Sinha, Murli M. and Brian Berry. 1991. "Ethnicity, Stigmatized Groups and Social Distance: An Expanded Update of the Bogardus Scale." Paper presented at the annual meetings of the American Sociological Association, Cincinnati, August 23-27.

Smith, Tom W. 1990. "Ethnic Images." *GSS Topical Report No. 19,* National Opinion Research Center, University of Chicago.

Sniderman, Paul M. and Michael G. Hagen. 1985. *Race and Inequality: A Study in America n Values.* Chatham, NT: Chatham House.

_____. et al. 1991. "Political Culture and the Problem of Double Standards: Mass and Elite Attitudes Toward Language Rights in the Canadian Charter of Rights and Freedoms." *Canadian Journal of Political Science* 22(2):259-284.

Swan, Neil, et al. 1991. *Economic and Social Impacts of Immigration: A Research Report Prepared for the Economic Council of Canada.* Ottawa: Supply and Services Canada.

Terkel, Studs. 1992. *Race: How Blacks and Whites Think and Feel about the American Obsession.* New York: Doubleday Anchor.

Turner, Margey Austin, Michael Fix and Raymond J. Struyk. 1991. *Opportunities Denied, Opportunities Diminished: Discrimination in Hiring.* Washington: Urban Institute Project.

3

The Contours of Racialization: Structures, Representation and Resistance in the United States

Stephen Small

This chapter examines patterns of race relations in the United States of America in the 1980s and 1990s, with a particular focus on the experiences of African Americans. It considers some key facts of race relations, a number of key incidents which reflect these broader facts, as well as the responses of African Americans to them. I suggest that race and racism continue to play a decisive role in Black peoples' lives, but because of the intricate relationships between racism and economic and political power, a new conceptual framework is needed to provide a better understanding of how this unfolds. A framework of racialization is introduced, in which the concepts of racialized barriers and racialized hostility (including racialized structures, images, ideologies and identities) are defined and examined. Each of these terms are defined and examples are provided. I argue that, while we cannot reduce the problems which Blacks face to economics and politics alone, we cannot focus exclusively on racism. A better approach is one which considers racialized hostility alongside a broad array of economic and political factors.

Considering the patterns of "racialized" inequality in the United States offers a number of useful insights into what is going on in Canada, and in other capitalist societies in which "racialized" and ethnic minorities are to be found. Comparison reveals a number of common features, even though the specifics of each nation varies because of the unique historical background. This can serve to offer a fresh and challenging perspective to the context at home.

The Racialization Problematic

Although the terms *race relations*, *race*, *racial*, *racism* and *racist* are commonly used, the precise meanings *and* significance of them is hotly contested. For example, do races exist as distinct biological groups? Or do they simply reflect the social definitions and constructions of different groups? If we call a relationship racial, does that mean it was determined by race? Or that ideas and beliefs about race shape the relationship in some way, and often not even in the most important way? Is there one racism or several different racisms? If we can identify racism, does that mean we can identify non-racism? Can we distinguish the content of racism, from the intentions of racists and from the outcomes or consequences of racism? And does the term *race relations* mean that relationships between Blacks and Whites are relationships between biological distinctive races?

In recent decades, more and more social scientists have questioned the language and the concepts used to analyze what was previously called race relations (Banton, 1977; Miles, 1982, 1989; Satzewich, 1988; Winant, 1994). I have also been a critic of this language (Small, 1989, 1991, 1993, 1994b). Along with these authors, I believe that these words or concepts, and the assumptions underlying them, create more problems than they solve. The words *race* and *racial* suggest the existence of discrete biological races, and imply that anything which is racial results primarily from this fact. For example, the idea of racial conflict suggests conflict results mainly from contact between races in and of themselves, rather than because of other factors, such as economics and political competition. But the vast majority of scientists, genetic and social, agree that discrete biological races do not exist, and that biological distinctiveness bears little relationship to the racial identities of communities scattered across the world today (Banton, 1977). In addition, Williams has argued that the origin of slavery had to do primarily with economics: "it had to do not with the colour of the laborer, but the cheapness of the labor" (Williams, 1944:19). Since slavery became overwhelmingly identified with Africans, "a racial twist has thereby been given to what is basically an economic phenomenon" (Williams, 1944:7).

The words *racism* and *racist* suggest that there is one type of racism and that individuals are either racist (such as the Ku Klux Klan) or non-racist. The reality is far more complex. We cannot say a person who opposes Affirmative Action or who favours tighter immigration controls is racist, because this opposition may be motivated by a wide variety of factors. For example, some people genuinely believe in treating all individuals equally without regard to ethnicity or race. On the other side, we cannot say that a person who expresses support for colour-blind policies is non-racist. In 1988, President Bush openly supported colour-blind policies and said he did not want race to enter into his campaign, yet he condoned the use of negative stereotypes of Black crime in strengthening his political campaign (Small, 1994b:89). The intentions people hold and what they do can be markedly different from what they say they will do. As we will see in the following sections, attitudes and ideologies that might be called racist can take different forms and be motivated by many different factors.

Because it owes its origin to mistaken assumptions from the past, the language of race relations fails to acknowledge these kinds of complexities and often leads to an oversimplified focus on race while ignoring the complexities of economics, political and social power and the consequences of the routine operation of key institutions in contemporary life. This is a language that we cannot afford to employ if we wish to understand such complexities, or bring about change.

I believe a better approach is provided by working within the racialization problematic or framework. This framework is a set of assumptions and key concepts which explores the multiple factors that shape what has previously been called race relations. Some of these factors entail explicit reference to race, such as beliefs about the existence of races, prejudice and discrimination based on such beliefs. But other factors—such as competition for economic and political resources (education, jobs, housing elected office)—may seem to have no racial reference. The racialization problematic enables us to draw out the relationship between these seemingly unrelated variables, and, importantly, to begin to assess the significance of each of them. In sum, analysts working within the racialization problematic are able to ask the question: "If 'race relations' are not the relationship between biologically different races, then what are they?" This turns our attention to economics, politics, power; and to the ways in which structures, images and ideologies operate to sustain inequality and injustice.

The key concept within the racialization problematic is the process of racialization (and thus of racialized relations) which has been defined in a number of ways but refers primarily to a historically specific ideological process, and the structures that accompanied this process (Omi and Winant, 1994; Small, 1994b). This process refers to the ways in which diverse ethnic groups from Europe and Africa came to be defined as the White race and the Black race in the colonization and conquest of the Americas (Banton, 1977; Miles, 1982). It also refers to the institutional arrangements which accompanied these processes: the legal system (in slavery, and Jim Crow segregation); the economic system (the plantation economy, and the distribution of jobs); and housing (with Blacks confined to the ghetto). The laws and policies, such as Civil Rights legislation, voting rights laws, and Affirmative Action, that were introduced to end segregation continue processes of racialization, though their goals are clearly in a different direction.

Rather than referring to race and racial, I talk about racialized groups. As well as moving away from the notion that Blacks and Whites are biologically discrete groups, it emphasizes how definitions of who is White and who is Black vary from context to context. Rather than talking of racism or racist and non-racist, I believe it is more useful to discuss the intentions, content and outcomes of ideologies and actions, and how they impact upon groups defined by race in different ways. In this way, interactions between groups that are defined as races are seen as racialized relations. It is assumed that ideas and beliefs about race, both at present and in the past, have shaped these relationships, and that other factors, such as economics, class and gender are central. But there is no presumption that racism is the primary or most important variable. The concrete examples provided in this chapter demonstrate that this is not simply a matter of changing the words or playing semantics; it is rather a matter of challenging the assumptions and of improving the analysis by identifying as central a number of variables that are usually ignored, neglected or obscured.

The concepts of racialized barriers and hostility (including structures, images and ideologies) emphasize the systemic and sustained obstacles to Black aspirations. They refer to the activities of key institutions and the actions of those who work in them, which result in the exclusion or victimization of African Americans. It is important to note that "hostility" is not used in its usual sense of explicit and direct violent or aggressive action, but rather to mean "attitudes and actions where the intentions and/or outcomes are detrimental to Black people" (Small, 1994b:210, fn6).

Finally, racialized identities refers to how groups and individuals embrace the idea of race and difference in their efforts to compete and succeed. Developing organizations around a common and shared experience—a Black identity—is a primary example of this, particularly for African Americans who have sustained resistance to hostility, discrimination and exclusion of various kinds (T'Shaka, 1990).

Inequality and Institutional Practices

Racialized structures are the institutional pillars of society. They are the routine, recurrent and organized features of contemporary life. The idea of racialized structures has two key components. First, it refers to the distribution of valuable resources such as political power, employment, education and housing. Primarily this aspect involves who owns what, who works and lives where, and who has good health. Second, it refers to the normal, recurrent and routinized procedures of institutions that shape and constrain our daily lives, from politics (voting and political representatives), economics (businesses, employment); education (universities, schools); health (hospitals); and other spheres of social life (family, media, music, sport). These behaviours and actions sustain the distribution of resources. The practices of key institutions in the contemporary United States shape and determine who succeeds and who fails, who is rewarded and who is punished.

Racialized inequality is revealed in differences in the share of, and access to, valued resources. It is captured in the notion of a "colour line," that is, of material disparities between Blacks and Whites (Small, 1994b:15). What it means is that, on the basis of all the key indicators, Blacks are at a disadvantage compared to Whites. A recent study of Black and White wealth argued that "materially, whites and Blacks constitute two nations ... two middle classes" (Oliver and Shapiro, 1995:7). Whites have far more wealth than Blacks, and rich Whites have far more wealth than rich Blacks. When compared with the richest Blacks, the richest Whites "controlled four times as much wealth as Blacks with the same degrees" (Oliver and Shapiro, 1995:8). Middle-class Blacks earn only 70 cents for every dollar earned by middle-class Whites (Oliver and Shapiro, 1995:7). Not only do Whites benefit from better earnings; they also benefit from a tax system that affects them less adversely. Whites benefit from low taxes on capital gains, from real estate taxes and from the tax deduction for home mortgages (Oliver and Shapiro, 1995:43). Wealth is important, not only because it reveals the greatest disparities, but also because wealth "captures the historical legacy of low wages, personal and organizational discrimination and institutionalized racism" (Oliver and Shapiro, 1995:5). It is testimony to the fact that the analysis of the present cannot begin without some consideration of how it is shaped by the past.

For Blacks as a whole, income is almost 60 percent that of Whites, but this understates the disparities; the median net worth of Black households (that is, total assets less liabilities) at the turn of the decade was only about one-tenth that of Whites (O'Hare et al., 1991:30). In 1989, the median annual income for Black families amounted to $20,200, while for White families it was substantially higher (O'Hare et al., 1991:27). Similar disparities can be found in patterns of employment. White men are still twice as likely as their Black counterparts to work in administration, management or a profession (O'Hare et al., 1991:25).

Residential segregation remains widespread. Blacks and Whites are to be found in different neighborhoods, regardless of their levels of earnings or occupations (O'Hare et al., 1991:9). Furthermore, the proportion of Blacks residing in high-poverty areas (defined as census tracts with at least 20 percent of the residents in poverty) increased by almost 20 percent during the 1980s (O'Hare et al., 1991:9). The pattern of segregation is so entrenched and severe that it has led two authors to call it "American Apartheid" (Massey and Denton, 1993). The picture is the same in education and health, and in experiences with the criminal justice system. White students are twice as likely as Blacks to graduate from college, while around 20 percent of Whites earn a degree as compared with 11 percent of Blacks (O'Hare et al., 1991:22). Young Black people experience more health problems and have more conflicts with the criminal justice system.

The racialized structure of inequality reflects not only disparities between Blacks and Whites, but also those within the Black population. The 1980s and 1990s has seen the internal stratification of African Americans intensify, as educational, occupational and economic upward mobility of some Blacks has continued alongside the continued entrenchment of the majority in poverty or in low paying, dead-end and part-time jobs. This stratification has pronounced gender dimensions. Black married couples are the most economically successful families, while so-called "female-headed" families experience the most economic hardship. Black families comprised of married couples, and in which the head of household is twenty-five to forty-four years old and a college graduate, have median incomes of $54,400; that is 93 percent of Whites' medium income of $58,800 (O'Hare et al., 1991:28). At the same time, 26 percent of Black families revealed incomes below $10,000 (O'Hare et al., 1991:27). Women are more likely to earn less, to find themselves in part-time jobs (most often without health benefits), and to be in poverty, especially if they head families with children. The median income of Black female-headed households is less than $12,000, compared with nearly $19,000 for White female-headed households (O'Hare et al., 1991:28).

On the whole, then, Blacks are at considerable disadvantage when compared to Whites, and face problems of racialized hostility which Whites do not face. But Black efforts to survive and succeed have produced varied results. While the majority of institutions are still dominated by Whites, Blacks, in small number, can still be found among executives and managers, and there are Black businesses which control limited but significant resources. This is particularly important in cities such as New York, Washington, Detroit, Chicago and Los Angeles, where Blacks constitute a majority or a very substantial proportion of the residents. Blacks can be found working in, managing and even controlling television and film media (such as Black Entertainment Television, films like *Devil in a Blue Dress* and *Waiting to Exhale*) print media (such as *Ebony*, *Jet*, and an array of Black newspapers) and music videos (Rose, 1994). The significance of this presence is important when we seek to understand the dominant images and representations of Black people in American society. This is discussed in the following section.

Racialized discrimination is widespread and continues to constrain the aspirations of Black people, in all class positions and for both genders. This includes violence, attacks, exclusion and (verbal) abuse. A 1991 study of 6.4 million applications for home mortgages, carried out by the Federal Reserve, found that banks "rejected Black applicants twice as often as whites nationwide" (Oliver and Shapiro, 1995:19). Blacks who do qualify, moreover, pay higher interest rates on home mortgages than whites (Oliver and Shapiro, 1995:8). This was true regardless of financial status because the same study also suggested that "the poorest white applicant ... was more likely to get a mortgage loan approved than a Black in the highest income bracket" (Oliver and Shapiro, 1995:19-20). The authors concluded that "discrimination follows Blacks no matter where they want to live and no matter how much they earn" (Oliver and Shapiro, 1995:20). Discrimination within the real estate industry—via subsidies to those who live in the suburbs, mainly Whites, and penalization of those who seek inner-city housing, mainly Blacks—has long historical precedent (Massey and Denton, 1993).

This hostility is also reflected in a number of internationally covered incidents, such as the Stuart case in Boston, the Rodney King beating and the riots that followed the court case, the implementation of Proposition 187 in California in 1994, mobilization around the so-called "Civil Rights Initiative" (which calls for the abolition of Affirmative Action), as well as in attitudes towards the O.J. Simpson case and the Million Man March (Small, 1994b; Feagin and Vera, 1995; *Time*, October 30, 1995).

Another element of racialized structures that must be considered is the increased importance of other ethnic groups and their salience in the political arena (Jennings, 1994). Minorities like Asians and Latinos have grown dramatically in number and economic and political significance—particularly at the regional level, as in the southwestern states—and their presence has made analysis of racialized and ethnic inequality that much more complex (Chang and Leong, 1994). These groups face extensive hostility, exclusion and victimization of various kinds. They are important because Blacks alone can no longer set the political agenda, are more often out-numbered, demographically and in terms of resources, and because there is often competition between Blacks and other groups for the same resources (Jennings, 1994; Small, 1994b).

Finally, it is important to recognize the international context as a decisive factor in the unfolding of these processes. Dramatic international changes have had an impact on the racialization of social relations: the rise of transnational corporations and global competition; the massive innovations in computer technology and communications; military involvement in the Gulf War, Somalia, Haiti and Bosnia; the disintegration of the Soviet Union; the unification of Germany; the European Union (Small, 1994b; Lusane, 1994; Oliver and Shapiro, 1995); and international terrorism. This context shapes the attitudes of government and business executives and the policies and strategies that they decide appropriate for domestic policies of education, employment, welfare and policing. It is fear of global competition—especially from Japan and the European Union—which has encouraged a preoccupation with the budget deficit, changing policies of education and skills training, a restructuring of employment and a strengthening of resolve to reduce expenditure on welfare in general, and Affirmative Action in particular. These are patterns exemplified elsewhere in the world, particularly in Europe (Wrench and Solomos, 1993). In a world of increasing inter-dependence and competition—and a dizzying array of factors that shape racialized and ethnic relations—international factors can only become more important (Rattansi and Westwood, 1994; Winant, 1994).

Screening the Images

The images of Black people that are prevalent in U.S. society are a central factor in shaping relations between Blacks and Whites and in shaping relations within the Black community, because they influence the attitudes, expectations and responses of the various communities. By image and representations, I refer to the roles in which Blacks are found in television, film and print media (newspapers, magazines, books). These images are also important because they do not reflect the general experience of Black people—they abbreviate it, encapsulate it, and in doing so, distort it. Though they appear to present a range of roles, such images are overwhelmingly narrow, unrepresentative and stereotypical. This means that, given the dramatic patterns of residential segregation, most views and beliefs held by Whites about Blacks come not from personal experience but from the media. In the United States today there is so little opportunity for whites to meet and interact with Blacks, and in fact, at Universities across the USA that Blacks and whites are often interacting in a meaningful way for the first time when they attend college. And one reason that the O.J. Simpson trial was so important is that it provided a channel through which Whites and Blacks interacted, and disagreed so vehemently.

A dominant set of images concerns Black success: in sport, music and television, and to a lesser extent in politics and business. Shows such as *The Cosby Show*, *Arsenio Hall*, *Oprah Winfrey*, outstanding athletes (Michael Jordan, Jerry Rice), entertainers such as Whitney Houston, film stars such as Denzil Washington, Wesley Snipes and Angela Bassett, highly visible Black newsreaders such as Bryant Gumbel and Bernard Shaw, all lead to an impression that African Americans have achieved equality. For example, a study of White attitudes towards *The Cosby Show* demonstrated that Whites felt any Black American could make it to the top (Jhally and Lewis, 1992; Small, 1994b). But the facts contradict this. These images do not reflect the experiences of the vast majority of African Americans, and most African Americans are either excluded from these industries or occupy subordinate and powerless roles (Rose, 1994; Guerrero, 1993; Omi, 1989). A second set of images concerns Black failure: reluctance and laziness around the issue of work, and welfare dependency, especially welfare mothers (Small, 1994b: Glenn, 1994). Black men are presented as unwilling to work and dependent on the mothers of their children, with the mothers themselves dependent on the largesse of government handouts (Jewell, 1988).

A third set of images is of Black crime. In the United States, crime is pervasive—there is not a social class or racialized group which is free from crime. Yet, if one reviews stories on crime in the media, one could not be blamed for believing most crime is committed by Blacks. In fact, most crime is committed by Whites, and the crime which costs society the most is committed by middle-class Whites—that is, corporate crime, laxity in health and safety provisions and tax evasion (Mokhiber, 1988; Simon and Eitzen, 1993). Media images distort this picture. However, these images, while biased, are not entirely inaccurate—that is, though Blacks are less likely to commit certain crimes, they are more likely to be arrested. For example, the U.S. government estimates that from 15 to 20 percent of American drug users are Black. Yet in certain regions, Blacks are overwhelmingly arrested for drug crimes—in New York in 1989, 92 percent of those arrested were African American or Latino (Duster, 1995:22). Punishments also vary tremendously; possession with intent to distribute five grams of cocaine brings "a variable sentence of 10 to 37 months," while possession with intent to distribute five grams of crack "brings a mandatory minimum five-year sentence" (Duster, 1995:23).

A final image that must be considered is that of reverse racism: so-called excesses of Affirmative Action; of White victims of reverse discrimination being denied jobs and education; of the financial burden of race-specific policies, of incompetent Blacks and other minorities being admitted to jobs and colleges; and of Black racists. These images are pervasive in debates on higher education, on unemployment and the budget deficit and, of course, of the unfairness of the O.J. Simpson decision and the largely Black jury that proclaimed it. The ideologies and activities of Minister Louis Farrakhan of the Nation of Islam figures prominently here—as a fanatic, anti-Semite and hater of Whites, fomenting racial dissent, and damaging race relations.

Related to these images is the fact that so-called "Black conservatives" have been given substantial time on television to argue that Black leaders such as Jesse Jackson and organizations such as the National Association for the Advancement of Colored People (NAACP) are antiquated and out of touch with the majority of the Black community. People such as Shelby Steele and Thomas Sowell, both academics, and Alan Keyes, candidate for the Republican nomination for president for 1996, join in the chorus against Affirmative Action, insisting, contrary to the evidence, that racialized discrimination has ended or is less relevant to the Black experience, and that Black laziness, dependence and a culture of poverty is to blame for continuing inequality (Boston, 1988; Small, 1994b:90). The fact is that individuals with these attributes represent a tiny and unrepresentative section of the Black community. And it is no joke that one finds so many of the television shows about Black people to be situation comedies, many of them involving professional comedians and/or rap artists (*The Fresh Prince of Bel Air*, *Family Affairs*, *Martin*, *Roc* and others). Collectively these programs contribute to the impression that Black people are comedians and their lives, experiences and attitudes are not to be taken seriously.

Where are the images of racialized hostility and exclusion? Of Black resilience and strength, of moral courage and stamina against all the odds? They are there, to be sure, but sandwiched infrequently and irreverently between this larger picture of sloth, undeserved privilege and hatred.

The overall impact of such images is more difficult to ascertain. Guerrero has argued that:

> The representation of Black people on the commercial screen has amounted to one grand, multifaceted illusion. For Blacks have been subordinated, marginalized, positioned, and devalued in every possible manner to glorify and relentlessly hold in place the white-dominated symbolic order and racial hierarchy of American society (1993:2).

Wong has studied images of people of colour in some of the most important, widely seen and successful films of the 1980s, such as *Driving Miss Daisy, Clara's Heart,* and *The Hand that Rocks the Cradle* (Wong, 1994). She demonstrates that Blacks in particular, and people of colour generally, are caste in roles as caregivers and nurturers, looking after, assisting and helping White families. She suggests that there is a common underlying purpose in such images—they serve "to allay racial anxieties; those who fear the erosion of their dominance and the vengeance of the oppressed can exorcise their dread in displaced forms" (Wong, 1994:69). They also create an "illusion of equality and reciprocity with the caregiver" (Wong, 1994:69). In the 1990s many films continue to fulfil a similar function.

Masking and Unmasking Ideologies

The notion of racialized ideologies refers to the systematic statements and elaborations about the way in which society is organized, or ought to be organized, if it is to function well. Statements about free-market principles, about the appropriate size of government, about individualism and family values and morality, all exemplify the dominant ideologies of capitalist societies such as the United States. These ideologies shape our lives. Ideologies that make explicit reference to race are the most obvious examples of racialized ideologies, closely followed by those in which it is clear that race is indirectly referred to, or implied. But all ideologies are racialized in that they have differential consequences for populations called Black and White.

Among these ideologies are statements about fairness, equal opportunities and racism. It used to be useful to talk about racist and non-racist ideologies in a context in which the expression of racist sentiment by those with power was accepted, expected or condoned, especially prior to the 1960s (Wilson, 1978). But this is no longer the context—the successes of the Civil Rights Movement has made such actions unacceptable. Those who harbour hostility to Black people, especially those who have power, are less likely to use overt, explicit language to express this anger (Omi and Winant, 1994:ch. 6). But many statements which lack explicit reference to ideas and beliefs about race continue to be made in which it is possible to identify hostility to Blacks. They are more likely to be covert and indirect, argue Omi and Winant, to rearticulate racism by using codewords and double entendres (1994:123). This makes it more difficult to identify so-called racists.

Furthermore, there are many ideologies in which no racial content is found, or where open opposition to racism is expressed—as in the demand for colour-blind policies—but which nevertheless can have major adverse consequences for Black people. The idea that all applicants to college should be treated equally, that there should be no Affirmative Action, despite the fact that Blacks have faced and continue to face extensive discrimination and inequality, is but one example.

In this context—and I believe this is the main context of the 1990s—the argument presented here is that it is not useful to approach ideologies by asking whether they are racist or non-racist. It is more useful to acknowledge the varied ideologies and to examine them for their racialized intentions, content and consequences. In other words, it is more useful to consider all ideologies in terms of the intentions of those promoting them, the content of the ideologies and the outcomes they have or are likely to have for different racialized groups. When we consider the content of ideologies I suggest that we should analyze those with explicit racialized reference those with coded racialized reference and those without any racialized reference but in which we can identify hostile intentions of those advocating them, or adverse consequences of the ideology for Blacks. This approach builds upon the innovative analysis on the changing nature of racism in the 1980s, carried out by Omi and Winant (1994). Consider some concrete examples.

One example of a straightforward expression of a racialized ideology is when extremist groups such as the Ku Klux Klan or the White American Resistance (WAR) make openly hostile statements about Blacks. Engaging in a different rhetoric in mainstream politics provides a different kind of example, as when President Bush and Vice-President Quale explained the 1992 riots in Los Angeles as an outcome of liberal policies which somehow favoured minorities (Lusane, 1994). Similarly, Pat Buchanan, a leading Republican who had previously worked for Nixon and Reagan, offers a related example. He claims to be in favour of equal opportunities but advocates policies that oppose Black and Latino interests generally by implying that all Mexican immigrants are undocumented. Closely related are arguments that policies around welfare, crime, and Affirmative Action favour Blacks and minorities and harm Whites.

We can also examine ideologies with coded racialized reference, which entail what Omi and Winant call the "re-articulation" of racism. This is the rearrangement of ideas and assumptions about policies such that, although no reference is made to race, the words themselves are heavily saturated with such meanings and interests (Omi and Winant, 1994). When politicians highlight crime in the inner city, the burden on the welfare state, reverse racism or when they say anti-discrimination policies are un-American, these are understood to have racialized reference. They are understood to be promoting policies believed to benefit Whites, while penalizing Blacks. For example, when advocates proposed the so-called Civil Rights Initiative currently under consideration in California, their goal was and is to abolish race-specific policies, and their argument is based on a notion that Blacks and other minorities get undeserved and unnecessary preferential treatment while the White majority faces reverse racism as a consequence.

There are also ideologies without any racialized reference, but in which we can identify the hostile intentions of those advocating them, or adverse consequences of the ideology for Blacks. For example, when a local bus company in Richmond, California, wanted to abandon several bus routes as unprofitable and inconvenient, it was clear that it was motivated by a desire to prevent young Black shoppers—the group most dependent on the bus service—from frequenting the shopping mall. Similarly, a decision to produce a list of young Black men barred from shopping in their stores by a group of store owners in a mall in Georgia had clear racialized intent, though the owners vehemently denied it.

Finally, one step further removed are those policies which openly claim to be anti-racist—for example, colour-blind policies and even free-market polices. These are presented as impartial, unbiased, even anti-racist, because they treat everyone equally, regardless of colour, nationality and racialized identity. But to treat all equally, while denying the very real evidence of racialized discrimination at present and in the past, is to effectively treat them unequally. The significance is to be found not in the content but in the outcomes they have, or are likely to have, for different racialized constituencies. It is widely agreed that the decision to abolish Affirmative Action at the University of California—although proclaimed in the interests of fairness and equality—will have a substantial adverse impact on the likelihood of Blacks entering and graduating from the university.

Resisting the Onslaught

Despite the many obstacles which confront them, Black people continue to resist injustice in various ways. This resistance entails collective and individual, physical and ideological strategies, many of which are articulated around the organizations and institutions of the Black community, and the cultural patterns prevalent within it. Activism and leadership have always been present in this opposition to injustice, and Black women have been central to all these activities, as well as developing a distinctive tradition of their own. The various forms of resistance present in the contemporary United States reflect traditions of resistance and resilience by Africans and African Americans to European conquest and colonization (Marable, 1992; Small and Walvin, 1994).

It used to be possible to classify the goals and strategies of African Americans in the simple notions of integration and/or separatism; but today the range and diversity of goals and strategies defies such a framework. Blacks have various goals, and employ various strategies; among the goals are integration and incorporation in the present system, primarily focusing on overcoming the starkest feature of discrimination and injustice; others seek fundamental change in the current system; still others see the way forward in developing distinctive Black institutions and communities (T'Shaka, 1990). The strategies vary—some see broad alliances with other people of colour, and with Whites, as in the Rainbow coalition strategy of Jesse Jackson (Collins, 1986; Lusane, 1994); others call for the resuscitation, consolidation and expansion of Black organizations and the regeneration of self-reliance and self-dependence. This is a strategy best exemplified in the work of Louis Farrakhan's Nation of Islam, but certainly one widely endorsed by a diverse array of Black organizations—such as Baptist and Methodist Churches, educational and community organizations—which may be at odds with the tactics and spirit of Farrakhan.

Many African Americans seek to work within the system. Like the majority of Americans, they seek success in education, employment and in political representation and participation. Socialized in the United States, they seek the goals and rewards promised to all Americans—a good education, a secure well-paying employment position and a home of their own. Some seek to achieve these though the ethos of a colour-blind meritocracy, downplaying race, and trying to swim or sink on merit and hard work alone. Others use the few measures currently available to them via Affirmative Action.

Community organizing is central to the strategies embraced by African Americans. In cities across the nation, community groups, institutions and cooperative societies plan daily for their assault on inequality and injustice. In education, health and welfare, the criminal justice system and housing, these groups fight poor schooling and health facilities, inadequate finances and homelessness. This community organizing is tied into a national network of organizations—such as the Children's Defense League, the National Association for the Advancement of Coloured People, the Urban League and others. Needless to say, Black churches—Baptist, Methodist and African Episcopalian, and the Nation of Islam—are key. Frequently, local community organizing assumes new proportions—the Million Man March in Washington, D.C., in October 1995 is only one in a long history of marches that epitomizes the centrality of mass mobilization in African American protest. The backbone of such organizing is, of course, Black families. In light of the many obstacles which Black families face, it is a surprise that there has not been much more devastation. Too many analysts have focused on damage and destruction; and far too few on the resourcefulness and resilience of Black families, argues Billingsley (1992).

Black theorists and analysts have developed an array of literature which systematically analyzes the problems confronting Black people, and offers ways of moving beyond them. These analysts offer insights, counter-explanations and evidence to challenge dominant views. They articulate and elaborate philosophies which challenge the crude and simplistic images of free-market competition, individualism and colour blindness that bombard Black communities, suggesting alternative goals and strategies—from multiculturalism to nationalism and racialized identities (T'Shaka, 1990; Hine, 1995; Lusane, 1994). Black women have been central here, among them Barbara Christian, Angela Davis, June Jordan and bell hooks. And collections of writings and analyses by Black women—which highlight the concerns and priorities of Black women—continue to be produced (Hine, 1995; Guy-Sheftall, 1995).

Similarly, in film, Blacks have worked to produce counter-images to the simplistic and stereotypical ones which flow out of Hollywood and the main television networks (Diawara, 1993). Spike Lee's *Crooklyn*, John Singleton's *Higher Learning*, Mosley's *Devil in a Blue Dress*, Haile Gerima's *Sankofa*, and Julie Dash's *Daughters of the Dust*, all reflect the values and priorities of Black life and its many links across the world. Though they do not have the extensive distribution of Hollywood, they offer real alternative renditions of family, community and identity among African Americans.

It is clear that activism and leadership have been central planks of these strategies, at the level of both formal and community politics. Lusane has suggested that there are five tiers of Black leadership in contemporary America (1994:29-31). He identifies national umbrella organizations such as the Black Leadership Forum; at the federal level, the Congressional Black Caucus; organizations of Black elected officials, including the National Conference of Black Mayors; the systematic efforts of churches, evident in the National Baptist Convention; and local leaders such as city elected officials, civil rights organizations and radical groups. Collectively such groups form a redoubtable challenge to injustice.

Black women have been, and remain, central to all these traditions of resistance; in fact, in the activities just described, they have often been in the majority. However, their contribution and their modes of organization have differed, because of the additional problems they have faced (Guy-Sheftall, 1995; Hine, 1995). While Black men have faced racialized and class hostility, and White women have faced sexism and class hostility, Black women have also faced sexism, much of it coming from Black men, and racism, much of it from White women (Glen, 1994). Social analyses have tended to ignore their unique position (Collins, 1991, 1994). In this way, Black women have occupied a unique intersection of hostilities, and have had to develop strategies accordingly. The attempt to exclude women from the Million Man March is reflective of this.

Patricia Hill Collins suggests that Black women's involvement in struggle has been primarily mobilized around group survival and institutional transformation (Collins, 1991). Their priorities have grown out of their awareness that they occupy a unique location in American society, at the intersection of racism, sexism and class hostility, one in which they face problems which White women in general do not face—including physical survival, powerlessness and identity—as well as facing the problems that White women do face, but to a greater degree (for example, sexual objectification, discrimination, failure to provide support for child care) (Collins, 1994). Black women have struggled to ensure their own physical survival and that of their children; to change institutions such as schools, hospitals and the workplace; and to create a sense of self- and collective identity which can withstand the array of negative images which pervade American institutions (Christian, 1994).

Conclusion

Patterns of racialized relations in the United States are more complex than ever before. The links between racialized hostility, economics and politics have never been so intricate, nor has the relationship between structures, images an ideologies. The tactics of those hostile to the African American presence have taken a greater range of forms, and the African American population manifests greater stratification than ever before, while national and international factors shape one another in ways previously absent. Racialized processes are more intricate and illusive, yet the old atrocities and entrenched inequalities persist. This makes it more difficult to analyze, and it requires a clear grasp of the facts, a clear conceptual framework for analysis and a clear understanding of theories.

In light of these developments, this chapter has suggested that analysis of racialized images and ideologies should not be divorced from the realities of racialized structures involving resource allocation, ownership and control; nor from the mobilization around racialized group membership and identities. It becomes clear that the best understanding of racialized processes will be derived from an examination of the multiple factors involved. An exclusive focus on the distribution of resources alone, or on how images and ideologies are articulated alone, may result in losing sight of the how each set of forces has an impact on the other.

Racialized structures shape many images and ideologies. Poverty causes material hardship, and in a society in which a premium is put on material possessions, Black people are led to doubt their own self-worth. For example, ownership and control of media institutions shapes how certain images prevail and others are ignored, neglected or discarded. Control of government institutions affects the policies that prevail, just as control of businesses hinders or helps opportunities. These same institutions are positioned so as to restrict or expand the incidence of racialized discrimination. In the Black community, the never-employed, the unemployed, the unskilled and the skilled continue to face hostility. And members of the Black middle class—the group that is supposed to demonstrate that meritocracy rules supreme—are tired of being subjected to second-class treatment: professors being treated as if they were students; air pilots as if they were attendants; even Jesse Jackson being mistaken for a porter. Were these incidents isolated and infrequent, one might look upon them with alacrity—but they are systemic, routine and endemic (Benjamin, 1991).

Similarly, racialized images and ideologies shape structure. Black people continue to be subjected to the most pernicious degradation and vilification of colour and culture in images disseminated by politicians, press, television, literature and popular culture, so that White people despise Black people and even Black people can despise one another. The psychological consequences are immense (Akbar, 1984). Ideologies of colour blindness create the appearance of equality and fairness, while hiding practices of discrimination. The case of the Stuart family in Boston—in which a young, middle-class White man shot his pregnant fiancée, and blamed it on a Black man—exemplifies these problems. The image of Black criminality so common in the United States led the Boston police to believe this man's story, to harass the entire Black community in Boston and to arrest an innocent man (Feagin and Vera, 1995). A similar event happened in New York city, when a white couple from Canada murdered their child in Central Park and then told police that a Black man had kidnapped him.

One outcome of these racialized practices is that Whites have an understanding of the experiences and treatment of Black people that is largely at variance with the understandings expressed by Blacks. Whites regard racialized discrimination as minimal and irrelevant, and consider Affirmative Action unjust; most Blacks see discrimination as a major reason for the problems they continue to face, and believe Affirmative Action, or similar policies, are indispensable for progress (Small, 1994b). This divergence in views was reflected in the O.J. Simpson trial decision, in which Whites overwhelmingly believed he was guilty and the jury biased, while Blacks felt he was innocent and the jury impartial.

It may be of no comfort to acknowledge the persuasiveness of racialized structures, images and ideologies in the United States today, or, for that matter, in the contemporary world. However, we do an injustice to ignore their ubiquity. Only by acknowledging both the crude and the subtle workings of these processes can we begin to understand the complexities underway, and begin the more difficult task of arresting, containing and reversing their effects.

REFERENCES

Akbar, Na'im. 1984. *Chains and Images of Psychological Slavery.* Jersey City: New Mind Productions.

Almaguer, Tomas. 1994. *Racial Faultlines. The Historical Origins of White Supremacy in California.* Los Angeles: University of California Press.

Banton, Michael. 1977. *The Idea of Race.* London: Tavistock.

Bell, Derrick. 1992. *Faces at the Bottom of the Well. The Permanence of Racism.* New York: Basic Books.

Benjamin, Lois. 1991. *The Black Elite. Facing the Color Line in the Twilight of the Twentieth Century.* Chicago: Nelson Hall Publishers.

Billingsley, Andrew. 1992. *Climbing Jacob's Ladders. The Enduring Legacy of African-American Families.* New York and London: Simon & Schuster.

Boston, Thomas. 1988. *Race, Class & Conservatism.* London: Unwin Hyman.

Chang, Edward T. and Russell C. Leong, eds. 1994. *Los Angeles-Struggles toward Multi-ethnic Community: Asian American, African American and Latino Perspectives.* Seattle: University of Washington Press.

Christian, Barbara. 1994. "An angle of seeing: Motherhood in Buchi Emecheta's Joys of Motherhood and Alice Walker's Meridian." In Evelyn Nakano Glenn, Grace Change and Linda Rennie Forcey, *Mothering. Ideology, Experience, and Agency.* New York and London: Routledge.

Collins, Patricia Hill. 1991. *Black Feminist Thought: Knowledge, Consciousness, and the Politics of Empowerment.* New York and London: Routledge.

_____. 1994. "Shifting the center: Race, class, and feminist theorizing about motherhood." In Evelyn Nakano Glenn, Grace Change and Linda Rennie Forcey, *Mothering. Ideology, Experience, and Agency*, New York and London: Routledge.

Collins, Sheila D. 1986. *The Rainbow Challenge. The Jackson Campaign and the Future of U.S. Politics.* New York: Monthly Review Press.

Darder, Antonia, ed. 1995. *Culture and Difference: Critical Perspectives on the Bicultural Experience in the United States.* Westport, Connecticut, and London: Bergin and Harvey.

Diawara, Manthia, ed. 1993. *Black American Cinema.* New York and London: Routledge.

Duster, Troy. 1995. "The new crisis of legitimacy in controls, prisons and legal structures." *The American Sociologist* Spring:20-29.

Edsall, Thomas B. and Mary D. Edsall. 1991. *Chain Reaction: The Impact of Race, Rights, and Taxes on American Politics.* New York and London: W.W. Norton & Company.

Feagin, Joe R. and Hernan Vera. 1995. *White Racism: The Basics.* New York and London: Routledge.

Glenn, Evelyn Nakano, Grace Chang, and Linda Rennie Forcey. 1994. *Mothering: Ideology, Experience, and Agency.* New York and London: Routledge.

Guerrero, Ed. 1993. *Framing Blackness: The African American Image in Film.* Philadelphia: Temple University Press.

Guy-Sheftall, Beverly. 1995. *Words of Fire: An Anthology of African-American Feminist Thought.* New York: The New Press.

Hacker, Andrew. 1992. *Two Nations: Black and White, Separate, Hostile and Unequal.* New York: Charles Scribner's Sons.

Hadjor, Kofi Buenor. 1995. *Another America: The Politics of Race and Blame.* Boston: South End Press.

Herrnstein, R. J. and Charles Murray. 1994. *The Bell Curve: Intelligence and Class Structure in American Life.* New York: The Free Press.

Hine, Darlene Clark, Wilma King and Linda Reed. 1995. "We specialize in the wholly impossible." *A Reader in Black Women's History.* New York: Carlson Publishing, Inc.

Jennings, James, ed. 1994. *Blacks, Latinos, and Asians in Urban America: Status and Prospects for Politics and Activism.* Westport, Connecticut, and London: Praeger.

Jewell, K. Sue. 1988. *Survival of the Black Family: The Institutional Impact of U.S. Social Policy.* New York, Westport, Connecticut and London: Praeger.

Jhally, Sut and Justin Lewis. 1992. *Enlightened Racism: The Cosby Show, Audiences and the Myth of the American Dream.* Boulder: Westview Press.

Landry, Bart. 1987. *The New Black Middle Class.* Berkeley, Los Angeles, and London: University of California Press.

Lusane, Clarence. 1994. *African Americans at the Crossroads: The Restructuring of Black Leadership and the 1992 Elections.* Boston: South End Press.

Massey, Douglas S. and Nancy A. Denton. 1993. *American Apartheid. Segregation and the Making of the Underclass,* Cambridge, MA: Harvard University Press.

Marable, Manning. 1992. *The Crisis of Color and Democracy: Essays on Race, Class and Power.* Maine: Common Courage Press.

_____. 1995. *Beyond Black and White: Transforming African-American Politics.* Verso: London and New York.

Miles, Robert. 1982. *Racism and Migrant Labour.* London: Routledge.

_____. 1989. *Racism.* London: Routledge.

Mokhiber, Russell. 1988. *Corporate Crime and Violence: Big Business Power and the Abuse of the Public Trust.* San Francisco: Sierra Club Books.

Morrison, Toni, ed. 1993. *Race-ing Justice, En-Gendering Power: Essays on Anita Hill, Clarence Thomas and the Construction of Social Reality.* London: Chatto & Windus.

Murray, Charles. 1984. *Losing Ground: American Social Policy, 1950-1980.* New York: Basic Books.

Oliver, Melvin L. and Thomas M. Shapiro. 1995. *Black Wealth, White Wealth: A New Perspective on Racial Inequality.* New York and London: Routledge.

O'Hare, William P., Kelvin M. Pollard, Taynia L. Mann and Mary M. Kent. 1991. *African Americans in the 1990s.* Population Reference Bureau, Vol. 46, No. 1., July.

Omi, Michael. 1989. "In living color: Race and American culture." In Ian Angus and Sut Jhally, eds. *Cultural Politics in Contemporary America.* New York and London: Routledge.

_____ and Howard Winant. 1994. *Racial Formation in the United States: From the 1960s to the 1980s.* 2nd edition. London and New York: Routledge.

Orfield, Gary and Carole Ashkinaze. 1991. *The Closing Door: Conservative Policy and Black Opportunity.* Chicago: University of Chicago Press.

Pohlman, Marcus D. 1990. *Black Politics in Conservative America.* London: Longman.

Rattansi, Ali and Sallie Westwood. 1994. *Racism, Modernity and Identity on the Western Front.* London: Polity Press.

Rose, Tricia. 1994. *Black Noise: Rap Music and Black Culture in Contemporary America.* Hanover and London: Weysleyan University Press.

Satzewich, Vic. 1988. "The Canadian state and the racialization of Caribbean migrant farm labour, 1947-1966." *Ethnic and Racial Studies* (11)3:282-304.

Simon, David R. and Eitzen, D. Stanley. 1993. *Elite Deviance*, 4th edition. Boston: Allyn and Bacon.

Small, Stephen. 1989. "Racial differentiation in the slave era: A comparative analysis of people of 'mixed-race' in Jamaica and Georgia," unpublished Ph.D. dissertation. University of California, Berkeley.

_____. 1991. "Racialised relations in Liverpool: A contemporary anomaly." *New Community* (11)4:511-37.

_____. 1993. "Unravelling racialised relations in the United States of America and the United States of Europe." In John Wrench and John Solomos, eds. *Racism and Migration in Europe.* Oxford and New York: Berg Publishers Inc.

_____. 1994a. "Concepts and terminology in representations of the Atlantic slave trade." *Museum Ethnographers Journal* 12:1-14.

_____. 1994b. *Racialised Barriers: The Black Experience in the United States and England.* New York and London: Routledge.

_____ and James Walvin. 1994. "African resistance to enslavement." In Tony Tibbles, ed. *Transatlantic Slavery: Against Human Dignity,* September, pp.42-49. Merseyside Maritime Museum.

Steele, Shelby. 1990. *The Content of Our Character: A New Vision of Race in America.* New York: St. Martin's Press.

Taylor, Ronald L. 1995. *African American Youth: Their Social and Economic Status in the United States.* Westport, Connecticut and London: Praeger.

Thiong'O, Ngugi Wa. 1993. *Moving the Centre: The Struggle for Cultural Freedoms.* London: James Currey; London.

T'Shaka, Oba. 1990. *The Art of Leadership.* Volume 1. Richmond, California: Pan Afrikan Publications.

Tucker, M. Belinda and Claudia Mitchell-Kernan, eds. 1995. *The Decline in Marriage Among African Americans: Causes, Consequences and Policy Implications.* New York: Russell Sage Foundation.

Turner, Patricia. 1994. *Ceramic Uncles and Celluloise Mammies.* London and New York: Routledge.

Walvin, James. 1973. *Black and White: The Negro and English Society 1555-1945.* London: Allen Lane.

Williams, Eric. 1944. *Capitalism and Slavery.* London: Andre Deutsch.

Wilson, William Julius. 1978. *The Declining Significance of Race: Blacks and Changing American Institutions.* Chicago: University of Chicago Press.

_____. 1987. *The Truly Disadvantaged.* Chicago: University of Chicago Press.

Winant, Howard. 1994. *Racial Conditions: Politics, Theory, Comparisons.* Minneapolis: University of Minnesota Press.

Wrench, John and John Solomos. 1993. *Racism and Migration in Europe.* Oxford and New York: Berg Publishers.

4

Racism and Immigration Policy

Alan Simmons

Racism ... operates by constructing impassable symbolic boundaries, and its typically binary system of representation constantly marks and attempts to fix and naturalize the difference between belongingness and otherness (Hall, 1988).

Critical anti-racism moves beyond a narrow preoccupation with individual prejudices and discriminatory actions to the examination of the ways that racist ideas and individual actions are entrenched, linked and [un]consciously supported in institutional and society structures (Dei, 1996:252).

Racism is based on "othering"—that is, on a process involving mental images in which people who have some distinctive physical attributes (such as skin colour) and who may also have associated ethnic characteristics (accent, or style of dress) are viewed as different, less deserving, suitable only for low-wage jobs and as outsiders with respect to the normal benefits of membership in a given society. When racism enters into state policies, a second, subordinate class of citizens is created and kept in place through institutional practices. Nations with racist policies regarding their own citizens invariably apply them to foreigners who would like to become permanent residents and citizens. Potential immigrants are assessed in terms of racist criteria. Those who have no possibility of admission generally do not even apply. Others are permitted to enter on short-term visas for low-wage and/or dangerous work. Still others are allowed to take up permanent residence, but as minorities without full political rights. Only those who meet the standards of racial desirability will be allowed to enter and become full citizens.

When racist states decide voluntarily or through external pressure to abandon discriminatory practices, their first task is to revise laws and regulations in order to eliminate racial bias in all state policies, including those covering immigration. Such a step covers the distance from being racist to that of being non-racist. However, as this paper will make clear, a non-racist policy still falls short of an anti-racist policy. Nations wishing to further distance themselves from a racist or ethnocentric past would do this by establishing new programs to eliminate racist practices in society as a whole. Such policies would include those to overcome racial stereotypes and biases that affect state decisions on immigration targets, categories of admission and so on.

Over thirty years ago, Canada abandoned an explicitly ethnocentric and implicitly racist immigration strategy and officially adopted a non-racist stance. As one might expect, the adoption of a non-racist immigration policy did not fully or immediately end the influence of racism in the selection of immigrants. For example, several years after the new policies were introduced, immigration officials in the Caribbean continued to use racist criteria in accepting some applicants rather than others (Satzewich, 1988). Perhaps this was an instance where policy changes took some years to become institutionalized, yet this is only one possibility. Is there any evidence that such biases in selection are still present? If present, what explains their continuity, given the long-established history of non-racist policy?

Previous research has also noted some important ways in which immigration policy after the 1960s continued to reinforce certain kinds of stereotyping and discrimination. The most noteworthy example is the continuation (to the present) of policies to admit domestic workers (maids and nannies who work in private homes). Those admitted are women; most are non-European and non-White; they generally work under contract for very low wages, and they frequently experience abuse. Studies of this program have noted the way in which it arises from sexist and racist stereotypes and, by its outcomes, tends to reinforce these stereotypes (Calliste, 1989; Bakan and Stasiulis, 1994; Arat-Koc, 1992). What other features of immigration policy have such outcomes? Have such policies changed in response to the criticism of them?

Going beyond the need to update the historical record on concrete links between racism and Canadian immigration policy, this chapter is also concerned with understanding the origin of these links and why they persist. Do racist outcomes from policy arise from intentional racism on the part of (at least some) voters, politicians or state officials? Or, more frequently, are these outcomes unconscious and unintended consequences of deeply embedded institutional practices, as is the case with much racism? If so, in what sense and why are the links unconscious? If unconscious means ignored and not discussed in dominant policy discourse, how is it that such racism remains unconscious when critics seek to point it out? What is so important about existing institutional practices and their objectives that racist outcomes from them are not anticipated or dealt with through revisions to these practices?

The preceding questions raise larger theoretical issues about social structural and ideological forces that either generate racism or seek to avoid recognizing and dealing with it. This is a very large topic and so my treatment of it in this chapter will be limited. Stated very generally and briefly, I argue that contemporary Canadian immigration policy is characterized by neo-racist elements. These arise when immigration strategy is inserted in a dominant policy discourse and ideology that greatly privileges other goals, particularly national economic performance, efficiency and cost-benefit maximization. From the perspective of political leaders, racist influences and outcomes in immigration within this framework are secondary, unwelcome aspects that are troublesome to address without challenging major assumptions in the framework itself. The racist aspects remain ignored and unconsidered (or "unconscious," following Dei, 1996) in the dominant discourse. This contemporary situation is an important variation (or phase) within a longer history of racism in Canadian nation building (Stasiulis, 1997; Simmons, 1998).

The chapter is organized into three sections. The first clarifies the distinctions between racist, non-racist and anti-racist immigration policy, and sets forth a number of empirical indicators of each type relevant for historical and contemporary analysis. The second section briefly examines the evolution of Canadian immigration policy, and critically reviews explanations that have been proposed to account for those changes that affect racist influences and outcomes. The third section both reviews previous research on racism in Canadian immigration policy and examines some evidence on dimensions that have not been given much attention.

I. Racism and Immigration Policy

For research purposes, at least four kinds of immigration policy can be distinguished: racist, non-racist, anti-racist, and neo-racist. These are expressed as pure-types, but in practice, a given historical case of immigration policy can include a mix of contradictory elements.

1. Racist Policies

Official policies of the state play a pivotal role in racism. At one extreme, the state can reinforce and institutionalize existing racist biases in society, building discrimination against minorities to new heights. This is what happened in Nazi Germany under Hitler, and in South Africa during its long history of apartheid. These and other racist political regimes typically enact legislation that restricts the access of minorities to property, housing, employment and even to public beaches. Other laws dictate who is eligible to marry whom, and who can claim legal residence and full citizenship. Foreigners can become permanent residents and citizens only if they fit the criteria of the racist state.

2. Non-Racist Policy

Progressive nations enact laws and programs which seek to eliminate the ideology, stereotypes and practices that constitute institutionalized racism. Steps in this direction may be viewed as cumulative. The fundamental goal is to remove racial discrimination from all aspects of state policy. All citizens are to be treated as equals under the law, regardless of skin colour or minority affiliation. State policies covering the hiring of civil servants, access to state-supported schooling and social services must ensure that all members of society are treated in the same way. Logically as well, non-citizens who would like to enter the nation as immigrants must be selected without any reference to any signifier of race. To do otherwise would erode efforts to eliminate racism within other aspects of the law.

A related step is to seek to counter-institutionalized racism in major non-governmental institutions that receive licenses to operate from the state. Such institutions include large corporations, professional associations that license doctors, engineers, lawyers, accountants and other professionals, labour unions and private schools. These institutions also include real-estate agencies, since they operate under state authority in listing and selling property. This step involves the enactment of laws which prohibit discrimination against minorities by all such institutions. Recent immigrants who have not yet been granted citizenship would be fully covered by such laws. Failure to cover immigrants would allow them to be subject to racist treatment in society and would undermine the broad thrust of progressive policy.

From the above, it is evident that eliminating all signifiers of race from immigrant selection procedures does not necessarily mean that racism has been fully removed from immigration policy, nor that anti-racist programs are receiving support. Immigrant selection policy which ignores race may still be partially racist if the "intended or unintended consequence is to put certain ... groups at a disadvantage while making it easier for others to gain admission ..." (Richmond, 1994:155). Similarly, Bolaria and Li (1988:ch.1) and Jakubowksi (1994) argue that any immigration practices that result in some ethnic minorities being ghettoized and restricted to low-wage jobs are part of a systemic pattern of "racial oppression." When such racist influences and outcomes are common, yet ignored or denied within a "non-racist" discourse, it is more appropriate to refer to the resultant immigration policy as "neo-racist."

3. Anti-Racist Policies

As a complement to judging immigration policy in terms of what it must do to overcome racism, it is important to ask what positive steps it also takes in the area of anti-racist programs. A *non-racist immigration policy* can leave intact and unchallenged racism in civil society and in the international system. An *anti-racist immigration policy* would include various steps to address these problems, such as the following:

(a) Initiate programs to break down racial stereotypes affecting the integration of immigrants. Efforts in this area will necessarily address racism affecting Native peoples that may have emerged historically through colonization and the repression of Native culture. The full range of efforts will include programs that help the citizens to understand immigrants and to treat them as equals. Given that some immigrants may come from racist countries and backgrounds, the programs will also seek to help various groups of immigrants accept other groups of immigrants and the citizens as equals.

(b) Adjust immigration selection procedures so that minorities who have faced racial discrimination in their home countries are not excluded on the grounds of their lower levels of schooling or low incomes, when these are documented outcomes of the discrimination they have faced.

(c) Promote international agreements with other countries in which racism in immigration policy is condemned and anti-racist activity is supported.

(d) Apologize to (and, if appropriate, compensate) those who have suffered from racism in past immigration policies.

4. Neo-Racist Policy

Neo-racist immigration policy is one revealing significant racist influences and outcomes within a framework that claims to be entirely non-racist. Such a policy is characterized by a contradictory policy process—anti-racist forces may be dominant, yet systemic aspects of racist influence and racist outcomes are still evident. In effect, this policy category is one in which both racist and non-racist elements co-exist, despite tensions. It is an important addition to the typology because it seems to apply well to Canada in the period since 1962. Neo-racist immigration policies arise when the broader discourse on nation building and national survival (in times of crisis) give very high priority to other objectives and to a need among national leaders to deny (and ignore) racist influences and outcomes. The following tendencies would each be considered indicators of neo-racist tendencies:

(a) Yielding to racist sentiment to reduce overall levels of immigration. When this happens state officials are generally tempted to claim that they are reducing immigration levels for "economic" or some other "legitimate" reason, while denying that racist pressures in society had any influence in the decision.

(b) Making immigration from certain regions of the world more difficult by not providing equal access to immigration officers and application procedures. Such policies tend to deny that racism is involved and point to other considerations, such as the job skills of the potential immigrants in each region, as explaining why certain regions receive less attention. In a racist world system, where national levels of education and job skills still reflect historical patterns of racism and colonial exploitation, it is difficult to separate policies that address national skills from racism.

(c) Excluding asylum seekers and other classes of migrants on the basis of fears of racist "backlash" among citizens. This is neo-racist, because it admits to the power of racism without adopting measures to counter it.

(d) Not acting quickly to protect the rights of foreign workers and immigrants when they face violence at the hands of racist groups, or when they face discrimination by employers and housing agencies. Here the state is, in a sense, an accomplice of racist elements in society.

(e) Accepting opportunism and racism in a national police force that leads disproportionate focus on "immigrant crime" and on crime in certain national-origin groups who are more visible due to skin colour, accent or dress.

(f) Ignoring inter-ethnic rivalry and competition in which some groups are more likely to end up as "losers," confined to immigrant and ethnic ghettos and limited to low-wage employment.

(g) Adopting non-racist policies for the admission of certain categories of foreigners, such as domestic workers, knowing that such policies will contribute to racism and sexism in Canada, but maintaining these policies in any case. Racism and sexism in the international system and in Canada ensures that domestic workers are primarily non-White and female. Low wages and exploitative conditions for then reinforce pre-existing racist and sexist stereotypes.

Much of the analysis in this chapter explores the hypothesis that neo-racist elements are widespread in Canadian immigration policy, and that understanding why this is the case involves an analysis of "imagined futures" and the dominant ideologies of national development.

II. Three Phases of Canadian Immigration

The history of Canadian immigration is well described in other works. In this chapter, attention can be directed to a summary of the major historical phases of immigration, with the phases defined in terms of characteristic patterns of racist influence and outcome. I will argue that Canadian immigration, when viewed with a focus on its links to racism, can be summarized in three historical phases. Each historical phase has been characterized by an "imagined future"—a vision promoted by political leaders—of the nation within the international system. Such visions may be understood as nation-building ideologies and strategies. The three phases are:

Neo-Colonial (1870s to the early 1960s)

This long period of history witnessed many specific changes in Canadian immigration volume, from huge inflows to settle the prairie provinces in the late nineteenth century and early part of the twentieth century, to scarcely any immi-

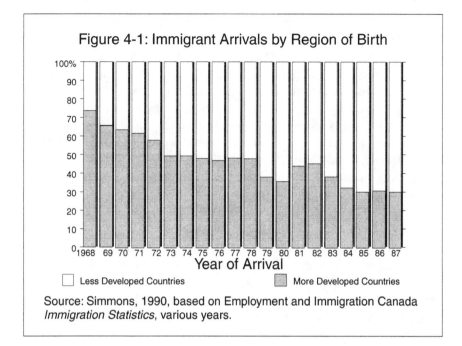

Figure 4-1: Immigrant Arrivals by Region of Birth

Year of Arrival

☐ Less Developed Countries   ▨ More Developed Countries

Source: Simmons, 1990, based on Employment and Immigration Canada *Immigration Statistics*, various years.

gration during the 1930s depression and the Second World War, then a resurgence of immigration after that war. Yet, throughout the entire period, Canadian immigration policy was set within a largely unchanging view of the nation: Canada was understood by its leaders to be a new European and Christian nation in the Americas. This view was consistent with how the major world powers (Europe and the United States) viewed Canada. Underlying the image of Canada was a set of reciprocal interests among business and state leaders in Canada and outside. Canada was rich in resources and a huge potential source of low-cost raw exports, but it was short of workers, farmers and financial capital. Europe had many unemployed workers and capital that it could export, but it was short of farm land and in need of low-cost resources, including grain for food. There is little debate that these complementary circumstances were linked through Canada's imagined future, including its Eurocentred immigration, capital dependence on Europe and the United States, and exports to European markets.

Emerging Middle Power (early 1960s to the recession of the early 1980s)

Prior to the shift to a non-racist immigration policy in the early 1960s, the vast majority of immigrants to Canada came from Europe or European-origin nations overseas (such as the United States and Australia). Within ten years of the adoption of the changes, two-thirds or more (currently around 75 percent) of all immigrants came from Asia, the Caribbean, Latin America, Africa and other non-European sources (see Figure 4-1). Immigrants from non-European sources constitute, in the 1990s, more than 5 percent of the total Canadian population and 15 percent or more of the population in major Canadian cities.

Three somewhat overlapping yet essentially different explanations seek to interpret the radical change in immigration policies and practices that emerged in the early 1960s. Two of these are well established in the literature. The third, in my view the most promising, deserves more attention. It is developed further in my own work as part of a more general approach to understanding the determinants of immigration policy (Simmons, 1998). The three are: (a) Labour Demand, (b) Enlightened Leadership, and (c) Canada as an "Emerging Middle Power."

The *Labour Demand* approach argues that post-War recovery in Europe eventually led to a drying-up of this region as a source of immigrant labour under conditions where labour demand in Canada, driven by profit-seeking investment, remained high. This contradiction was resolved by turning increasingly to other regions as sources of immigrant labour. The pressures leading to this trend began earlier with respect to work that European immigrants did not want. By the late 1950s, the domestic workers program was operating and encouraging Caribbean women to come to Canada on fixed-term employment visas to do this work. A similar program was later instigated to bring in temporary farm workers from the Caribbean and Mexico. The real shift, however, came when workers and their families from all parts of the world were admitted under annual immigration "targets" based on trends in labour demand.

The *Enlightened Leadership* interpretation arises from the very detailed account by Hawkins (1988:ch.5) of the various problems faced by the Department of Citizenship and Immigration and the governments in power in the late 1950s and early 1960s, and how key state officials—such as Davie Fulton and Ellen Fairclough, in the roles as Ministers of this department—carried out policy changes that were consistent with their commitments to "justice" (Fulton was later Minister of Justice) and other values (Fairclough wanted to be viewed as "humane and sympathetic," *Ibid.*:124). The key changes arising from their efforts came in 1962 when immigration regulations "removed racial discrimination as the major feature of Canada's immigration policy ...." (*Ibid.*:125). Particularly important for this argument is the way in which their changes were introduced: at the top, with consensus among leaders of the main political parties, and without much discussion or debate in parliament. The leaders sought to resolve various issues through these changes, including the inability of the system at the time to deal with the demand from Canadians to sponsor relatives from certain countries that fell outside the previous Eurocentred policy, and the need for Canada to shed its racist policy in the context of shifting international circumstances and rising anti-racist sentiment among Canadians. Hawkins does not explain these latter trends; had she sought to do so, her argument would have moved towards a more general explanatory framework of the kind I propose.

Canada as a New Middle Power. The two preceding explanations are both compelling, but they are partial views that need to be joined together and extended by other arguments within a nation-building framework. My approach is indebted to the Canadian Political Economy tradition (Harold Innis) but remains broad within this tradition and does not reduce the arguments simply to labour demand, as some interpretations have done (see the different interpretations of Canadian political economy and immigration reviewed by Stafford and McMillan, 1988). Stasiulis (1997) provides an excellent review and interpretation of political-economic links between nation building, immigration, racism, class formation and sexism, but again I feel that this interpretation is too restricted to questions of labour demand and immigrants and immigrant women as a "reserve army" of workers. In the Innis tradition, the specifics of labour demand and supply, as important as they are, need to be put into a broader political economy that includes particularly international trade and Canada's place in the international system. Such a broader framework suggests ways in which immigration policy is also a way of promoting national values, addressing internal contradictions within the nation and promoting the nation externally.

The late 1950s and early 1960s was, from the above perspective, an important moment of change in the perception by Canadian political and business leaders about the role of the nation in the international system. Canada's rising wealth, its role in the Second World War, and its place as a Commonwealth nation at a moment when former colonies of Britain in Asia, the Caribbean and Africa were becoming independent nations, created significant opportunities for Canada to take on new leadership in the international system in areas such as peace keeping, international development, and anti-racism. To leaders of the time, the imagined future of the nation necessarily included a shift first to non-racist immigration, then later the promotion of multiculturalism (1971) and the official incorporation of humanitarian principles governing refugee admission and family re-unification (1978). The non-racist thrust of policy over the 1960s and 1970s, however, never did develop any strong anti-racist elements, and policy remained open to charges that racist sentiments and practices were deeply structured into immigration practice, including particular practices that admitted non-European workers into lower-wage occupational niches (Stasiulis, 1997).

Sophisticated Global Niche-Player (late 1980s to the present)

A third wave of policy change began in the late 1980s and is projected to continue to evolve in the same direction to the year 2000 (see EIC, 1992, and CIC, 1994). It consists of efforts to rationalize the immigration framework within a pay-for-service, entrepreneurial focus (Simmons, 1995). The main elements of current policies and advanced proposals for policy change are:

(a) The establishment of moderately high targets (in historical terms) for immigration intake. For example, the targets for 1990-1995 were initially set in 1989 in the range of 250,000 per year (EIC, 1992). More recently these targets have been modified downward by about 15 percent, raising questions of possible racist influences in policy process (see below). The revised target for 1995 (set in 1994) was a range from 190,000 to 215,000 (CIC, 1994). The target for 1998 is slightly higher: up to 220,000 (CIC, 1997). Targets of this kind have been set since 1989 without the kind of annual adjustment based on employment trends that were systematically applied in previous years.

(b) The proportion of economic immigrants—namely skilled workers and business investors—is currently targeted to increase gradually over the next few years. In 1994 such migrants constituted 43 percent of the total; by the year 2000 they are to constitute 53 percent of the total (CIC 1994). The proportion of sponsored kin (migrants not selected on performance criteria) is to fall over the same period.

(c) Skilled workers are required to have higher levels of proficiency in English or French and higher levels of schooling than in the past. Under proposals that have been advanced for discussion in 1998, immigrants would have to have efficiency in one of these languages prior to arrival, or be prepared to privately pay for their own language instruction.

(d) Immigrants must pay a higher proportion of the costs related to processing their applications. Under the new fee structure, an immigrant family consisting of a couple and two children will pay $3,150 for an application and landing fees (Marchi, 1994). About one-third of this is for fees alone and is not refundable to unsuccessful applicants. Most surprising to many observers is the ruling that refugees must also pay these costs, although they may first borrow the money from the government and pay it back after arrival.

(e) Family re-unification policies continue, but the family in Canada that initiates the sponsorship of a relative abroad will have to demonstrate a much higher level of earned income (income from employment, business or investment, rather than from welfare, unemployment insurance or other state transfers). Under a change that came into effect in 1996, a family of four seeking to sponsor a single relative from abroad needs to have an annual income around $41,000 or more, up from the previously required $34,000 (Sarick, 1995a). The objective is to ensure that sponsors can pay for the needs of those they invite. This would reduce the welfare burden of sponsored immigrants who cannot find employment.

None of the preceding policy developments, and a number of others that are not mentioned, signal any overt racism or racial bias in immigration policy. Rather all are explicitly directed towards economic efficiency and reducing the costs of state programs within a broader state-policy framework that gives high priority to these concerns. Canadian immigration policy initiatives arising over the past decade are promoted by the state largely as complements to general efforts to increase the competitiveness of the economy and to make Canada more attractive to foreign investors by reducing public expenditures, budgetary deficits, the costs of immigration and burden of foreign-born criminals. A large volume of highly skilled, wealthy, entrepreneurial and self-financed immigrants represents the not-so-hidden objective of current policy. At the same time, the public and private "downsizing" creates insecurity and a potential for anti-immigrant sentiment. These conditions create a context for greater racist influence and outcomes in what would otherwise be a non-racist agenda. At the same time, a neo-liberal ideology and a related future image of the nation currently dominate political discourse and ignore outcomes of current policy that increase ethnic competition for jobs and widen income disparities in ways that negatively affect non-Whites (including Native peoples and immigrants) among others. The next section appraises possible racist influences in policy and possible racist outcomes from policy over the 1980s and 1990s.

III. Evidence Regarding Racism in Immigration Policy

This section examines the way Canadian immigration policy affects and is affected by racism in Canadian society. My objective is to explore various possible links through an examination of indicators of non-racist, anti-racist and neo-racist policies, as previously outlined. The analysis covers the entire period since 1962, but gives greater focus to the 1980s and 1990s. It is organized in two parts, one at the level of discourse and the other at the level of policy process and racist outcomes. An emphasis on coverage of a wider range of issues has the advantage of pointing to the broader picture. Much of the available evidence is partial, so that the review is intentionally directed to developing hypotheses for future research.

Non-Racist Policy and Racist Discourse

A non-racist immigration policy may be considered to be at the mid-point in a classification which runs from racist at one extreme to anti-racist at the other. From this perspective, one would anticipate that the current Canadian policy directions—which are largely characterized by a non-racist orientation and rejection of race and ethnicity as criteria—would be extremely troubling for bigots who would like to attack immigration on racist grounds. They will naturally be obliged to hide their racist sentiments in other arguments. But what other arguments will they use? Consistent with the "imagined futures" approach to the interpretation of Canadian immigration policy and racism, one would argue that racists will tend to camouflage or hide their sentiments by employing arguments consistent with dominant values. Thus, non-European immigrants might be opposed on the grounds of arguments that they are "burden" on public welfare expenditures that cannot be afforded in times of cutbacks in state social expenditures.

Nearly all of what Canadians have had to say in public on immigration over the past several decades has been couched in economic terms, particularly how immigrants affect economic growth and the employment prospects for Canadians who are unemployed or insecure in their jobs. This economic focus reflects both a real concern on the part of many, and a pseudo or false concern on the part of some racist and ethnocentric Canadians who do not like immigrants for reasons of skin colour or cultural difference. In fact the false economic concern is often so well masked in "legitimate" (acceptable in political debate) economic arguments that it is difficult to tell how extensive racism is, and how racism relates more generally to xenophobia (a general dislike of foreigners), regardless of race. Cross-national attitude polls give at best a rough indication.

In a 1990 cross-national representative poll of Canadians, some 46 percent expressed the view that Canada should admit fewer immigrants, while only 16 percent said more should be admitted (Windsor, 1990). In a similar poll taken a year later, about 31 percent of respondents indicated that they ascribed to the view that it would be "better not to have so much racial diversity because it tends to cause social problems" (Mitchell, 1991). The less educated were most likely to express both anti-immigrant and racist views. People living in regions which receive few immigrants were also more likely to express both these views—a fact which seemingly relates to their lack of direct experience with recent immigrants.

The non-racist thrust of contemporary Canadian immigration policy has had four important effects. First, it reinforces efforts to remove racist language from the public stage. People who might be tempted to use the vocabulary of racist "othering" hesitate to do so. Second, non-racist policy has brought native-born into closer contact with large numbers of immigrants from diverse regions of the world and, in so doing, seems to have created understandings that promote acceptance of the foreign-born and racial tolerance. Third, the emphasis on attracting highly skilled immigrants from those countries where such immigrants can be found has led to a rising immigration of non-White professionals and entrepreneurs. The first wave of Caribbean immigrants, for example, was not only predominantly Black, but included a significant middle-class component of nurses, school teachers and other skilled workers and professionals (Simmons and Plaza, 1990ℭ). Immigrant families from Hong Kong are selected on the basis of educational background and entrepreneurial experience. Visible images of middle-class and elite non-White immigrants help to fracture old stereotypes. Of course, the entry of non-Whites into middle- and upper-class occupations and residential areas can also spark new racist backlash from some native-born in these social strata. It can also create competition and conflict between minorities who enter into very different strata of Canadian society (Reitz, 1988). Finally, however, all the preceding points must recognize that the non-racist policy has also not directly sought to eliminate racist sentiment. As a result, racism continues to exist, even though its expression tends to be expressed through arguments more consistent with dominant ideology and accepted values.

Racism and Immigration Policy Process and Outcomes

Various questions have been raised about the extent to which an explicitly non-racist policy may continue to be shaped by racist forces in society and the international system. Racism can influence various aspects of immigration policy, including: (a) immigration targets, (b) access of foreigners to Canadian immigration information and services, (c) selection of immigrants from all those who apply, (d) the settlement and economic integration of immigrants, and (e) the expulsion or deportation of undesirable immigrants. Each of these possibilities needs to be examined.

(a) Racist Influence on Immigration Targets?

One way a government can give in to racist pressure while claiming that it has not done so is to reduce overall immigration levels and to provide a bogus explanation for this policy direction. Such a ploy is possible in countries like Canada where immigration is mostly non-White. Whether racist influences on Canadian immigration policy have been hidden from sight in this manner is difficult to assess. Governments deny that they are subject to racist pressures and official immigration targets are set on various criteria, hence it is hard to figure out which of the stated reason are the real ones. For example, the state may be concerned that high immigration will increase unemployment and racist backlash. A decision to reduce immigration may be based on both concerns, but only the economic reason is likely to be admitted in public. This said, the evidence that racist pressures may have played a role in setting immigration targets is at least strong enough to warrant further research.

Consider the issue immigration targets for Canada and for Quebec. Since 1989, immigration planning in Canada has been based on the assumption that the "ideal" number of immigrants admitted each year should be just under 1 percent of the total population of Canada. This suggested ideal targets of approximately 250,000 per year for the five-year period of 1990-1995 (EIC, 1992). It was understood that this ideal would then be treated as an upper level to be sought only if economic conditions were promising. In fact, the actual targets set each year for the following period have been well below the ideal level (CIC, 1994). This made sense in terms of the recession from 1989 to 1993, but it has made less sense subsequently due to evidence that (a) the economy was beginning to grow again and (b) immigrants tend to create jobs rather than increase unemployment.

Questions have been raised about the extent to which the real reason for lower levels (relative to previously established ideals) are really based on economic considerations. Does such a trend actually reflect a political response to rising political pressure on the government from anti-immigrant political groups, particularly the Reform Party, as some like Cardozo (1992) suggest? Economic concerns and fear of racist reaction may both be involved. In 1991, the Economic Council of Canada recommended to the government that it slow immigration "because failure to do so would lead to a rise in unemployment and in racism" (Oziewicz, 1991a). The state did later lower its targeted immigration levels, but claimed that it did so only for economic reasons.

One of the more controversial issues in the area of immigration targets concerns those established by Quebec. Under current federal-provincial arrangements, any province can work out an agreement with the federal government with respect to joint responsibility for immigrant targets and increased provincial responsibility for immigrant settlement programs. Quebec formalized a basic agreement in 1978 and a revised agreement in 1990 (see Hardcastle et al., 1994). In the current accord, immigrants who indicate that their intended destination is Quebec are subject to the targets and special criteria set by that province. Quebec is particularly keen on skilled migrants who are fluent in French. The supply of such migrants in the world is limited: hence, Quebec has tended to admit many immigrants with the necessary work skills, provided that they have at least some French or show a strong willingness to learn French. The assumption is that French-speaking immigrants will integrate fully into Quebec society and its political structures, but this assumption has not always been borne out.

Adoption and use of French by immigrants to Quebec is a complex matter. It seems that the majority of immigrants arriving in recent decades do in fact learn French, at least to the point of being able to work in the language. Certainly their children learn French, since they are required to go to Francophone schools. At the same time, most continue to speak their own language at home. In addition, many learn English, which is useful in the workplace and is the dominant language in North America. Even more important, they predominantly identify with the federalist position and so do not support the separatist option promoted by the Parti Quebecois (PQ).

A 1991 decision by the PQ to back away from previously planned increases in immigration and its 1995 decision to actually reduce immigration inflows to

Quebec has been viewed by some as an effort to reduce the ranks of those opposed to sovereignty. PQ members who are committed to immigration and to support of minority cultural communities responded by arguing that the reductions in immigration targets were motivated entirely by the depressed circumstances of the provincial economy. Yet, PQ Immigration Minister Monique Gangnon-Tembley offered a more complex and revealing explanation. While denying that racism had anything to do with the policy shift, she clearly admitted that the policy direction was based on the "social consensus" and the "rhythm of the evolution of mentalities," since the government is convinced that "immigration does not create unemployment and brings much-needed skills and capital to the province" (Oziewicz, 1991c). Subsequently, PQ leaders and supporters became furious when some observers charged that significant elements of the party are deeply ethnocentric and at least quasi-racist. The clash of views escalated sharply when the former Premier of Quebec, Jacques Parizeau, argued that the 1995 sovereignty referendum was lost due to "money and the ethnic vote."

A number of informed observers in Quebec, including Anglophones, have argued that the racist charges against the PQ were primarily efforts to score political points and that the ethnocentrism and racism in Quebec is no greater than in other parts of Canada (Conlogue, 1966; Philpot, 1995). Of course, the latter argument is not necessarily flattering to Quebec. This said, it is clear that any future research on the way in which racism and ethnocentrism influence immigration policy decisions in Quebec and elsewhere in Canada will have to take into account that political parties, like the Parti Quebecois, are far from homogeneous. For example, the intellectual leadership and major policy directions of the Parti Quebecois are clearly non-racist and incorporate a pro-immigration philosophy and the ideals of cultural diversity (Simmons, 1995). However, such an official policy direction does not mean that all voters who support the party or its sovereignty platform agree with these goals. Some supporters may be anti-immigration and anti-racist at the same time. Many others may be anti-immigration and racists, given that these sentiments are typically related. If so, what may be taking place in Quebec would indeed be no different than what appears to be taking place elsewhere in Canada. The answers to such questions need further study.

In the 1976 Immigration Act (still in effect), individuals who meet the requirements of the points system on the basis of their own attributes are accepted as Independent Immigrants. Points are given for occupational skills, ability to speak English or French, being an adult under a certain age and so on. If the individual is married, with or without children, he or she is considered to be the Principal Applicant, while the spouse and any dependent children are considered immediate family members and allowed to enter within the Family Class without any review of how they measure on the points system. If other more distant relatives (brothers, sisters, parents) not included in the narrow definition of "family" apply to immigrate after the principal applicant has "landed," they are given additional points for being related to a Canadian resident. If successful, the more distant relatives immigrate to Canada within the class of Assisted Relatives.

The definition of Family Class, and who is eligible for consideration as an Assisted Relative, have been matters of considerable debate. Immigrants from countries with non-European family patterns have claimed that the definition of family in Canadian policy is narrow and ethnocentric. Some have argued that parents should be included, as should children over the age of twenty-one if they are still living at home, since these are people who live in the same household and are economically and emotionally interdependent in their home country. On the other side, a number of policy critics argue that the family policy creates a large inflow of individuals who do not meet the skill requirements of the points system. They point to periods, such as the early 1980s, when in fact the Family Class and Assisted Relatives far exceeded the number of Independent Immigrants, particularly among those immigrants originating in less developed countries. Efforts by such critics to reduce immigration within the Family and Assisted Relatives classes were, in turn, viewed by ethnic minority communities in Canada as ethnocentric and racist. They saw the policy criticism as an effort to indirectly slow immigration from non-European source countries.

In the late 1980s, the debate moved in the direction of widening the definition of family to include unmarried children over the age of twenty-one and to give more points to more distant relatives (brothers, sisters and parents) who were seeking to enter in the Assisted Relatives Class. The points given to parents was particularly central in the debate, since an adult child could "assist" the immigration of a parent, who could then immigrate with a wife and younger children (under age 21), and so on. By 1992 the first of these provisions was rescinded (permitting only unmarried children under age twenty-one to enter with their parents) while the second one was watered down (parents in particular get fewer points to enter in the Assisted Class).

As with many features of Canadian immigration policy, the evidence regarding the role of racism in the definition of "family" and the points to be given to Assisted Relatives is ambiguous and inconclusive. This is because all the explicit arguments leading to narrowing of the definition of family or downplaying points to be given to other relatives were stated in terms of concerns about "skill" levels among immigrants. While some of the supporters of such arguments may have been motivated more by racist considerations, this was kept carefully hidden.

(b) Unequal Access to Immigration Services?

Different regions of the world are not served equally by immigration officers in Canadian embassies and consulates. In 1980, nearly twenty years after immigration policy had shifted away from a country-preference system, the distribution of Canadian immigration officials throughout the world was still clearly biased towards Europe. Of the one hundred and eighteen posts for immigration officers abroad, thirty-nine were located in Europe, while another two were located in Australia, a country of largely European settlement (Table 4-1). Only four were allocated to sub-Saharan (Black) Africa. Paris alone had six officers, even through relatively few French citizens have migrated to Canada in modern history.

These may exaggerate the European bias of policy implementation to some degree, since a few of the positions in Europe were devoted in part to Third World immigration. An officer in Marseilles covered Algeria and Morocco, while one of the officers in Rome shared responsibility with an officer in Cairo for immigration from Libya (a minimal responsibility, given that hardly any migrants come to Canada from that country).

A reading of the country-by-country distribution of immigration officers shown in Table 4-1 suggests various possible interpretations regarding the nature of official staffing decisions. While Black Africa is clearly ignored, the Caribbean is not. While large parts of South Asia are clearly understaffed relative to the size of the population in that region, Hong Kong is a major location for immigration officers. These patterns suggest a strong bias towards staffing immigration posts in countries which score highly on a mix of explicit and unstated objectives. Staffing is allocated to countries with medium-high to high levels of education and occupational skills, capacity in English or French, a history of institutional and cultural contact and a high level of interest in emigration to Canada. On these grounds, Europe came out with an exceptionally high allocation of immigration officers in 1980, even though interest in emigrating to Canada from that region had been declining for a number of years and was at a much lower level than the allocation of staff would warrant. In the period around 1980, about a quarter of all immigration to Canada was from Europe, while two-fifths of immigration officers were stationed in that region. But the Caribbean and Hong Kong also came out high, for although they are not European-origin countries, they have been shaped historically through European colonial institutions, educational systems and language. Most importantly, in the period around 1980 they were middle-income countries facing political uncertainty for different reasons—in the Caribbean this was largely due to political instability and violence in the context of stagnant development efforts, and, in Hong Kong, this was due to its uncertain future in relation to China. Interest in emigration was high in both cases. If there is a racist element in the staffing bias outside Europe, then it would be one strongly moderated by other considerations, particularly the explicit "skill," "language," and "target" features of immigration policy.

Table 4-1: Canadian Immigration Officers by Location, 1980

Location	Number	Percent
EUROPE	**46**	**39.0**
Austria	2	
Belgium	2	
Britain	13	
Sweden	2	
France	7	
Germany	4	
Greece	2	
Italy	4	
Yugoslavia	3	
Netherlands	2	
Spain	4	
Switzerland	1	
OTHER DEVELOPED COUNTRIES	**4**	**3.4**
Australia	2	
Japan	2	
SOUTH EAST ASIA	**26**	**22.0**
Thailand	8	
Hong Kong	10	
Singapore	6	
Korea	1	
Philippines	1	
SOUTH ASIA	**10**	**8.5**
Pakistan	3	
India	7	
WEST ASIA	**5**	**4.2**
Israel	2	
Lebanon	3	
CARIBBEAN	**11**	**9.3**
Jamaica	5	
Trinidad	6	
LATIN AMERICA	**8**	**6.8**
Mexico	2	
Argentina	2	
Chile	2	
Colombia	2	
AFRICA	**8**	**6.8**
Ivory Coast	2	
Kenya	4	
Egypt	2	
TOTAL	**118**	**100**

(c) Biased Selection of Immigrants?

A neo-racist immigration policy may also arise when the state does not monitor and thoroughly control racism among public officials who are expected to implement immigration law. Satzewich (1988) noted that Canadian immigration officials working in the Caribbean in the late 1960s, some years after the law had been changed towards a non-racist stance, still revealed significant racism and racist imagery in their description and official treatment of non-White applicants. Such prejudice and bigotry soon after the law had changed may have been a dying ember of the old way of thinking. Unfortunately, it is difficult to ascertain whether such attitudes and behaviours persist. The officially non-racist policy climate in federal bureaucracies no longer allows for the explicit expression of racist sentiment, hence any residual racism will tend to be carefully hidden.

(d) Racism in the Economic Role of Immigrants?

A number of studies have argued that Canadian policy is a integral component of a racist system of immigrant recruitment and employment (Jakubowski, 1994; Bolaria and Li, 1988). Similar arguments have been advanced for the United States (Sassen, 1983, 1985). The argument is in several parts. Certain employers in wealthy nations would like to take advantage of "cheap labour" in immigrant and minority communities within their own countries. These employers recognize that racism in society can work as their ally. Immigrants who face discrimination typically find that to get any employment at all they have to accept the lowest paying jobs, or lower pay than other workers doing the same job. By offering low-wage and low-status employment to immigrant and minority workers, these employers perpetuate the stereotyping and segregation of minority workers, and thereby assure themselves of a continuing supply of low-wage labour. Such a system does not require that immigration policies themselves be racist, only that there be a continuing immigration of non-White or ethnic minority workers. If the employment system is discriminatory along both race and gender lines, the best inflow would be that of female, minority immigrants, as this would provide workers at the lowest cost. Employers benefiting from such arrangements will prefer a non-racist immigration policy, since this will provide legitimacy to the admission of minority workers and divert attention away from their racist practices. From this perspective, a non-racist policy can be simply an opportunity for continued exploitation of immigrants as a source of low-cost labour.

The "systemic racism" argument outlined above requires that one look for racist bias in immigration policy by examining evidence of employment and wage segregation among immigrants and minorities. This is a very broad research area. By way of summary, it may be noted that existing studies in this area do point to evidence that immigrant men and women typically have employment income below the level of Canadian-born mean and women with similar training and of a similar age (Beaujot, Basavarajappa and Verma, 1988; Richmond, 1990, Simmons and Plaza, 1995). However, the disadvantage of immigrants tends to disappear over time. In addition, the time required for immigrants to reach or surpass the wage levels of comparable Canadian-born workers varies by gender and ethnicity. Women of Caribbean and South Asian background, for example, tend to achieve and then exceed the wage levels of comparably trained Canadian women within a few years (Richmond, 1990). Men from these backgrounds take longer. Black men of Caribbean origin seem to carry a long-term disadvantage and may never reach the wage level that one might expect (Simmons and Plaza, 1995). In contrast, the very high incomes of recent immigrants from Hong Kong and Taiwan suggest that they immediately arrive in the upper economic strata of Canadian society, even if they face problems of social and cultural acceptance.

From the above evidence we may conclude that immigrant workers in Canada are not part of a uniform low-wage pool. Outcomes seem to be very uneven. For this reason, a number of studies have focused on particular classes of immigrants where low wages and discrimination seem indisputable.

One such group that has received particular attention is that of minority visa-workers, particularly domestics. The current trade and export-led thrust of inter-national business and Canadian economic policy has led to a rapid rise in the number of visa workers coming to Canada in recent years (Michalowski, 1996). Most of these workers are from more developed countries; they are highly skilled; and their visit is to work as a trainee or to offer management and profes-sional services in branch plants or home offices of an international firm with operations in Canada. However, Canada has a long history with a very different kind of visa worker. For several decades, Canada has pursued policies which admit domestic workers (nearly all of whom are non-White women) and sea-sonal farm workers (most of whom are Caribbean Blacks or Mexicans) on sea-sonal work visas (Satzewich, 1989, 1991). As Satzewich (1988) and others have argued, such policies seemingly arise from a desire to obtain low-wage labour without having to worry about growth in a resident non-White working class.

Calistste (1989), Arat-Koc (1992) and Bakan and Stasiulis (1994) have noted that the visa system for domestic workers has made them fearful and submissive to employers, some of whom badly exploit their employees. This was particu-larly the case in the 1980s when the domestic workers were dependent on keep-ing their work contract with their original employer in order not to face deportation. Public outcry about the many abuses of this system led the state to institute reforms. Domestic workers may now change jobs and complain about abuses, but whether these measures are fully effective is unknown. Many domes-tic workers on temporary visas may feel too insecure to take advantage of the reformed policies.

Another feature of the domestic-workers program is that it is an exception to the rule that all prospective immigrants must apply for immigrant status from outside Canada. In order to entice domestic workers to accept low wages and often oppressive working conditions, the state allows them to apply for immigrant status provided that they successfully complete their work contracts and, in addition, show evidence that they have developed skills (language abilities, job credentials) suitable for living and working in Canada. Many domestic workers treat this incentive as the most important feature of their contract. This may reduce their desire to complain about abuses.

The fact that a high proportion of domestic workers apply to become landed immigrants has also raised policy concern. To ensure that visa workers would have desirable skills for the Canadian economy, policies were changed to provide visas only to foreign nannies with specialized education in child care and/or equivalent prior experience. The requirements were raised so high in the early 1990s that the supply of nannies dried up. The government had to revise the skill requirements downward to more reasonable levels. This said, there is some evidence that a certain proportion of nannies are women with higher-than-required levels of training, often in other fields. They come as domestic workers because they lack the language skills or face other circumstances (some are single mothers, and so on) that would prevent them from entering as regular immigrants. Such a system tends to promote de-skilling and an underevaluation of the value of prior schooling and training of female, non-White, immigrant workers.

(e) Selective Deportation of Visible Minorities?

Among various minority groups, Blacks in Canada have in particular claimed that they receive unfair treatment by police. The press continually publish news reports on cases where Black men have been shot and killed by police under circumstances where they were unreasonably suspected of crimes they did not commit, and in cases where the offenses would not seem to warrant such an extreme reaction. The problem seems to be linked to racist stereotypes, shared by some police officers. According to the imagery prevalent in certain milieux in Toronto, for example, crime is very widespread among young Black males, and almost universal among those of recent Jamaican origin (Appleby, 1992). The topic is sensitive. First, it stereotypes all Black males, particularly the Jamaican-born, and as with all stereotypes it is grossly unfair to the majority of such people. Second, however, even the Black community in Toronto is appalled by the criminal activity of certain of its own members and feel that this must be addressed in its own right, by non-racist policing (*Ibid.*).

The role of the police in the above context is to move in two directions simultaneously. It must firstly ignore the stereotype and avoid any actions based on racist imagery. At the same time it must uphold laws and protect the public.

The problem is that police and other officials may sometimes fail to do the first of these in their desire to do the latter.

When crime becomes viewed as a problem caused by new immigrants, then the federal government may choose to appease public sentiment with new laws to crack down specifically on criminal immigrants by deporting them. The federal government has recently passed Bill C-44 with these objectives in mind. However, the legislation may have gone too far. A major objective of the law is to increase the powers of immigration officers to investigate and deport individuals who moved as adults to Canada in order to commit crimes. However, the law also applies to Canadian residents who were born abroad, but who have lived from childhood on in Canada. Any crimes they commit would seem to be an entirely Canadian problem. By classifying their crimes as those of "immigrants," the law tends to exaggerate the extent to which immigrants are criminals and to reinforce public stereotypes concerning the foreign and immigrant nature of Canadian crime.

There is some evidence that police and other officials in Canada tend to target certain minorities when trying to meet arrest quotas. For example, in 1991, Canada was the destination of large numbers of asylum seekers. In some cases, the claims were judged by authorities to be "false" or "bogus." These included Portuguese asylum seekers claiming they had suffered persecution on religious grounds, and Trinidadians claiming they were fleeing political harassment and violence. After their claims were rejected, many of the claimants disregarded instructions to leave the country and instead went "underground" by finding inconspicuous jobs, while hiding from the police. When immigration officials were instructed to find the illegal migrants, the Association of Friends of Trinidad and Tobago proclaimed that "Trinidadians are being singled out for special treatment" (Oziewics, 1991b). The association apparently felt that all Trinidadians were being targeted in the searches, even though only a few of them were illegal migrants. Given the fact that false refugee claims had also been submitted by individuals from many other nations, this was viewed as unfair. Officials denied any biases in the search, yet a reporter who accompanied immigration officers in the search for illegal migrants found that the search, that day at least, concentrated entirely on Trinidadians (*Ibid.*). This focus ambiguously supported both the "targeting" charge and the official explanation that many Trinidadians were in violation of the law.

Recent changes in immigration policy tend to accentuate performance criteria. Entry criteria stress increasingly higher levels of schooling, language skills and business experience. The imposition of application-processing fees is an indirect requirement for past performance: only those with higher incomes and savings will want to risk submitting an application. Relatives who wish to sponsor the immigration of kin living abroad must also perform well with respect to income earned in Canada. Critics have pointed out that policies which raise performance criteria tend to discriminate directly against the poor, and indirectly against minorities (Sarick, 1995a). This is the case when the poor are potential immigrants who have experienced racial oppression abroad or immigrants who have low incomes in Canada due to prejudice within the country. The effect of the policy is to discourage immigration of minorities who are poor as a result of either international and/or domestic bigotry, leading some to charge that the policy is racist (Philpot, 1995). While discouraging minorities may not have been the objective, that fact that it will likely do so cannot be ignored in evaluating the fairness of the policy.

Increasing the performance requirements for immigrants may shift the relative size of immigrant flows from different regions of the world. For example, one would anticipate that the 1995 proposal to further raise language-skill and educational requirements for immigrants will reduce flows from regions where English and French are not widely spoken. These proposals will likely also tend to reduce flows from regions where educational levels are low. Countries with low levels of schooling and where neither English nor French is spoken would presumably face the greatest reduction. Under these circumstances, flows from Central America would decrease while the proportion from Asia would rise, since Central American immigrants to Canada have much lower levels of schooling than those from Asia. In general, Canadian immigration would come more from countries with higher levels of schooling, but should have no specific ethnic or racial implications. The latter conclusion may well be wrong.

The anticipated decline in Central American immigration would arise not only because educational standards are low in that region, but would also arise due to the selective nature of emigration. Emigrants from Central America are largely poor peasants (Simmons, 1993). Those from Guatemala also include people of indigenous background who face racial oppression in their home country. Many of these immigrants to Canada came as refugees, while more recent immigration has also included sponsored kin. Many other friends and relatives might wish to immigrate to Canada, but cannot do so because they do not have the education and job skills necessary to immigrate through normal channels, or they have close family in Canada, but the family does not have the resources to meet currently high sponsorship criteria. In other words, they fail to meet Canadian immigration criteria due to the historical legacy of class, ethnic and racial oppression in their home countries. Contrast this with the case of Hong Kong immigration. This is a movement of elite professionals and successful entrepreneurs. In sum, the rising skill requirements of Canadian immigration policy do not discriminate against non-Whites, but the policy can indirectly reduce the inflow of minority groups who remain disadvantaged as a result of discrimination in their home countries.

Anti-Racist Policies

Efforts to undermine the base of racist imagery in civil society and systematic features of racism in the international community mostly take place outside the framework of immigration policy itself, in areas such as multicultural programs and the development of cross-cultural education modules in schools. Such efforts are crucial for supporting the role which immigration policy itself can play in countering racism. The topic of anti-racial programs in society at large falls outside the focus of this present paper. At the same time there are some anti-racist actions which can be taken within the framework of immigration policy.

In recent years, Citizenship and Immigration Canada has provided some modest grants to immigrant groups to document and bring to light instances of discrimination. For example, CIC, along with Canadian Heritage and the United Way of Metropolitan Toronto, have jointly funded a $243,000 project called Nation of Immigrants. The project provides resources to immigrant groups so that they can document prejudice affecting their well-being. This seems in principle to be a progressive step, although little is known about the content and effects of the program, other than occasional press reports that provide, at best, mixed reviews (e.g., Valpy, 1996).

The selectivity of immigrants in certain cases reflects well-known, extreme cases of racial oppression abroad. The case of South African immigration to Canada provides a case in point. Nearly all of the fairly sizable number of South Africans who have migrated to Canada in the past twenty years are Whites. Many of them are European-born persons who first emigrated to South Africa and later, in the context of the anti-apartheid struggle and other problems in that country, re-emigrated to Canada. It is also known that many of these immigrants are very progressive people, disappointed with the economic prospects and violence in that country, and supportive of the end of apartheid. The question then arises why so few South African Blacks have come to Canada. One hypothesis is that few Blacks in South Africa have the education and capital to meet Canadian entry requirements. Thus, while Canada's foreign policy gave strong support to the anti-apartheid movement, immigration policy tended to ignore the links and solidarity which might have been generated with the then-oppressed peoples of that country had immigration policy been constructed to give special consideration to victims of racial oppression.

Discussion and Conclusions

Is Canadian immigration policy rife with self-serving racist bias as some would contend, or is it simply negligent, preoccupied with other priorities and oblivious to systemic racism affecting policy outcomes as others contend? The historical record prior to 1962 does support the "self-serving racism" argument (Bolaria & Li, 1988:ch.10). Furthermore, Jakubowksi (1994) and Stasiulis

(1997) have interpreted several features of immigration policy after 1992 as indicating a continuation of self-serving racism. Others, such as Richmond (1996:ch.9) point to a more nuanced interpretation of the shifting links between racism and immigration policy. He notes the extent to which Canada has made important progress along a non-racist agenda, acknowledges that Canada is far more open and progressive than European nations such as Britain, yet pointedly draws attention to some hypotheses concerning the influence of systemic racism on Canadian policy directions and outcomes. Conclusions arising from this chapter are consistent with Richmond's assessment, yet go beyond it. This chapter identified and examined a broader range of hypotheses on racism in Canadian immigration and an overall interpretation of these hypotheses within an "imagined futures" perspective on nation building.

It is difficult to summarize the evidence on the many claims regarding racism in post-1962 Canadian immigration policy. In part, the problem is one of establishing an analytic framework for evaluating the extent of racism in state policies. To date, researchers have tended to differ in their approaches. From one perspective, a policy which is far from pro-racist but which is not anti-racist either provides a space in which racism in the international system or in society at large can continue to function. Those who adopt a non-racist standard will be concerned about the racist influences in the policy process and outcomes, but will also view the state's actions in largely positive terms, noting the powerful role that a non-racist stance has played in countering racism. At the same time, anti-racists will see this kind of a policy as insufficient and therefore still racist. Only a clearly pro-active policy to eliminate all racist influence and outcomes in state policy processes and in society at large would meet the standards they seek. This point of view is favoured by minority groups in Canada, but has not received priority in immigration policy to date.

Much of the evidence on racism in Canadian immigration policies is ambiguous. In a world where racism is widely condemned in public discourse, finding evidence of racism in state policy formation is particularly difficult. The evidence that does exist, therefore, tends to be in the form of diverse *intimations* of neo-racism. These offer suggestive but uncertain indicators of racist influences and biases in a policy which is officially non-racist. The intimations are less impressive taken one by one, but more plausible when interpreted together.

In many instances the evidence available is subject to more than one interpretation. Such debates are characterized by an "either/or" vocabulary. Thus, opposing sides argue whether immigration targets are reduced *either* because of public fear concerning immigrants as "job thieves," *or* because of racism. It may be that a "both/and" approach would serve better. Immigration targets are reduced below ideals established within the current logic of national development objectives because of public fear concerning job threat, *and* also quite likely because of pressure from racist elements in society.

It seems that we can benefit from a refined classification of immigration policy with respect to racism. The question should not be simply whether immigration policy is or is not racist. This is too crude a differentiation for both research and action. Rather, the questions should be: To what extent and in which areas are racist influences and outcomes evident in policy process? Is immigrant selection racist, non-racist or anti-racist? What about immigration targets, or visa policies for domestics and farm workers? From this perspective one might come to conclusions such as the following:

- Canadian immigration policy is non-racist with respect to the formal procedure of immigrant selection. The increasing focus on highly skilled immigrants, however, means that people who have low levels of schooling due to racist oppression in their home country or in the international system are less likely to be accepted to Canada. This outcome reinforces racial inequality in the world and is a neo-racist element in policy.

- The policy is also largely non-racist with respect to immigration targets in that these are largely set within a national development ideology focused on economic issues. At the same time, the hypothesis that immigration targets have a neo-racist element cannot be discounted, given the suggestion that targets are often lower than they ideally would be (in state planning ideology) due to public pressure, some of which is clearly racist.

- Visa policies for domestic workers and seasonal farm workers are clearly neo-racist in character, since they address non-racist goals (filling a gap in the labour market) through mechanisms that reinforce the "low status" stereotyping of non-White women and men.

What is perhaps most clear from the analysis, however, is that the overall policy framework—explicitly non-racist but showing in fact many indicators of a neo-racist underlying process—has not incorporated a strong anti-racist stance. Rather, it has tended to deflect and deny racist influences and outcomes by focusing on nation building and national economic development discourses and associated imaged futures, such as Canada as a sophisticated niche player. In this regard, the racist elements remain deeply entrenched in ideology and practice. As such, they are ignored and unconscious (at least in dominant political discourse). The challenge, then, is to counter the dominant ideology, its related institutional practices and the "blinders" it imposes. Such an effort requires the promotion of new concerns and greater awareness of racist biases in current structures.

REFERENCES

Appleby, Timothy. 1992. "Crime story: the Jamaica connection." *Globe and Mail,* Toronto, July 13, A1.

Bakan, Abigail and Daiva Stasiulis. 1994. "Foreign domestic worker policy in Canada and the social boundaries of modern citizenship." *Science and Society* 58:7-33.

Basok, Tanya and Alan Simmons. 1993. "Refugees in Canada: A review of the politics of refugee selection." In Vaughn Robinson, ed. *The Global Refugee Crisis: British and Canadian Responses.* U.K.: Oxford University Press.

Beaujot, Roderic, K.G. Basavarajappa and Ravi Verma. 1988. *Income of immigrants in Canada: A census data analysis.* Ottawa: Statistics Canada.

Bolaria, B.S. and Peter Li. 1988. *Racial Oppression in Canada,* 2nd edition. Toronto: Garamond Press.

Borowski, Allan, Anthony Richmond, Jing Shu and Alan Simmons. 1994. "The international movements of people." In Howard Adelman et al., *Immigration and Refugee Policy: Australia and Canada Compared,* vol. 1, pp.31-62. Melbourne: Melbourne University Press.

Breton, R., W. Isajiw, W. Kalback and J. Reitz. 1990. *Ethnic Identity and Equality: Varieties of Experience in a Canadian City.* Toronto: University of Toronto Press.

Calliste, Agnes. 1989. "Canada's immigration policy and domestics from the Caribbean: The second domestic scheme." In J. Worst et al., eds. *Race, Class and Gender: Bonds and Barriers.* Toronto: Between the Lines Press.

Cardozo, Andrew. 1992. "Reform calls the tune and Ottawa plays along." *Globe and Mail,* Toronto, July 13, A15.

Cernetig, Miro. 1995. "White flight." *Globe and Mail,* Toronto, Sept. 30, D1.

CIC (Citizenship and Immigration Canada). 1994. *A Broader Vision: Plan 1995-2000.* Ottawa: Supply and Services Canada.

Conlogue, Ray. 1996. "The misleading question of Quebec racism." *Globe and Mail,* Toronto, March 26, C1.

Calliste, Agnes. 1989. "Canada's immigration policy and domestics from the Caribbean: The Second Domestic Scheme." In Jesse Vorst et al, eds. *Race, Class, Gender: Bonds and Barriers,* revised 2nd edition. Toronto: Garamond Press.

Das Gupta, Tania. 1994. "Political economy of gender, race and class: Looking at South Asian immigrant women in Canada." *Canadian Ethnic Studies* 26:59-73.

Dei, George J. Sefa. 1996. "Critical perspectives in antiracism: an introduction." *Canadian Review of Sociology and Anthropology* 33(1):247-62.

EIC (Employment and Immigration Canada). 1992. *Managing Immigration: a Framework for the 1990s.* Ottawa: Employment and Immigration Canada.

Hall, Stuart. 1988. "New Ethnicities." In *Black Film, British Cinema,* pp.27-31. London: Institute for Contemporary Arts.

Hardcastle, Leonie, Andrew Parkin, Alan Simmons and Nobuaki Suyama. 1994. "The making of immigration and refugee policy: Politicians, bureaucrats and citizens." In Howard Adelman et al., eds. *Immigration and Refugee Policy: Australia and Canada Compared,* vol. 1, pp.95-124. Carleton, Victoria: University of Melbourne Press.

Hawkins, Freda. 1988. *Canada and Immigration: Public Policy and Public Concern,* 2nd edition. Kingston and Montreal: McGill-Queen's University Press.

Jackubowski, Lisa. 1994. *Immigration and the Legalization of Racism.* Toronto: York University (PhD dissertation, Sociology).

Marchi, Sergio. 1994. "Changes to the Fees charged for immigration services and changes to the Adjustment Assistance Program (AAP)." Press Release, April 15. Ottawa: Citizenship and Immigration Canada.

Michalowski, Margaret. 1996. "Visitors and visa workers: Old wine in new bottles?" In Alan Simmons, ed. *International Migration, Refugee Flows and Human Rights in North America: the Impact of Trade and Restructuring,* pp.104-22. Staten Island: Center for Migration Studies.

Mitchell, Alanna. 1991. "Sixty-three percent like multiracial Canada: Country's needs should come first in immigration policy." *Globe and Mail,* Toronto, Nov. 5, A1-A2.

Nash, Alan. 1989. *International Refugee Pressures and the Canadian Public Policy Response.* Ottawa: Institute for Research on Public Policy, Discussion Paper 89. B.1.

Oziewicz, Estanislao. 1991a. "Ottawa urged to slow immigration: Racism, unemployment will grow otherwise, study says." *Globe and Mail,* Toronto, Feb. 21, A1.

_____.1991b. "All in a Sunday's work for immigration enforcement teams." *Globe and Mail,* Toronto, Mar. 18, A4.

_____. 1991c. "Quebec freezes immigration level: Reaction prompted partly by perceived threat." *Globe and Mail,* Toronto, July 5, A3.

Philpot, Robin. 1995. "Look who's engaging in ethnic politics." *Globe and Mail,* Toronto, Nov. 20, A15.

Reitz, Jeffrey. 1988. "The institutional structure of immigration as a determinant of inter-racial competition: A comparison of Britain and Canada." *International Migration Review* (22):117-46.

Richmond, Anthony. 1990. "The income of Caribbean immigrants." In Shiva Halli, Frank Trovato and Leo Driedger, eds. *Ethnic Demography*, pp.363-80. Ottawa: Carleton University Press.

_____. 1994. *Global Apartheid: Refugees, Racism, and the New World Order.* Toronto, New York, Oxford: Oxford University Press.

Sarick, Lila. 1995a. "Increase in fees for immigrants called new 'Chinese head tax'." *Globe and Mail,* Toronto March 1, p.A6.

_____. 1995b. "Family reunification rules tightened." *Globe and Mail,* Toronto, Dec. 15, A13.

_____. 1996. "New immigration rules called overkill: Among Somalis, stricter standards mean 'Nobody will qualify to sponsor his relatives'." *Globe and Mail,* Toronto, Jan. 19, A8.

Sassen (Sassen-Koob), Saskia. 1983. "Labour migrations and the new international division of labour." In June Nash and Maria Patricia Fernandez-Kelly, eds. *Women, men and the international division of labour.* Albany: State University of New York.

_____. 1985. "Capital mobility and labor migration." In Steven E. Sanderson, ed. *The Americas in the new international division of labor,* pp.226-252. New York and London: Holmes and Meier.

Satzewich, Vic. 1988. "The Canadian state and the racialization of Caribbean migrant farm labour, 1947-1966." *Ethnic and Racial Studies* 11(3):282-304.

_____. 1989. "Racism and Canadian immigration policy: The government's view of Caribbean migration, 1962-1966." *Canadian Ethnic Studies* XXI(1):77-97.

_____. 1991. *Racism and the Incorporation of Foreign Labour: Farm Labour Migration to Canada Since 1945.* London: Routledge.

Simmons, Alan. 1990a. "Immigration: Pressures on the system." *Human Rights Forum* (Fall):4-5.

_____. 1990b. "'New wave' immigrants: origins and characteristics." In S. Halli et al, eds. *Ethnic Demography.* Ottawa: Carleton University Press.

_____. 1994. "Canadian immigration policy in the early 1990s: A commentary on Veuglers and Klassen's anlaysis of the breakdown in the unemployment-immigration linkage." *Canadian Journal of Sociology* 19(4):525-34.

_____. 1995. "Economic globalization and immigration policy: Canada compared to Europe." Paper prepared for the Organizing Diversity: Migration Policy and Practice, Canada and Europe. Berg en Dal, Netherlands, Nov. 8-12. 31 pp.

_____ and Dwaine Plaza. 1995. "Breaking through the glass ceiling: the pursuit of university training among Afro-Caribbean migrants and their children in Toronto." A paper presented at the Annual Meeting of the Canadian Population Society, Montreal. Mimeo.

Stafford, J. and B. McMillan. 1988. "Immigration and the two schools of Canadian political economy: A Report to the National Demographic Review." Lakehead University. Mimeo.

Stasiulis, Daiva. 1997. "The political economy of race, ethnicity and migration." In Wallace Clement, ed. *Understanding Canada: Building on the New Canadian Political Economy.* Montreal and Kingston: McGill-Queen's University Press.

Valpy, Michael. 1996. "The immigration cheerleaders." *Globe and Mail,* Toronto, Mar. 26, G1.

Veuglers, John and Thomas Klassen. 1994. "Continuity and change in Canada's unemployment-immigration linkage (1946-93)." *Canadian Journal of Sociology* 19(3):351-70.

Whitaker, Reg. 1987. *Double Standard: The Secret History of Canadian Immigration.* Toronto: Lester and Orpen Dennys.

Windsor, Hugh. 1990. "Forty-six percent want immigration levels reduced, poll finds." *Globe and Mail,* Toronto, Oct. 29, A7.

5

The Market Value and Social Value of Race

Peter S. Li

The notion of *race* is commonly accepted as an ascribed feature of people in that it signifies certain physical and cultural characteristics which are associated with people at birth. One of these characteristics is skin colour, which is often seen to provide a logical basis for classifying people, and for understanding why people behave differently. In reality, there is nothing rational about using superficial physical features to sort people into groups. Thus, the social import of race has to do with society giving significance to people according to selective phenotypic characteristics, and treating the resulting groupings as though they are naturally constituted in and of themselves.

The process by which society attributes social significance to groups on superficial physical grounds is referred to by social scientists as *racialization*; people so marked may be referred to as racialized minorities in terms of their relation to a dominant group, which has the power to set the terms and conditions of racial accommodation. Over time, racialization systematically pairs superficial features of people with social characteristics that are often undesirable to give the false appearance that the social import of race comes from a natural origin, and not society's attribution.

This paper shows that racialization, or the social construction of race, produces two major outcomes in Canadian society. First, there is a social hierarchy of races, which is manifested in Canadians' view of which groups are socially desirable or undesirable according to racial origin. Second, racial groupings are associated with unequal earnings in the labour market, with those of European origin having higher average earnings than non-White Canadians. The disparity persists even after inter-group differences in schooling and other factors are taken into account. The social value and market value associated with racial origins are indications of how a society has developed concrete manifestations of what otherwise would be an abstract notion of race.

Race and its Social and Market Value

Many authors have pointed out that there is no scientific basis to justify using superficial features such as skin colour to categorize people as though the resulting groupings are logical genetic classifications (Rex, 1983:1-5; Miles, 1989:41-50; Bolaria and Li, 1988:14-25). However, since the term *race* is used both as a folk and a scientific concept, there is confusion between the phenotypic traits used to justify the construction of race on the one hand, and the social attributes given to racial groupings on the other (Banton, 1979). Some authors prefer to use the term *social race* to highlight the fact that selected phenotypic attributes are important only in the social construction of racial categories, but otherwise trivial in genetic classifications (Banton, 1979; Miles, 1989:69-73). In other words, physical and cultural traits of people being racialized take on specific meanings such that race becomes what Banton (1979:129) calls a "role sign," and that superficial physical variations serve as markers of racial roles.

In short, while superficial physical features of people do not provide the scientific grounds for classifying them into logical genetic groups, phenotypic features are used in the social construction of race. Over time, as it becomes socially acceptable to consider people on racial grounds, physical and cultural characteristics which are originally trivial become socially significant, since they represent convenient markers by which people and groups, and their implied characteristics, can be distinguished.

To the extent that it is socially meaningful to regard people on racial grounds, it implies that society has attributed normative values and expectations to people of certain identifiable features that are primordial in origin. Such a normative scheme provides people with a rationale and a guide for evaluating race and racial origin. Over time, as certain ideas of race take root in the minds and hearts of people, and as social actions continue to reflect the meaning of race, the normative order associated with race becomes a part of the culture which people internalize in their way of life and perpetuate through socialization.

The racially based normative order is also manifested in many aspects of life; for example, as racism in the ideological realm and as social practice embedded in social institutions of society. In short, racialization makes it socially meaningful to regard people on racial grounds, and it attributes social value to people according to racial origin. In this sense, race can be considered as having a social value, not so much as deriving from the essential nature of race, but from society's placing relative social worth on superficial physical and cultural characteristics of people.

The social worth placed on race is only one manifestation of how race has assumed social importance in the lives of people. After all, the idea of race cannot sustain itself as a meaningful concept unless it is also supported by social actions which reflect the relevance of race. In this respect, racial ideas and social practices mutually reinforce each other. Thus, in addition to its articulation in the ideological domain, race can be manifested as a social feature in politics, the economy and other aspects of society.

One social context in which the relevance of race is articulated is the labour market. The unequal market worth given to people of different racial origins is one indication of how the labour market has come to recognize the relative economic value of race. In this sense, race can be seen as having a market value in that the origin of some people adversely affects their economic returns in the labour market, while that of others improves the outcomes of their market participation. Hence, the earning differentials attributed to race provide a basis for assessing the market worth of race in a society which upholds its social importance.

The Social Value of Race

Historically, Canada has maintained discriminatory policies and practices towards people of certain racial origins, with the result that the racial origin of members of such groups and their social conditions became inseparable in defining the meaning of race. In this way, race was given social importance in that it provided the ground for segregating people for differential treatment as well as for justifying such actions. The history of Canadian Aboriginal peoples, for example, was characterized by the domination of Europeans, which led to the destruction of their livelihood and the loss of autonomy (Patterson, 1972). The Indian Act of 1876 legalized the distinction between Indians and the rest of the population, since the Act formally established what Indian status was, and placed Indians under the legislative and administrative control of the state. With the decline of the fur trade and agricultural expansion into western Canada, the Aboriginal peoples lost further control over their land, their livelihood and their political future. Even today, the marginal social and economic position of Aboriginal peoples in Canadian society makes them dependent on the state for survival (Frideres, 1993; Satzewich and Wotherspoon, 1993). Thus, the term *Indians* or *Native peoples* becomes associated not only with a racial origin of a remote past, but also signifies a contemporary people which is economically deprived, socially marginal and politically militant. Canada's past policies and treatment of Asian Canadians also reflect how the public and the state resorted to using the notion of a foreign race to manage and control a marginalized segment of the population (Li, 1998). Throughout the latter half of the nineteenth century and early twentieth century, Asians in Canada were viewed as an inferior race, with loathsome values, customs and behavioural standards that would corrupt the morality and culture of Europeans (Anderson, 1991; Li, 1998; Roy, 1989; Satzewich, 1989). By the early part of the twentieth century, the notion of Asians in general, and Chinese in particular, as racially distinct and culturally inferior was well entrenched in the ideology and practice of Canada; as well, the view of a racial hierarchy that favours Occidental culture and the White race was prevalent in Canadian society (Anderson, 1991; Berger, 1981; Li, 1998). Canada's historical treatment of racial minorities has imputed many deep-seated symbols and meanings to the notion of race in Canadian society. However, in the decades after the Second World War, Canada also developed legal protection and public policies to safeguard basic human rights. Some of the major statutes include the Canadian Charter of Rights and Freedoms in Part I of the Constitution Act of 1982 (Statutes of Canada 1982, c.11), the Employment Equity Act of 1986 (Statutes of Canada 1986, c.31) and the Multiculturalism Act of 1988 (Statutes of Canada 1988, c.31). These statutes in particular formally affirm the fundamental rights of the individual to equality without discrimination; the Multiculturalism Act endorses the policy of the federal government to recognize and to promote cultural and racial diversity of Canadian society as the individual's freedom of choice. At the same time, there are some indications that racialized minority groups, such as the Chinese and Japanese, which historically were marginalized and discriminated, have been upwardly mobile in terms of educational level and occupation status (Li, 1990). As well, the First Nations became more assertive in their claims of Aboriginal recognition and constitutional entitlement in the post-War decades; consequently, they have gained some political concessions from both federal and provincial governments when it comes to Aboriginal title and Aboriginal rights (Boldt, Long, and Little Bear, 1985). On the surface, it would appear that the post-War social conditions are more favourable towards racial minorities than the historical ones. As a result, the social import of race may have receded as human rights are entrenched in Canadian society.

Some authors have argued that despite the legal protection of human rights and the general acceptance of the principle of equality in Canadian society, racism continues to be manifested in the ideas of people and in practices of social institutions (Henry et al., 1995; Li, 1995; Zong, 1994). Henry et al. (1995:17) use the term *democratic racism* to refer to the contradictory way in which racist ideologies are articulated in Canadian society, which also upholds egalitarian values of justice and fairness. Democratic principles and racist ideologies can co-exist, especially when some people rely upon their stereotypes of race to make sense of their everyday experiences, since they provide the grounds for simplistic but convenient explanations of complex economic and social problems. Ironically, the entrenchment of individual rights and freedoms in Canadian society in the post-war decades also gives added legal ammunition to extremists to advocate racial supremacism in the name of freedom of speech (Li, 1995). As Canadians face an uncertain future due to economic re-structuring, it is appealing to accept a rationale which allows those who feel their traditional economic and social security being eroded to blame racial minorities and immigrants for their woes (Li, 1995). In this way, the historical construction of race in Canada is given a contemporary reality, as it offers a simplistic but meaningful solution to people in dealing with the hardships and contradictions they face (Li, 1995).

There is substantial empirical evidence to indicate that Canadians continue to attribute unequal social worth to people of different racial origin despite the public's awareness and general acceptance of democratic principles of equality and justice. For example, Berry, Kalin and Taylor (1976) reported data from a 1974 national survey to show that Canadians tended to rank people of European origin much higher than racial minorities in terms of whether they were considered "hardworking," "important," "Canadian," "clean," "likable," "interesting" and other qualities. Among the groups with the lowest ranking were "Chinese," "Canadian Indian," "Negro," and "East Indian" (Berry, Kalin, and Taylor, 1976:106).

Other studies have also produced evidence to show that Canadians tend to project a lower social image on racial minorities (Driedger and Peters, 1977; Filson, 1983; Li, 1979; Pineo, 1977; Richmond, 1974). For example, Pineo (1977) reported findings from a national study to show that English Canadians regarded "Negroes," "Coloureds," "Canadian Indians," "Chinese" and "Japanese" to have the lowest social standing, while French Canadians gave "Chinese," "Negroes," "Coloureds," and "Japanese" the lowest social ranks. Filson (1983) indicated that Canadian respondents in a 1977 national survey showed most hostility towards immigrants from India and Pakistan, followed by those from the West Indies; in contrast, British and American immigrants received the least hostility. Foschi and Buchan (1990) studied perceptions of university male subjects to see how much they perceived their partner as competent to perform a task on the basis of the racial origin of the partner, and found that the subjects were more influenced from a partner portrayed as White than from one portrayed as East Indian.

In 1991, a national attitudinal survey was conducted by Angus Reid Group on behalf of Multiculturalism and Citizenship Canada to find out how Canadians felt about multiculturalism and ethnic diversity (Angus Reid Group Inc., 1991). The results indicate strong public support for various elements of the Multiculturalism Policy; as well, they suggest the notion of race is meaningful to Canadians in two major ways. First, as many as 45 percent of the respondents agreed that discrimination against non-Whites is a problem in Canada, and 36 percent agreed that it is more difficult for non-Whites to be successful in Canadian society than Whites (Angus Reid Group, 1991:50). In other words, a substantial segment of the general population thought that race was a barrier for non-Whites in Canadian society. Second, respondents themselves displayed different degrees of "comfort" towards individuals of various ethnic groups. Ethnic groups of European origin had higher social rankings than those of non-White origin, mostly Asians and Blacks, in terms of having a larger percentage of respondents report the highest comfort levels while being with them (Table 5-1). For example, 83 percent of respondents said they had the highest comfort levels with immigrants of British origin, as compared to 69 percent who said so for Chinese, and 48 percent for Indo-Pakistani. The lower rankings of non-White ethnic groups relative to White ethnic groups held true irrespective of whether individuals of the group being evaluated were immigrants or native-born. This kind of public opinion surveys indicates that racial minorities have a lower social standing in Canadian society than those of European origin.

The same survey also indicates that Canadians showed contradictory tendencies with respect to the principle of equality and support of minority rights. For example, 85 percent of the respondents indicated that they support a multiculturalism policy which promotes equality among all Canadians, regardless of racial or ethnic origin (Angus Reid Group, 1991:24). At the same time, 28 percent of the people surveyed said "people who come to Canada should change to be more like us" (Angus Reid Group, 1991:35). Another survey, conducted by Ekos Research Associates in 1994, found that most respondents agreed that there are too many immigrants, especially from visible minority groups, and 60 percent of respondents agreed that "too many immigrants feel no obligation to adapt to Canadians values and way of life" (*Globe and Mail*, 1994). These results confirm that a segment of the Canadian public sees visible minorities as being the major problem of immigration, and that their alleged unwillingness to adapt to Canadian values and lifestyle is threatening Canadians' traditional way of life.

The findings from the foregoing studies also suggest that despite the existence of multicultural policy and the legal entrenchment of human rights in the postwar decades, Canadians continue to consider it meaningful to use race as a basis to evaluate the social standing, competence and desirability of others.

The Market Value of Race

The social importance of race is manifested in many facets of life in Canadian society. One such facet is in the labour market, where race affects the opportunities of individuals and their economic outcomes. Many studies have reported findings which indicate that there are differences in occupation and earnings associated with the racial and ethnic origin of Canadians. Historically, members of racialized minorities, such as the Chinese, were systematically paid less than White workers, and they were hired in labour-intensive projects when White workers were hard to find (Li, 1998). But as soon as White workers became readily available, Chinese labourers became the targets of racial exclusion and were blamed for taking away the jobs of White Canadians and depressing their wages (Li, 1998).

Porter's systematic study of the relationship between ethnic origin and occupational status shows that certain racial and ethnic groups were underrepresented

Table 5-1: Ranking of Selected Immigrant Ethnic Groups and Canadian-Born Ethnic Groups According to the Percent of Respondents Who Indicated Having the Highest Comfort Levels Being Around Individuals from Each Group

Origin Being Evaluated	Respondents Indicating the Highest Comfort Levels Towards:	
	Immigrant Ethnic Group (%)	Canadian-Born Ethnic Group (%)
British	83	86
Italian	77	83
French	74	82
Jewish	74	78
Ukrainian	73	79
German	72	79
Portuguese	70	76
Chinese	69	77
Native Canadian	...	77
West Indian Black	61	69
Moslem	49	59
Arab	52	63
Indo-Pakistani	48	59
Sikh	43	55

Source: *Multiculturalism and Canadians: Attitude Study 1991 National Survey Report*, submitted by Angus Reid Group, Inc. to Multiculturalism and Citizenship Canada, August, 1991, p.51.

in professional, managerial and technical occupations, but overrepresented in labouring jobs, and that the occupational disadvantages associated with racial and ethnic origins persisted from 1931 to 1961, the period being studied (Porter, 1965). A number of people have reconsidered Porter's thesis and have since found that he overstated the magnitude of the relationship between ethnic affiliation and social class (Brym with Fox, 1989; Darroch, 1979). However, despite disagreements over the precise magnitude of influence of ethnic origin on socioeconomic performance, many studies have shown that race affects one's market outcomes such that non-Whites are often disadvantaged in occupational status and earnings (Lautard and Loree, 1984; Lautard and Guppy, 1990; Li, 1988; Satzewich and Li, 1987; Geschwender, 1994).

For example, using data from the 1981 Census, Li (1988) showed that Canadians of European origin had an income advantage over those of Black origin or Chinese origin, even after differences in education and other factors had been taken into account. Data from the 1986 Census also indicated that an earning disadvantage was associated with non-White origin, while an advantage was linked to White origin, despite controlling for social class, and adjusting for differences in education and other variables (Li, 1992). Non-White women in particular were most affected by income disadvantage that could be attributed to race and gender (Li, 1992). These studies show that there is a market value being attached to racial origin, and that people of different origins are being remunerated in unequal terms in the Canadian labour market.

The 1991 Census provides further evidence for estimating the market value of race. The 1991 Census allowed respondents to be classified according to whether they belong to the visible minority category or not. A person is defined as belonging to the visible minority category if the person claims a single or multiple origin of the following groups: Black, South Asian, Chinese, Korean, Japanese, South East Asian, Filipino, Other Pacific Islanders, West Asian and Arab and Latin American (Statistics Canada, 1994b:56). On the basis of the 1991 Census data on origin, respondents can be classified as White Canadians, visible minority and Aboriginal peoples.

The 1991 Census shows that White Canadians account for 87 percent of the total population, Aboriginal peoples, 3.7 percent, and visible minorities, 9.3 percent. White Canadians and visible minorities can be further classified into those born in Canada (native-born) and those born outside of Canada (foreign-born).

Table 5-2 lists the employment earnings of groups classified according to racial origin and nativity from the 1991 Census. The data show that there are marked income differences among these groups. For example, the average earnings for Aboriginal peoples is $5,992 below the national mean of $23,740, and that for native-born and foreign-born visible minorities is $4,894 and $2,710 below the mean, respectively. In contrast, foreign-born White Canadians' average income is $4,171 above the national average; and native-born White Canadians earn just marginally below the national average.

Although these income disparities indicate how much each group actually earns on average in the labor market, some of the differences are due to groups having unequal levels of education and other individual and market characteristics. However, when inter-group differences in education, age, gender, occupation, industry of work and duration of work have been statistically adjusted, the data still show that there are residual income differences that can be attributed to the racial origin and nativity of groups. The last column of Table 5-2 indicates that foreign-born visible minorities have the lowest average income, which is over $3,000 below the national average, followed by the income of Aboriginal peoples, which stands at $1,122 below the mean. As well, native-born visible minorities also have below average earnings, but not to the same extent as those born outside of Canada. White Canadians, both foreign-born and native-born, show an income advantage over other groups.

It should be pointed out that the gross income differences are the actual income disparities among the various groups, and the statistics clearly show that non-White Canadians, irrespective of nativity, earn less than white Canadians. However, some of the earning disparities can be attributed to differences in

Table 5-2: Average Employment Earnings of Groups According to Racial Origin and Nativity, Canada, 1991

Racial Groups	N	*Employment Earnings As Deviations Above (+) or Below (-) National Mean*	
		Gross	Net
Native-born White Canadians	341,670	-$57	$204
Foreign-born White Canadians	51,921	$4,171	$1,027
Native-born visible minorities	5,755	-$4,894	-$654
Foreign-born visible minorities	34,269	-$2,710	-$3,068
Aboriginal peoples	12,698	-$5,992	-$1,122
Average employment earnings (all groups)		$23,740	$23,740
Total	446,313		

Note: Gross earnings in deviations are actual differences from the mean when variations in other variables have not been statistically accounted for. Net earnings in deviations are residual differences after variations in year of education, age, nativity, full-time/part-time employment, gender, industry of work, occupation, and number of weeks worked have been statistically controlled.

Source: Statistics Canada, *1991 Census of Canada*. Public Use Microdata File on Individuals, 1994.

educational levels and other demographic and market factors. Thus, the net differences are produced under the hypothetical condition that the five racial groups have similar levels in other variables, and the residual earning gaps can be attributed to racial origins as defined by nativity and origin. The net differences suggest that native-born visible minorities would have less income disadvantage if they were to have the same educational level and the same average demographic and market characteristics as others. Similarly, foreign-born visible minorities would have earned less if their educational level were not higher than others, and their other characteristics were not the same as other groups.

Table 5-2 also shows that about 87 percent of White Canadians were native-born, whereas about 86 percent of visible minorities were foreign-born. These demographic differences reflect the historical bias in the immigration system in favouring European immigrants over those from Asia and Africa, and that it was only after the changes in the immigration policy of 1967 that racial minorities were able to immigrate to Canada under the same selection criteria as others. The unequal demographic distribution between White Canadians and visible minorities means that comparisons between the two groups are necessarily confounded by nativity. Furthermore, in a society which evaluates racial minorities on a lower standing than the White majority, there are many grounds to believe that visible minority status and foreign-born status together would produce an interaction effect, placing persons in this situation at a greater disadvantage than the sum total disadvantage of what nativity and race would produce. For example,

Table 5-3: Gross and Net Employment Earnings of Racial and Ethnic Groups as Deviations from the Mean, Canada, 1991

Racial and Ethnic Groups	Number	Employment Earnings As Deviations Avove (+) or Below (-) National Mean	
		Gross	Net
White Canadians			
British	166,281	$1,018	$567
French	104,384	-$630	-$310
Dutch	6,408	$865	$596
German	17,052	$233	-$469
Hungarian	1,908	$1,888	-$769
Polish	4,405	$350	$1,038
Ukrainian	7,221	$1,397	-$54
Balkan	2,459	$397	$204
Greek	2,696	-$3,417	-$1,316
Italian	13,692	$1,330	$1,486
Portugal	4,100	-$2,314	$2,451
Spanish	606	-$1,954	-$1,338
Jewish	3,927	$11,503	$5,376
Other European	9,524	$2,772	$292
British and French	23,606	-$1,601	$173
Other single and multiple origins	25,260	$1,459	$899
Non-White Visible Minorities			
Arab	2,059	-$2,948	-$4,384
West Asian	1,168	-$3,917	-$4,445
South Asian	7,004	-$2,235	-$2,366
Chinese	9,376	-$2,074	-$3,056
Filipino	2,962	-$4,365	-$3,910
Vietnamese	1,234	-$5,775	-$3,707
Other South/East Asian	2,145	-$1,245	-$1,994
Latin American	874	-$9,382	-$5,894
Black/Caribbean	5,240	-$3,828	-$2,682
Other single and multiple origins	7,893	-$3,212	-$1,974
Non-White:Aboriginal Peoples	12,698	$5,986	$1,096
Average Employment Earnings (all groups)		$23,735	$23,735
Total	446,182		

Note:
Gross earnings in deviations are actual differences from the mean when variations in other variables have not been statistically accounted for. Net earnings in deviations are residual differences after variations in year of education, age, nativity, full-time/part-time employment, gender, industry of work, occupation, and number of weeks worked have been statistically controlled.

Source: Statistics Canada, *1991 Census of Canada*. Public Use Microdata File on Individuals, 1994.

EXAMINATION COPY/EXEMPLAIRE POUR VÉRIFICATION

DATE 5/26/98

74840-6654

QUANTITY 1
QUANTITÉ Small

TITLE/TITRE FITTING TASK TO THE HUMAN 5TH

AUTHOR/AUTEUR TAY FRAN LTD UK

PRICE/PRIX 75.00

CONTACT S.HOPKINS 05-20-98

Scot Hopkins
447-5101

IRWIN
PUBLISHING
1800 Steeles Ave. West
Concord, Ontario L4K 2P3

foreign accents would affect non-White immigrants more negatively than White immigrants due to the unequal way racial origin is being evaluated in Canadian society (Scassa, 1994). These subtle differences would explain why there are substantial earnings disparities between foreign-born and native-born visible minorities. Even though both groups earn less than the average when other differences are accounted for, foreign status probably interacts with racial origin in such a way as to make it easier for racial minorities to be discriminated against on the basis of language problems, the lack of Canadian experience and other stereotypes about many alleged incapacities of non-White immigrants. In the case of native-born visible minorities, discrimination on the grounds of language and Canadian experiences become more difficult to justify.

Further evidence is provided in Table 5-3, which demonstrates the market worth of specific ethnic and racial origins before and after controlling for inter-group differences. The data indicate that, even before any differences in education and other factors are taken into account, all non-White groups, whether of visible minority or Aboriginal origin, have average earnings which fall below the national average; in most cases the differentials are substantial. White Canadians, except those with South European origins (such as Greek, Portuguese and Spanish), have average income levels above the national average. These differences are actual disparities among groups according to origin. Again, some of the income gaps are probably due to differences in the levels of human capital and demographic characteristics of the groups.

When inter-group differences in education, occupation, industry of work and other job-related features are artificially adjusted, non-White groups still have income levels substantially below the national average (Table 5-3, last column). For example, those of Latin American origin have an average income $5,894 below the Canadian average, while those of Arab or West Asian origin have earnings over $4,000 below the national mean. As well, those of Chinese, Filipino or Vietnamese origin earn, on average, over $3,000 less than what an average Canadian earns, even after educational and other differences have been accounted for.

Although all visible minorities earn less than the national average after inter-group differences are adjusted, some earn more than before while other earn less. For example, the Chinese and the Arabs earn even less, and those of Filipino, Vietnamese, Latin American or Black origin earn relatively more after other variations are controlled. One reason for these changes has to do with the differences in educational levels of various groups. The reason that some groups, such as the Chinese, earn more before controlling for other variations is because they have relatively high educational levels. But when their educational level is assumed to be the same as the national average, they suffer a larger income disadvantage. In other words, the reason the Chinese earn only $2,074 (gross) less than the national average is because they have higher average education; but if their educational advantage is removed, then they would earn even less (net). Conversely, a group such as Blacks earn less than the national average in part because of their relatively low education level. When their educational level is assumed to be the same as others, their income improves, but not to the extent that it matches the national average. The data are unequivocal in showing that non-White origin creates a penalty for all visible minorities in the labour market.

In contrast, White Canadians tend to have an average income level above the national average, except for those of certain Southern European and Eastern European origins. For example, those of Polish, Greek, or Spanish origin show an income disadvantage that is over $1,000 below the national average. However, those of Portuguese origin show an income advantage of $2,451 after other differences are adjusted, suggesting that some of the original income disadvantage may be due to their lower educational level and other demographic variations. It is not entirely clear why some European groups from southern and eastern Europe earn less than those from western and northern Europe, although in the past, those from southern and eastern Europe also tended to do less well than those from western European origin in occupational status and income level (Porter, 1965; Li, 1988b). By and large, White Canadians' average income tends to be above the national mean. Even in those European-origin groups whose income falls below the average, the deviation tends to be much less than non-White Canadians.

These data clearly indicate that there are unequal market values associated with different racial origins in the Canadian labour market. Since these income differentials are maintained after adjusting for other differences, it can be said that non-White Canadians, both Aboriginal peoples and visible minorities, are penalized in terms of receiving a lower income that is attributed to their origin. By comparison, most White Canadians enjoy an income premium due to their origin.

Pendakur and Pendakur (1996) also analyzed the 1991 Census data using a different model, but came to similar conclusions with respect to earning disparities between White Canadians and visible minority Canadians. The authors wrote: "Even when controlling for occupation, industry, education, potential experience, CMA (Census Metropolitan Area), official language knowledge and household type, we find that visible minorities earn significantly less than native-born White workers in Canada" (Pendakur and Pendakur, 1996:19).

Many other studies have produced evidence to suggest that life chances for various racial and ethnic groups are not the same, and that visible minorities such as Asians and Blacks have lower earning returns in the Canadian labour market than White Canadians (Reitz and Breton, 1994; Satzewich and Li, 1987; Abella, 1984). Several factors have been identified as creating barriers of employment and social mobility for non-White Canadians, especially those who are immigrants. These factors include the difficulty faced by many non-White immigrants in having their credentials fully recognized in Canada (McDade, 1988), and employment discrimination against racial minorities with identifiable linguistic characteristics and racial features (Henry and Ginsberg, 1985; Henry, 1989; Scassa, 1994).

The point about foreign credentials was also made by Basavarajappa and Verma (1985), who, based on their analysis of Asian immigrants in Canada in the 1981 Census, argued that the insistence by employers on having Canadian experience as a condition of employment and the fact that foreign credentials were not being fully recognized would explain why Asian immigrants were less likely to be in professional and managerial jobs despite their relatively high educational attainment. Rajagopal (1990) produced data from the 1986 Census to indicate that although Indo-Canadians in Ontario were more likely than the general population in Toronto to have completed university, Indo-Canadians in Toronto had a lower annual income level than immigrants and non-immigrants in Toronto. Rajagopal (1990) suggested that one of the barriers had to do with Indo-Canadians' foreign credentials being highly discounted or not recognized by business and educational institutions, and evaluators using prejudicial opinions and not objective criteria in assessing Indian applicants.

Henry and Ginsberg (1985) conducted a field study in Toronto and found that non-White Canadians were less likely to be hired than White Canadians in the Toronto job market. Their study used matched Black and White job seekers to apply for entry positions advertised in a newspaper, and White job seekers received three times more job offers than Black job seekers. Furthermore, Henry and Ginsberg (1985) reported that telephone callers with an Asian or Caribbean accent were often screened out when they called about a job vacancy. A follow-up study of employers and personnel managers of large businesses and corporations in Toronto revealed that 28 percent of the respondents felt that racial minorities had less ability than White Canadians to meet performance criteria (Billingsley and Muszynski, 1986).

Besides direct job discrimination, Canadians of non-White origin often face other obstacles in the labour market. Scassa (1994) argued that non-native speakers of the dominant language encounter discrimination in employment and in access to services because of their language characteristics, and that their lack of fluency, their accent of speech and their deviation from the language standard of the dominant group can be used as bases of unfavourable treatment and as surrogates of racial discrimination. Ethnographic accounts by immigrant women in Fredericton also indicated that their accent and "colour" set them apart from mainstream society, despite their ability to speak English (Miedema and Nason-Clark, 1989). These studies offer some explanations as to how those of non-

White origins are associated with a lower market value; in essence, it has much to do with racial minorities being disadvantaged in the labour market as a result of racial discrimination, or differential treatment based on superficial differences.

Conclusion

Superficial physical differences such as skin colour do not provide sound scientific grounds for classifying people into logical genetic groupings. Nevertheless, phenotypic traits are used in the social construction of race, with the result that superficial physical and cultural characteristics are systematically associated with social features to produce racial categories which are meaningful to people. Canada has a long history of maintaining discriminatory policies and practices towards Canadians deemed to be racial minorities based on skin colour and other superficial features. Over time, differential treatment and unfavourable policies targeted towards racial minorities became in themselves identifiable characteristics of these groups. In this way, superficial characteristics of racial minorities are inseparable from unfavourable social features attributed to them. Throughout the nineteenth and twentieth centuries, White people, mainly of European origin, were socially accepted in Canadian society as more desirable than non-White minorities.

There is substantial evidence to indicate that this is still the case today. Canadian society continues to attribute unequal social value to people of different origins. Many studies have shown that Canadians regard non-White minorities as socially less desirable and less favourable than people of European origin, and that the notion of race remains meaningful to many people as a means to make sense of their everyday experiences.

Several studies have also indicated that there are unequal market values attached to various racial origins, and that people of non-White origin suffer an income disadvantage in the labour market, while those of European origin enjoy an income advantage that can be attributed to their origin. Data from the 1991 Census confirm that such a hierarchy of market value exists in accordance to White and non-White racial origins, and that non-White groups suffer an income penalty while most White Canadians receive an income premium as a result of their racial origin. Other studies have argued that discrimination based on racial origin, language standard and credentials tends to adversely affect the job opportunities of racial minorities. Consequently, they suffer from having lower remuneration as a result of their racial origin being negatively evaluated and discounted in the Canadian labour market.

Finally, it should be recognized that the social value and market value attached to racial origin are related. It can be seen that economic disadvantages associated with certain racial origins reinforce their low social standing since people so marked carry a lower market worth. In the long run, economic disparities according to racial origins help to maintain the social reality of race by giving a discounted market value to certain racial groups. In turn, the low social value given to certain racial origins creates obstacles which further limit the market outcomes for people being racialized.

Acknowledgment: Research for this paper was funded by a grant from the Social Sciences and Humanities Research Council of Canada. The 1991 Census data used in this paper are based on the 1991 Public Use Microdata File on Individuals supplied by Statistics Canada and made available to the author through the University Library of the University of Saskatchewan as a member of a consortium of the Canadian Association of Research Libraries. The author is solely responsible for the use and interpretation of the census data. The helpful comments of Vic Satzewich and three anonymous reviewers is gratefully acknowledged.

REFERENCES

Abella, Rosalie S. 1984. *Report of the Royal Commission on Equality in Employment.* Ottawa: Minister of Supply and Services.

Anderson, Kay J. 1991. *Vancouver's Chinatown: Racial Discourse in Canada, 1875-1980.* Montreal and Kingston: McGill-Queen's University Press.

Angus Reid Group. 1991. *Multiculturalism and Canadians: Attitude Study 1991 National Survey Report.* Submitted to Multiculturalism and Citizenship Canada.

Banton, Michael. 1979. "Analytical and folk concepts of race and ethnicity." *Ethnic and Racial Studies* 2:127-138.

Basavarajappa, K.G. and R.B.P. Verma. 1985. "Asian immigrants in Canada: Some findings from 1981 Census." *International Migration* 23(1):97-121.

Berger, Thomas R. 1981. *Fragile Freedoms: Human Rights and Dissent in Canada.* Toronto and Vancouver: Clarke, Irwin and Company Limited.

Berry, John W., Rudolf Kalin and Donald Taylor. 1976. *Multiculturalism and Ethnic Attitudes in Canada.* Ottawa: Minister of Supply and Services Canada.

Billingsley, B. and L. Muszynski. 1986. *No Discrimination Here.* Toronto: Social Planning Council of Metro Toronto and the Urban Alliance on Race Relations.

Bolaria, B. Singh and Peter S. Li. 1988. *Racial Oppression in Canada.* 2nd edition. Toronto: Garamond Press.

Boldt, Menno, J. Anthony Long, and Leroy Little Bear. 1985. *The Quest for Justice: Aboriginal Peoples and Aboriginal Rights.* Toronto: University of Toronto Press.

Driedger, Leo and Jacob Peters. 1977. "Identity and social distance." *Canadian Review of Sociology and Anthropology* 14(2):158-173.

Filson, Glen. 1983. "Class and ethnic differences in Canadian's attitudes to native people's rights and immigrants." *Canadian Review of Sociology and Anthropology* 20(4):454-482.

Foschi, Martha and Sari Buchan. 1990. "Ethnicity, gender and perceptions of task competence." *Canadian Journal of Sociology* 15(1):1-18.

Frideres, James S. 1993. *Native Peoples in Canada: Contemporary Conflicts.* 4th edition. Scarborough, Ontario: Prentice-Hall.

Geschwender, James A. 1994. "Married women's waged labor and racial/ethnic stratification in Canada." *Canadian Ethnic Studies* 26(3):53-73.

Globe and Mail. 1994. "Canadians showing signs of cultural insecurity." March 11, A6.

Henry, Francis. 1989. *Who Gets the Work in 1989?* Ottawa: Economic Council of Canada.

_____ and Effie Ginsberg. 1985. *Who Gets the Work? A Test of Racial Discrimination in Employment.* Toronto: Social Planning Council of Metro Toronto and the Urban Alliance on Race Relations.

_____, Carol Tator, Winston Mattis and Tim Rees. 1995. *The Colour of Democracy: Racism in Canadian Society.* Toronto: Harcourt Brace & Company, Canada.

Lautard, Hugh and Neil Guppy. 1990. "The vertical mosaic revisited: Occupational differentials among Canadian ethnic groups." In Peter S. Li, ed. *Race and Ethnic Relations in Canada,* pp.189-208. Toronto: Oxford University Press.

_____ and Donald J. Loree. 1984. "Ethnic stratification in Canada, 1931-1971." *Canadian Journal of Sociology* 9:333-343.

Li, Peter S. 1979. "Prejudice against Asians in a Canadian City." *Canadian Ethnic Studies* 11(2):70-77.

————. 1988. *Ethnic Inequality in a Class Society*. Toronto: Thompson Educational.

————. 1990. "The emergence of the new middle class among Chinese in Canada." *Asian Culture* 14 (April):187-194.

————. 1992. "Race and gender as bases of class fractions and their effects on earnings." *Canadian Review of Sociology and Anthropology* 29(4):488-510.

————. 1995. "Racial supremacism under social democracy." *Canadian Ethnic Studies* 27(1):1-18.

————. 1998. *The Chinese in Canada. 2nd Edition*. Toronto: Oxford University Press.

McDade, Kathryn. 1988. *Barriers to Recognition of the Credentials of Immigrants in Canada*. Ottawa: Institute for Research on Public Policy.

Miedema, Baukje and Nancy Nason-Clark. 1989. "Second-class status: An analysis of the lived experiences of immigrant women in Fredericton." *Canadian Ethnic Studies* 21(2):63-73.

Miles, Robert. 1989. *Racism*. London: Routledge.

Patterson, E. Palmer II. 1972. *The Canadian Indian: A History Since 1500*. New York: Collier-Macmillan of Canada Limited.

Pendakur, Krishna and Ravi Pendakur. 1996. "Earnings differentials among ethnic groups in Canada." Ottawa: Strategic Research and Analysis, Department of Canadian Heritage.

Pineo, Peter. 1977. "The social standings of racial and ethnic groupings." *Canadian Review of Sociology and Anthropology* 14(2):147-157.

Rajagopal, Indhu. 1990. "The glass ceiling in the vertical mosaic: Indian immigrants to Canada." *Canadian Ethnic Studies* 22(1):96-105.

Reitz, Jeffrey G. and Raymond Breton. 1994. *The Illusion of Difference: Realities of Ethnicity in Canada and the United States*. Toronto: C.D. Howe Institute.

Rex, John. 1983. *Race Relations in Sociological Theory*. London: Routledge.

Richmond, Anthony. 1974. *Aspects of Absorption and Adaptation of Immigrants*. Ottawa: Minister of Supply and Services Canada.

Roy, Patricia E. 1989. *A White Man's Province: British Columbia Politicians and Chinese and Japanese Immigrants, 1958-1914*. Vancouver: University of British Columbia Press.

Satzewich, Vic. 1989. "Racism and Canadian immigration policy: The government's view of Caribbean migration, 1962-1966." *Canadian Ethnic Studies* 21(1):77-97.

Satzewich, Vic, and Peter S. Li. 1987. "Immigrant labour in Canada: The cost and benefit of ethnic origin in the job market." *Canadian Journal of Sociology* 12:229-241.

Satzewich, Vic and Terry Wotherspoon. 1993. *First Nations: Class, Race and Gender Relations*. Scarborough, Ontario: Nelson Canada.

Scassa, Teresa. 1994. "Language standards, ethnicity and discrimination." *Canadian Ethnic Studies* 26(3):105-121.

Statistics Canada. 1982. *Statutes of Canada. Charter of Rights and Freedom in Part I of the Constitution Act*, Chapter 11.

————. 1986. *Employment Equity Act*, Chapter 31.

————. 1988. *Multiculturalism Act*, Chapter 31.

————. 1994a. *1991 Census of Canada. Public Use Microdata File on Individuals*. Ottawa: Minister of Industry, Science and Technology.

————. 1994b. *Public Use Microdata File on Individuals. Final Edition*. Catalogue: 48-039E. Ottawa: Minister of Industry, Science and Technology.

Zong, Li. 1994. "Structural and psychological dimensions of racism: Towards an alternative perspective." *Canadian Ethnic Studies* 26(3):122-134.

6

Race and Canadian Education

Scott Davies and Neil Guppy

E ducation matters in Canada. Access to quality schooling greatly improves chances in today's job market. Though acquiring school credentials no longer guarantees secure employment, opportunities for those outside the educational competition are thinner than ever. Good jobs requiring only minimal levels of education are disappearing. As well, schooling has a heightened non-economic role. In a globalizing world, identity politics are amplifying our sense of self and our definition of the collectivities with which we identify. Schools can promote or erode cultural identities, and they have become a prime institutional arena for waging these culture wars. Since any social group that faces disadvantages in our schools will likely also face problems in the labour market and in cultural spheres, Canadians are rightly sensitive to issues of bias and discrimination.

Racism has been understood historically as an attribute of individuals, a belief that people of other biological types are inferior. Though such beliefs have been long discredited, they were common in many nations, including Canada, in the nineteenth and early twentieth centuries. History shows unquestioned examples of racism in Canadian education. Almost from the outset, European settlers deemed Aboriginal culture to be inferior and set out to "civilize" the indigenous population. The early missionaries zealously promoted Christianity and attempted to assimilate Aboriginals by using residential schools. Beginning in the 1880s and lasting until the 1970s, many Aboriginal children were removed from their homes and sent great distances to boarding schools. This distancing was a deliberate strategy to not only immerse Aboriginal children in an English-speaking environment, but to shatter most links with their own traditions. The goal of the residential school program was to "Canadianize" Aboriginal children, but as the historical record and testimonials of Aboriginal people reveal, it created a marginalized, excluded people. In addition, Stanley (1995) has found some examples of segregated schools for Chinese immigrants in British Columbia during the 1920s (though they were partly a response to these children's needs for English-language training) and a few separate schools persisted for Blacks in southwestern Ontario and Nova Scotia until the 1960s (see Goulbourne, 1993).

These examples suggest that these racial minorities experienced profound dislocation through schooling in the nineteenth and early twentieth centuries, though the treatment of Aboriginals in residential school represents a unique case of cultural degradation and exclusion from mainstream opportunities. Black and Chinese children surely faced expressions of bigotry from teachers and fellow students, though not the same type of institutionalized "solution" by educational authorities.

The situation in Canada today is very different. Most non-Aboriginal racial minority children are now immigrants or the children of immigrants, and are schooled in modern, urban institutions. Involuntarily segregated schooling is a relic of the past. Yet, accusations of racism in Canada have, if anything, increased in recent years, and the concept of institutional racism has gained a currency in academic and political circles. How can an institution, as opposed to a living, breathing person, be racist? To some degree this trend reflects changing standards of what is racist. In today's context, allegations of institutional racism in Canadian education usually touch on two major areas.

The first is that racism is manifested in differential access to schooling. Using the principle of proportional representation, activists assume that non-discriminatory practices result in school outcomes such as dropping out or attending university that are roughly equal among groups, and that group representation in various educational realms ought to reflect their proportion in the population. All groups are presumed to strive for the same material rewards in society, and given a total absence of discrimination, each group would have similar rates of educational attainment. Any disparity is taken as direct evidence of institutional racism and discriminatory practices (James and Braithwaite, 1996).

Canadian activists assert in categorical terms that Whites have far better educational opportunities than visible minorities. Our schools are said merely to offer the appearance of equal opportunity (Ghosh, 1996:1), disguising a reality of limited avenues for economic and social advancement for minorities (Alladin, 1996:2,4). Students who fail in school, according to many observers, are usually poor students, ethnic minorities and females (Ghosh, 1996:33).

The second claim is that our schools implicitly promote the superiority of a culture that Canadians inherited from Europe. The Canadian education system stands accused of being "predominately Eurocentric, Judeo-Christian, middle class, white, and male" (Ghosh, 1996:3). According to this view, most school structures and practices have been devised for this majority, at the expense of minorities. Merit standards, instructional techniques and curricula content are said to be designed to ensure the academic advantage of White students, particularly Anglo-Saxons, and to systematically disadvantage minority students. Youth who do not trace their ancestry to Europe are said to lack connection and identification with the public school system. This type of subtle racism, according to this argument, is not overt, nor is it expressed as hatred. Nevertheless, it is said to be potent, because it "disables" minority students, socializes them into failure and condemns them to permanent marginality in the labour market (Ghosh, 1996:33).

One of the more puzzling aspects of these claims, however, is their lack of supporting evidence. Despite the ready availability of census data and national educational surveys, none of the above authors refer to published statistics on educational achievement. Also, other assertions about school practices are not backed by detailed studies. Dei's (1994) accusations that White teachers have low expectations of Black students, that minorities are denied respect in Canadian schools and that curricula are little more than "White studies" are accompanied by neither classroom observation studies nor systematic content analyses of textbooks. Ghosh (1996:32,45,47) cites only American writings to infer that Canadian minorities internalize the inferior status attributed to them by school officials and asserts, without evidence, that racial bias is still common in textbooks and that this bias has destructive effects on students. Varpalotai (1995:246) claims that ethnic minorities get differential treatment and that this is "well documented," though she cites no such documentation.

Are contemporary Canadian schools racist? Our aim is to examine the evidence and reasoning that underpin claims of institutional racism in Canadian education. We present and assess quantitative evidence on equal opportunity in contemporary Canadian education. Following that, we examine the evidence and logic of scholars who claim that Canadian schools are culturally racist. Next, in light of the new "politics of difference," we attempt to explain why education in Canada is becoming increasingly racialized, and outline two prominent school reforms that seek to institutionalize racial differences. We end with a cautionary discussion about possible future directions in our schools.

Before launching this investigation, we need to clarify the standards of reasoning and evidence that we apply in this chapter. Charges of institutional racism ought to be based on systematic evidence of objective discrimination that is rooted specifically in race and not some other social category. We reject four types of reasoning and forms of evidence that are common in the literature on race and education. First, the mere existence of educational disparities for some minority groups does not in itself constitute direct evidence of discrimination. The principle of proportional representation lacks realism when applied rigidly. As sociologists we are ever wary of "blaming the victim," but it is unrealistic to completely disregard the role of particular group traditions, conditions and histories. Many refugees entering Canada, for instance, are impoverished, suffer deep emotional scars and thus have considerable difficulties in adjustment. If their initial school attainment falls below the national average, it makes little sense to lay all blame on Canadian schools. But further, as we will see below, Canadian-born White students achieve, on average, less in our schools than do immigrants and visible minorities. Though it would be consistent with the principle of proportional representation, few would conclude that Canadian education is systematically biased against Whites, Anglo-Saxons, and the native-born. The point is that the burden of proof is on demonstrating a group's repeated neglect *vis-à-vis* other groups. To do otherwise is to engage in a crude politics of blame and to merely re-label disparities due to a range of other factors as racism.

Second, we are sceptical of the increasingly common practice of using students' subjective feelings as full evidence of racism in schools. Perceptions of racism ought to be verified with objective measures. For instance, if someone "feels" unemployed, a researcher might check whether this person indeed has a job. Similarly, if someone "feels" poor, but we discover that they actually have a tidy middle-class income, it is wise to be sceptical of this person's claim. This has relevance for education, since, as we will see below, researchers have often made claims about teachers based on student perceptions without observing the teachers themselves. To consider racism as simply in the eye of the beholder, rather than as an objective state of affairs, is to dilute and trivialize the concept.

Third, anecdotal evidence does not provide adequate support for claims of institutional racism. Such claims ought to be backed with systematic evidence. When discussing institutional racism, for instance, noting that "hot dog days" are more frequent that "chow mein days" (Alladin, 1996:12) is to stretch the meaning of the term unless it is backed with more data.

Fourth, forms of disadvantage rooted in non-racial social conditions, and which are experienced similarly by Whites who share that condition, do not constitute racism *per se*. For instance, if an immigrant minority group with a lower-than-average economic standing has a university attendance rate below the national average but above that of Whites of similar socio-economic status, we would consider their educational problems to be rooted in socio-economic status rather than race. Conversely, the history of Aboriginal people sent to residential schools represents a stark case of racism, since similarly placed Whites were not subjected to the same treatment. The latter is a clear case of discrimination based on race.

Race and Educational Attainment: Past Studies and The 1991 Census Profile

We begin by reviewing attainment studies and discussing our own analysis of 1991 census data.[1] Research from the 1980s suggests patterns of attainment that

---

1
  We focus on equality of educational opportunity as manifested by the amount of schooling accumulated by different groups. Exposure is a necessary, although not sufficient, condition for the attainment of a good formal education, and that is why we emphasize it. Not everyone at the same level of schooling has the same experience of schooling, nor have they necessarily had the same quality of education. Unfortunately, we, like virtually all researchers, lack good measures of the quality of schooling experience.

are in direct contrast to those assumed by many scholars. The 1981 census shows that most ethnic and racial minorities achieved higher levels of schooling than the average Canadian, as well as people of Anglo-Canadian heritage. Pooling immigrants and the native-born, Black and Chinese Canadians, especially the latter, had above-average high school and university completion rates. Among the Canadian-born, both Chinese and Black Canadians exceeded the national average in years of attained schooling (Li, 1989:76-78).

In Ontario, a province with large concentrations of minorities, studies conducted in the mid-1980s showed that few dropouts were immigrants or minorities. Over 90 percent of young high school dropouts were White, Canadian-born youth who spoke English or French as their primary language (Radwanski, 1987). Minorities and immigrants had lower dropout rates than the White, native-born majority. The lone exception to this pattern was found among a particular segment of visible minorities—those who had been in Canada for less than four years. The Canada-wide *School Leavers Survey*, conducted in 1991, also found that youth who were not born in this country had lower dropout rates than Canadian-born youth, regardless of whether the youth spoke English or French as their first language, or another language. However, Aboriginal youth had dropout rates that were more than double the national average (Gilbert et. al, 1993:23).

The City of Toronto Board of Education now reports educational achievement by race and other social categories (e.g., Yau, Cheng, and Ziegler 1993:24). They find that Asian students do better than Whites, and that Blacks are over-represented among low-achieving, bottom-stream, "at-risk" students (those failing to graduate from high school in five years; the study did not measure dropout rates directly). To explain these group differences, the authors note (*Ibid.*:32) that parental occupation greatly affects who proceeds satisfactorily, implying that much of the educational disadvantage of Blacks may be a socio-economic effect, since the latter more than most other groups hail from disadvantaged socio-economic origins. Nevertheless, current Toronto patterns for Blacks may be unique from the rest of Canada.

We turn next to our own examination of the 1991 Canadian census. We compare groups on three different measures—high school completion, years of schooling, and university degree attainment—to develop a comprehensive portrait of educational attainment.[2]

Who graduates from high school? The second and third rows of the Table 6-1 compare completion rates of visible minorities and other Canadians (see the

---

[2] Where possible, we distinguish the attainments of the foreign-born from the Canadian-born. Since average attainments of ethnic groups with large proportions of immigrants are greatly influenced by their schooling (or lack of schooling) elsewhere, group disparities may largely reflect differences between groups upon entering in this country. We raise this point because, like much existing research, we are unable to make this distinction for some measures.

Table 6-1: Percentage of Canadians Twenty Years of Age and Above with Secondary School Graduation Certificate by Visible-Minority Status, by Immigration Status, and Sex, 1990

	Women		Men	
	Native-born	Foreign-born	Native-born	Foreign-born
All Canadians	**54.5**	**50.7**	**51.5**	**54.2**
Visible-Minority Population	69.6	57.7	68.6	64.5
Non-Visible Minority Pop.	54.3	46.9	51.3	48.7
Korean	83.3	75.0	92.5	86.1
Chinese	80.4	53.5	79.4	61.5
Filipino	78.1	77.7	73.3	79.6
South Asian	75.5	57.3	72.6	66.3
West Asian & Arab	73.2	62.5	70.8	72.3
Latin American	71.4	55.9	64.1	60.6
Japanese	69.2	69.8	69.1	72.3
Other Pacific Islanders	61.3	58.4	54.2	59.8
Blacks	57.6	55.2	55.4	60.1
South East Asian	53.3	39.5	50.0	48.6
Multiple Visible Minorities	73.2	65.2	70.7	66.0

Source: Unpublished data from Census Analysis Division, 1991 Census, Statistics Canada.

Notes: Visible-minority status is coded in accordance with the Federal Government's Employment Equity Act (1986). No 1991 Census question asked about race or colour. Visible-minority status was derived by Statistics Canada, from responses to ethnic origin, language, place of birth, and religion questions. Ethnic categories have been collapsed so that, for example, Black includes people of African, Caribbean, American, and Canadian descent, while South East Asian includes people of Vietnamese, Thai, Laotian, Cambodian, and Indonesian descent. Black was explicitly identified on the 1991 Census questionnaire, while South East Asian responses required people to write in information in a "Please specify" section.

notes to Table 6-1). The table shows that visible minorities, whether born here or not, male or female, are more likely than other Canadians to have graduated from high school. As one example, among Canadian-born visible-minority women, 69.6 percent have completed high school as compared to 54.3 percent of other Canadian-born women. Table 6-1 further highlights the graduation rates for different visible-minority groups. For example, 83.3 percent of Canadian-born Korean women have graduated from high school. Among Canadian-born Chinese, the figure is 80.4 percent, while for West Asian and Arabian Canadians, it is 73.2 percent. What is most striking is that fully ten of eleven visible-minority groups have high school graduation rates that are superior to other Canadians. It is important to note that Blacks, foreign-born or Canadian-born, have graduation rates that are superior to other Canadians. Notice too that individuals who belong to more than one visible-minority group (i.e., having parents from different backgrounds), here classified in the Multiple Visible Minorities category, also have superior levels of high school graduation. The lone exception are Canadian-born

Table 6-2: Percentage of People Holding University Degrees by Ethnic Group, Age Group and Sex

Ethnic Group	Women		Men	
	25-34	55-64	25-34	55-64
Jewish	49.6	5.0	55.0	34.1
Chinese	28.9	5.9	37.6	14.3
Filipino	28.8	23.7	20.8	30.5
Greek	21.4	1.8	24.0	3.5
Polish	19.8	4.8	18.3	10.9
Italian	18.6	1.0	18.8	2.3
Hungarian	18.6	7.0	17.2	11.2
Ukrainian	17.1	3.1	16.2	9.1
Scottish	16.3	6.3	15.7	11.8
Irish	15.4	5.4	14.8	10.1
Dutch	14.9	3.1	12.9	7.8
Scandinavian	14.4	4.6	12.5	8.1
French	12.6	3.4	13.0	7.2
Spanish	11.7	6.3	11.5	13.8
English	11.0	4.3	11.7	9.3
Black	9.8	3.7	12.9	13.9
Portuguese	6.4	0.5	4.5	1.2
Aboriginal	2.6	0.7	1.9	1.1
All Canadians	15.7	5.0	15.9	10.1

Source: Unpublished data from Census Analysis Division, 1991 Census, Statistics Canada.

Notes: Ethnicity is measured by self-report. Only individuals listing a single ethnic origin are included in the table. The smallest number in any specific cell of the table used in calculating the percentages is for Portuguese women between 55 and 64 with university degrees (N=55; out of a total of 10,330 such women). NB: Both foreign-born and native-born people are included.

women of South East Asian descent, who have lower graduation rates than other women, and this difference is quite small (53.3% to 54.4%).

By including everyone over the age of nineteen, Table 6-1 mixes persons of widely varying ages, and it also lumps together all non-visible minorities. Table 6-2 compensates for both of these weaknesses by comparing persons from a wider range of ethnic backgrounds, while at the same time examining patterns for younger (twenty-five to thirty-four) and older (fifty-five to sixty-four) groups. This table uses the percentage of persons with a university degree as a measure of educational achievement. We compare group rankings between the younger and older cohorts as a proxy measure of change (note here the limitation of mixing the foreign-born and the native-born).

For both men and women, Chinese and Filipino Canadians are among the groups most likely to have a university degree, especially in the younger cohort. In contrast, Blacks have lower-than-average attainments, with the exception of the older male cohort, although among men, Blacks had similar or higher per-

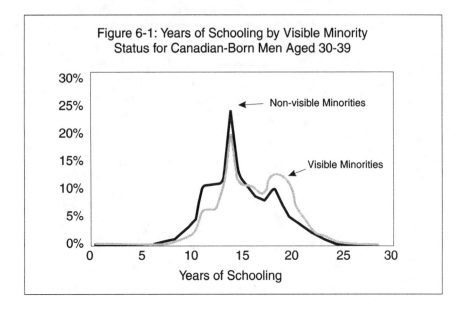

Figure 6-1: Years of Schooling by Visible Minority Status for Canadian-Born Men Aged 30-39

centages of degree attainment than English, Dutch, Portuguese, Spanish, and Scandinavian Canadians in both age cohorts. Most striking is the far-below-average attainment of Aboriginal Canadians. In all but one cohort, Aboriginals receive the smallest share of university degrees.

Figures 6-1 and 6-2 graph years of schooling completed as a third way of illustrating educational achievements. Here only Canadian-born citizens aged thirty to thirty-nine (the youngest cohort for whom most people will have completed schooling; the relative patterns are not different if we choose an even younger cohort) are compared. Three patterns are very clear. First, for both women and men, the majority population is more likely than visible minorities to have dropped out before completing twelve years of school. Second, among both women and men, majority members are more likely to have stopped their schooling at twelve years (note the higher peaks). Third, among both women and men, visible minorities are more likely to have continued in school beyond twelve years (ie., into post-secondary education).

A further way to investigate the effects of race and immigration status is to do a multivariate analysis—to compare groups in their years of schooling while simultaneously taking into account many other factors. While a full accounting of this question cannot be addressed with *any* existing data set in Canada, we approximate such an analysis for a delimited number of variables. In particular, it allows us to explore a key issue; whether the attainment of many minorities is a consequence of their high socio-economic status upon entering Canada. Since

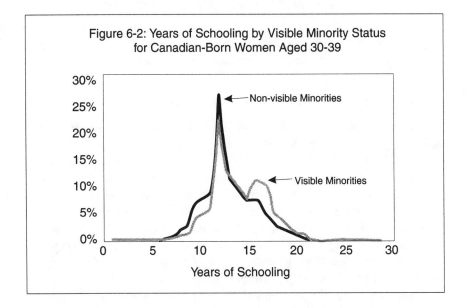

Figure 6-2: Years of Schooling by Visible Minority Status
for Canadian-Born Women Aged 30-39

immigration policy now favours better-educated and wealthier immigrants, it is reasonable to hypothesize that the success of the children of immigrants could be due to their advantaged class background.

To investigate this hypothesis, we estimated the average number of years of schooling acquired by people living in Canada in 1994 using regression models that controlled for sex, region, mother's birth place, family structure and parental socio-economic status (table not shown; available upon request). We found that even controlling for these variables, students with Asian mothers have significantly higher attainments, and students with Canadian-born parents have significantly lower attainments.

These findings taken as a sum lead us to two conclusions. First, the evidence is overwhelming that racial minorities as an aggregate, both native- and foreign-born, have attainments that are superior to Whites and to the Canadian-born. Using a variety of measures, no case can be made for claims of across-the-board discrimination blocking the educational attainment of visible minorities or immigrants in comparison to other Canadians. Indeed, in many respects, these patterns of advantage and disadvantage are the reverse. This is not to deny that some visible-minority Canadians may face forms of discrimination and harassment in schools, but it is to say that such problems do not result in inferior levels of schooling. Second, crucial distinctions must be made among racial minorities. Asians appear to be advantaged on all measures; Blacks have mixed attainments (above-average high school completion rates; below-average university completion rates); and Aboriginals rank near or at the bottom on all measures. The only clear case of blocked attainment can be made for the First Nations.

Is There Institutionalized Cultural Racism in Our Schools?

The conclusions of the previous section do not preclude the possibility that non-Aboriginal minorities, though attaining superior levels of schooling, may face a different set of problems. As we discussed at the outset, many activists and academics contend that Canadian schools have institutionalized a form of cultural racism. Their claim is not merely that immigrants encounter a strange new culture in our schools, nor that Canadian schools could improve the way they integrate newcomers. Rather, they contend that by reflecting the majority experience, and by focusing more on Canada than on other countries, Canadian school curricula degrade non-White cultures, implicitly promote White cultural supremacy and injure the collective self-esteem of minorities.

The starting point for this claim is a sweeping assertion: that the standards and structures of Canadian schools are essentially rooted in a White, Judeo-Christian, male culture (Ghosh, 1996). Everything from rules, goals, notions of development, teaching methods and discipline codes are said to have a White, European essence that is foreign to minorities. These alien conditions may not prevent minorities from graduating from high school and attending post-secondary institutions, but is said to send a hidden message that minorities possess an inferior cultural heritage.

This position is best substantiated by the experiences of Native children in the pre-Second World War era. As discussed above, residential schools were forcibly imposed upon a largely reluctant Aboriginal population, and the aim of these schools was to suppress Aboriginal cultures. The dominant majority was largely oblivious to the damage of this cultural imposition because they deemed the imposed culture to be superior. But this claim is also extended to current practices for non-Aboriginal minorities. Can the grave historical mistreatment of Aboriginals be equated with the experience of other minorities in contemporary schools?

Some scholars offer an elaborate rationale for this claim. Dei (1994), for instance, borrows the American multiculturalist view of North American culture as derived from four continents, each presumably rooted in ancient civilizations (see Manning and Baruth, 1996). White children are said to share a European-Canadian culture; Black children share an African-Canadian culture, Aboriginal children share a single Native North American culture, and finally all children who trace their origins to Asia hold an Asian-Canadian culture. Children from each "culture" are presumed, without evidence, to think and learn differently, regardless of how long their families have been in North America. Dei (1994) alludes here to an "African epistemology," asserting that children of African descent think and learn differently from White children, who think and learn in ways that are essentially European. Canadian schools, deemed to be entirely European, are urged to change their staffing, pedagogy and curricular content, or else be culturally racist and Eurocentric.

But consider the problematic premises of this position. To see world culture as divided into four archetypes, derived from four continents and racial groupings, is to assume that all racial groups retain a separate, unchanging cultural essence derived from ancient civilizations. Black Canadians, for instance, are asserted to relate better to African writers and African traditions, regardless of their individual ancestry. Even if school practices have constantly changed over the past one hundred years, today's schools are seen to retain an European, and thus White, essence. Any book written by a White Canadian such as Margaret Atwood is deemed European, and hence foreign to minority Canadians, even if the latter are born and raised in Canada.

The accusation of cultural racism is thus premised on racial essentialism. Many readers may find it difficult to see just how the teaching of Grade 12 physics, or Grade 2 phonics, is "White" or "Christian" in essence, and may recall when notions of race-specific thinking patterns were rightly denounced as racist just twenty years ago. But rather than dismiss these charges outright, we argue that they ought to be tested in various ways. One could conduct international, cross-cultural comparisons of contemporary schools. If Canadian schools are indeed structured in ways that are alien to non-Aboriginal minority students, then one ought to present examples of modern schools in other nations that (a) differ widely from the Canadian model, and that (b) give students an education that is clearly superior to that they receive in Canada. To our knowledge, no multicultural or anti-racist educator has presented such evidence.

In fact, our reading of the international research literature suggests that contemporary Canadian schools, like schools elsewhere, are constantly influenced by transnational trends in education. Over the past century, our schools, like those in most modern countries, have undergone continual transformation and have gradually but continually shed an ethnic-specific character. Gone are semblances of the Christian school of the British empire ("God Save the Queen," the Lord's Prayer). Their missions, pedagogy and content have constantly evolved because today's schools are dynamic institutions embedded in a transnational system of professional education.

Comparative sociologists have shown that forms and content of modern educational institutions around the globe have continually converged since the 1940s. Schools systems in countries across the Third World and Europe, as well as Canada and the United States, have adopted remarkably similar methods and practices, regardless of their level of industrialization, urbanization or political structure (Benavot et al., 1991). These processes of standardization have their origins in an evolving world polity that promotes common patterns of institution building. Educational innovations and state-of-the-art theories of pedagogy diffuse rapidly as educators compare their practices to those in other countries, and follow the advice from international organizations such as the UN, UNESCO, UNICEF, and OECD. In turn, the professionalization of education has fostered the formation of professional networks spanning the globe (Meyer, 1980). Consequently, Canadian schools, as one node in this vast network, are *modern* institutions with increasingly transnational cultural orientations and content.

Coupled with this is the fact that virtually all non-Aboriginal minority groups in Canada now share the modernist ethos of public schooling. Compare the outlook of today's Asian immigrants versus the Mennonite and Hutterite immigrants who arrived from Europe in the early 1900s. The latter held a pre-modern outlook, rejected technology, city life and consumerism, and segregated themselves to keep these modern ills at bay. Contemporary immigrants, in contrast, enter Canada precisely to attain the fruits of contemporary capitalism—urban affluence, worldly success and careers. For all of the talk of "cultural diversity," the vast majority of Canadians, regardless of their ethnic ancestry, share a bourgeois, middle-class orientation (Howard, 1996). With education so essential for a variety of life chances, few of today's immigrants demand to be left out of public schooling. Indeed, class and socio-economic background are stronger predictors of school outcomes than are race and ethnicity, and thus the types of cultural aspirations and aptitudes that schools reward are probably much more differentiated by socio-economic status (SES) than race or ethnicity. This sheds light on why most ethnic groups, even those lacking English skills and familiarity with existing Canadian culture, from the European Jews of past waves of immigration to the Asian immigrants of today, have typically outperformed Canadian-born students.

Given the international influences on Canadian schools, and given the similar cultural orientations towards schools among most groups, we are sceptical of sweeping claims that today's minorities face culturally alien schools. Rather than containing some primordial Anglo-Saxon essence, our schools are the on-going product of internationally oriented education professionals. Despite the heated rhetoric, most race-related battles in today's schools take for granted the broad institutional form of modern education. Conflicts erupt over relatively circumscribed issues, such as the demographics of school staffing, access to language programs and the content of literature and history. We turn to these specific issues next.

The more particular allegations of cultural racism are four-fold: (a) public schools are said to not give enough coverage to the role of racial minorities in the history of Canada; (b) the existing coverage of minorities is insulting and demeaning; (c) there is too much emphasis on Canadian and European history and literature, and a lack of coverage of Native, Asian and African history and literature; and (d) the sum total of these biases is that public schools tacitly tout White, European culture as superior, damaging the collective self-esteem of minorities.

All four claims appear to ring true for Aboriginals, at least prior to the past few decades. Older textbooks taught that North America was "discovered" by European explorers; Natives were portrayed as playing a minor role in Canadian history, and their portrayal was often as either child-like innocents or wild savages. The attempt to suppress traditional Native cultures and to assimilate them into a English-speaking, Christian culture has had devastating effects. However, much has changed; First Nations' civilizations, conquest and the historical legacies of that conquest are now openly discussed in our public schools.

These allegations are on shakier ground when we turn to non-Aboriginal minorities. Claims of contemporary biases are asserted without systematic analyses of textbooks; claims of damaged self-esteem among non-Aboriginal minorities are also offered without detailed examples or psychological studies. While not necessarily denying these claims, we note their lack of supporting evidence at this time.[3]

Moreover, we question some claims of bias in older textbooks. One popular account of pre-modern textbooks is offered by Stanley (1995), who describes how British Columbian school texts extolled the virtues of British patriotism, enterprise and skill, and depicted Asians as the "Yellow Race" that included some of "the most backward" peoples in the world. He quotes from a 1880s school reader that describes China as a "land of oddities and contrarieties," where "everything seems to be the exact opposite of what we have in this country.... A Chinese begins to read a book from the end; and he does not read across the page, but up and down. The wealthy classes have a soup made of bird's nests" (1995:47). Stanley argues that these quotes constitute an unambiguous form of racism by making the Chinese exotic, "the other." He also presents a diagram that teaches students about the different races of the world. Subtly, he argues, this process of "othering" promoted white supremacy.

The irony of Stanley's interpretation is that the "othering" he denounces is typical of contemporary multicultural education. Multiculturalists routinely identify racial groupings, and urge teachers to recognize the cultural uniqueness of each. Compare the 110-year-old B.C. text to a recent American teacher's manual for multicultural education. Teachers are warned not to stereotype students, but are then informed that "Asian Americans come from cultures that often view children's behaviour as the result of a lack of will or supernatural causes" (Manning and Baruth, 1996:120; no supporting evidence is offered for this assertion). The same authors further instruct, again without evidence, that "in Asian fami-

---

3
    Recent debates about classic American texts offer a cautionary note. When seeking to validate claims of bias, some researchers find them either exaggerated or highly inaccurate. See Hoff Sommers, 1994:85; Ravitch, 1978:122; and Lerner, Nagai and Rothman, 1995.

lies, females do not receive the respect that males receive. Females are valued less than males" (*Ibid.*:114). The book also quizzes teachers on their multicultural sensitivity. Apparently, the correct answers to the question "Which of the following characterize Asian Americans?" are "soft, well-modulated voices," and "modest in dress, manner and behaviour" (Dotson, 1996:26). Similarly, a popular textbook in the sociology of education, written by socialist-feminist enthusiasts of multiculturalism, offers this: "European-American children tend to be intimidated by African Americans, and to feel threatened by the noise and movement *natural among African Americans*" (de Marrais and LeCompte, 1995:233; our emphasis).

If written one hundred years ago, these statements would be dismissed today as offensive racial stereotypes. Yet today's multiculturalists insist that they are true "differences." It is thus strange to condemn a 110-year-old text—from an era when Canadians had far less information and knowledge about different cultures—for engaging in a practice echoed by today's anti-racists. In current lingo, those B.C. texts were "acknowledging differences" between Canada and China, albeit in a way that reflected the information restrictions and idioms of the times. But moreover, even if these depictions were inaccurate, Stanley does not explain just how they promoted "White supremacy" or denigrated Chinese students, nor does he show them to be representative of nineteenth century texts.

Things have certainly changed. School boards in many districts are re-writing Canadian history; some have added courses on Black history and some offer instruction in many different languages. In addition, English as a second language (ESL), multicultural initiatives and other special programs in Ontario mean that schools with high concentrations of minorities receive more money than others. North York schools, for instance, receive over $2,000 per student more than rural schools.

Next, consider the underlying logic behind some of the claims of cultural racism. Advocates presume that it is unreasonable for a curricula to reflect the experience of the majority of the population. Canadian historians are accused of de-emphasizing the contributions of Asians and Blacks and for overemphasizing the role of European nations in shaping our history. But, as historians are pointing out, to do otherwise is to distort Canadian history. Until recently, less than 2 percent of the population had Black or Asian heritage. England, France, and the U.S. played by far the most pivotal roles in the formation of modern Canada as a political entity.

Few multiculturalists directly deny these past realities, but many offer a different rationale: Canadian history ought to be re-written to make it more relevant to the present. Minority students need positive role models with whom they can identify, so history is to be taught according to the principle of proportional representation (using current proportions). According to this view, educators should purposefully search out and select historical events and heroes by race. Here, multicultural critics seem to be blaming Canadian educators for not using race as the sole organizing principle for writing history. It is curious to accuse educators of racism for insufficiently racializing history, for not using history and literature for political goals and for being historically accurate.

In sum, Aboriginals were undeniably subjected to virulent forms of cultural racism in the past. Even though most residential schools have been closed for over thirty years, and insulting textbook depictions and other forms of cultural racism have been purged from the school system, this past has retained a menacing presence for Aboriginal youth. In contrast, there is far less evidence of institutional racism against other minorities, at least as we define the term. Claims of cultural racism have either lacked supporting evidence, have been based on questionable reasoning, or represent the re-labelling of non-racial problems, such as difficulties of adjustment for recent immigrants. This is not to deny that racism may exist in varying degrees in other institutional realms, such as the justice system or the labour market, nor that individual students experience incidents of personal bigotry in Canadian schools. Rather, we are noting the dearth of strong evidence of institutional racism in our schools, and we question the reasoning and logic that underlie some of those claims.

There is, nevertheless, little doubt that Canadian education is becoming increasingly *racialized*. When the issues of disparity and cultural incompatibility in schools are raised, they are increasingly framed in racial terms, despite the fact that other criteria, particular class and socio-economic status, are usually more crucial sources of these problems. Where do these racialized perceptions come from? Why are racial interpretations of school phenomena accepted so readily by politicians, educators, activists and academics? In the next section we present a few illustrations of racialization, and attempt to shed light on social factors that promote racialization in contemporary education. By necessity this is a speculative effort to develop a framework for thinking about current trends in educational politics.

The Racialized Context

Virtually all national-level indicators of school attainment show non-Aboriginal minority students exceeding the average. Yet, as we saw in the introduction, many advocates and multicultural experts are convinced that the opposite is true. The same data show that Black students exceed national averages on some indicators, and are not ranked near the bottom on any measure of attainment. The City of Toronto data cited above suggested that much of the disadvantage of Black students was related to their overrepresentation among low SES and single parent families, and that similar patterns of disadvantage were found for Portuguese students. Students whose parents had low socio-economic status or were single parents had lower achievements, regardless of student skin colour. Immigrants and students who did not speak English as their first language did not achieve less in Toronto schools. Females scored higher than males.

Yet, despite this assortment of empirical patterns, the study gained attention almost entirely for its conclusions regarding race. *The Toronto Star* (1995), Canada's largest daily newspaper, summed up the results with the title "The Colour of Learning." Activists used these findings to press for separate schools for Black students. Ontario's Royal Commission on Learning concluded from these data that there was there is a "crisis among black youth with respect to education and achievement" (*Ibid.*).

North York's Flemington School has a successful program geared to integrating immigrants. The school uses translators to write report cards in many languages and to improve parent-teacher communication, and it has a home reading program for ESL students and various community support programs (Moodley, 1995). All of these worthy initiatives are aimed at easing the difficulties of transition experienced by all recent immigrants, regardless of skin colour, who lack proficiency in English. Yet, these measures are housed within an "anti-racism" program, and are construed as racial matters. Similarly, programs that aim to combat alienation among Black dropouts focus entirely on racism as the source of alienation (e.g., Dei, 1996), ignoring studies which show that dropouts of any colour are alienated (e.g., Radwanski, 1987; Gilbert et al., 1993).

These illustrations show how many difficulties in Canadian schools are being increasingly interpreted as racial matters and not problems connected to non-racial categories, such as SES, single parent status, or recency of immigration. Complex situations and solutions are largely reduced to a question of race. Why?

To comprehend how contemporary education politics have become increasingly racialized, we need to examine how educational processes are shaped by the wider context of race relations, economic prospects and cultural identities. Here, a bedrock idea needs introduction: education is *embedded* in social relations linked to the wider economy, cultural struggles, and to some degree, race relations. A student's expenditure of effort in school, like any goal-seeking behaviour, is not merely a matter of individualistic competition. It is a social act infused with cultural norms and meanings (see Granovetter, 1985; Portes and Sensenbrenner, 1993). The social ties among students, parents and teachers shape the behaviours that constrain or enable good relations between public schools and various communities. Context is crucial.

For instance, racial and ethnic patterns in Canadian education reflect historical segregation and enclave activity. Much schooling is motivated by economic ends, so it is not surprising that ethnic patterns in education have reflected economic niches. For example, the overrepresentation of some Jewish and Chinese Canadians at higher levels of professional education reflects their collective solutions to past discrimination, real and perceived. Education was part of a collective strategy of using self-employment to ensure some market place autonomy. Conversely, the past educational underachievement among some European ethnic groups occurred in a context of plentiful blue-collar jobs that did not require educational credentials. As the stock of those jobs dwindled, the educational attainment of these groups rose (Guppy and Davies, forthcoming).

However, school achievement relies on good social relations characterized by trust and mutual obligation. Students bear a set of school-related resources and cultural meanings, and schools' practices are based on assumptions about these resources and meanings. One of our key ideas focuses on the quality of the match between a minority group's school-related meanings and these institutional expectations.

Coleman (1988) conceptualizes "social capital" as the set of collective expectations within a community that affect the goal-seeking behaviour of its members. In education, a community has social capital when there are durable and reciprocal norms of obligation among parents, community members, students and schools. These norms establish strong bonds of trust and cooperation, and breed mutual respect among students, educators and parents. Conversely, if a group has little trust in their local schools, students and educators will be less committed to their educational goals. If there is discord between schools and a particular minority group, racialization can occur.

Coleman's thesis prompts a key question: from where does collective distrust stem? Suggestive American and Canadian illustrations are offered by Lareau's (1993) and Dei's (1996) interviews with teachers, students and parents. Both researchers found relations to be much more strained between Black parents and White teachers than between same-race parents and teachers. Black parents were more likely to believe that White teachers were biased and insensitive, hence they were more likely to challenge teachers' assessments of their children. Dei (1996) points out that many Blacks distrust their schools, believing that teachers hold low expectations and perceive Black students and parents as "trouble-makers." This lack of trust harms the quality of parental involvement in terms of monitoring homework and supporting teachers. Both Dei and Lareau report that some teachers felt many of Black parents' challenges were erroneous and unhelpful since it undermined their authority and made it difficult for them to teach.

Dei and Lareau trace the source of these conflicts beyond the school to the broader setting of race relations. In Toronto, for instance, it is impossible to separate the lack of trust between Black community leaders and professional educators from the strained relations between Blacks, the justice system and the police. Relations in one institutional realm can spill over into another. Such conditions, Lareau argues, make it difficult for Black parents to comply with the teacher's standards of the helpful parent, because these parents distrust "White" institutions and perceive parent-teacher relations through the lens of racial injustice. While Dei's and Lareau's studies do not allow us to judge how representative such sentiments are among teachers, parents or students, the existence of such sentiments certainly affects race relations in schools. Mutual distrust can weaken the bonds between the school and these minority families. One does not have to take sides to acknowledge the harmful effects of a breakdown of trust.

But what are the contingencies of trust among minority groups? Certainly not all minorities have adversarial relations with the school system. John Ogbu (1987) argues that various minorities develop their own "folk understandings" of schools, society and their place within society. Most immigrants are said to share the dominant belief that society offers great opportunities provided one works hard and gets an education. Language barriers and other cultural adjustments are perceived as hurdles that can be surpassed with time and effort. Since immigrants move voluntarily to North America for a better life, they are able to compare their current situation and imagined future to their former lives, and most often this is a favourable comparison. Further, Ogbu claims that immigrants enter countries like Canada with a relatively well-developed sense of self and cultural assurance. To adopt standard ways of speaking English or to defer to White authority figures in schools is not threatening to their identity, in the sense of making them "less" Ghanian, Korean or Pakistani. Minorities who hold this folk understanding place their faith in schooling, even with little knowledge of the system, and this faith facilitates work habits conducive to school success. This description of pragmatic trust appears to apply to the educationally successful minorities in Canada.

Conversely, Ogbu argues that "non-voluntary minorities," such as Black descendants of slaves and North American Aboriginals, view society differently. Blacks and Aboriginals, he argues, have had their identities formed historically as subordinates in White-dominated societies, often having lost their original languages and religions. Their sense of self and group distinctiveness are in many respects acquired in opposition to Whites. Moreover, their collective memories of slavery and conquest lead them to perceive widespread discrimination and social barriers. Lacking a "homeland" for comparison, they are readier to interpret difficulties as evidence of institutionalized discrimination, and less prone to see their situation as mutable by hard work and education alone. Consequently, there is an undercurrent of distrust of public schools among these minorities. Instead of placing faith in public schools as an avenue for social advancement, they stress collective efforts such as self-segregation in economy, and sometimes, as we will see in the next section, separate education.

These speculations shed light on the tension between family and school underlined by Lareau and Dei, though Ogbu's categories need to be modified for the Canadian case. In this country, Aboriginals represent "involuntary minorities." Virtually all other racial minorities in modern Canada are "voluntary." Nevertheless, some of Ogbu's ideas are applicable. James (1993) and Dei (1996) suggest that in Canada, Black identity is constructed in light of the troubled status of Blacks in the Western world as a whole. They argue that today's Black youth construct their "Blackness" in response to dominant stereotypes, which are more intensely negative for them than for other non-Aboriginal minorities. Dei similarly reports that among Black youth in Ontario, a constant concern is whether they are "Black enough." Black dropouts, he argues, often resent their peers who act "too White." For these youth, speaking standard English, or being a diligent student is to "act White" like an "Uncle Tom" or a "wannabee." Some Black youth interpret the archetypal student role as part of "White culture," something that threatens their identity and group solidarity. Euphemisms such as "wannabee" serve to police individual effort and exercise social pressure. To the extent that a minority youth group's solidarity has its base in adversarial relations to the mainstream, there will be an acute cultural discord between that group and public schools.

Of course, among Black youth there is a wide variety of orientations to school; far from all think this way, and Ogbu has been criticized for exaggerating the degree of oppositional sentiment among minority youth. James (1993) depicts young Blacks as viewing Canadian society as having discriminatory elements, yet as offering opportunities as well. These students blend oppositional and aspirational folk understandings into a cautious optimism. But an oppositional stance can be a powerful presence in school, even if held by only a few students. Teenagers can be torn between parental expectations of school success and a youth subculture that denies that such success is possible or desirable. As an example, Solomon (1994) found that in a Toronto high school, West Indian youth congregated in a sports subculture because they considered academics and other extra-curriculars to be "White activities." Sports became a refuge for those with little interest in school work, and formed the basis for an all-Black clique that did not seek integration in the rest of the school.

In sum, the current racialized context in Canadian schools reflects the interplay of folk understandings, youth peer pressures and the broader context of race relations. As a consequence of our racialized context, activists are urging educators to re-build trust and legitimacy among minorities. As Canada's population becomes increasingly diverse, they argue, reforms that "recognize difference" are essential. We discuss two of these reforms, and examine the sociological milieu in which they have emerged. We argue that contemporary politics of race and education do not merely reflect responses to local problems, but are also enmeshed within deep ideological shifts among Western societies in thinking about citizenship, national cultures and state-citizen relations. These reforms, we argue, will likely promote further racialization.

Institutionalizing "Difference": Multiculturalism/Anti-Racism and School Choice

Canada has always been pluralistic, from its origin as three-nations-within-a-nation (Aboriginal, English and French), to the integration of mainly European immigrants, to the recent influx of immigrants from around the world. What is new is the official embrace of pluralism by politicians, bureaucrats and intellectuals in the guise of multiculturalism. Multiculturalism has become Canada's self-defining slogan, extolled by state officials and media as our major (and perhaps sole) collective virtue. To declare one's loyalty to "diversity" has become a latter-day piety.[4]

Within the circles of professional educators, multiculturalism is championed under the rubric of anti-racist education (see Moodley, 1995, for a critical review). Invoking the watchwords "difference," "diversity," and "inclusion," multicultural educators work to revise teaching styles, re-write history and literature and diversify the demographic composition of school staff with the hope of building a more inclusive school climate and fostering inter-group respect and harmony. An underlying assumption is that if minority youth hear about their own cultures in public schools they will develop the pride and enhanced self-images that will enrich their school experience.

But multicultural education is not merely a response to minority-group advocacy or local problems in schools. It has affinities with international institutional movements from which Canadian policy makers take their lead, and with shifts in an intellectual *zeitgeist* that extend far beyond Canada's borders. Canadian multiculturalists have borrowed from British, Australian and American efforts to deal with new immigration patterns and, in turn, Canadian activists earn exorbitant consulting fees for exporting Canadian multicultural programs to eager international customers.

Bureaucrats, educators and intellectuals are re-thinking ideas of nation building and citizenship. Historically, schools helped construct national polities by inculcating notions of rights, obligations and loyalty to the nation. Schools promoted an individualistic identification with the nation-state. For instance, fifty years ago Canadian schools would portray a virtuous person as God fearing, patriotic and hard working. Since the Second World War, universalism, individual rights and colour blindness have been the building blocks of a liberal, progressive stance on racial issues. Yet, multiculturalists have declared this old-style

---

4

The multiculturalism movement in English Canada draws strength from our weak national identity. Without a strong national myth or an essential ethnic character, the English Canadian political class, unlike the Germans or the French for instance, rarely proclaim a singular and renowned cultural tradition that is worthy of preservation. In sharp contrast, Quebec's political elites, with their potent ethnic nationalism and sovereignist aspirations, do not embrace the multiculturalist ethos because they perceive any undue prominence of other cultures as a threat to their survival as a French-speaking enclave.

patriotism and universalism as narrow, parochial and even dangerous. This is where multicultural education enters the story.

For its advocates, multiculturalism better embodies what modern nations are becoming and what they should strive to be. Multiculturalists encourage minorities to identify primarily with their ethnic, racial or linguistic group, and to let this identification mediate their relation to the nation-state. This new form of citizenship, for its advocates, is more effective than the older, individualist version. In this vision, institutions are increasingly centred on groups and the recognition of cultural difference, in whatever way "difference" is defined. Since the accommodation of racial differences is at the heart of multiculturalism, and since schools are major levers of change in society, race and education is a focal point of a re-thinking of what social institutions ought to be.

A typical text for multicultural teacher training proclaims the need "to create a more just society through major reforms to education" (Miller-Lachman and Taylor, 1995:6). Schools are to help construct a pluralist polity by cultivating each student's identification with a particular ethnic community, and by teaching the primacy of "diversity," "tolerance" and "equity," all understood increasingly as characteristics of groups rather than individuals. Gone is old-fashioned patriotism, replaced by ideals of anti-racism, environmentalism and global citizenship (Schuyler and Schuyler, 1989; McLeod, 1992). For many educators, diversity and equity are the lone common ideals that can forge social bonds among citizens in a fragmented polity. As universal public spheres shrink, we need "unity through diversity," a commitment to a new sense of universal justice that declares ethnic-based self-esteem, self-respect and community ties as primordial needs shared by all. As an institution, multicultural schools attempt to command authority and legitimacy by claiming to be *truly* responsive to these needs.

Multicultural educators justify their programs with appeals to national reconstruction and survival. Educators assert that greater appreciation and tolerance of racial diversity is needed for Canadians to thrive in a new era of global competition. They promise that economically, multicultural education will foster international trade links and bring Canada to the fore of new ways of doing business. Domestically, it is trumped as a well-spring of unity, sensitivity and harmony between ethnic groups.

"School choice," a second policy now receiving critical attention, is more controversial than multiculturalism because it directly confronts the liberal creed of social integration. Choice is premised on the idea that different types of students thrive in different settings, and that there is no single best model of public education. Rather, a truly effective and fair public system is said to maximize variety in educational content, goals and methods. Further, since parents are said to know their children far better than education officials, they should be able to choose to which school they will send their children.

Choice advocates come in a variety of stripes, but only recently have many minority groups in Canada demanded their own publicly funded schools. Representatives from Black, First Nations, Chinese, Hindu and Muslim groups are all demanding public school choice initiatives to complement their existing private schools. In Toronto, a "Black Focus" school has been established, and more have been proposed. Heritage language schools promote Chinese cultural traditions in British Columbia; Sikhs and Hindus in Ontario have joined the Multi-Faith Coalition for Equity in Education to lobby to attain separate public schools. For Aboriginals, band-controlled schooling through self-government initiatives is now common in most provinces. These schools are characterized by a special emphasis on Aboriginal cultures and heritages. Many universities, especially on the prairies, have established programs designed to support Aboriginal students in their educational quests.

School choice for racial minorities is premised on the idea that current arrangements fail to address these groups' special needs and wants. Racially homogeneous school communities would allow minorities to feel less different and feel more comfortable, advocates argue, and would provide the type of congenial and caring learning environment that many minority youth do not see in the current public system (Dei, 1996). These advocates envision an array of schools tailored to various religions, languages and cultures; otherwise their cultures will flounder and eventually dissolve into the majority. Public funding is needed because the financial cost of private schools forces most students to attend mainstream schools.

While many choice advocates support the all-inclusive multicultural model for public schools, they have some reservations. For them, official multicultural education is too diluted and superficial to be effective: by trying to accommodate all, multiculturalism accommodates no one. How can a Hindu child, for instance, really learn anything of substance about Hinduism and the history of India in a multicultural public school? As just one of the school's customers among many, the teaching of Hindu culture would amount to little more than tokenism. Instead, a genuine multiculturalism retains and cultivates "real" differences through a variety of schools rather than one school for all.

While school choice and multicultural education are not inherently incompatible, their visions of accommodating race in schools ultimately clash. Multiculturalists envision re-constructed universal institutions that promote inter-group mingling and a new global culture. School choice threatens the goal of exposing all youth to a diverse student body and curriculum, and raises the spectre of segregation. In contrast, choice advocates regard the all-inclusive school as a form of assimilation into an internationalist culture that is hardly neutral or faceless, and is even hostile to cultures with traditional religious dimensions. For choice advocates, authentic diversity and pluralism must be institutionalized through a wide variety of separate schools. Only choice makes everyone an equal partner in a truly pluralistic, multicultural and democratic society, they say.

Conclusion

In international comparison, Canadian schools enjoy a strong record on race relations. Non-Aboriginal minorities and immigrants tend to fare better in our schools than others. Yet, claims of institutional racism have escalated. This is undoubtedly because the politics of race and education are far more complex than in the past. Until recently, these politics largely centred on improving accessibility within an unchallenged liberal framework of equal opportunity and individual rights. The new politics of race, which entail creeds of pluralism and identity politics, are now transforming these struggles.

The new politics may benefit our country in some ways, but we need to recognize that these politics are fraught with tensions and contradictions. Racial diversity is often equated with cultural diversity, which in turn is presented as a national resource that will invigorate our culture and our international trade links. But race is also presented as a potential source of strife—the spectre of Toronto's Yonge Street riots looms here.

Both school choice and multicultural education are building momentum as programs that reflect the changing politics of race. What is the potential impact of these policies? Are these initiatives, now in their infancy, progressive steps that will benefit all Canadians or could they backfire?

Both deserve their share of scepticism for a variety of reasons. The ever-increasing promotion of racial identities in our schools may encourage a more racialized system. Separate schools, for instance, could fuel the very intolerance they aim to avoid. The multicultural acknowledgment of so-called group traits seems to repeat old stereotypes. State-sponsored multiculturalism has been sharply criticized for promoting a retrograde cultural retention instead of the similarities of Canadians. The continual preoccupation with race and ethnicity deflects attention from issues of socio-economic status and rural-urban differences, which are far more enduring sources of educational inequality. These movements may be inconsistent with the worthy goals of making social life in Canada colour blind, where each person is treated according to their individual merit, and where programs are directed to those Canadians who are truly most in need.

Similarly, is it really possible to celebrate and respect *all* diversity? Should public schools celebrate traditions that do not share the multicultural ethos of anti-sexism or gay rights? What if some traditions run counter to the teachings of others? Christian parents in Abbotsford, B.C., recently demanded that science classes in their public schools teach Creationism along with evolutionism. The effort was squashed by the Ministry of Education, but it highlights issues of incompatible curricular issues. Must an all-inclusive school system accommodate all perspectives, from Christian evangelism to Rasta power? How do such schools justify the exclusion of some perspectives? Where and how does a multiculturalist draw the line?

Canada's changing racial composition has certainly influenced our institutions, but activists, bureaucrats and educators in turn influence how race is perceived and institutionalized in schools. Schools must continue to respond to the needs of students as the student population changes, but accommodation is one thing, racialization another. As we have tried to show in this chapter, the pains and joys of Canadian schooling are more evenly distributed across racial lines than many interested parties are willing to admit. Any sound education policy that truly seeks to promote equity must look unflinchingly at these realities, and must design programs accordingly. It is unclear where to go from here. We are at a crossroads, and we need to make some wise choices.

REFERENCES

Alladin, M. Ibrahim. 1996. "Introduction." In M. Ibrahim Alladin, ed. *Racism in Canadian Schools*. Toronto: Harcourt Brace Canada.

Benavot, Aaron, Yun-Kyung Cha, David Kamens, John W. Meyer and Suk-Ying Wong. 1991. "Knowledge for the Masses: World Models and National Curricula, 1920-1986." *American Sociological Review* 56(1):85-100.

Bennett, deMarrais and Margaret D. LeCompte. 1995. *The Way Schools Work: A Sociological Analysis of Education*, 2nd edition. White Plains, NY: Longman.

Coleman, James S. 1988. "Social Capital in the Creation of Human Capital." *American Journal of Sociology* 94:S95-S121.

Dei, George. 1996. "Black/African-Canadian Students' Perspectives on School Racism." In M. Ibrahim Alladin, ed. *Racism in Canadian Schools*. Toronto: Harcourt Brace Canada.

Dotson, Jennifer. 1996. *Instructor's Manual with Tests for Manning and Baruth*. Needham Heights: Allyn and Bacon.

Gilbert, Sid, Lynn Barr, Warren Clark, Matthew Blue and Deborah Sunter. 1993. *Leaving School: Results from a National Survey Comparing School Leavers and High School Graduates 18 to 20 Years of Age*. Ottawa: Government of Canada.

Ghosh, Ratna. 1996. *Redefining Multicultural Education*. Toronto: Harcourt Brace Canada.

Goulbourne, Michelle "The Persistence of Separate Schools in Ontario, 1850-1965." Unpublished paper, Department of Sociology, McMaster University.

Granovetter, Mark. 1985. "Economic Action and Social Structure: The Problem of Embeddedness." *American Journal of Sociology* 91:481-510.

Guppy, Neil and Scott Davies (forthcoming). *Education in Canada: Recent Trends and Future Challenges*. Statistics Canada.

Hoff Sommers, Christina. 1994. *Who Stole Feminism? How Women Have Betrayed Women*. New York: Simon and Schuster.

Howard, Rhoda. 1996. "Ethnicity and Group Rights Claims." Paper presented to the annual meetings of the Canadian Sociology and Anthropology Association, St. Catharines, Ontario.

James, Carl E. 1993. "Getting There and Staying There: Blacks' Employment Experience." In Paul Anisef and Paul Axelrod, eds. *Transitions: Schooling and Employment in Canada*. Toronto: Thompson Educational.

_____ and K. Braithwaite. 1996. "The Education of African Canadians." In K. Braithwaite and C. James, eds. *Educating African Canadians*. Toronto: James Lorimer and Co.

Lareau, Annette. 1993. "Race, Social Class, and Family-School Relationships: The Impact of Race on Social Reproduction." Paper presented to the annual meetings of the American Sociological Association, Miami.

Lerner, Robert, Althea K. Nagai, and Stanley Rothman. 1995. *Molding the Good Citizen*. Westwood, CT: Praegar.

Manning, M. Lee and Leroy G. Baruth. 1996. *Multicultural Education of Children and Adolescents,* 2nd Edition. Needham Heights, MA: Allyn and Bacon.

McLeod, Keith. 1992. "Multiculturalism and Multicultural Education in Canada: Human Rights and Human Rights Education." In Kogila A. Moodley, ed. *Beyond Multicultural Education: International Perspectives.* Calgary: Detselig.

Meyer, John. 1980. "The World Polity and the Authority of the Nation-State." In Albert Bergesen, ed. *Studies of the Modern World-System,* pp.109-38. New York: Academic Press.

Miller-Lachman, Lyn and Lorraine S. Taylor. 1995. *Schools for All: Educating Children in a Diverse Society.* Albany: Delmar Publishers.

Moodley, Kogila A. 1995. "Multicultural Education in Canada: Historical Development and Current Status." In J.A. Banks, ed. *Handbook of Research on Multicultural Education,* pp.801-20. New York: Macmillan Publishing.

Ogbu, John. 1987. "Variability in Minority School Performance: A Problem in Search of an Explanation." *Anthropology and Education Quarterly* 18:312-335.

Portes, Alejandro and Julia Sensenbrenner. 1993. "Embeddedness and Immigration: Notes on the Social Determinants of Economic Action." *American Journal of Sociology* 98(6):1320-50.

Radwanski, George. 1987. *Ontario Study of the Relevance of Education, and the Issue of Dropouts.* Ontario: Ministry of Education.

Ravitch, Diane. 1978. *The Revisionists Revised: A Critique of the Radical Attack on the Schools.* New York: Basic Books.

Roy, Patricia. 1980. "British Columbia's Fear of Asians, 1900-1950." *Historie Sociale/Social History* 12(25):161-72.

Schneider, Barbara and James Coleman, eds. 1993. *Parents, Their Children, and Schools.* Boulder, Colorado: Westview Press.

Schuyler, Patricia and George W. Schuyler. 1989. "Thoughts on Education for Global Citizenship." In Keith McLeod, ed. *Canada and Citizenship Education.* Toronto: Canadian Education Association.

Solomon, R. Patrick. 1994. "Academic Disengagement: Black Youth and the Sports Subculture from a Cross-National Perspective." In Lorna Erwin and David MacLennan, eds. *Sociology of Education in Canada: Critical Perspectives on Theory, Research and Practice.* Toronto: Copp Clarke Pitman.

Stanley, Tim. 1995. "White Supremacy and the Rhetoric of Educational Indoctrination: A Canadian Case Study." In J. Barman, N. Sutherland, and J.D. Wilson, eds. *Children, Teachers and Schools in the History of British Columbia,* pp.39-56. Calgary: Detselig.

The Toronto Star, February 11, 1995. "The Colour of Learning."

Varpalotai, Aniko. 1995. "Affirmative Action for a Just and Equitable Society." In Ratna Ghosh and Douglas Ray, eds. *Social Change and Education in Canada,* 3rd edition. Toronto: Harcourt Brace Canada.

Yau, Maria, Maisy Cheng and Suzanne Ziegler. 1993. *The 1991 Every Secondary Student Survey, Part II: Program Location and Student Achievement,* Research Services, Toronto Board of Education.

7

"Up to no good": Black on the Streets and Encountering Police

Carl E. James

They [police] have their stereotypes: If you are Black and male, the cops think that you are up to no good, and if you are Black and female, it's not so bad but we are still harassed.

One of the most controversial aspects of police discretion has been the right of police to stop, question and search citizens in public places. It is alleged that this aspect of discretion often constitutes harassment, which has contributed to strained relationships between police and particular communities. Newspaper reports in many Canadian cities, such as Toronto, Halifax, Ottawa and Montreal, have given accounts of numerous incidents involving racial minority youth and police. In Toronto, for instance, one reported incident was about two brothers who were harassed and assaulted by the police while they waited at a bus stop on their way from a church meeting one Friday evening. Another was an alleged police assault on a young man who was eventually found dead from drowning in the Ottawa River. And tensions between the youth and police in Cole Harbour, near Halifax, continue to undermine the building of trusting relationships. These incidents, along with police shootings of Black people,[1] have contributed to Black communities' concern about police-community relations and the criminalization of youth. It is a concern that must be addressed if we are to change Toronto Caribbean youth's view of "the police as the 'ultimate oppressor'" (Henry, 1994:202).

In this chapter, I explore the nature of Black people's encounters with police, and focus in particular on Black youth. I examine how the street is understood and experienced by the youth and police, since it is one of the major arenas in

---

[1]
Between 1978 and 1997 at least 13 Black people in Ontario have been shot and killed by police. Add to this another six who were injured, in some cases, paralysed, from police bullets. Of the 19 Black people injured and/or killed by police, 12 were young Black males (8 were killed) and one female. See the *Report* by the Commission on Systemic Racism in the Ontario Criminal Justice System, 1995: 378 which reports on shooting from 1978-1995).

which many of the encounters are played out initially. I argue that police and security personnel[2] discretion (i.e., stop, question and so on) in their encounters with Black youth on the streets and in shopping malls is an articulation of patriarchy and systemic racism, which is culturally embedded in a level of consciousness that constructs some members of Canadian society as more prone to crime and hence must be closely observed.

Racism, Policing and Black Youth

Colonial discourse provides a framework within which we might understand the experiences of Black youth and their encounters with police. According to Weis and Fine (1996:8), within this discourse Whites engage in a process of "othering" where "'White' becomes the norm against which all other communities of colour are judged (usually to be deviant)." Colonialism and neo-colonialism have contributed to "the marginalization of people of colour and the resulting normality of whiteness." Hence, the dominant "White" are able to engage in the process of establishing "boundedness."[3]

> Thus much of white identity formation, stemming from colonial times to the present, involves drawing boundaries, engaging in boundedness, configuring rings around the substantively empty category "white," while at the same time decisively constructing "others" (Weis and Fine, 1996:8).

Part of the process of social construction and marginalization is reflected, as Alan James (1981) demonstrated, in word usage. In his exploration of "the pejorative associations" of the English word *black* and its relationship to the social construction of Black people, James (1981:19) points out that "the offensive connotations of the word 'black' in English impose on the users of the language, black-skinned and white-skinned, an interpretation of reality that is hard to break." He goes on to say that the associations of the word *black* with, among others, "dirt and sin, evil and taboo" are so pervasive that people are tempted "to regard them as 'natural,' part of the commonsense knowledge of the world and our own humanity." With reference to the influence of Western Christendom, James demonstrates how Black people, as the "frightening and fascinating children of Cham," continue to be socially constructed by the "folk-racism" of medieval society. While the colour white is seen to represent "the unattainable ideal, virginal purity, bodily incorruption, social order and peace," on the other hand the colour black is seen to represent "the violent and disturbing urges of the human body and excretion ... [and] the repressed, dark elements of the mind, both fearful and fascinating" (James, 1981:29).

---

[2]
 We recognize the difference in the functions of police and security personnel. However, for the purposes of this discussion, we explore how both have used discretion in the process of "othering" and criminalization of Black youth.

[3]
 The concept, referenced by Weis and Fine (1996), is borrowed from Trim-Min-Ha who discusses the concept in *Women, Native, Other* (1989).

In Judith Butler's essay "Endangered/Endangering: Schematic Racism and White Paranoia," in which she discusses the case of Rodney King, the African American man who was beaten by the Los Angeles police, she points out that even in its indefensible state, the Black male body is seen as a physical threat (1993:16). She states that "this is not a simple seeing, an act of direct perception, but the racial production of the visible, the working of racial constraints on what it means to 'see.'" Further, Butler writes:

> In Fanon's citation of the racist interpellation, the black body is circumscribed as dangerous, prior to any gesture, and raising of the hand, and the infantalized white reader is positioned in the scene as one who is helpless in relation to that black body; as one definitionally in need of protection by his/her mother or, perhaps, the police. The fear is that some physical distance will be crossed, and the virgin sanctity of whiteness will be endangered by the proximity. The police are thus structurally placed to protect whiteness against violence, where violence is the imminent action of that black male body. And because within this imaginary schema, the police protect whiteness, their own violence cannot be read as violence; because the black male body ... is the site and source of danger, a threat, the police effort to subdue this body, even if in advance, is justified regardless of the circumstances (1993:18).

These constructions of Black people as "other," as "physical threats" and as "violent" help to justify the ways in which they are managed, contained and policed by Western law enforcement and security personnel. In their research comparing African Americans' and White Americans' relations with police, Browning and colleagues (1994) conclude that police were more likely to hassle minorities without cause. And in large urban settings where racial minorities constitute a higher percentage of the population, they are more likely to be targeted by police, and once targeted, they are likely to receive harsh treatment (Dannefer and Schutt, 1982; see also Lieber, 1994; Anderson, 1990; Staples, 1975). In Britain, Norris et al. (1992) found that Black people, particularly young Black males, were more than twice as likely to be stopped by the police (see also Landau and Nathan, 1983). As in Britain and the United States, Canadian studies show that racial minorities, and Black youth in particular, have experienced differential treatment in their contacts with police (Head, 1975; James, 1990; Henry, 1994; Neugebauer-Visano, 1996; The Commission on Systemic Racism, 1995). In the study in which she compared Black and White male youth experiences with the police in Toronto, Neugebauer-Visano (1996) found that Black youth were treated with "contempt" by police. While young White males were stopped occasionally, young Black males were stopped as a matter of routine; and their experiences with police often involved harassment, mistaken identity and arbitrary arrest resulting in harsher penalties at all stages of the criminal justice system. Neugebauer-Visano argues that a "folk history" of frightening experiences with the police have become part of a collective consciousness shared by Blacks even in the absence of direct personal experience with police.

The nature of policing in Canadian, as in other stratified societies, "inevitably leads to policing the poor and minorities rather those in social classes capable of creating problems if they are heavily policed" (Chambliss, 1995:256). For young, Black, working-class males whose lives are tormented by overpolicing, current police and security personnel practices help to elicit from them hostile responses (Chambliss, 1995; Henry, 1994) as they resist the "confinement and definition" that are imposed upon them by police. As Walcott (1995:49) argues, "by resisting imprisonment within the boundaries and borders, black cultures refuse to accept what Frantz Fanon called 'amputation.'"

As part of this "amputation" or "othering," the images of Black people as working class and immigrants[4] persist even though Blacks have resided in Ontario since 1628, and many who are immigrants today entered Canada with professional qualifications and ambitions to work and many hold responsible positions in society (Plaza, 1996; Henry, 1994). So, even though police are likely to have had contacts with many middle-class professional Black people, the entrenched historical construction of Blacks as "criminals" remains (James, 1997; Henry, 1994, Gilroy, 1987) and is articulated in the complex constructions of police discretion. And as Franklin (1996:142), writing about the situation of African-Americans, argued, in the 1990s "many whites are having status anxieties in a global context of rapid technological and social change. Fear of unemployment and downward mobility contributes to white scapegoating" of racial minorities including Blacks and new immigrants. This situation does not leave the Black middle-class unscathed. In fact, as Franklin also argued, "regardless of their occupational success, the black middle class does not escape from the various forms of race exclusion and insults" (p.139).

This is why, in *The Toronto Star* (1985) "Minority Report," Canadian Black community members were reported to have expressed the belief that the police operate on stereotypical images of Black people, particularly males, thinking of them as making money primarily through hustling, pushing drugs or pimping for prostitutes. The study participants claimed that regardless of social class status and education, Black people had to deal with police images and stereotypes of them as "criminals, layabouts and disruptive elements." In the words of one participant, "You're always under suspicion" (Ward, 1985:6). This finding is corroborated by Henry (1994), Ginzberg (1985) and Head (1975), whose studies have reported on the differential ways in which Black people are represented in the media and their negative experiences with police in Toronto.

From her study on Caribbean people in Toronto, Henry (1994:224) concludes that police-Black community relations are "fraught with tensions." She explains that "the increased policing of the Black community, the stop-and-search procedures, and other forms of harassment have become so severe that tensions have been exacerbated," and these in turn have contributed to the criminalization of

---

4

   This perception of Black people as immigrants re-enforces "their inside/outside position" in Canadian society (Walcott, 1995:52).

young, Black, working-class males. The same conclusion was reached by the Commission on Systemic Racism in the Ontario Criminal Justice System. It reported that police discriminatory practices, particularly against Black men, were evident in the police exercise of discretion to stop and question citizens. Specifically, "about 43% of black male residents, but only 25% of white and 19% of Chinese males report being stopped by the police in the previous two years. Significantly more black men (29%) than white (12%) or Chinese (7%) report two or more police stops in the previous two years" (1995:ix). In accounting for the particular encounters and negative experiences that racial minorities have with the police in Canadian society, researchers, such as Henry and colleagues (1995), Vincent (1994), Henry (1994), Forcese (1992), Desroches (1992) and Andrews (1992), point to "police culture" as the basis for their attitudes and behaviours. In his audit of the Metropolitan Toronto Police force, Andrews, writes that "the culture of police forces in general tends to produce a 'we and they' philosophy. Part of this is probably necessary, related to the need to maintain a detached view of the world being policed; part is brought about over time by virtue of the high level of contact with people who break the law; part is undoubtedly due to the image of policing as portrayed on television and other the media" (1992:17). Similarly, Desroches argues that the negative stereotypical images that police hold, particularly of ethnic minorities, helps them to make the group's behaviour "more understandable and predictable, thus reducing the unexpected," which in turn predisposes enforcement agents to enter encounters with members of "ethnic minority groups with a negative and closed-minded attitude" (1992:53).

These cultural attitudes, views and behaviours of police are related to their backgrounds, and the patriarchical and gendered-nature of law enforcement and the justice system (Brophy and Smart, 1985; Harris, 1993; St. Lewis, 1995). According to Forcese, "most police in service have been recruited from working-class and lower middle-class backgrounds, and there is little reason to expect them to have attitudes other than those associated with such class backgrounds. These attitudes include distrust of immigrants and minorities, and outright racism" (1992:76). Socialized within a male, Anglo-Celtic, para-military culture, police are expected to control and maintain order in society, a society that is stratified by, among others, race, class, and gender.[5] And as Henry et al. point out, "the 'street' is exalted as a *raison d'être* of policing, and the 'street' experience is asserted to be the foundation of police knowledge" (1995:120). Perceiving themselves as "pseudo-police," security personnel, many of whom have similar backgrounds as police (and in some cases are ex-police officers), tend to

---

[5]
    Black police officers and security personnel are socialized within this dominant culture and therefore are as likely to act in similar ways as their white counterparts (see Henry et al., 1995; Henry, 1994; Forcese, 1992; Desroches,1992).

have similar understandings of, and approaches to, the enforcement of law, regulations and policies.

The Streets, Police and Youth[6]

The streets serve many purposes. For the car owner or drivers, the street may be the "public" asphalted path used to drive from one place to another and/or a place to park one's vehicle. For pedestrians, particularly those with no alternatives, the street, or more specifically the sidewalk, is much more. It is a public path to move about, get from one place to another, and a social space; probably the most available, accessible and relatively non-restrictive social space in which to meet, "hang out," and converse. For some "street users," particularly young, working-class apartment dwellers, because of their limited access and opportunities to alternative leisure and recreational spaces, the sidewalk, the street, the street corner and the mall become an integral part of daily living and a part of cultural life. These are social and recreational spaces that are free from the adult-controlled rigid organizations that are often culturally indifferent and insensitive to youth's needs and interests, and into which they have little input.

In patriarchal societies such as Canada, the streets as public spaces are typically the domain of males, where many have grown up participating in recreational and sport activities. For poor and working-class young males generally, and apartment dwellers in particular, the streets are for many the only free and available spaces in which they have been able to, in Carrington's (1983) word "colonize, " and which affords them the opportunities for recreational and social activities on their terms.

Shopping malls can be seen as "roofed streets" and "street corners," where "outside" has been turned into "inside";[7] and where public spaces have been turned into private spaces. And given weather conditions, especially in the winter, these covered spaces offer much-needed shelter from the cold and rain. It is in these busy shopping malls that we are likely to find video arcades, cinemas and fast food restaurants, which, for the most part, constitute entertainment for many youth. It is inevitable, therefore, to find youth congregating in the malls. But insofar as malls are indeed private spaces, business owners and mall authorities, through their "legal right" and private security agents, are able to enforce formal regulations on behaviour, dress, congregation and attitudes of the "street users" who might be outside police jurisdiction. In other words, these security personnel have the authority to enforce the very things that the police have been enforcing on the "public" streets. Here the "enforcement of the law" becomes problematic when one considers that the "right to evict from private property"

6
  My colleague Tony Xerri particularly helpful in assisting me with the development of this section.
7
  These descriptors were offered by Tony Xerri.

has now come to include what had been the street prior to "the roofing"—the only way to get from one shop to another, or attend the cinema, or other places of business and entertainment, and at the same time window-shop, meet and talk with friends and engage in what the youth might have regarded as honest and legal activities.

This interpretation of the street, the street corner and mall as a meaningful part of life for a sector of the community contrasts significantly with the "accepted" view that has been traditionally held. This view, perpetuated and maintained by those more privileged, is rooted in the assumption that leisure and recreational spaces and activities are accessible to all; therefore there is no need for people to be on the streets. In other words, it is believed that there are enough community and recreational centres, parks, clubs and other inexpensive resources that cater to the needs and interests of those who currently use the street. Hence, people who use the street in ways that are contrary to what is "acceptable" are seen as unlawful, "up-to-no-good," suspicious characters that need to be controlled and contained. And, often it is not what the youth are doing but their perceived lack of activity (Brodgen, Jefferson and Walklate, 1988), or their engagement in perceived "inappropriate" activities that are at issue. As Brodgen, Jefferson and Walklate (1988) write:

> Just walking round the streets "doing nothing," or "simply hanging around," felt inno-
> cent enough to the youths themselves. But, to a police force imbued with the virtues of
> useful toil, and its corollary—"the devil finds work for idle hands"—such unstructured,
> unsupervised and essentially "disorganized" inactivity is always vaguely suspect, and
> potentially threatening. "Doing nothing" is all too close, from a police viewpoint, to
> "loitering with intent"—especially if you belong to a group, male youth, with a "known"
> propensity for crime....

Informed by this view, and given the nature of policing and the laws concerning property[8] and normative behaviour with which they are charged to enforce, the police are likely to target particular groups of people, in this case Black youth, for special attention, believing that in taking pre-emptive or deterrent action, they are preventing crimes from happening and/or escalating (Brodgen et al., 1988). These pre-emptive actions by police are often regarded as proactive policing; and as Hagan (1994) points out, this policing of youth occurs in "offensible space," where police believe that a disproportionate amount of crime occurs. Smith (1986) suggests that the result of such scrutinization results in a process of "ecological contamination" in which all residents of designated areas are stereotyped as potential suspects. But as Brodgen et al. (1988) argue, this over-attention that youth receive from police may well create the very culture that the police are supposedly trying to stop from developing. Further, the impo-

---

[8]
In her article " Whiteness as Property," Harris (1993:1731) makes the point that "when the law recognizes, either implicitly or explicitly, the settled expectations of whites built on privileges and benefits produced by white supremacy, it acknowledges and re-enforces a property interest in whiteness that reproduces Black subordination."

sition of a disreputable label contributes to the stigmatization of an individual (Goffman, 1961; 1963), and the self-fulfilling prophesy wherein individuals internalize the label and react to the police accordingly.

For racial minority youth, social ideologies and cultural and generational differences influence police perceptions, attitudes and actions towards them. In other words, racism and stereotyping operate to "form at one and the same time both instigation for the initial contact by the police and the treatment received by the youth upon contact" (Brodgen, Jefferson and Walklate, 1988). It is through these contacts that the criminalization of Blacks, especially working-class youth, is effected, as police, in the case of Toronto, carry out their "war on drugs" (Henry, 1994). But while working-class communities might be the target, middle-class youth do not escape similar practices.

In my work on Black youth experiences with racism in Toronto, one research participant reported that he was stopped by police while walking in his middle-class neighbourhood, because the police believed that he did not live there. The participant commented that the police suspected him of committing a crime while not holding the same suspicion of his white friends with whom he was walking. These experiences with police were found to be fairly common; so too were the explanations that youth received from the police as reasons for being stopped. These reasons included claims that the youth "looked like" someone that the police were seeking (James, 1990:22). In their study of Black high school dropouts in Toronto, Dei et al. (1995:51-52) quote one young woman as saying, "When you're a Black male ... you don't have to do anything.... You could be a good student, you could be a good father or whatever, [but] when you're out on the street, you're seen as a criminal ... a drug dealer." In naming this social construction of Blacks as a "problem," one high school student commented that "there is no positive image of Black people," and as a result police "assume all Black people are the same" (Frater, 1991:68).

In an economically and racially stratified society where stereotyping, classism, sexism, racism and discrimination inform institutional policies and practices, it is quite easy to attribute negative police-youth encounters to those questioned, arrested and otherwise singled out by the law enforcement officers. And while the officers' practices might be attributed to their "just doing their jobs," their practices do not always justify or legitimate their actions. For as Forcese points out:

> The police officer is a very powerful person. He [sic] has the delegated right to arrest persons, even to use force against persons. An officer's interventions are usually discretionary, in that he or she must decide whether the conduct warrants police action ... [and] generally persons subject to police interventions are very vulnerable. The citizen carries the burden of reacting to police, who carry the full weight of social authority, and who have the benefit of a high degree of public and court confidence (1992:49).

So, while there is a tendency to believe that the person that has been stopped by the police must have done something wrong in the first place (cited in Amour,

1984:34), we must be conscious that policing can and sometimes does initiate a "self-fulfilling prophecy" (Brodgen, Jefferson and Walklate, 1988:112). That is, once perceived to be potential law breakers and therefore targeted, once stopped by police, the youth's actions in their vulnerable state, might then fit the stereotype as they react to police attitudes and behaviours towards them.

In proceeding, we present the narratives of Black youth as they report on their experiences with, and perceptions of, police. More precisely, we focus on what the youth had to say about their encounters with police on the streets, the nature of these encounters, and their views of the perceptions that police have of Blacks generally. The data was collected through focus groups and individual interviews in six Ontario cities (Toronto, Ottawa, London, Windsor, Hamilton and Amhurstburgh). About seventy racial minority youth participated in the interviews that were conducted in community centres, malls and on "the streets." Here we focus on the contributions of the approximately fifty Black youth (60 percent males and 40 percent females) who participated in the discussions. They represent a diversity of backgrounds in terms of social class and birthplaces. While the majority were born in Canada, their parents are largely from the Caribbean (for example, Jamaica, Trinidad, Guyana and others), and Africa (for example, Somalia). The discussion which follows attempts to show how the youth's encounters with police contribute to a criminalization process (Henry, 1994) and cultural struggles on the part of both the youth and police.

Black Youth Experiences with, and Perceptions of, Police

"They look at colour first"

Many of the youth who participated in this study stated that being stopped and questioned by the police was a common occurrence for them. There was a consistent belief that colour of skin was a primary determinant in attracting police attention and suspicion. One youth expressed this sentiment poignantly when he said, "You can't win. As long as you are Black you are a target." Another youth argued that Black youth were stopped more often because of the negative stereotypes that were used by the police: "I think they think that once there is a group of Black youth, they think that there is going to be some sort of violence, some fight or something like that."

While most youth argued that the clothes they wore increased their chances of being stopped by the police, some were adamant that it was colour or race and not merely clothes that was the prime determinant of police action towards them. On this point, and with reference to his own experiences with police, one youth commented that it was "not the clothes we wore. Standing waiting for a bus around nine in the evening, two police came up and asked us what we were doing; where we were going; and which bus we were taking. I wasn't wearing any hat, hood or anything." There seems to be consensus among the youth that they were not judged by the clothes they wore but by the colour of their skin. The following comments further make this point:

> They drive by. They don't glimpse your clothes, they glimpse your colour. That's the first thing they look at. If they judge the clothes so much why don't they go and stop those white boys that are wearing those same things like us?

> I think that if you are black and wearing a suit, they would think that you did something illegal to get the suit. They don't think that Black people have money.

> If you're a Black youth with a white person, the white person is not approached usually. White youth can dress the same as Black youth and not be harassed; other than to be told by police that they should not be hanging out with Black youth.

> Clothes is nothing. It's your colour, your colour, and it's your colour ....

"It also depends on what you are wearing and your hairstyle"

Suggesting that clothes, jewellery and hairstyles were used by police to reinforce their stereotypical images of Black youth, many of those interviewed alleged that it was on this basis that they, as well as their relatives and/or friends, were stopped and harassed by the police. They felt that hairstyles, particularly "locksy hairstyle," dress and jewellery were used by the police as indicators of the fact that they were suspicious persons in suspicious activities. In other words, they were perceived as "candidates for crime." The following comments are illustrative:

> If you dress in a suit everyday, with a nice haircut, they won't harass you.

> ... with Black youth, you see them wearing baggy clothes, lots of rings and necklaces, they automatically think that they are drug dealers.

> There is the stereotype of Blacks—baggy pants, flashy jewellery, baseball caps, flashy colours and so on. All Black people dress like this are [seen] as pimps or drug dealers. White people dress like this too, [but are] not seen as pimps etc.

> It's all how you present yourself. If you look like a rude girl, lots of gold chains etc., you'll get harassed. But if you are in your church clothes—pleated skirts—they won't trouble you.

> The chances of me catching a policeman's eyes increases with how I dress, and what I am wearing. If I am wearing a cap etc. has a lot to do with how I am treated.

> I have been stopped on the street many times. I guess it's just the way I look—my hairstyle, the kind of people I hang out with. I go to a lot of parties, for example, and we are always being stopped for one thing or another. I guess my hairstyle attracts attention—the different colours.

> A bald head is a message. If you are white and you have a bald head, you are probably seen as a skin head. If you are Black and you have a bald, you will probably be [seen as] a gang member.

> If you cut your hair low, cop ask you why you cut your hair like that. Are you trying to be like Ice Cube? Or say: "Nice hair cut, who are you trying to imitate, Michael J.?" They will always find something to say to you—Tie, suit, hair, no hair, big Afro, whatever.

"Not just colour but also your socio-economic level"

Some of the youth who participated in the study felt that other factors such as socio-economic status also contributed to the way they were perceived by the police. They believed that police typically held the perception that Black people were poor and therefore were unable to buy and wear expensive clothing. The youth reasoned that all these factors go together to influence police perceptions of, and their actions towards Black people. One youth articulated this sentiment in the following way:

> I think that a lot of the times police look at someone and just because they are of another race or colour, and they are wearing expensive clothes, they are wondering "How did they get these clothes?" Or if you are not wearing clothes that are expensive, they think that they must be up to trouble. A lot of times, it's not even your colour but your socioeconomic level. If you are poor looking, they are going to think that you are up to no good.

"We fit the description"

Many of the youth claimed that the police were indiscriminate in stopping them, either claiming that "it is a routine check," or because they "matched the description of a crime suspect." The youth saw this as racism because in these cases police were operating on the notion that "all Blacks look alike." As one participant sarcastically remarked, "It is funny how White officers think that every Black male looks the same." Noting that police perceptions were influenced by media images of Blacks, one youth argued that when the media described, for example, a robbery suspect as "Black male, six foot something, hundred and something pounds," often police took this to mean that every Black male fitting this description is a possible suspect without giving consideration to further descriptors. The youth claimed that this is not the case for White youth. In their case, further descriptions were taken into consideration.

Reflecting on their experiences of the treatment that they received from police, because police perceived Blacks to be "bad people" who were likely "to steal and kill people," some of the youth said:

> There was a robbery in the area. The cop pulled me over and all of a sudden a whole swarm of cops came. It was eight cops. I was with three guys. The cops said that we fit the description of the robbers who were five in number but we fit the description of three. They surrounded us and asked us to lie on the ground and they had their guns out....

> Once we were stopped by police because they said that we fit the description of robbery suspects. The description was that the robbers were Black. The cops asked us to open our bags and they took everything out. There were also people with suitcases and they searched them too.

"Black, immigrant, and ..."

The youth believed that all Black people are perceived as "immigrants" by most Canadians and police in particular. But while this construction of Black people was often generalized to the entire population, there were some constructions (or stereotypes) that were held of particular Black immigrant groups that affected how they were perceived and treated by the police. Jamaicans and Somalis were two of the groups that were named. Jamaicans were perceived as "drug dealers and gangsters." On this basis, the participants claimed that police often made the association between criminal activities and national origin and/or immigrant status. The youth suggested that "even if you are not Jamaican, if you're Black, [you are] considered Jamaican"; and it is on this basis that the police proceeded to deal with them.

Most of the youth who participated in the study and were familiar with So-malis agreed that police perceptions of Somalis, while different, were not any better than those held of Jamaicans. In fact, as one Somali participant stated, while "as Somalis we don't have that much criminals—we don't do drugs and all that, we stick to religion—it does not matter. We get the image—all the stereo-types—like the last set of Black people. We inherit the perceptions or the views that the police have of the last group of [Black immigrant] people." Other Somali youth who participated in the study said that they were generally perceived as refugees who were "violent, crazy, bad tempered, less educated, terrorists with guns"; and who were "living off the taxes" of Canadians. They felt that they had "double pain" in addition to being Black—i.e., "the pain of being Somali and being immigrant." For these reasons, there was a tendency among some Somali youth to think that police treated them "worse" than other Blacks.

> No matter what the situation that you're in, what your dress is like … they will find a negative way of thinking about you, because you're Black, and secondly because you're Somali, and thirdly because you're an immigrant and you speak a different language.

> I was stopped by the police… for nothing…. He asked me when I came to Canada, how long I had been here, am I on welfare assistance? Questions I was not expecting from a police officer. Then I told him that "that doesn't concern you," and he just said have a nice day and left.

"White people window-shop, Black people loiter"

Based on the "stereotypes" that police and security personnel have of Black people, and youth in particular, the youth believed that unlike their White peers, police operated with the assumption that any "standing around" of one person, or a number of Black youth, meant that "something is going down." For this reason, their presence on the street or in a mall was always suspect, particularly when they were believed to be "doing nothing." As one youth explained:

> When I was in grade 9… everybody used to go downtown after school, and it used to be a bunch of Black girls…. We weren't allowed to "linger" in one area. If we were in the food court, you had to eat your food and "done." You couldn't stay around for nothing. You couldn't stay in front of the mall. You know how you are waiting for a friend at the side and talking; you couldn't do that. You stay there for five minutes and all of a sudden a security guard comes up and tells you: "What are you doing here? You are loitering. Get outside." And then if there are too many of you, all of a sudden you see cruisers circling J_____ Square. Next you know, there's police in the mall.

"If you are Black and female, it's not so bad. But still we are harassed"

It was noted that while females were also viewed with the same suspicion as males, they were harassed less often and, in cases where they were stopped, they were dealt with differently than the males. In the words of one participant, "Like if a bunch of girls is standing there, [the police] won't search the girls but, if a group of guys is standing next to them, they would go directly to the guys." The participants reasoned that this was so because many of the stereotypes that police had of Black people tend to be related to Black males as opposed to Black females. They further reasoned that fear of being accused of "sexual harassment" probably deterred police, particularly in cases which involved searching females. But as one young woman claimed, "nowadays ... sometimes [girls] are treated the same way [as guys] because you could get a woman and a male cop working together so the woman cop would do the searching." So today there is no escape for Black females from receiving somewhat similar treatment to Black males.

Location was believed to play a role in the females' chances of being stopped, searched and harassed. As one participant remarked, "I think that girls get harassed now by the police but I think in different settings. I think in schools and in malls, they get harassed just as much as the guys. This is because mall security guards think that the girls have the money and the boys don't." Another participant said, "The security guards think that the girls are okay because they go to school." According to the youth, stereotyping underlies the perceptions that were held of Black males and females and thus the treatment they were likely to receive from police.

Discussion

Criminalizing the young Black male or protecting him from himself?

Within racist colonial discourse, as Gilroy (1987) and Thornton (forthcoming) among others have argued, the streets and indeed "private roofed streets" (i.e., malls) are racialized spaces. They are White defined locations, which are to be used in culturally prescribed manners. Insofar as Blacks, and young Black males in particular, violate the cultural norms of the streets and malls by their presence and actions, either alone or in groups, they will be targets. They will be targets of police officers and mall security personnel who operate within the dominant construction of Black young males as "up to no good," security risks and potential law breakers (see also Dei et al., 1995; Commission on Systemic Racism in the Criminal Justice System, 1995; Henry, 1994; Four-Level Government, 1992; James, 1990; Head, 1975). As the youth have so eloquently argued, it is not a matter of clothes, jewellery or hairstyle, but a matter of race and colour. And as they further argued, race, gender, social class and "perception of being immigrants" are intricately linked and together form the basis of the assumptions and stereotypes by which the police and security personnel exercise discretion.

Why were Black males more likely to be stopped by the police? Franklin (1996:138), with reference to Black youth in the United States, offered the following reason: "Whites fear young Black males." In fact, historically, Black young men have been represented in Canadian society as potential criminals that should be feared (James, 1997). This racist representation[9] of Black young men coupled with what may appear to be their aimless strolls or congregation on the streets contribute to their images as potential criminals. But as Brogden, Jefferson and Walklate point out, "once a group has been statistically identified as criminal, and satisfies other criteria such as low status and relative powerlessness, the resulting police 'over-attention' begins to produce the sorts or results that justify the original over-attention. This then leads to continued over-attention" (1988:112).

What about Black females? It is in Dei et al's (1995:52) work that a young woman is quoted as saying that just being a young Black man on the street is enough for him to be regarded as a criminal or drug dealer. Evidently, many of the youth who participated in this study concur, for they too pointed out that "it's not so bad for females." They suggested that while young Black women tended to be harassed less often than males, that is changing. Police and mall security personnel are beginning to suspect females as potential law breakers. Females are also being searched, more likely by female officers, if only to avoid accusations of sexual harassment. But why this increased suspicion of Black females? Is it that they too are also to be found on the streets and in shopping malls in larger numbers than before? Is it that, with increased confidence of their citizenship rights, young Black females today, like Black males, are asserting their rights to be on the streets and in malls? Are police increasingly constructing young Black women as criminals insofar as they are perceived as supporting males in their criminal activities?

Consistent with other studies (Henry, 1994; James, 1990), the findings in this study demonstrate that Black, middle-class young men were just a likely as working-class young men to be stopped, questioned, harassed and searched by law enforcement personnel. This is understandable, since style of dress and/or jewellery are today no indication of socio-economic status. And as Walcott (1995:36) suggested, clothing has become "one of the new markers for blackness."[10] So it is more than, as the youth suggested, being perceived by police as

---

9

Butler (1993: 18) also makes the point that "white male's racist fear of the black male body" is also, to some degree, based on homophobia, which in turn contributes to their anxiety.

10

Walcott (1996) argued that the wearing of jewellery can be read as the youth assertion of their status in society, and a type of Black nationalism and Afrocentrism. He continued to say that "style and fashion carry for diasporic blacks important cultural practices and signifiers that tell us about their histories and desires. In particular, such practices can be read as signifying black histories of domination and subordination, suggesting

poor immigrants who do not have the financial means to afford the same clothes and styles as their White counterparts; and unlike their white counterparts, it is believed that Black youth do not have the money to shop in the malls. Therefore, whatever the class background or attire, and regardless of the community in which young Black males and females stroll, they will be regarded as suspect. It is understandable then, that being Somali, Jamaican, Muslim or Christian did not make a difference in the experiences of the youth's encounters with police. They were all subjected to the existing social construction of Black youth.[11]

One of the curious ironies of police claims to be astute observers of people's appearances, behaviours and movements is the repeated mistakes they make with regard to Black youth fitting the descriptions of the suspects they sought. But were they really mistakes? Or is this phrase part of the racist discourse where, once having stopped the youth, the police must account for their actions and hence give their "best" line? Interestingly, every youth knows "the line" and police seemed not to be shy in saying it (Neugebauer-Visano, forthcoming). Police rationalization that the youth "fit the description" is in fact part of the process of "othering," whereby the police engaged in bounded actions that serve to marginalize Black youth. In some cases, the youth's responses to their marginalization are expressed in hostility that sometimes resulted in them being charged—a further component of the marginalization process.

As in other studies (Head, 1975; James, 1990; Henry, 1994), the youth in this study who reported that they were often stopped, questioned, searched and harassed by police were predominantly male, and they were often perceived to be working class, "immigrants" and/or "refugees." To suggest that it is because these individuals defy laws and/or regulations that necessitate them being stopped and questioned does not tell the entire story of why they were stopped in the first place, neither does it justify the actions of many of the law enforcement personnel. Once stopped for questioning, the act of having been stopped does not only come to represent the police as "doing their job," but it further adds to the layered and constructed image of young Black males as a "troublesome" group of people. For as Snider (1983:433) argued, this is not "as arbitrary and irrational a focus as it would at first appear; indeed it is a rational, though not humane, way of preserving the status quo" to target a certain type of people who commit a certain type of crime, thus "leaving the majority of lawbreakers virtually unscathed."

---

some of the ways in which black cultural practices respond by revising dominant symbolic orders" (Walcott, 1996: 131).

11

In discussing the ways in which Blacks are criminalized, Henry et al. (1995:113) pointed out that "police and some members of the justice system commonly believe that Blacks are responsible for more crimes and that Blacks come from a crime-prone culture, notably Jamaica."

Despite vociferous public outrage expressed by Black people for a number of years, indeed decades, regarding police actions (Henry, 1994; Four-Level of Government, 1992), it is evident that very little or nothing has changed. In fact, even after receiving cross-cultural, race relations and/or anti-racism training (Fleras, 1992; Andrews, 1992; Forcese, 1992; Race Relations and Policing Task Force, 1989), police continue to construct Black youth as potential trouble-makers who need to be constantly policed. Much of the overattention given to the youth on the streets or in shopping malls as a result of this social construction has little to do with any statistical evidence of their overrepresentation in crimi-nal activities.[12] Rather, this over-attention reflects structural and institutional as-sumptions about these youth that are rooted within the colonial discourse of policing which legitimizes "othering" of Black youth in their encounters. Within this discourse, any suggestions that police and security personnel's actions are based on racism and discrimination would be seen as an attempt to shift the issue from "the one stopped for questioning" to the police or security personnel. For it would be generally accepted that police base their actions upon social norms which are not considered to be racist. Hence, in this regard, Andrews (1992) in his audit of policies, procedures, programs and practices of police is able to conclude that

> we found no evidence at all of organized, intentional prejudice or bias against racial minorities. Nor did we find evidence that the force attracts individuals who are overtly racist. We did find evidence that, over time, officers develop strong feelings and beliefs as to attributes of individuals based on factors such as appearance and racial background. These attitudes, when taken collectively, can and do produce a bias which produces unequal treatment of individuals of different cultural or racial background.

Essentially, in policing Black youth—stopping, questioning and harassing them, and placing the onus on them to prove that they are not the "suspects" that the police seek—law enforcement agents engage in a process of othering which in turn contributes to their criminalization of the youth. This is reflective of the formal social control mechanisms by which the law enforcement agents operate, which are, in fact, an extension of historical and colonial attitudes towards Black people, and their use and abuse of power informed by racist ideologies (Harris, 1993).

The perception of Black youth on the street as "up to no good"—a theme that captures their perception of how police see them—becomes a self-perpetuating, cyclical phenomenon founded on four conditions: First is the notion of the street as "white property" to be protected by police; second is the concomitant issue of how and why the spaces where the youth congregate come to be recognized as

---

12

The value of collecting and reporting data on criminal activities based on race has been debated strongly. While it would be useful to ascertain statistically the extent to which police overattention to youth is justified, Blacks are reluctant to support this practice. They understand that any analysis and reporting of such information must be contextualized by the colonial and racist discourse that inform police cultural practices, the construction of Black people, and their responses to their criminalization.

"in need of policing"; third is what gets defined as "criminal activities"; and fourth is how the overattention given to the youth and the areas they traverse increases the probability of contact, thus initiating and perpetrating this cyclical process.

Hidden within this cycle is how perceptions of the youth mirror the perceptions the police have of them. Although it may sound superfluous to ask which comes first, it is not difficult to see that it is the youth who end up being in a reactive position, not only due to their discriminatory treatment by the law enforcing agents (and the *a priori* negative assumptions that both guide and lead to the treatment), but also to their treatment by the society around them. All this acts as a backdrop to what many of the youth told us was simple, wholesome, normal travelling on their own, or social interaction with friends on the street. Evidently, the youth's perceptions of their behaviour is in sharp contrast to that of the police. As Corrigan argued,

> The boys see trouble as something connected purely with the police.... At no stage do they perceive it as doing wrong, or breaking rules.... What wrongs are they doing if they just walk around the streets and the police harass them? The reasons for the harassment lie with the police, and NOT inside any rule that the boys are breaking, since for the boys the streets are a "natural" meeting place (1979:139).

The adversarial nature of the youth's encounters with the police contributes to their hostility towards the police, a hostility, as Smith (1991) argues with reference to African Caribbean Blacks in Britain, that is related to the assertion of their identity as Blacks and citizens.

Given that most police officers and security agents operate on the dominant White, Anglo-Celtic, middle-class, patriarchal cultural values of Canadian society, we can see how a situation involving police patrolling the streets where youth are present can turn into "an incident with the law." For young members of communities judged to be different from the "norm," in particular, working-class Black youth, contact with police becomes even more dangerous. It is dangerous because the constructions of age, race, gender and social class converge to form a "suspicious image" for the police, which in turn "trigger" their expectations and actions. The problem is, there is nothing the youth can do (even if they wanted to) to escape the "up to no good" label and overattention they receive. While they might be able to change their clothes or attire, they can do nothing about their colour or their class position and what they signify.

Despite the possibility of being stopped, questioned, detained and harassed by police while on the streets and in shopping malls, the Black youth with whom we spoke did not give any indication that fear of law enforcement and security personnel would make them change their practices. They saw their dress, behaviours and congregations as cultural practices and expressions of their identity. And insofar as they are denied the right to express their cultural identity, then they will struggle. Much of this struggle will continue to occur in these public arenas—the streets and the malls. For the youth, it is a struggle over identity, representation and the right to public space; a struggle in which they resist their "confinement and definition" in Canadian society (Walcott, 1995). For the law enforcement personnel, it is a struggle to exercise their power and control over the streets and the malls as "public"[13] spaces which must be used in particular ways. Their irritation with the youth is likely to produce periodic explosions, and their encounters continue.

To address these negative experiences that Black youth have with the police, educational and legal institutions must take steps to change what these Black youth have identified as the limited knowledge and misinformation on which Canadian people in general, and police in particular, operate in their dealings with them. We can think of how frightening, but more so vexing, it must be for the youth to live constantly with the trepidation and knowledge that, in taking a walk down the street, unless they are White, they might be perceived as "law breakers" and the police will treat them accordingly. It becomes a sad commentary on our institutions when one realizes that the rationale used to justify the policing of certain streets and spaces and particular groups is one of the ways in which racism and discrimination are disguised and consciously and unconsciously practiced. Having identified, explored and researched the issues relating to police-minority community relations, numerous commissions have made dozens of recommendations, including anti-racism and cultural training and local community-based policing structures (see The Commission on Systemic Racism, 1995). While these are useful, they must be accompanied by changes to the para-military approach to policing and the creation of a justice system that takes into consideration the ways in which the social construction of race in Canadian society affect the development and enforcement of laws.

REFERENCES

Anderson, E. 1990. *Streetwise: Race, Class and Change in an Urban Community.* Chicago: University of Chicago Press.

Andrews, A.G. 1992. *Review of Race Relations Practices of the Metropolitan Toronto Police Force.* Toronto: Metropolitan Audit Department, The Municipality of Metropolitan Toronto.

Armour, M. 1984. "Visible Minorities: Invisible: A Content Analysis of Submissions to the Special Committee on the Participation of Visible Minorities in Canadian Society." *Currents: Readings in Race Relations.* The Urban Alliance on Race Relations (Spring) 2:1.

Brodgen, M., T. Jefferson and S. Walklate. 1988. *Introducing Policework.* London: Unwin Press.

Brophy, J. and C. Smart, eds. 1985. *Women in Law: Explorations in Law, Family and Sexuality.* London: Routledge.

Browning, S.L., F.T. Cullen, L. Cao, R. Kopache and T.J. Stevenson. 1994. "Race and Getting Hassled by the Police: A Research Note." *Police Studies* (Spring) 17(1):1-11.

Butler, J. 1993. "Endangered/Endangering: Schematic Racism and White Paranioa." In R. Gooding-Williams, ed. *Reading Rodney King, Reading Urban Uprising,* pp.15-22. London: Routledge.

13

It should be noted that "public" is inscribed in gender, race, class and generational terms. In some cases malls are thought of as private spaces.

Corrigan, P. 1979. *Schooling the Smash Street Kids.* London: Macmillan.

Chambliss, W.J. 1995. "Crime Control and Ethnic Minorities: Legitimizing Racist Oppression by Creating Moral Panics." In D.F. Hawkins, ed. *Ethnicity, Race, and Crime: Perspectives across Time and Place,* pp.235-258. Albany: State University of New York Press.

The Commission on Systemic Racism in the Ontario Criminal Justice System. 1995. *Report.* Toronto: Queen's Printer for Ontario.

Dannefer, D. and R. Schutt. 1982. "Race and Juvenile Processing in Court and Police Agencies." *American Journal of Sociology* (March) 87(5):1113-1132.

Dei, G.J.S., L. Holmes, J. Mazzuca, E. McIsaac and R. Campbell. 1995. *Drop Out or Push Out? The Dynamics of Black Students' Disengagement from School.* Toronto: Department of Sociology in Education, Ontario Institute for Studies in Education, October.

Desroches, Frederick, J. 1992. "The occupational subculture of the police." In Brian K. Cryderman, Chris N. O'Toole and Augie Fleras. *Police, Race and Ethnicity: A Guide for Police Services.* pp.45-54. Toronto: Butterworths.

Forcese, D.P. 1992. *Policing Canadian Society.* Scarborough: Prentice-Hall Canada Inc.

Franklin, R.S. 1996. "The response to black youth crime by a new breed of bleeding heart conservatives." In *Race, Gender & Class: An Interdisciplinary & Multicultural Journal* 3(3):137-146.

Frater, T. 1991. "Just my opinion." *Racism & Education. Our Schools/Our Selves* 3(3).

The Four-Level Government/African Canadian Community Working Group. 1992. *Towards a New Beginning: The Report And Action Plan.* Toronto. November.

Gaskell, G. and P. Smith. 1985. "How young blacks see the police." *New Society* (August) 73(1182)23:261-263.

Gilroy, P. 1987. *"There ain't no black in the union jack.": The cultural politics of race and nation.* Chicago: University of Chicago.

Ginzberg, E. 1985. *Power without Responsibility: The Press We Don't Deserve.* Toronto: Urban Alliance on Race Relations.

Goffman, E. 1961. *Asylums.* Chicago: Aldine-Atherton.

_____. 1963. *Stigma: Notes on the Management of Spoiled Identity.* New Jersey: Englewood Cliffs.

Hagan, J. 1994. *Crime and Disrepute.* Thousand Oaks, CA.: Pine Forge Press/Sage.

Harris, C. 1993. "Whiteness as property." *Harvard Law Review* 106:1709-1791.

Head, W. 1975. *The Black Presence in the Canadian Mosaic: A Study of Perception and the Practice of Discrimination Against Blacks in Metropolitan Toronto.* Toronto: Ontario Human Rights Commission.

Henry, F. 1994. *The Caribbean Diaspora in Toronto: Learning to Live with Racism.* Toronto: University of Toronto Press.

_____, C. Tator, W. Mattis and T. Rees. 1995. *The Colour of Democracy: Racism in Canadian Society.* Toronto: Harcourt Brace & Company Ltd.

James, A. 1981. "'Black': An inquiry into the pejorative associations of an English work." *New Community* 9(1):19-30.

James, C.E. 1990. *Making It: Black Youth, Racism and Career Aspirations in a Big City.* Oakville, ON: Mosaic Press.

_____. 1997. "The distorted images of african canadian: Impact, implications and responses." In Charles Green, ed. *Globalization and Survival in the Black Diaspora.* Albany, NY: State University of New York Press.

Landau, S. and G. Nathan. 1983. "Selecting delinquents for cautioning in the London Metropolitan Area." *British Journal of Criminology* (April) 23(2):128-149.

Lieber, M. 1994. "A comparison of juvenile court outcomes for native Americans, African Americans and Whites." *Justice Quarterly* (June) 11(2).

Neugebauer-Visano, R. 1996. "Kids, cops and colour: The social organization of police-minority youth relations." In G. O'Bireck, ed. *Not a Kid Anymore: Canadian Youth, Crime and Subcultures.* Toronto: Nelson Canada.

_____. (forthcoming). *Police-Community Relations; The Impact of Culture on the Control of Colour.* Toronto: University of Toronto Press.

Norris, C., N. Fielding, C. Lemp and J. Fielding. 1992. "Black and blue: An analysis of the influence of race on being stopped by the police." *British Journal of Sociology* (June) 43(2):207-224.

Plaza, D. 1996. *The Strategies and Strategizing of university Education Black Caribbean-born Men in Toronto: A Study of Occupation and Income Achievements.* (Unpublished). Ph.D. Dissertation. North York: Department of Sociology, York University.

The Race Relations and Policing Task Force. 1989. *Report.* Toronto: Solicitor General, Queen's Park.

Skyes, R. and J. Clark. 1975. "A theory of defence-exchange in police-civilian encounters." *American Journal of Sociology* 81(3):584-600.

Smith, D. 1986. "The neighborhood context of police behaviour." In A.J. Reiss and M. Tonry, eds. *Communities and Cities*. Chicago: University of Chicago Press.

_____. 1991. "The origins of black hostility to the police." *Policing and Society* 2(1):1-15.

Snider, L. 1988. "The criminal justice system." In D. Forcese and S. Richer, *Social Issues: Sociological Views of Canada*, pp.287-320. Scarborough: Prentice-Hall Canada Inc.

St. Lewis, J. 1996. "Race, racism, and the justice system." In C.E. James, ed. *Perspectives on Racism and the Human Services Sector: A Case for Change*, pp.104-119. Toronto: University of Toronto Press.

Staples, R. 1975. "White racism, black crime, and American justice: An application of the colonial model to explain crime and race." *Phylon* (March) 36(1):14-23.

Thornton, A. D. (forthcoming). "Driving the lane against the raptor: The production and racialization of (transgressive) subjects on the streets of Toronto." In R. C. Wilcox, D. Andrews, and R. Pitter, eds. *Sport in the City*. University of Memphis.

Vincent, C.L. 1994. *Police Officer*. Ottawa: Carlton University Press.

Waddington, P.A.J. and Q. Braddock. 1991. "Guardians or bullies?: Perceptions of the police amongst adolescent Black, White and Asian boys." *Policing and Society* 2(1):31-45.

Walcott, R. 1995. "'Voyage through the multiverse': contested Canadian identities." *Border/Lines* 36:49-52.

_____. 1996. *Performing the Post-Modern: Rap, Hip-Hop and the Black Atlantic*. (Unpublished) Ph.D. Dissertation. Toronto: Ontario Institute for Studies in Education/University of Toronto.

Ward, O. 1985. *A Minority Report*. Toronto: *The Toronto Star*.

Weis, L. and M. Fine. 1996. "Notes on 'White' as 'Race'." *Race, Gender & Class: An Interdisciplinary & Multicultural Journal* 3(3):5-9.

NOTE: I wish to acknowledge the contributions of my colleagues Tony Xerri, Robyn Neugebauer, Joy Mannette and Rinaldo Walcott who gave generously of their time and provided critical comments and suggestions.

8

Racism in Justice: Perceptions

Commission on Systemic Racism in the Ontario Criminal Justice System

Our justice system can survive, only so long as it continues to have the confidence of the public it is designed to serve.... That confidence, however, must be earned and not assumed...[1]—*The Honourable Charles L. Dubin, Chief Justice of Ontario.*

Do Ontario residents think there is racism in the criminal justice system? The Commission conducted consultations and surveys to answer this question. At the most general level, we asked Ontarians to write or call us, and to share their views at public forums held in urban centres throughout the province. We also hosted or sponsored a large number of consultations with members of the public, lawyers, police officers, justices of the peace, probation officers, government policy makers, prison workers and managers, members of Ontario's board of parole, academic experts, equity workers and representatives of community organizations involved in the criminal justice system.

These consultations produced rich and vital information about people's beliefs and experiences. They alerted us to the complexities of our task, highlighted important differences in perspectives and gave us a better understanding of problems and possible solutions.

At the same time we realized that these methods, when used to research inequality and discrimination, are often controversial. They may be criticized as too selective or biased. They are said to result in overrepresentation of the views of those most interested in the issues and underrepresentation of what the average person thinks. Critics frequently dismiss these findings as anecdotal and unscientific. We do not accept this dismissal of personal testimony, but we do recognize that this type of research has limits.[2]

To avoid fruitless debates about how many people really think racism is a problem in Ontario's criminal justice system, and because we recognize that it is

---

1
  Hon. Charles L. Dubin, Chief Justice of Ontario, "The Future of Our Profession and of Our Justice System," *The Law Society Gazette*, Vol. 28 (1994), pp.203-4.

2
  Earl Babbie, *The Practice of Social Research*, 6th Edition (Belmont: Wadsworth Publishing Company, 1992).

useful to look at this question from different research perspectives, we conducted and commissioned several opinion surveys. Each deals with several themes, resulting in data that will appear in subsequent chapters. Here we present findings about what people inside and outside the justice system think generally about racial and other forms of discrimination in Ontario's criminal justice system.

First, we describe the survey results of what was formerly Metro Toronto residents' views on whether judges treat people equally. We focused on judges because of their special role in criminal justice. To many people, judges *are* the criminal justice system. They are expected to epitomize its values and to stand for the system's commitments to integrity and impartiality. People have high expectations of judges and want to think well of them:

> The black accused sees the judge as standing between him and the oppressive power of the state. He ... expects the judge to be neutral and impartial ... [and] expects the trial judge to exercise discretion without fear or prejudice.[3]

Second, we present findings from the Commission's surveys of Ontario's trial judges and criminal lawyers. We asked these legal professionals about specific concerns that people had brought to our attention, and also encouraged general comment on the issues raised by our inquiry.

After briefly describing the roles of the different legal professionals, we report the perceptions by those surveyed of differential treatment and systemic discrimination, illustrated by selections from their direct comments. In presenting these comments, our goals are to represent fairly what we were told and to provide opportunities for lawyers and judges to speak directly to those they may see as their critics, as well as to one another. Though we organize the comments under themes, the Commission makes no attempt, at this stage, to analyze individual remarks. Later in the Report we return to some of these perceptions in discussing specific aspects of the administration of criminal justice.

Perceptions of Racial Inequality

In essence, our surveys of the general population and legal professionals show:

- widespread perceptions among Black, Chinese and White Torontonians that judges do not treat people equally;

- widespread perceptions among Black, Chinese and White Torontonians that judges discriminate on the basis of race;

3
  Castor F. Williams, "Sentencing—Blacks in Nova Scotia," prepared for the Nova Scotia Judicial Education Seminar, Feb. 20-22, 1992 (on file), pp.7-8.

- much more widespread perceptions among Black than among White or Chinese Torontonians that judges discriminate on a variety of grounds, and specifically because of race;

- substantial variation among justice professionals in their perceptions of racial discrimination in Ontario's courts;

- strong resistance by some judges and lawyers to any suggestion of racial discrimination in Ontario's criminal courts.

Metro Toronto Residents' Perceptions

To find out what members of the general public think about discrimination in Ontario's justice system, the Commission asked an independent research body, York University's Institute for Social Research, to survey adults from three significant groups in Metro Toronto. In addition to perceptions, the survey asked respondents about their experiences with some aspects of the criminal justice system. Reference will be made to these in subsequent chapters. The survey was carried out by telephone interviews, in English or Chinese, with randomly selected individuals who identified themselves as Black, Chinese or White.[4]

The survey focuses on Metro Toronto rather than all of Ontario because of the high concentration of racial minority people living there. Canadian census estimates for 1991 indicate that racial minority communities now comprise 29 percent of the population of Metro Toronto, as compared to 14 percent of the population of Ontario as a whole. Moreover, over half of Ontario's Black (54%) and Chinese (61%) populations live within Metro Toronto.[5]

Black residents were selected because our Terms of Reference directed the Commission to focus on anti-Black racism and because Black people are the largest racial minority group in Ontario. Chinese residents were selected because they make up the second-largest racial minority group in Ontario. White residents were selected to provide a comparison of their opinions and experiences with those of members of racial minority groups.

Ideally, the Commission would have surveyed opinion among all racial minority populations in Toronto, but resource limitations prevented us from pursuing a more comprehensive project. In order to make statistically accurate generalizations, we needed a minimum of four hundred respondents from each group surveyed.[6] Confronted with the cost estimates of finding a sufficient num-

---

4

Random digit dialling was used to select the households, so that all members of the Black, Chinese and White communities in Metro Toronto had an equal chance of being chosen for interview.

5

Statistics Canada 1991 census, special tabulation for the Commission (manuscript on file).

6

Using data from the 1991 Canadian census, we estimated that it would take approximately 5,700 random telephone calls to find 400 Black people, and 5,000 calls to find 400 Chinese people. Locating the same number of South Asian people would have required 6,700 calls, and identifying 400 Vietnamese respondents would have required 50,000 calls.

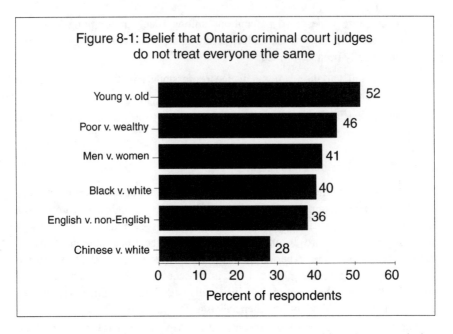

Figure 8-1: Belief that Ontario criminal court judges do not treat everyone the same

ber of respondents from smaller racial minority communities, the Commission decided to restrict our study to three groups.

Interviews were completed with 417 Black, 405 Chinese and 435 White residents (all self-identified), for a total of 1,257 persons. General demographic characteristics of persons in the sample—such as income, age and education—are consistent with the most recent census data, which indicates that the sample is representative of Black, Chinese and White Metro Toronto residents. Since the survey randomly sampled more than four hundred people in each of the selected racial groups, the findings or estimates for each group are said to be accurate, plus or minus 5 percent, 95 times in 100.

In this chapter we present findings about perceptions of unequal treatment by judges. This aspect of the survey addresses three general questions:

- How extensive are perceptions of unequal treatment in Ontario's criminal justice system?

- Do these perceptions vary among racial minority and white communities?

- Are some racial minority communities perceived as more likely to receive discriminatory treatment than others?

Although racism is the key subject of this report, our Terms of Reference also directed us to pay special attention to women and youth. Therefore, we also asked about perceptions of differential treatment by judges because of age and gender. In addition, because many judges and lawyers had suggested that income is the real explanation for what might appear to be racial discrimination in the criminal justice system, we asked about perceptions of differential treatment due to income.

What Metro Toronto Residents Think about Judges

We asked the residents surveyed if they think, in general, that judges treat people in the different comparison groups the same. Those who responded negatively were then asked if they think one group is treated better or worse than another, and how frequently they think differential treatment occurs. As a whole, our findings show that a large proportion of the Metro Toronto population think Ontario's criminal court judges do not treat everyone the same. For each comparison, at least one-quarter of the people in the sample perceive differential treatment.

People who think judges do not treat people equally believe:

- Young people are treated worse than older people.
- Poor people are treated worse than wealthy people.
- Men are treated worse than women.
- Black people are treated worse than White people.
- Chinese people are treated worse than White people.
- People who do not speak English are treated worse than people who do speak English.

When comparing judges' treatment of Black people and white people:

- More than five in ten (52%) Black respondents, three in ten (31%) Chinese respondents and more than three in ten (36%) White respondents believe judges do not treat Black people the same as white people.
- Among those in each group who perceive differential treatment of Black and White people, at least eight in ten—87% of Black, 85% of Chinese and 80% of White respondents—believe judges treat Black people worse or much worse than White people.

When those who believe judges do not treat White and Black people the same were asked how frequently they think differential treatment occurs:

- 58% of Black, 36% of Chinese and 43% of White respondents think judges "often" treat Black people differently than White people.
- Another 30% of Black, 25% of Chinese and 28% of White respondents think differential treatment of White and Black people occurs "about half the time."

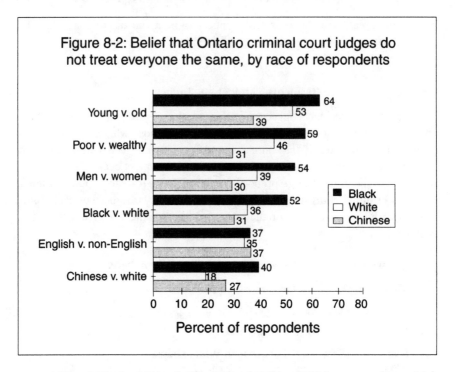

Figure 8-2: Belief that Ontario criminal court judges do not treat everyone the same, by race of respondents

- 10% of Black, 31% of Chinese and 26% of White respondents think differential treatment of White and Black people is rare (occurring "once in a while" or "almost never").

When comparing judges' treatment of Chinese people and White people:

- Four in ten (40%) Black respondents, close to three in ten (27%) Chinese respondents and about two in ten (18%) White respondents believe judges do not treat Chinese people the same as White people.

- Among those in each group who perceive differential treatment of Chinese and White people, eight in ten—81% of Black, 80% of Chinese and 79% of White respondents—believe judges treat Chinese people worse or much worse than White people.

When those who believe judges do not treat White and Chinese people the same were asked how frequently they think differential treatment occurs:

- 35% of Black, 29% of Chinese and 28% of White respondents think judges "often" treat Chinese people differently than White people.

- Another 39% of Black, 31% of Chinese and 37% of White respondents think differential treatment of White and Chinese people occurs "about half the time."

- 23% of Black, 35% of Chinese and 33% of White respondents think differential treatment of White and Chinese people is rare (occurring "once in a while" or "almost never").

Of the three groups in our sample, Black residents are consistently more likely to perceive differential treatment than either White or Chinese residents. As Figure 8-2 indicates, Black residents are more likely than White or Chinese residents to perceive discrimination because of age, sex, wealth and language.

Black residents are also more likely than White or Chinese residents to think discrimination occurs frequently and results in a substantial difference in treatment. For example, 59 percent of Black respondents, compared with 31 percent of Chinese and 46 percent of White respondents, think judges do not treat poor people the same as wealthy people. Of those who think judges do not treat wealthy and poor people the same, 51 percent of Black respondents, compared with 26 percent of Chinese and 30 percent of White respondents, think discrimination occurs "often"; 30 percent of Black respondents but only 7 percent of Chinese and 13 percent of White respondents said judges treat poor people "much worse" than rich people.

Summary of the Metro Toronto Residents Survey

What should we make of these perceptions of inequality in the criminal justice system? First, the survey shows that a significant proportion of Metro Toronto residents do not believe the justice system in practice treats everyone equally. Beliefs that judges discriminate on the basis of race are strongest among Black respondents, but significant proportions of the city's White and Chinese communities share this view.

Second, the survey shows that respondents of all three groups are more likely to perceive discrimination against Black people than against Chinese people. This finding suggests people perceive a hierarchy of discrimination.[7]

Third, the extent to which Black Metro residents perceive bias based on age, wealth, gender and language—as well as race—indicates a widespread lack of confidence in the fairness of the criminal justice system within this community. These data clearly show that a majority of Black residents perceive racial bias in the criminal justice system,[8] and many members of Metro Toronto's Black communities are also convinced that other forms of bias exist.

---

[7] This hierarchy is similar to the hierarchy of prejudice documented by many researchers. Studies in both Canada and the United States show that White people generally view Black people as less "acceptable" than members of other ethnic groups. See, for example, Jeffrey G. Reitz, *The Illusion of Difference: Realities of Ethnicity in Canada and the United States* (Toronto: C.D Howe Institute, 1994).

[8] The study confirms findings reported in Stephen Lewis' report to the Premier of Ontario (June 9, 1992), p.3, and implied in "The Report of the Race Relations and Policing Task Force," Clare Lewis, chair (1989), pp.12-14.

Since these findings deal with perceptions, they do not measure racial differences in the daily practices of the criminal justice system and their consequences. But findings of opinion are no less important than data about differential outcomes. What people think about the criminal justice system matters, because the justice system, more than many other institutions, depends on the confidence of the community. This evidence that many people lack confidence in the justice system is a reason for grave concern and a call for action.

Judges' and Lawyers' Perceptions

We separately surveyed crown attorneys, defence counsel and judges concerning several issues, producing data that we present throughout the report. Here we focus on what judges and lawyers think about racial discrimination in the criminal justice system.

Judges and lawyers have strong personal and professional interests in the Commission's work. As actors in the system, they may feel that any problems we find reflect on them personally. Few people enjoy public criticism of an institution they identify with, however constructively such criticism is intended. Criticism that centres on racism is particularly hard to accept. Atrocities such as the European enslavement of African people, the Holocaust against European Jews, South Africa's former policy of apartheid, the destruction of Aboriginal societies throughout the world and activities of groups such as the Ku Klux Klan commonly come to mind when people think of racism.

The Commission's inquiry focuses on different expressions of racism—those that may be unintended and that are implicit in practices rather than explicit in motives (see chapter 3 of the Commission on Systemic Racism in the Ontario Criminal Justice System). Even so, it would not be surprising if judges and lawyers found it hard to accept that the criminal justice system may reflect systemic racism. In a British context, Mr. Justice Henry Brooke made the point effectively when he said, "[F]air-minded people are so very easily offended at the very slightest suggestion that they have behaved in a way which other equally fair-minded people might describe as racist."[9]

In addition, judges and lawyers have a strong interest in maintaining public confidence in the system. That people believe the justice system to be fair and impartial is essential to its integrity. As the recent report of the Martin Committee notes, "without integrity, no system of justice, no matter how ingeniously designed and lavishly funded, can function."[10] Perceptions of discrimination and

---

9
  Mr. Justice Henry Brooke, "The Administration of Justice in a Multicultural Society," Kapila Lecture by the chairman of the Ethnic Minorities Advisory Committee, Judicial Studies Board, United Kingdom, Nov. 18, 1993 (manuscript on file).

10
  Province of Ontario, Attorney General's Advisory Committee on Charge Screening, Disclosure and Resolution Discussions, *Report*, chair, G.A. Martin, (*Martin Report*) (Toronto: Queen's Printer for Ontario, 1993), p.26.

other forms of unfairness, no less than racist practices—however unintended—are simply incompatible with this notion of integrity. As a senior police official told the Commission, "While the justice system is wrapped up in procedure, substantive law and a valued history of independence, the only true test of its integrity is its *credibility within the community it serves*" (emphasis in original).

Judges and lawyers also have a particular interest in the Commission's work because they will be held responsible for many of the problems we have found, and will be expected to implement changes that may flow from our recommendations. Finally, as people whose professional lives are spent in Ontario's courts, judges and lawyers are well placed to identify some types of subtle practices that may be less visible to those outside the system. By encouraging them to respond to our questions frankly, privately and anonymously, we hoped to gain access to this rich source of information.

For all these reasons the Commission felt it was important to understand how judges and lawyers see the problems, to learn of any insights they might have about these issues, and to find out to what extent they are open to change.

What Crown Attorneys Think

Crown attorneys are lawyers who act for the state in the criminal justice process. Through the Ministry of the Attorney General, the Province of Ontario employs more than five hundred full-time crown attorneys and sometimes hires additional lawyers in private practice to do this work for a daily fee. Ontario's full-time and part-time crown attorneys deal with Criminal Code offences, while lawyers hired by the federal government are responsible for the prosecution of drug charges and other offences contained in federal laws apart from the Criminal Code.

As lawyers for the state, crown attorneys "are granted a broad and generous area of unfettered discretion,"[11] which they exercise within a framework of legal rules and Ministry policy. This discretion influences many aspects of the criminal prosecution process. Crown attorneys may, for example, screen charges to decide which should proceed to trial, seek to have an accused detained before trial or establish conditions for release, discuss with defence counsel the pleas, facts and sentences to be jointly presented in court, and suggest appropriate sentences for convicted persons.

When exercising their many discretionary powers, crown attorneys face complex and conflicting demands. As "effective advocates" for "the active denunciation of criminal wrongdoing,"[12] they must "prosecute vigorously those accused

---

11

John Clement, former Attorney General of Ontario, in a 1975 speech, quoted in Phillip C. Stenning, *Appearing for the Crown* (Cowansville, Que.: Brown Legal Publications Inc., 1986), p.311.

12

Martin Report (note 6), p.32.

of crime"[13] and "discharge [their] duties with industry, skill and vigour."[14] By contrast, as "public officer[s] engaged in the administration of justice,"[15] their role "excludes any notion of winning and losing."[16] A crown attorney's duty "is not so much to obtain a conviction as to assist the judge and the jury in ensuring that the fullest possible justice is done. His [or her] conduct before the court must always be characterized by moderation and impartiality."[17] It is difficult—some have suggested almost impossible—for crown attorneys to fulfil both of these roles simultaneously.[18] Vigorous advocacy appears to conflict with impartiality. Though the expectations are stated clearly, the implications for practice are professionally challenging.

We asked crown attorneys if they think that, "in general, racial minorities are treated the same as white people" in Ontario's criminal court system.[19]

- The vast majority—three in four (74%)—agree, or strongly agree, that the courts generally treat White and racial minority people the same.
- Only one in eight (13%) disagrees.

We also asked crown attorneys about the extent of such discrimination.

- Most—three in five (61%)—think "discrimination exists, but only in a few areas and only with certain individuals."
- A minority—about one in five (18%)—think "there is no discrimination against racial minorities in the Ontario criminal court system."
- Fewer than one in ten (7%) think "discrimination against racial minorities is widespread, but subtle and hard to detect."
- Only 1% think "discrimination against racial minorities is widespread and easy to observe."

Many crown attorneys responded to our invitation to offer their personal comments on racism in the criminal justice system. As might be expected from the answers summarized above, most said that, in general, racism is not a problem in Ontario's courts. These crown attorneys wrote about:

13
   Province of Nova Scotia, Royal Commission on the Donald Marshall, Jr. Prosecution, Findings and Recommendations, *Report*, Vol. 1 (Halifax: 1989), p.241.
14
   R. v. Savion and Mizrahi (1980) 52 C.C.C. (2d) 276 at 289 (Ont. C.A.) per Zuber J.A., cited in *Martin Report* (note 5), p.31.
15
   Ibid.
16
   Boucher v. The Queen (1959) 110 C.C.C. 263, per Rand J. at 270.
17
   Ibid., per Taschereau J. at 267 (translation).
18
   J.A. Sutherland, "The Role of Crown Counsel: Advocate or Minister of Justice?" (LL.M. thesis, University of Toronto, 1990).
19
   Survey questionnaires were mailed to 483 provincial crown attorneys. After extracting one incomplete response, a sample size of 193 was left, a 40 percent response rate. Our Technical Volume contains further details and a copy of the questionnaire. See Appendix B [*not reproduced in this volume—editor*].

- **the good faith, education and professionalism of individuals who work for justice**

Duty and honour are two concepts I sincerely believe are not foreign to the performance of one's function as a professional involved in our criminal justice system, whether you are a judge, counsel, support staff or police officer. Each of these positions are populated in the 1990s by the best-educated people ever. Therefore I find it hard to believe that while incidents of racism may occur ... they are anything more than rare.

My impression of the criminal justice system is that it is not systemically racist, based upon my understanding of the term. Neither is the justice system rife with racists. By and large, it would appear that most of the participants in the criminal justice system are individuals committed to the fair and impartial application of the criminal law.

Racism in the justice system is far less than in the general population. This is perhaps attributable to the fact that by and large the system is populated by intelligent and well-educated individuals. I am not aware of a single situation [in which] a minority accused was dealt with unfairly by the system simply because he/she was a member of that minority group.

While I think it is a given that most people in society and therefore in the criminal justice system have certain biases, I think that only in a fraction of those cases are those biases actually reflected in the treatment of individuals. In fact, I think most officers of the courts probably bend over backwards not to let any biases they may have negatively influence their conduct, and are conscious that it appear that justice is being done.

While some individuals in the criminal justice system no doubt harbour racist views to some extent, I have never seen an accused, witness or complainant receive less courteous treatment or a less fair hearing solely because he or she is a member of a racial minority.

There are very few racists in the justice system. Most judges, crowns and defence lawyers work very hard to do a good job. The level of dedication is extraordinarily high [among] all involved. Mistakes are made, but for the most part all persons involved in the system are remarkably decent, caring people.

- **the lack of opportunity for racism to influence key decisions in the treatment of accused persons**

Many plea negotiations take place without the crown being aware of the accused's race or place of origin. Such issues are irrelevant. Crowns making these decisions will often never ... see the accused.

When decisions are made in the bail court, there is simply no time at all to consider anything other than the offence and the offender's antecedents. The colour of a person's skin is never a factor.

Prosecutorial decisions are almost exclusively based on "paper" that reveals no racial make-up.

- **the influence of factors other than race itself, particularly class or poverty, on the treatment of accused persons**

Criminal activity is strongly correlated to class, and visible minorities, particularly first-generation blacks, are largely poor in relation to the rest of the population. They are accordingly over-represented in the criminal courts. Before concluding that there is racism in the court system, it is very important to compare your minority group stat[istics] with a similarly situated white group in terms of all socio-economic data, family background and criminal antecedents.

Generally, persons of low socio-economic background have greater problems in the system than those of higher socio-economic background. People who have been in Canada longer, speak English better, have family, jobs [or] property are all treated better than those who do not. However, new Canadians with family and community supports and jobs are also well treated.... New immigrants who commit criminal offences are not well looked-upon. White and other long-term welfare recipients with [criminal] records are also not well treated. There is bias in the system. It is not always racially motivated.

While I do not have the benefit of statistical data, and my observation and views are based upon my own experience and information obtained from others, it would appear that racial minority accused are not discriminated against on the basis of race but because they are disadvantaged, as whites are, when it comes to issues like bail by the fact that they perhaps more frequently lack family support, strong community ties and stable employment. These disadvantages would appear not to be race-based, but rather a function of the length of time the accused has been resident in the community and his or her employability.

Race has rarely if ever been an issue in courtrooms.... The true difficulties our middle-class courts have are in dealing with or understanding poverty and non-Canadian cultures. The colour of skin is not an issue, or this misdefines the issue."

Some crown attorneys who think there is no racism in the justice system expressed strong disagreement with the Commission's mandate and work. They maintained that people who believe there is systemic racism in the criminal justice process:

- **do not understand the justice system**

  The idea that there is widespread racism in the administration of justice is patently false. These ideas result from an ill-informed, politically correct minority who, I believe, have no experience in the criminal justice system.

  Whining about supposed discrimination is a waste of time. The suggestion of discrimination is unfounded.

- **are making "excuses"**

  Since time immemorial, persons accused of crime have utilized whatever means necessary to divert attention from the charges they are facing, and in these days of "political correctness," bureaucrats have allowed, nay encouraged, the view of the forest to be artificially obscured by the trees.

  The accusation of "racism" is often used as the last refuge of the scoundrel.

  It is far too easy in our society to cry "racism" and not address the real reason for which one is in trouble with the law.

- **are following a misguided or illegitimate political agenda**

  You are creating racism by falsely accusing people of being racist. Racial minorities should receive training in Canadianism. You are creating expectations that people who come to Canada have a right to their own piece of their old country in Canada. This creates and perpetuates racism.

From what I have observed, I do not see that racism is as great a problem in the justice system as [do] the media and some individuals and self-serving interest groups.

Those who are the most vocal in the criticism of the judicial system are the ones most likely to ensure that what racism there is will continue and perhaps increase. These are the persons whose living and standing in the community are dependent on finding racism everywhere, for without this spotlight they are nothing.

- **have so intimidated judges that the more serious problem today is discrimination against White persons**

  In our jurisdiction there is "reverse" discrimination.... A white person will get a jail sentence for an offence and a racial minority will not, because the court is afraid if the person is jailed the court will appear racist.

Other crown attorneys, however, are convinced that racism is a genuine problem in the justice system. They talked about:

- **the subtlety of racism**

  Overt examples of racism in the criminal justice system are rare. It is the subtle examples that are rampant.

  With respect to the trial process itself, I have found that racist elements tend to be very subtle.

  The only large group of racial minority clients we have here is [from] an Indian Reserve. The witnesses are not abused, but they are treated with condescension—they are on average less likely to be believed.

  There are racist comments by police officers... [but these are] not in my experience limited to race. Comments about women or gay people also come up.... The defence, crowns and court personnel are too aware to voice similar views, but give messages more subtly.

- **the individuals and officials responsible for racism in the justice system**

  Regional directors of crown attorneys set the tone for the office. Where they fail to establish that racism in whatever form (comments, behaviour, exercise of discretion) will not be tolerated, you see an increase in an atmosphere of intolerance.

  Judicial conduct needs to be better scrutinized. Where judges or [justices of the peace] make inappropriate comments, etc., the matter should be dealt with. At present, although certain individuals are notorious, nothing is done by the system. By tolerating their behaviour it is condoned, continues and increases.

  The legal profession and the criminal justice system take their lead from the judges, who rule the courtroom. At both the provincial and general division levels, but particularly the provincial division, the bench is saturated with elitist, racist and sexist individuals.... Accused persons, victims and witnesses are daily subjected to humiliation and degradation at the hands of such judges.... Until the courtroom becomes an impartial arena, no amount of education or infringement of crown discretion will address the existing racist and sexist biases within the system.

  As a woman and a member of a religious minority.... I have experienced some very glaring examples of overt racism and sexism from judges.... But these individuals are the minority—most people are very aware of the special needs of minority persons and are not racist. In particular, I have found that the police go out of their way to treat [minority] accused persons fairly in most cases. Most racist behaviour, unfortunately, stems from the bench.

It is my general impression that the alleged racist bias of police officers is in fact exaggerated. It is my general impression that the alleged racist bias of certain defence counsel is underrated. By far the most likely of all court "people" to utter racist comments are a minority of vocal defence counsel. The Law Society should be sensitized to this problem.

I have heard defence counsel go on in an extremely racist fashion, and it disgusts me because these people are their clients.

What Defence Counsel Think

Defence counsel are independent professionals who act for persons charged with criminal offences. Their main discretionary powers include negotiations with crown attorneys about pleas, facts and sentences; development of trial strategy; and gathering and presenting information about the accused that might influence sentencing.

In exercising these discretions, defence counsel are guided by the law and practice, clients' wishes and their professional obligations to serve the client and the court simultaneously. Their duty to the client is

to raise fearlessly every issue, advance every argument, and ask every question, however distasteful, which the lawyer thinks will help the client's case; and to endeavour to obtain for the client the benefit of every remedy and defence authorized by the law.[20]

As these words suggest, defence counsel are largely free, and expected, to advocate vigorously on behalf of their clients. But as lawyers, they are also "officers of the court concerned with the administration of justice." In this role, the lawyer is said to have

an overriding duty to the court, to the standards of [the] profession and to the public, which may and often does conflict with [the] client's wishes or with what the client thinks are his [or her] personal interests.[21]

We asked defence counsel if they think that, "in general, Black and other racial minorities are treated the same as White people [in] the court system in Ontario."[22]

- Five in ten (50%) defence counsel agree that Black and other racial minorities are treated the same as White people.

20
Commentary to Rule 10 of the Law Society of Upper Canada, Professional Conduct Handbook (Toronto: Law Society, 1978), para. 2, adapted from *Rondel* v. *Worsley* [1969] 1 AC 191 at 227-228, cited in *Martin Report*, p.30.

21
Rondel v. *Worsley*, ibid.

22
We reached defence counsel through the Criminal Lawyers Association, a voluntary association of defence lawyers. At our request the Association labelled envelopes and mailed questionnaires to 800 lawyers on its membership list. Extracting five incomplete responses left a sample size of 343, a response rate of about 43 percent. See our Technical Volume for further details and a copy of the questionnaire.

- Four in ten (40%) defence counsel disagree.

This question, like many others, prompted different patterns of responses from lawyers with substantial racial minority clienteles (40% or more of their clients) compared with those from lawyers with a smaller proportion of racial minority clients.

- Five in ten (52%) lawyers with larger racial minority clienteles think that Black and other racial minority people are not treated the same as White people, compared with three in ten (34%) defence counsel with smaller racial minority clienteles.

- Four in ten (38%) lawyers with larger racial minority clienteles think Black and other racial minority people are treated the same as White people, compared with six in ten (56%) defence counsel with smaller racial minority clienteles.

Like the crown attorneys who responded, many defence counsel used the survey as an opportunity to offer written comments. Drawing on their experience of the administration of criminal justice, some said they **do not see any racism in Ontario's courts**.

I have never witnessed any racially motivated differences in how discretion is exercised. All have depended on the facts and passed [sic] records—not the individual.

In 17 years of practice representing members of both the majority and ... minorities as you have defined them, I have never once seen any racially motivated exercise of discretion by either the crown's office or court personnel.

My experience has been that accused persons regardless of the[ir] race, ethnic origin or background are treated fairly and equally by all in the administration of justice.

Complaints of racial minorities that they have received discriminatory treatment, in my personal experience, have inevitably been the product of dissatisfaction with being caught and suffering the penalty—just another reason to use to cause the justice system to "back off" their case a touch or completely....

The courts today are sensitive to the needs of all accused and particularly to the perceptions the minorities have of their treatment. I ... see little evidence to indicate minorities are subjected to prejudice, bias or slurs of any kind. The system ought to be proud of this general appearance of fairness and respect for all who come before the courts.

So far as judicial proceedings are concerned, I believe there is no evidence of systemic racism in the Ontario criminal justice system.

This Commission is virtually a waste of time and money, as I perceive there to be no racism ethnically in the judicial process. The only obvious prejudice that exists is against white Anglo-Saxon males.

My observation: you are investigating a non-existent problem. My prediction: you will recommend an elaborate set of measures to deal with the [non-existent] problem.

Other lawyers clearly had different experiences with the administration of criminal justice. They talked about:

- **subtle biases against racial minority clients**

The system—from police through to crowns—has targeted minorities with a broad brush. More difficulty arises for defence counsel in presenting the "human being" to them when the client is a member of a racial minority.

One never discusses racism but it is clear that issues such as credibility, guilt beyond a reasonable doubt, and innocent till proven guilty become unclear if your client is black or yellow. The problem is not only police- and crown-related.

The problem is not that judges are overtly discourteous to non-white participants. The problem is that they are less likely to believe them. Again the relevant factors are intangible: the empathy and identification factors are lacking.

Very little of the real racism is blatant. Racial minorities know they are treated unfairly. But the unfair treatment is not consistent throughout the province.

- **the exercise of discretion**

The ubiquitous exercise of so many discretions—which permeate the system from arrest through incarceration—permit the free play of racial stereotyping and prejudice in so subtle a manner as to make it elusive.... Ontarians must be persuaded of the subtle forms of racism as opposed to thinking of racism as gross and exaggerated displays by extremists.

There is a bias with some judges against racial minorities when it comes to judicial interim release [bail]. They take that long look at the accused in the dock and, in the final analysis, it comes down to an [exercise] of discretion based on submissions and intuition. Too often, I feel, intuition is a cover for institutionalized discrimination. I have even heard judges give voice to that discrimination in a way which was supposed to be humorous.

Assumptions are made by police, crowns and judges that certain racial minorities are more likely to be guilty of certain categories of offences, and discretion is exercised or restricted accordingly.

- **stereotyping of persons from racial and ethnic minority communities**

Comments often flow from crowns and police officers re various communities and stereotypes—e.g., Jamaicans, Portuguese.

Judges are more likely to stereotype minority accused in the questions, comments and findings of fact than to make overt comments, although they do that as well.

- **racist conduct behind closed doors**

Pressure placed on defence counsel in back-room dealings provides cover for racist attitudes of the judiciary. If more were done in open court, either a judge would have less opportunity to give effect to the racism or it would become apparent on the record.

I am often appalled that judges, crowns, police officers and even defence counsel assume they are speaking to someone who agrees with their racist point of view.

Police attitudes are the worst. Many officers with racist attitudes have learned over the last few years to "conceal" this unless among people they consider to share similar views. It's very instructive to share a coffee with a few officers and to pretend to be "one of the boys" and then listen to the racial invectives spewing forth. It's harder to detect now, but the mindset has changed very little.

- **the responsibilities of police officers, judges and to a lesser extent crown attorneys and defence counsel for racism in the criminal justice system**

In many cases I have had, I am sure the police would not have charged the person if the person was white. It seems to me that the police are more willing to resolve disputes (assaults, theft, threatening) [without] charges being laid if the person is white. I often think my clients should enter a guilty plea to being black, as that is really why they are in court. To me, it is the racism of the police in exercising their discretion which must be examined. Giving blacks criminal records seems to be the goal of too many police officers.

The biggest problem with racial discrimination in the criminal justice system lies in the original laying of the charge—i.e., the police. They seem to pride themselves on being experts about the "way of life" of particular races and areas of the city. They typically do not use discretion in laying charges, particularly with Jamaicans, Afro-Americans and Portuguese.

Any racism that exists in the courts is, in my view, mostly related to the manner in which police investigate and arrest members of the community, the charges they lay and the police recommendations for the detention of the accused and/or bail conditions to be requested if accused is released. More and more racial minority accused advise counsel they have been hassled and at times abused for no reason, they have been searched illegally, [or] they have been denied their rights to retain and instruct counsel without delay; and a sizeable number insist that the police have planted drugs on them. I realize that some allegations of maltreatment by police could well be fabricated, but the allegations occur in patterns with the same officers, and [are] so similar in detail that it is difficult to discount the majority of these claims.

In general the police treat my minority clients differently. The police single out minority accused. The police lay charges. The police suggest conditions upon release that are impossible for an accused to meet, or [recommend] no release. The police fabricate circumstances on the synopsis[23] to aggravate a possible release situation. The police show up at more minority bail hearings to give "valuable" evidence. The same officers attend at pre-trials and often hinder possible resolution. More of my visible minority clients are beaten by the police. A large number of my visible minority young offenders and their families are less educated and less aware of their rights. The police take advantage of this ignorance.

If there is significant discrimination against minorities, it is worst against blacks. Police have a perception of the black community as a criminal sub-culture.... Mercenary, high-volume legal aid defence counsel are even less likely to be concerned for the rights of black clients if those rights get in the way of expediency and a fast buck.

Judges seem to me the worst offenders. Perhaps part of it is that, burdened with a multi-trial list, they have no patience or courtesy to spare for those who have difficulty making themselves understood. While many (crowns and judges) are pretty even-handed with respect to complainants, there is less tolerance for minority defence (as opposed to crown) witnesses and far less for minority accused. Maybe this is just part of the general contempt for the accused and his/her witness that I find almost commonplace in the courtroom.... (regardless of race).

Most judges do not see colour, but some do. Get rid of the bigots! Better appointments, based on merit not race, etc., is the way to go. Good judges treat each person the same.

"Generally speaking, I do not see any racist behaviours by judges and court staff. On the other hand, I do see racist attitudes and behaviour by police on a routine basis.

23

The synopsis is a written summary of the case and the background of the accused, prepared by the police immediately after arrest. It is intended to assist the crown attorney who will conduct the bail hearing.

> Judges often become irritated with West Indian witnesses because the judges are unable to understand the accent. It would be a good idea to introduce programs to educate justice system personnel to West Indian culture.... Police probably reflect racist attitudes in society.... The police seem to be the main problem with racist behaviour and attitudes.

Several defence lawyers perceived systemic biases in the justice system and the vulnerability of racial minority accused to these biases, but said disadvantageous treatment is mostly or really due to reasons other than race:

> I think racism plays only a small part.... The greater problem is class. Those on welfare, [the] unemployed, [the] underemployed or [those] on government benefits fare poorly.

> Discretion seems largely to depend on economic factors—poor accused, whether or not they are minorities, seem to be treated alike—increased police suspicion and surveillance, more charges, less discretion. Middle-class or high-income minorities tend to be treated as well as middle-class whites. Discretion and much of the other aspects correlate more closely with economic factors than race, although some may confuse hostility towards the former for hostility to the latter.

> The differences seem to me very much "systemic"—that white accused are able to show more often than racial minorities those things (wealth, employment, drug rehabilitation, family support, community support, etc.) which impel crowns, police and judges to extend bail or sentencing leniency. Class biases overlap with racial biases.

> I do not think the issue is the bias of the individuals who work in the system. The bias [is] in the system.... In other words, a white or black from the "projects" gets a bad shake in court, not because he is white or black, but because he is from the projects.

> There is a strong tendency for crowns and police to develop racial/ethnic animosities. I suppose the nature of the job attracts certain authority types and that the pressure leads to frustration. The end result is that lower SES [socio-economic status] groups are condescended towards. Wealthy, white anglos are better treated. Poor, uneducated immigrants are at the lowest end. I think race is not as big a factor as income level and language skills.

> Poor people are ... disproportionately black, and poor people are often before the criminal courts. The reasons involve cultural issues as well as some level of systemic racism, both in our society and in the police. I see systemic racism less in our courts than elsewhere in our society.

> Class and income play a part in determining who comes before the courts. That should be the subject of consideration. One cannot point to a percentage of "minority" accused and say this is racism. The issue is more complex. Social structure must be addressed.

What Judges Think

Ontario's criminal trial judges are former lawyers called to a provincial bar for at least ten years before their appointments. As judges they may be members of the General Division or the Provincial Division of the Ontario Court of Justice. Judges who sit in the General Division are federally appointed, while appointments to the Provincial Division are Ontario's responsibility.

Judges may participate in pre-trial meetings with crown attorneys and defence lawyers at which agreements are sometimes made about which issues will be contested in court. They are responsible for ensuring that trials are fair, for convicting or acquitting accused persons, and sentencing people convicted of criminal offences. In fulfilling these roles they exercise discretion.

Although these general functions are the same for all trial judges, there are important differences in the roles of general and provincial division judges in Ontario's criminal justice system. For example, only provincial division judges conduct preliminary inquiries. They also conduct trials without juries, while general division judges may conduct trials with or without juries. In addition, provincial division judges conduct trials of youths aged twelve to seventeen charged with any criminal offence. By contrast, general division judges try only youths aged over fourteen charged with very serious offences, and only if a judge has decided that the accused should be tried as an adult.

We asked judges if they think "in general racial minorities are treated the same as White people in Ontario's court system."[24]

- The majority of provincial division judges—about three in five (64%)—and general division judges—three in four (72%)—agree that the courts generally treat White and racial minority people the same.

- One in five (19%) provincial division judges and one in ten (10%) general division judges disagree.

We also asked judges if they think "systemic discrimination is a serious problem in [Ontario's] criminal justice system."

- One in four (25%) provincial division judges, but fewer than one in ten (7%) general division judges, agree that systemic discrimination is a serious problem in the criminal justice system.

- About five in ten (45%) provincial division judges and three in four (76%) general division judges disagree.

These questions, like many others in the survey, prompted different patterns of responses from provincial division judges appointed before and after important changes were made to the appointment procedures. The new process, intended to eliminate any suggestion of patronage,[25] includes people who are not lawyers, judges or politicians in selecting new judges; affirms the merit principle as the main qualification for appointment; introduces clear, public criteria for evaluating candidates; and considers diversity as a factor. Using as our dividing point 1989, the year in which the changes were introduced, we found:

24

The survey was mailed to every general division judge on a mailing list given to the Commission by the office of the Chief Justice—253 names in total. Responses were received from 137, a response rate of 54 percent. Of the 265 surveys mailed to provincial division judges, on a mailing list given to the Commission by the office of the Chief Judge, 121 were returned—about 46 percent. Our Technical Volume contains further details and a copy of the questionnaire. See Appendix B [*not reproduced in this volume—editor*].

25

Attorney General Ian Scott, Ontario Legislature Debates 6835 (Dec. 15, 1988).

- Judges appointed under the new system are much more likely than their longer-serving colleagues to think there are racial differences in how people are treated in the courts. One in three (33%) of the more recent appointments, compared with one in ten (10%) of the longer-serving judges, disagree that White and racial minority people are treated the same.

- Judges appointed under the new system are much more likely to think there is systemic racism in the criminal justice system than their longer-serving colleagues. Close to two in five (37%) recently appointed judges, but fewer than one in five (16%) longer-serving judges, agree that "systemic discrimination is a serious problem in the criminal justice system."

Judges' comments raise similar themes to those of crown attorneys and defence counsel. The dominant view, especially among general division judges, is that concerns about racism or any other form of discrimination in Ontario's courts have no basis in fact. Judges said:

- **there is no evidence of discrimination in the courts**

   Counsel, prosecutors [and] court personnel tend to treat users of the justice system alike. I have seen no evidence of unequal treatment over a 33-year career as a lawyer and a judge.

   I strongly disagree with those who allege there is systemic discrimination and racism in the court system in Ontario. There will always be anecdotal statements to this effect, but the hard evidence is exactly to the contrary. My extensive experience is that judges, lawyers and court personnel treat all people coming into conflict with the law in the same way.

   My experience is that the court is colour-blind. For the most part I can honestly say that minority parties have been treated no differently than any other by judges, juries, courts staff, lawyers, etc.

   In 21 years as a judge, I have seen no racial discrimination in the courts nor in the verdict[s] of juries.... My experience, and that of judges I have talked to, is that racial discrimination does not exist in the courts.

   I have seen absolutely no evidence of any distinction between the way in which what you call "racial minority" persons are treated, and the treatment given to what you call "whites."

- **racial minority individuals tend to receive better treatment than white individuals in Ontario's courts**

   Ninety-nine percent of judges, counsel and court staff bend over backwards to be fair and not to appear racist. [They] often give non-whites more courtesy and consideration than whites.

   The fact is that certain racial minorities are given consideration that takes into account, in a way beneficial to the [racial minority] accused, the disadvantage generally experienced by that group.

   The individual needs of individuals are being addressed, and frequently I see greater efforts by court staff and crowns to accommodate the needs of those who don't appear to understand the process than would be made for an "average" person. This means frequently that poorer or less skilled or more recently arrived persons get better treatment, and frequently the beneficiaries are members of a "racial minority." If it didn't work that way in my Court, I'd make it work that way!

My general experience is that ... both judges and juries give members of racial minorities leniency as opposed to similarly placed accused from non-racial minority segments of the population. In effect they over-compensate for the perception that they may be prejudiced.

Most courts now are trying to be very careful not to be biased—possibly even leaning over the other way, which is equally unfair.

In the area where I preside, it is relatively rare to see an Oriental or black person in court. When they are present, the court staff and counsel appear to me to be more accommodating to them than to white persons.

- **allegations of racism are excuses for criminality**

Too many ethnic groups cry racism! And totally ignore the fact that their particular group is in fact committing a disproportionate number of serious crimes in a particular area.

The perception of unfair or unequal treatment of racial minorities is due to the disproportionate numbers who are brought into the system. The factors which bring them before the system are economic, social and cultural. Deal with the root causes and stop pointing the finger of blame at the people who are seriously trying to enforce the law.... Our courts attempt to serve with scrupulous fairness.

- **allegations of racism—and the work of this Commission—reflect a misguided political agenda, rather than a genuine problem in Ontario's justice system**

I do not agree that minority persons are badly treated in the provincial courts. As part of their defence "posture," minority persons frequently attempt to skew the case into racial lines. The socialist government has unfortunately encouraged this stratagem. The fault is not so much with the minority witnesses so much as it is in [members of] the left-liberal establishment [who] to perpetuate their own importance as "activists" encourage the very idea of racial inequality in the courtroom. The vast majority of players in the system bend over backwards to be fair and just to minorities as a matter of patriotism and personal decency.

This entire exercise is driven by an overreaction to a small segment of the population who would complain about the conditions in heaven. Not to say we should be complacent or over self-congratulatory; but come on—is it [so] bad that we should throw so much tax money away on yet another commission, study and survey? Wake up and smell the coffee!

The very existence of this Commission, its mandate and terms of reference, promotes rather than discourages racism... Any recommendations which require us to look at and deal with apparent difference[s] will further promote racism.

I anticipate that the Commission, driven by the force of political correctness, will find that racism is rampant in the justice system.... a conclusion that will not be based on hard evidence but, like Stephen Lewis' letter, on anecdote and unsubstantiated complaint. Failing all else the Commission will find invisible racism—visible only to the Commissioners.

By contrast, some judges said racism and other forms of discrimination are a reality in the administration of justice:

If it's not discrimination against colour, it's discrimination against the poor, the underprivileged and the weak. We go to great lengths to try to justify our positions, yet we all suffer from the same common denominator—prejudice—and we're not prepared, as a society, to do anything about it.

I am of the view that there exists systemic racism in the Ontario court system. While many might disagree, awareness programs for those involved in the administration of justice would likely help eliminate the unconscious discrimination. I'm sure many of us, from court personnel to judge, discriminate without being aware of it. Stereotyping is a strong influence we surely suffer without knowing. To a certain extent the more we are exposed to these minorities, the more we can understand.

My experience has been that we are all—whites, blacks, Oriental, etc.—racist to some degree. We are all more comfortable, other things being equal, with people who are like ourselves. I witnessed black and Oriental (Asian) racism when I worked in an African country when I was younger. I have certainly seen white racism in its more negative forms. Consequently any training which helps to sensitize us to the "other" and his or her fear and biases or perceived biases cannot but help us to avoid misconceptions and problems in dealing with races different from our own. Talking about these problems is a good thing even if it is sometimes unpleasant.

If most of the faces you see are black, there is a temptation to think there is a problem with that community. This would explain the attitude of some judges and crowns. The problem is the police. The police are homogeneous, closed [and] resistant to change.... Not all police are racist but a substantial portion are. There are lots of influences on judges and prosecutors to reduce racist attitudes....

Summary of Judges' and Lawyers' Perceptions

These findings make two important points. First, there is substantial variation among justice professionals in their perceptions of racial discrimination in Ontario's criminal courts. Significant proportions of defence lawyers and recently appointed judges of the provincial division think the criminal justice system does not treat White and racial minority accused the same. However, only about one in ten crown attorneys, general division judges and provincial division judges appointed before 1989 share this view.

That judges and lawyers by no means speak with one voice shows that these justice professionals are not a homogeneous group. Though they may have a common interest in how the justice system is perceived, they have different views about the extent to which racial discrimination permeates Ontario's criminal justice system today.

Second, as the quotations from the surveys illustrate, many justice professionals reject—some flatly—even the possibility that systemic racism might be a genuine problem in Ontario's criminal courts. For some, the rejection of racial bias is but a part of their belief that the criminal justice system treats everyone the same. Others, however, acknowledge differential treatment based on class or poverty even as they reject the suggestion of racial discrimination.

Many of the survey comments suggest that class or income bias, though it may be regretted, is inherent in Canadian society and may be transmitted into the court system through the workings of other social institutions, such as the educa-

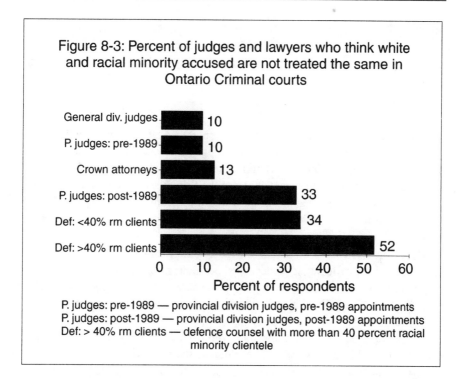

Figure 8-3: Percent of judges and lawyers who think white and racial minority accused are not treated the same in Ontario Criminal courts

General div. judges — 10
P. judges: pre-1989 — 10
Crown attorneys — 13
P. judges: post-1989 — 33
Def: <40% rm clients — 34
Def: >40% rm clients — 52

Percent of respondents

P. judges: pre-1989 — provincial division judges, pre-1989 appointments
P. judges: post-1989 — provincial division judges, post-1989 appointments
Def: > 40% rm clients — defence counsel with more than 40 percent racial minority clientele

tion system and labour markets. Class or income bias is not perceived to be caused by or the fault of justice professionals, nor is it necessarily influenced by dislike of poor people. Since the existence of class or income bias is not thought to reflect badly on individual judges or lawyers, it may be easier for justice professionals to acknowledge this problem without feeling personally responsible for it.

By contrast, many of the survey comments tend to treat any suggestion of racial bias in the court system as an attack on the personal integrity of the respondents. This response suggests that racial bias is understood to mean deliberately unfair decisions, made by specific individuals and motivated by negative judgments about races. There seems to be an attitude that somehow the legal system is immune from the consequences of racial inequality in Canadian society. Even when judges and lawyers are confident that their own conduct in the daily administration of criminal justice is beyond reproach, they seem to feel implicated when the integrity of the justice process is challenged. This narrow view—that any racial bias in the courts must reflect deliberate wrongdoing—has led to indignant denials of a general social or cultural problem that is endemic in Canadian society.

It is important to understand adverse consequences of racism even when they do not result from unfair motives. These more subtle forms of racism require greater effort to identify and eliminate. Cooperation and initiative from those most directly involved in the criminal justice system will be crucial to achieving the perception as well as the reality of true equality in Ontario's criminal justice system.

Conclusion

The Commission's findings show the importance of restoring public confidence in the criminal justice system's commitment to equality. We must not rest content that many residents of Ontario's largest and most racially diverse city appear to agree with a participant at one of the Commission's public forums who said, "We have two systems of justice within the criminal justice system. One is for the majority group in our society—people who have money, connections, etc.—and the other is for the racial minorities."

Much criticism has been levelled against some members of Ontario's Black communities for articulating concerns about racism within the system. These individuals have been dismissed as unrepresentative and described as speaking only for themselves. The Commission's findings show that a large proportion of Black Torontonians—who comprise just over half of all Black Ontarians—appear to have little confidence that the criminal justice system delivers justice equally. Many White and Chinese Torontonians share this view.

The Commission's findings also show that justice system officials are divided over whether the criminal justice system delivers equal justice to residents of Ontario. The findings suggest that a substantial proportion of all respondents feel that discrimination is common.

These findings should not be dismissed as attacks on the criminal justice system by those who do not understand it. They are a call to respond to the concerns raised, and to use available resources to improve and deliver what is now seen as only a promise of equality.

9

Racism, Ethnic Prejudice, Whiteness and the Working Class

Thomas Dunk

In both popular culture and academic social analysis, the working class, particularly the "White" working class, is frequently presented as having a unique relationship to racism and ethnic prejudice. There are competing conventional stereotypes and theoretical paradigms regarding the nature of the linkage between racism, ethnic prejudice and working-class experience. At one end of the continuum is the image of workers as the "salt of the earth" and a political and social theory that workers' class experience will inevitably lead to a class consciousness that transcends racial, ethnic and national differences. At the other end of the continuum is a commonsense view of workers as ignorant and/or authoritarian bigots, and social scientific hypotheses that, relative to other social classes, workers, whether because of their innately limited intellectual abilities or their social conditioning, are particularly prone to intolerance of various kinds.

These broad paradigms have been influential in discussions about working-class culture and in debates about racism and ethnic prejudice. In recent years many of the arguments about the relative significance of race, ethnicity and class as sources of identity have focused on the presence or absence of class consciousness among workers and how race and ethnicity influence its development or lack of development. There are two main aims of this chapter. First, it provides a critical review of the literature on racism and ethnic prejudice within working-class culture. Second, it offers a fresh perspective on how racism and prejudice within the working class can be explained without reproducing negative stereotypes of working-class culture and individuals.

I begin by situating the discussion of working-class racism within the two contrary paradigms already mentioned. One of these presents the working class as historically destined to transcend supposedly "irrational" forms of identity such as race, ethnicity and nationalism, while the other argues that workers are particularly prone to various forms of prejudice and intolerance. Empirical, theoretical and methodological problems with the view that racism and ethnic prejudice are more common among workers than among other social classes are also discussed.

Next, I describe and critically examine theories that have been developed to explain working-class racism and prejudice without taking either the position that it is inevitable or that the working class is necessarily immune to their influence. The split labour market thesis, the theory that racism is an ideology deployed to divide the working class and the notion that working-class racism can be explained either as an expression of deep-seated psychological longing for group homogeneity or as psychological compensation for low status are each found to have their strengths. Ultimately, however, they are limited by their tendency to reduce the complex articulations of racism, ethnic prejudice and class to an expression of either economic competition, false consciousness or mysterious psychological processes.

The chapter then discusses explanations of working-class racism that emphasize the way in which abstract and hard-to-grasp structural forces generate a concrete experience that is interpreted through frameworks and stereotypes derived from commonsense and popular culture. Such an approach emphasizes contextual specificities and avoids the reductionist tendencies of other models. I conclude by underlining the importance of conceptualizing race, ethnicity and class as processes, rather than static objects; processes that may be independent of one another, in contradiction or mutually reinforcing.

Working-Class Hero Versus Working-Class Bigot

It is useful for heuristic purposes to think about racism and ethnic prejudice among the working class in relation to two common images. On the one hand, workers have been represented in a romanticized heroic mode as the vanguard of the socialist revolution or as progressive populists leading a difficult struggle for democracy, justice and dignity against the entrenched hostile forces of capital and the state. Crucial to their struggle is their sense of a common identity as workers, a class consciousness which overrides the sense of racial, ethnic and national belonging.

On the other hand, there is the image of the authoritarian and prejudiced worker, a stereotype popularized in characters such as Archie Bunker from the 1970s television sitcom *All in the Family*. The underlying premise here is that, in the absence of a liberal education which teaches one better, workers' immediate loyalties fall with their own ethnic or racial group, and racial and ethnic "others" are treated with fear, disdain and, perhaps, even hatred. Racial and ethnic identities are conceived of as "primordial sentiments," to use the words of the anthropologist Clifford Geertz (1975), which stand in the way of the blossoming of a working-class consciousness.

The Revolutionary Worker

The romantic image of the worker as the vanguard of the revolution which would usher in a utopian world where each gives according to their abilities and receives according to their needs has its roots in the early writings of Marx and Engels. First- and second-generation Marxism was based upon the idea that changes in the economic structure of society which gave rise to the working class as a "class in itself" (a category of the population which shared a similar position in the relations of production) would, or should, generate a "class for itself" (a class which was conscious of itself as a collectivity with shared interests *vis-à-vis* its class enemies). Although they were critical of nineteenth-century capitalist society, Marx and Engels were also great admirers of capitalism because they viewed it as a progressive step on the evolutionary road to socialism. According to Engels, the Industrial Revolution shook workers out of "their silent vegetation" and forced "them to think and demand a position worthy of men [sic]" (Engels, 1969 [1844]:39). In *The Communist Manifesto* (1976 [1848]), Marx and Engels argued that as the remnants of feudalism disintegrated, two great classes, capitalists and the proletariat, were coalescing. They were locked in a struggle which inevitably would result in the transformation of society.

This vision of the evolutionary laws of social development and the potential for workers to become a progressive revolutionary force was formed in the context of the Industrial Revolution and the beginnings of the modern labour movement. It was based on speculation about the long-term consequences of these changes rather than an analysis of a mature capitalist society. At the moment of its birth, the working class appeared to some as a force with great potential for progressive change. As indicated in the work of both Durkheim (1933) and Weber (1978, vol. 2:926-40, 973-75), Marx and Engels were, however, by no means alone in assuming that the trajectory of social evolution was away from "irrational" forms of identity based on ethnicity and race.

Marx and Engels at times expressed an overly simplistic and optimistic vision of the political potential of the working class. They were also complex thinkers and their analysis of capitalism changed over time. Their representation of the class structure of nineteenth-century Europe and of capitalist England are far more complex in works other than *The Communist Manifesto,* which, after all, was originally written as a political platform. Marx recognized the divisions between Irish and English workers. He also realized that the existence of slavery in the southern United States had a negative impact on the development of working-class culture and politics (Allen, 1994:29). On the other hand, at least some of the racialized thinking of the nineteenth century is evident in their work. *The Condition of the Working Class in England* is rife with racist characterizations of the Irish. Marx's comments on the "idiocy of rural life" and his anti-Semitism are well known. As was common in nineteenth-century thought, the evolutionist bent of Marx's and Engel's thinking assumed the inevitable and progressive nature of the destruction of pre-capitalist societies. Thus the founders of Marxism, if not completely blind to the power of race and ethnicity as sources of identity, failed to give it the attention it deserved in their own social and political analyses and never transcended the racialized forms of thought typical of the time.

Irrational and Authoritarian Workers

Whereas socialist and communist critics of the new order celebrated the revolutionary potential of workers, many others, from liberal reformers to conservative defenders of the status quo, were less enthralled with the "dangerous classes," as workers were sometimes called. Indeed, during the nineteenth century the discourse on the working class was itself highly racialized. In the words of E.P. Thompson, the industrial working population was "regarded with an alliterative hostility which betrays a response not far removed from that of the white racialist towards the coloured population today" (1968:207). Even Engels (1969 [1844]) employs the imagery of racial degeneration in his descriptions of the conditions of the English working class, a practice that was common to the social critics and reformers at the time (McClintock, 1995:21-133).

Ideas such as the Great Chain of Being, Social Darwinism and scientific racism were applied to the social structure of the societies of imperialist nations as well as to the colonized peoples (Bynum, 1975:3-8). Nineteenth-century racist theories represented class divisions as rooted in the innate biological characteristics of individuals. The European elite in essence were perceived as a superior race of humanity. In de Gobineau's (1967) theory of history, the rise and fall of civilizations is the result of the conquest of an inferior population by a superior warrior race which eventually inter-breeds with the subject population. This miscegenation lowers the racial fitness of the ruling elite, thus leading to the decline and fall of the civilization. The importance of purity of race, a central feature of racist philosophies, is here also a theory of the need for purity of class.

English workers may have been higher on the evolutionary scale than Africans, New World Natives or the Irish, but they were not the equals of the dominant classes in their own society. Middle-class immigrants to North America compared their impoverished compatriots crowded into ships' steerage for passage to the New World unfavourably against a romanticized image of the noble savage (Dunk, 1991:125-9). Indeed, into the twentieth century, anthropologists explored the backward areas of Britain in search of the "dark people" and examined the physical structure of inhabitants of London's working-class East End for evidence of their non-Teutonic racial origins (Parsons, 1921; Bradbooke and Parsons, 1922).

Social Darwinism justified all social inequality, not just racial or ethnic in-equality, in terms of the survival of the fittest. William Graham Sumner, the American Social Darwinist, proclaimed:

> The class distinctions simply result from the different degrees of success with which men have availed themselves of the chances that were presented to them. Instead of endeavouring to redistribute the acquisitions which have been made between the existing classes, our aim should be to *increase, multiply, and extend the chances....* Such expansion is no guarantee of equality. On the contrary, if there be liberty, some will profit by the chances eagerly and some will neglect them altogether. Therefore, the greater the chances the more unequal will be the fortune of these two sets of men. So it ought to be in all justice and right reason (1952 [1883]:144-45).

Similar reasoning, of course, explained the relationship between imperialist and colonized society. The discourses of class, race, ethnicity (and gender) fed upon and reinforced one another (McClintock, 1995).

The existence of the proletariat generated a good deal of anxiety about the future of society. For many nineteenth-century liberals and reformers, the impact of the spread of democracy on culture and civilization depended on the extent to which the cultural level of the working classes could be raised. John Stuart Mill argued in 1848 that prospects for the future depended upon the degree to which the labouring classes could "be made rational beings" (cited in Kuklick, 1991:107). His position on women's suffrage and the capacity of descendants of African slaves in Jamaica for self-rule was similar (Hall, 1992:255-95). In *Culture and Anarchy* (1948 [1869]), Arnold posed what he perceived to be the options facing a society in which the old aristocracy had become corrupt, the new middle class was obsessed with pursuing financial gain above all else, and the working class was demanding more power. The "working-class question" was largely about whether and how to change the moral and cultural life of the working classes so as to make them conform to behavioural patterns essential to a capitalist system (Corrigan and Sayer, 1985:114-65, Stedman Jones 1971:239-336). Education came to be seen as a key element in moulding individual and group behaviour.

Once racism came to be seen as a social problem—an idea that took hold on a widespread scale only in the wake of World War Two and the revelations of the Holocaust, the growth of national liberation movements throughout the colonized world and the civil rights and other social movements of the 1960s—it was not long before it came to be seen as a problem of the lower, less-educated sectors of society. In diametric opposition to the view that the experience of workers in capitalist society would give rise to a collective sense of class belonging and interests is the thesis that working-class experience is more likely to generate authoritarian and prejudiced individuals. As Lipset expressed it:

> Gradual realization that authoritarian predispositions and ethnic prejudice flow more naturally from the situation of the lower classes than from that of the middle and upper classes in modern industrial society has posed a tragic dilemma for those intellectuals of

the democratic left who once believed the proletariat necessarily to be a force for liberty, racial equality, and social progress (1959:482).

Lipset's central concern was working-class support for communism, a phenomenon which, in the cold-war political climate of the 1950s, he interpreted as a sign of the anti-democratic nature of workers rather than as class consciousness and a critique of capitalism.

The working class is more drawn to totalitarian political movements and is more prone to ethnic prejudice because the conditions of their existence generate authoritarian "attitudinal predispositions" (Lipset, 1959:485, note 7). The specific elements of this condition are "low education, low participation in political organizations or in voluntary organizations of any type, little reading, isolated occupations, economic insecurity, and authoritarian family patterns" (Lipset, 1959:489). These aspects of working-class life give rise to characteristics such as anti-intellectualism, a desire for immediate gratification and an inability to take a long-term view of situations. Taken together, they generate a lack of sophistication which leads to a desire for simplistic solutions to political issues. There is a tendency to view things in terms of black and white, good and evil, and solutions in chiliastic terms. "Consequently, other things being equal, they should be more likely than other strata to prefer extremist movements which suggest easy and quick solutions to social problems and have a rigid outlook rather than those which view the problem of reform or change in complex and gradualist terms and which support rational values of tolerance" (Lipset, 1959:483).

Lipset realized that this vision of the working class did not fit with the historical role of working-class political movements in struggles for democratic rights. He solved this seeming contradiction by arguing that a distinction should be made between the leadership and official aims of political movements and the actual thought of members. It is also necessary to recognize the historical context within which the labour movement developed. In its early days, there was a direct connection between the goal of improving the lives of workers and the extension of political rights and freedoms. In the 1950s, this relationship did not necessarily hold. Protection of the working-class position in society or improving the economic situation of its members did not necessarily correspond with the protection and enhancement of political rights and freedoms in general.

Lipset clearly argues that working-class authoritarianism and ethnic prejudice arise from workers' social and material conditions, rather than from the inherent characteristics of individuals, and thus his interpretation should not be confused with the racialized image of workers expressed by some nineteenth-century thinkers. None the less, the picture of the poorly educated, prejudiced and authoritarian worker resonates with earlier representations of workers as irrational beings who pose a threat to society and culture.

Analyses which posit that the working class is particularly prone to intolerance and prejudice can be faulted on several grounds. Working-class history includes examples of cross-ethnic and race alliances and cooperation, as well as conflict, hostility and exclusion. In addition, other interpretations of authoritarian ideology and personality locate the cause or causes of this personality structure in particular family forms or in other social classes. Wilhelm Reich's (1970) analysis of the mass psychology of fascism identifies petty bourgeois merchants and farmers as the social categories which provided the base of Hitler's support. Adorno and his colleagues argued that there is a correlation between an authoritarian personality, support for fascism, anti-Semitism and ethnocentrism, a position which Lipset apparently follows in his assumption that authoritarian predispositions and ethnic prejudice necessarily go together. Among the trends they identify "underlying anti-Semitic ideology" is a "rigid adherence to middle-class values" (Adorno et al., 1950:100) but overall the analysis treats the relationship between class, authoritarianism, ethnocentrism and anti-Semitism as rather weak (Adorno et al., 1950:137, 192-3, 638-9).

As I have argued, education has been seen as one important element in the solution of "working-class problems" since the mid-nineteenth century. It is not surprising, then, that Lipset identifies low education as one of the factors contributing to the authoritarian dispositions supposedly characteristic of workers. The debate over the connection between education and prejudice is far from over. There are, however, grounds for being sceptical about the strength and meaning of this relationship. Barrett's (1987:35-38) study of the racist right wing in Canada found that it is not composed of poorly educated, blue-collar workers. Ellis Cose's (1993) research among African Americans who are well-educated professionals shows that they feel their White peers and colleagues do discriminate against them in both unintentional and intentional ways. Other recent American research suggests that levels of ethnic and racial intolerance may be rising among the young, even though they are better educated than older segments of the population (D'Alessio and Stolzenberg, 1991). At one time, higher education was a means by which one could move into occupations, income groups and neighbourhoods which were relatively homogeneous in terms of their racial and ethnic composition. As minorities gain access to these formerly closed social worlds, the kind of antagonism once thought peculiar to the ethnically and racially heterogeneous working-class may become more common. This is certainly one way of interpreting the backlash against affirmative action and other initiatives which seek to enhance equality of opportunity and outcome. Jackman and Muha (1984) argue that, to the extent that sociological survey research shows a relationship between greater tolerance and acceptance of racial and ethnic others and levels of education, the results may simply reflect the fact that the better educated are more sophisticated and careful about how they represent and defend their interests than those with less formal education. They have learned that explicit expressions of racial or ethnic antipathy are not wise from a strategic point of view.[1]

Definitive conclusions as to the relationship between social class, education and levels of prejudice are difficult to reach also because key concepts such as class, status and strata are confused or not employed consistently. Marxian-influenced writers see class as a power relationship between groups with differential access to the means of production, while non-Marxists view class as a position in a status hierarchy defined on the basis of criteria such as occupation, income and education. Individuals who are defined as working class in one theoretical framework are frequently categorized as middle class in the other. Lipset uses the terms *working class*, *lower class* (or classes), and *the poor* as synonyms. This only serves to muddy the waters, since it is not clear just who is being discussed. The poor, for example, may consist of a variety of social classes, if social class is defined in terms of the relationship to the means of production. Shop owners, independent farmers, artisans, wage labourers, students, the permanently unemployed, even down-on-their-luck, one-time nobles may all be poor, but they do not necessarily have much more in common. One has to avoid becoming overly pedantic about definitional clarity; at the same time, it is important that the meaning of concepts such as the working class are not ambiguous.

Finally, it has been demonstrated that working-class attitudes about racial and ethnic issues are heavily influenced by specific contextual interests and identities. Canadian research on the relationship between class, ethnicity and attitudes towards Native rights and immigration in Canada indicates that workers are not consistently less tolerant of racial and ethnic "others" than other segments of the population. "Relative to other classes, substantial percentages of the working class favour greater protection of native rights, want newcomers to try harder to be more like other Canadians, doubt the impartiality of the police and the courts in their treatment of immigrants, and vehemently oppose more immigration" (Filson, 1983:473). In other words, working-class opinion on these issues is more tolerant and open than some classes in certain cases and less so in others. Statements to the effect that the working class is more prejudiced than other classes are not justified. Working-class attitudes regarding race and ethnic relations vary with the situation. Thus, the issue is not whether and why the working class is more prone to racism and ethnic prejudice than other classes but why in certain contexts racism and ethnic prejudice seem to override or exist in common with class consciousness. I turn now to a discussion of more recent theories of racial and ethnic prejudice and their relationship to the issue of working-class culture and consciousness.

---

[1]
By way of comparison see Balibar's (1992a) commentary on the rhetorical strategies involved in contemporary "neo-racism."

Contemporary Theories of Working-Class Racism

The Split Labour Market Hypothesis

One of the most influential explanations of working-class racism and ethnic prejudice is that it is the product of antagonisms generated by competition for paid labour when there is a split labour market (Bonacich, 1972). A split labour market develops when two or more groups of workers do, or potentially do, the same work for different wages. It is in the interests of higher-paid labour to either exclude cheaper labour from the market altogether or to restrict it to certain kinds of work, thereby monopolizing better-paid work for itself. The Oriental-exclusion movement in Canada is an example of the former, whereas occupational and union restrictions on Asian and Black labour are cases of the latter.

According to Bonacich, the price of labour is determined by the standard of living of the country or region of origin, the information about a given labour market available to workers and the political resources available to workers to help them organize. The motivations of workers also affects their wages. Workers may enter a labour market with short-term economic goals and therefore be willing to accept whatever wages are offered, since they do not have a long-term reliance upon this source of income.

Bonacich argues that, in split labour markets, conflict develops between three classes which she refers to as business, higher-paid labour and cheaper labour (1972:553). Business is interested in keeping labour costs as low as possible; higher-paid labour is interested in keeping income derived from wage labour as high as possible. She sees both the exclusion of cheaper labour and restrictions on its occupational options and mobility as victories for higher-paid labour.

Ethnic or racial differences do not always generate a price differential among labour. Nor do split labour markets only develop where there are ethnic or racial differences between workers (Bonacich, 1972:552). Gender, region and differential political and legal status (e.g., prison labour) may also give rise to split labour markets. Split labour markets may generate ethnic-like distinctions and antagonisms where no ethnic differences previously existed. Moreover, and against Marxist theories which analyze racism and ethnic prejudice as elements of a dominant ideology, Bonacich maintains that the capitalist class is interested in paying as little for labour as possible regardless of ethnic or racial origins of the workers. Capitalists have and will undercut workers of their own racial or ethnic group if they can.

There are, however, several problems with the split labour market hypothesis. Bonacich asserts that one of the benefits of the split labour market hypothesis is that it explains variations in race and ethnic relations among nations. Following Marvin Harris's (1964) comparison of Brazil and the United States, she contends that where there is no split labour market there is much less racial or ethnic antagonism, even though the business class may be of a different ethnic or racial group than the working class. In these settings, she suggests a form of paternalism will develop.

However, working-class racism may, at times, be a metaphorical or direct expression of class struggle between the working class and the bourgeoisie. For example, anti-Semitism in Europe in the period from 1870 to 1945 may be analysed as a complex articulation of class struggle, nationalism and racism. Insofar as for some elements of the population, Jews served as a metaphor for a cosmopolitan international capitalism, anti-Semitism might be interpreted as a metaphorical anti-capitalism (Balibar, 1992b:205-6). According to Adorno et al., to "the true proletarian, the Jew is primarily the bourgeois. The working-class man is likely to perceive the Jew, above all, as agent of the economic sphere of the middle-man, as the executor of capitalist tendencies. The Jew is he who 'presents the bill'" (1950:638). Middle-class anti-Semitism is different: "they accentuate just the opposite of what workingmen are likely to complain about, namely, that the Jews are not real bourgeois, that they do not really 'belong'" (*Ibid.*). This example should remind us that ethnic and racial antagonism does not develop only among workers. It may be an expression, however deluded, of struggles between bourgeois and proletariat; it may also develop between segments of other classes. In other words, split labour markets do not explain all forms of racial and ethnic antagonism.

Versions of the split labour market hypothesis have been employed to explain the anti-Oriental movement and restrictions on the occupational choices of Asian contract workers and immigrants in the Canadian west, and what was effectively a colour-bar against Blacks on Canadian Railways (Calliste, 1987; Li, 1988:26). There can be no doubt that working-class involvement in the Oriental exclusion movement and White unionist's exclusion of Black members was motivated in part by a desire to defend occupations and wages. But anti-Oriental feelings and actions were not limited to the working class (Ward, 1978:14) and in the case of the railways, both management and some White workers opposed the merger of Blacks and Whites into one common union and promotional structure (Calliste, 1987:4-5, 15). In other words, racism was not unique to workers. The split labour market hypothesis, even though it seeks causes in economic forces rather than in the supposedly unique biological or cultural characteristics of the working class, once again lays the blame for racial antagonisms at the feet of workers. This is not to suggest that racism and ethnic prejudice do not exist among workers. It is, rather, to suggest that the issue is more complex.

The economic logic of the split labour market hypothesis has also been questioned. Reich (1986) and Syzmanski (1976) have argued that White workers economically do not gain from racism. Their American-based research suggests that racial discrimination divides workers, hinders their ability to organize to protect their interests and leads to lower wages and poorer public services for everyone except those at the very top of the income scale. Capitalists may not be responsible for the existence of racism and ethnic prejudice, but it is they who benefit from it.

Another contentious issue relates to the explanation of differential labour costs. Bonacich explains them in terms of the economic, knowledge and political resources available to different groups of workers and the variations in their motivations. It appears that it is merely circumstance or chance that in some cases the differential resources and motivations correspond to ethnic or racial distinctions. The problem with this is that economic, knowledge and political resources are themselves partly the product of ideological resources. It is no historical accident, as Bonacich herself recognizes but dismisses in a footnote (552, note 5), that skin colour and poverty are related. The paucity of economic resources available to many groups is directly or indirectly a function of European imperialism. Imperialism is, of course, profoundly influenced by economic interests but by no means is it only a product of economic forces. Ideas about colonized peoples cannot easily be separated from the economic rationale for imperialist ventures. A similar argument can be made about political resources. A group's ability to organize itself and fight for its rights is at least partly a function of the ideological resources available to it. Groups who have to defend or promote their interests in a cultural context where ideas about their inherent inferiority, lack of morality, dangerousness, hygiene and so on are common face a problem that others do not. White workers on the west coast of Canada who were concerned about being undercut by cheap Asian labour may only have contributed to this problem by demanding restrictions on the rights of Asian immigrants. In the absence of widespread negative stereotypes about Asians, it may have been easier for White workers to develop a more sophisticated analysis of their own labour market problems, one that did not focus on the presence of relatively small numbers of Asian workers.

Historians writing about the United States seem to agree, despite the differences in their interpretations, that Irish, Italian, Polish and other European "ethnics" could claim that their "Whiteness" made them similar to other whites regardless of class in a way that African Americans or Asians never could (Allen, 1994; Fields, 1990; Roediger, 1994, 1991; Saxton 1990). The ideology of race was one of the political resources available to them. As noted previously, trade union activists in Canada certainly invoked the commonality of White people in opposition to the supposed Asian menace as a means of uniting workers.

It required a combination of resources for different groups to be able to define themselves and have others recognize them as White. The split labour market hypothesis, in and of itself, cannot explain why some ethnic groups have been able to overcome the perception of them as competitors, even as non-Whites, and eventually be accepted as part of the "mainstream," while other groups continue to be subject to racialized forms of thought and action. There certainly were moral panics about the threat posed to British culture and social values by immigration from southern and eastern Europe. These concerns were not specific to the working class and were about much more than labour market competition (Avery, 1979; Valverde, 1991:104-128; Woodsworth, 1909:216-250). However, no European ethnic groups were subjected to the level and intensity of hatred reserved for Asian immigrants even though, in terms of overall numbers, there were many more immigrants from European nations than there were from Asian ones. Also, the level of state control and the extent of prejudice directed at Native people cannot be accounted for by labour market competition since Native people rarely competed with other groups for employment. Communities that were once seriously divided along ethnic lines have been transformed, such that second- or third-generation Canadian workers no longer see themselves as primarily Ukrainian, Italian, English and so on but do see the world as divided into Whites and Indians. White racism against Natives in these communities is generated by a complex of factors in which labour market competition plays only a little role (Stymeist, 1975; Dunk, 1991:101-31; 1993).

Workers, Racism and Social Control

As discussed, Reich (1986) and Syzmanski (1976) argue that, in the United States, racial discrimination hurts white workers as well as African Americans. For them, racism functions as a form of social control that benefits the capitalist class. I am aware of no Canadian study that explicitly adopts this approach in a systematic analysis of racism and prejudice. This maybe because the race issue does not have the prominence in Canada that it does in the United States. It may also reflect the pervasiveness of the political economy tradition in Canadian social science, a tradition that is more readily aligned to the split labour market hypothesis than to analyses that focus on ideology rather than economic issues. Thus, my exposition of this perspective will draw upon a work of American political and labour history. However, in so far as the focus of this study is the construction of "Whiteness" as an identity, it may be relevant to all "White-settler" nations.

Theodore Allen's *The Invention of the White Race* attempts to explain the transformation of Irish identity by their immigration to the United States in the nineteenth century. Given their experience in Ireland, one might expect that Irish immigrants, overwhelmingly poor and entering the lowest segment of the working class in the New World, would have identified with the plight of African-American slaves. Moreover, within Ireland abolition was a high profile cause vigorously promoted by some of the most important and well-known Irish politicians of the time. What actually happened, however, is, according to Allen, that "subjects of a history of racial oppression as Irish Catholics are sea-changed into 'white Americans,' into opponents both of the abolition of slavery and of equal rights of African-Americans in general" (Allen, 1994:159).

This was accomplished primarily by the political and ideological manoeuvres of the pro-slavery lobby. The lobby had three elements according to Allen: (1) the plantation bourgeoisie with its obvious and direct interest in the maintenance of slavery; (2) fractions of the northern United States bourgeoisie that in addition to the general bourgeois-class interest in defending the right to private property against state intervention, had business relations with the plantation bourgeoisie; and (3) the link between the plantation bourgeoisie and the labouring-class European-Americans.

The plantation bourgeoisie appealed to northern workers in two ways. On the one hand, they argued that they treated their slaves better than employers treated their workers, a message with the intended corollary that workers should not worry about the situation of the slaves since they were better off than the workers themselves. On the other hand, they argued that the abolition of slavery in the south would mean northern workers would have to compete against the newly freed African Americans and this would lead to a decline in White workers' economic and social status (Allen, 1994:165). Apparently this strategy worked. Irish immigrants and Irish Americans strongly supported the anti-abolitionist cause especially in New York City, which was a centre of bourgeois support for the pro-slavery cause and had the largest Irish population in the United States.

Allen rejects the argument that Irish-American workers were pro-slavery because of labour market competition with African Americans. He argues that other foreign-born European Americans, not to mention native-born American workers, were far more numerous as labour market competitors for the Irish than were African Americans (Allen, 1994:194).

Irish immigrants were interpellated by the ideology of White racial supremacy because they immigrated into a country which was already structured on racial lines. Prior to the American Civil War the privileges accruing to Whites were the assumption that they were free people with the right to emigrate to the United States and to be granted American citizenship (non-Whites were not allowed to do so under the U.S. constitution), with the right to vote, and with access to the political spoils system developed under the presidency of Andrew Jackson that operated in part along the lines of race (Allen, 1994:195). In other words, labour market competition was not the cause of hostility towards African Americans by Irish-immigrant and Irish-American workers. In a situation where political rights are defined on the basis of race, an ideological appeal to Irish workers on racial rather than class lines worked because workers gained something by identifying with other "Whites" as "Whites" rather than with workers as workers. Thus, here racism can be analyzed as an ideological and political system of social control instituted by the dominant classes or groups in society which divided workers among themselves on the basis of racial identification.

Allen's argument is compelling with regard to the specific issue of the transformation of the identity of Irish immigrants and, indeed, for understanding the appeal of "Whiteness" as a subject position for the working class in nineteenth-century America when racial discrimination was an explicit feature of the American political-legal scene. Moreover, there is no doubt that in both Canada and the United States the call to unite around or defend certain interests in the name of "Whiteness" frequently has been more effective than similar calls based on class. The benefits of Whiteness extend beyond strictly political or legal rights and privileges. They have real efficacy on many aspects of social and cultural status. As I have already briefly mentioned and will discuss in more detail below, European "ethnics" in Canada have in many regions more or less taken on an identity as Whites in opposition to "visible minorities."

None the less, the United States' history of slavery is relatively unique and plays such a critical role in Allen's explanation that it is not clear whether his analysis can be extended to nations such as Canada, where slavery was of less economic and historical importance. Allen's argument also is not directly applicable in the post-1945 era when, with the important exception of the apartheid period in South Africa, there have been moves to eliminate explicitly discriminatory policies and practices from political institutions in most White or White-settler nations. There is no longer any formal political advantage to being White[2]—indeed the rhetoric of the backlash against so-called political correctness and affirmative action claims that Whiteness is now a disadvantage—and as the work of Reich and Syzmanski show, it is at least arguable that White workers do not gain economically from racial discrimination. In this context, problems which plague all versions of the "dominant ideology thesis" becomes evident. Why do workers, or any other subordinate groups, believe the ideology? Why do they develop a "false consciousness" while critics see through the ideology for what it really is? Are workers that easily duped by ideologies promoted by the dominant class? Ironically, this perspective, which has its origins in Marxist theories of ideology, unintentionally leads us back to those negative stereotypes about unintelligent, undereducated workers that have previously been discussed.

White Workers, Social Psychology and Racism

At one level it is logical to suggest that if working-class racism and prejudice is not the product of workers' particular social conditioning, competition over

---

[2] To say this is not to suggest there is no longer discrimination or racial or ethnic preferences in the workings of the politico-legal system especially in areas such as immigration laws and regulations. It is simply to point out that now political institutions and parties proclaim their non-discriminatory nature whereas in the nineteenth and early twentieth century they were explicit about their racially and ethnically discriminatory policies.

employment or racist ideology promoted by the dominant class, then more fundamental psychological processes are at work.

One kind of psychological argument posits that people have a deep, ultimately irrational, yearning for social homogeneity. Ethnically or racially pluralistic situations generate feelings of insecurity and breed fear of otherness. For example, Ward concludes his study of west coast anti-Orientalism with the following argument:

> Ultimately, several sources fed the anti-Oriental impulse in Canada's westernmost province. Among the more important were western images of Asia, continued migration from the Orient, recurrent economic rivalry, and intermittent conflicts of custom and value. But what fused these disparate influences into a single racist imperative was one vital determinant much larger than all the rest: that psychological tension that inhered in the racially plural condition. White British Columbians yearned for a racially homogeneous society. They feared that heterogeneity would destroy their capacity to perpetuate their values and traditions, their laws and institutions—indeed, all those elements of their culture embraced by the White Canada symbol.... Fundamentally, then, racism was grounded in the irrational fears and assumptions of whites who lived in the farthest west (Ward, 1978:169).

The problem with this kind of analysis is that it is unclear why people yearn for racial homogeneity, especially homogeneity based on the identity of Whiteness. Despite Ward's statement that the fear was based on the idea that heterogeneity would destroy White culture and tradition, one of the virtues of his book is that he shows these fears were groundless. And why a concern with homogeneity should be constructed along the lines of race rather than, say, of class remains an open question (see also Anderson, 1991:18-20). There are now several studies of Whiteness which collectively show that the "White race" is a relatively recent historical construct. Racial categorizations are not culturally and historically transcendental identities that people long to maintain. The argument that race and ethnicity are primordial sources of identity is itself ultimately irrational insofar as it invokes mysterious psychological forces that exist only through inference.

A variant of the social psychological explanation of racism that focuses specifically on White workers is Roediger's (1991, 1994) interpretation of racism among the American working class. Roediger views racism as a pervasive theme in American working-class history that cannot be ignored or explained away as an expression of class consciousness. The American working class evolved in a nation where Black slavery was a fact. The early concern to dissociate free wage labour from the economic, cultural, social and political connotations of slavery was a determining fact of working-class history. Workers also had to come to terms with the cultural transformation they were experiencing as they were exposed to the cultural logic of industrial work and time. Racism against African Americans was one of the ways European immigrants dealt with the disciplining that was part of their inurement to the industrial capitalist world.

What gives force, poignancy and pathos to the process of choosing whiteness was that it not only enabled the not-yet-white ethnics to live more easily with the white American population but to live more easily with themselves and with the vast changes industrial capitalist America required of them. I have argued this case in some detail in my book *Wages of Whiteness*, but other later-coming groups also came to grips with their own (forced) acceptance of time discipline, loss of contact with nature and regimented work by projecting "primitive" values onto "carefree" African Americans (Roediger, 1994:192).

Groups of immigrants who were largely absorbed into the working class, such as the Irish, were concerned with being identified as White, because however low they may actually have been on the economic hierarchy, such identity raised them above stigmatized African Americans. Roediger follows W.E.B. Dubois in arguing that the status of being White provided a psychological compensation—a wage—for their otherwise low socio-economic status.

Roediger's historical narrative is masterful, and the fact of White working-class racism is undeniable. Once again, however, insofar as the history of slavery is a crucial component of his analysis, it may not be directly relevant to Canada, although, as I discuss below, the importance for White workers of separating themselves from those further down the social hierarchy should not be underestimated. However, the invocation of the notion of a psychological wage as a central part of the explanation does not avoid the problems of circular logic that plague split labour market theories and ideology-as-social-control models. Undoubtedly, in certain contexts the opportunity to claim an identity as "White" provided psychological comfort and a political resource for workers. It is not clear why claiming identity as a worker could not fulfill the same functions. Sufficient numbers of workers have to have absorbed the notion that the value of human beings can and should be ordered in a hierarchical manner according to perceived physical and cultural differences for the wages-of-Whiteness hypothesis to work at any level of generality. Again, we are mired in a circular argument where the explanation of White, working-class racial and ethnic prejudice assumes what it seeks to explain, namely, that the working class frequently chooses racial and ethnic rather than class images of society when it seeks to understand its own experience.

Working Class Culture, Racism and Experience

Each of the perspectives discussed so far has certain merits but none can serve as a general theory of working-class racism and ethnic prejudice. Racial and ethnic prejudice and the actions that follow from them are complex phenomena that are highly variable. Racialized and prejudicial discourses gain their purchase from the way in which they articulate with other discourses and experiences in specific contexts. In this sense, we do indeed have to speak of racisms rather than racism (Hall, 1980:336-337).

Thus, we need to examine the way in which abstract historical forces of both a material and ideal kind produce contextually specific experiences that generate racist and prejudiced understandings and reactions. For example, Phizacklea and Miles (1979: Miles, 1989:81-82) interpret working-class racism in an English inner city as the result of a unique combination of historical experience and racialized ideology. The racism inherent in the English national culture provides a backdrop and source of racialized imagery for this racism but does not in and of itself explain it. Their study was conducted in an area experiencing de-indus-trialization, which generated high levels of unemployment and other associated problems, such as a lack of decent housing. This happened to coincide with immigration to the area from the "New Commonwealth" nations. Both the economic decline of the region and the immigration to the region are the product of the uneven development created by the underlying structures and processes of capitalism. These structures and processes give rise to immediate experiences but remain relatively invisible to many of those who experience their effects. In this context, the racialized imagery and stereotypes present in the national culture provide tools with which workers make sense of their daily experience. "The working-class racist beliefs in the Willesden area are therefore an attempt to understand and explain *immediate daily experience*, while the real reasons for both the socio-economic decline and New Commonwealth immigration are to be found in much more abstracted and long-standing social and economic processes which cannot be grasped in terms of daily experience" (Phizacklea and Miles, 1979:118, emphasis in original).

As I have discussed in earlier analyses of male, working-class racism against Native people, the combination of specific class and regional conflicts with the racist imagery that is part of Canadian culture creates a potent fuel for reactionary beliefs (Dunk, 1991:101-31; 1993).

Northwestern Ontario is a resource hinterland both for the metropolitan areas of southern Ontario and increasingly for a globalized economy. The regional economy is still based significantly on old resource-dependent industries such as mining, timber production and pulp and paper, although tourism and public and government services became increasingly important in the 1970s and 1980s. The indigenous population of Cree and Ojibwa hunters and gatherers was overtaken demographically starting in the late nineteenth century by European immigrants, significant numbers of whom came from Finland and eastern and southern Europe and occupied unskilled jobs in the resource industries. In the early part of the twentieth century, many communities in the region were dependent on a single natural-resource-related industry. A limited range of occupations was available, and the labour market and the local communities were strongly seg-mented along ethnic lines. Interaction with the indigenous population was rela-tively limited and largely confined to reciprocal interactions whereby the local inhabitants exchanged money or other goods for the products of the Native bush economy (furs, fish, wild game, berries and crafts).

In the post-War era, much of this changed. Ethnicity declined as a source of social division between Europeans. The Canadian-born children of "ethnics" became part of "White" society. Education and medical services were extended to the Native population. Increasing numbers of Native people visited or moved into the White communities to escape the poverty and other problems of the reserves and to access the services and other cultural amenities which the White communities offered. Communities which had been segmented along ethnic lines evolved into communities divided racially between "Indians" and "Whites" (Stymeist, 1975).

"White" workers now interact with increasing numbers of Native people but often in contexts where Native people are utilizing services they are entitled to by treaty and by their rights as citizens and which they need because of the consequences of racism and colonialism. A long history of negative stereotypes about Native people within Euro-Canadian culture provides a racist framework to explain the perceived "dependent" nature of contemporary Native people.

But there is more to White workers' racism towards Native people than a history of racist imagery and Natives' perceived welfare dependency. White workers' own culture is profoundly marked by a sense of alienation from the southern-based power bloc. Widespread images of southerners as soft, liberal, middle-class bureaucrats express the way class and regional differences reinforce each other. In the post-War era, Native people, who stand lowest on the socio-economic hierarchy, have come to be seen in local White culture as a privileged minority favoured by southern-based liberal bureaucrats and activists who do not understand the problems of the local White community. White workers and petty commodity producers with a strong "productivist" sentiment interpret welfare and other state expenditures as a transfer of their wealth to Native people. White workers perceive themselves as victims of government policies and economic cycles that do not get the same level of attention as First Nations'.

The national and global processes that generate the state policies and eco-nomic cycles which are experienced by workers in the resource hinterland in an immediate and concrete sense are themselves abstract and opaque, as is the history of oppression that has generated the now all-too-visible problems of the First Nations. Daily experience is, however, refracted through discourses, catego-ries and stereotypes that are available in the local White culture. Long-standing racist ideas are elided with class and regional grievances, and these generate a backlash against the group that by any socio-economic measure is the poorest in the region.

In northwestern Ontario, then, White workers' racism cannot be explained solely in terms of either labour market competition, the hegemony of a racist ideology promoted by a dominant class, a psychological longing for racial purity or even the notion of a psychological "wage" derived from identification with "Whites" in opposition to "Indians." Nor is it useful in this context to think of class and race as competing sources of identity. Class and regional experiences are part, albeit only part, of the explanation of racism against Native people. Opaque historical forces and economic and ideological structures generate a class and regionally specific daily experience which is handled utilizing the conceptual and other cognitive tools available in the everyday culture of the White workers. It is the combination of these factors which needs to be empha-sized, rather than an argument in favour of the force of either a dominant ideol-ogy, the dull compulsion of economic competition or the inherent psychological needs of workers.

Conclusion: The Dialectic of Class, Race and Ethnicity

In Canada, working-class formation was and is inextricably bound up with racial and ethnic inequalities. The foundational act of European settler societies was the separation of the indigenous population from its land. Waves of emigra-tion to North America from Europe, Africa and Asia took place under different conditions. Most of the immigrants from Europe arrived as free labour, although they may have been fleeing political or religious persecution and economic hard-ship at home. The vast majority of Africans were brought as slaves, while signifi-cant numbers of Asians came as bonded labour and were often constrained in North America by legal restrictions placed upon their movements and activities. Working-class formation in Canada and the United States took place in a setting where significant variation in the legal status of segments of the population added another dimension to the cultural heterogeneity.

To add to the complexity, the racial identities that we now take for granted, especially those that are frequently treated as binary oppositions, such as Black versus White or White versus Indian, are not static entities. The boundaries and meaning of a concept such as Whiteness, or the White working class, are fluid and constructed in and through struggles between classes and racialized or ethni-cally defined groups. They are also influenced by other fractures within the working class, such as skilled versus unskilled and respectable versus rough. Where exactly groups such as the Irish, French Canadians, southern Italians and eastern Europeans, groups who often filled the least-skilled, poorest-paid, and most physically demanding occupations, fit within the racial categories was, in the nineteenth and early twentieth centuries, something of an open question.

While social scientists may make careful analytic distinctions between the meanings of terms such as *class*, *race*, and *ethnicity*, in popular speech the language of social distinction and hierarchy often reflects the way in which class and race or ethnic consciousness is inextricably bound together. In the United

States, White workers' perception of who workers are often excludes African Americans and Hispanics even though these groups may have an equally long history as wage labourers and union members (Halle, 1984). Others have argued that an "assertion of middle class status" can sometimes be "a metaphor for race privilege" (Frankenberg, 1993:24.). Mike Davis (1993a,b) has shown how terms such as *inner city* and *the suburbs* carry class and racial meanings such that politicians' discussion, or lack of discussion, of inner city problems is in essence a commentary on class and race relations.

In Canada, the articulation of racial and ethnic imagery with other repre-sentations of social divisions is equally elaborate.[3] Terms such as *taxpayer*, *homeowner*, *the middle class*, *single mother*, *welfare recipient* and so on play upon deeply rooted racial, ethnic and class meanings. Moral and economic pan-ics about single mothers, welfare, crime and taxes work in part because, in the popular imagination, welfare recipients, single mothers, and criminals are "oth-ers." They are not like "us," yet they supposedly live off "our" taxes. These categories easily elide with racial and ethnic imagery. As was explicitly asserted in a racist anti-Native pamphlet produced in the 1970s in northern Ontario, "taxpayer" means "White" in at least some local discourses (Jacobson, 1974). In communities where the actual biological history of the population is mixed and few can objectively claim "pure" racial or ethnic heritage, terms such as Indian, Métis, and White in the local parlance are descriptions of locations in the local social hierarchy rather than accurate portrayals of cultural or biological origin. They become explanations of inequality after the fact (St. Onge, 1989).

Perspectives that juxtapose race and ethnicity to class as necessarily contra-dictory must recognize that the boundaries, meaning and content of racial, ethnic and class categories are deeply intertwined and evolving. Discussions of racism and ethnic prejudice in working-class culture and politics must begin with the recognition that class formation and racial and/or ethnic formation are concurrent processes which operate at times against each other and at times reciprocally. The working class was and is spoken of in racialized language, just as workers often represent the boundaries between themselves and others in racialized and/or ethnocentric terms. Racial categories are economic and political catego-ries as much as anything, while popular representations of class may reflect perceived racial and cultural divisions. Understanding working-class racism and ethnic prejudice requires transcending all reductionisms whether they are based on race, ethnicity or class.

3

   Anderson's (1991) study of Vancouver's Chinatown is the best recent Canadian analysis of the contextually specific nature of racialization and its relationship to numerous other social divisions and categories.

REFERENCES

Adorno, Theodore, E. Frenkel-Brunswick, D. J. Levinson and R.N. Sanford. 1950. *The Authoritarian Personality.* New York: Harper and Row.

Allen, Theodore W. 1994. *The Invention of the White Race, Volume One: Racial Oppression and Social Control.* New York: Verso.

Anderson, Kay J. 1991. *Vancouver's Chinatown: Racial Discourse in Canada, 1875-1980.* Montreal: McGill-Queen's University Press.

Arnold, Matthew. 1948. *Culture and Anarchy.* Cambridge: Cambridge University Press.

Avery, Donald. 1979. *Dangerous Foreigners.* Toronto: McClelland and Stewart.

Balibar, Etienne. 1992a. "Is there a neo-racism?" In Etienne Balibar and Immanuel Wallerstein. *Race, Nation, Class: Ambiguous Identities*, pp.17-28. London: Verso.

_____. 1992b. "Class racism." In Etienne Balibar and Immanuel Wallerstein. *Race, Nation, Class: Ambiguous Identities*, pp.217-27. London: Verso.

Barrett, Stanley R. 1987. *Is God a Racist? The Right Wing in Canada.* Toronto: University of Toronto Press.

Bonacich, Edna. 1972. "A Theory of ethnic antagonism: The split labor market." *American Sociological Review* (October) 37:547-59.

Bradbrooke, W. and F.G. Parsons. 1922. "The anthropology of the Chiltern Hills." *Journal of the Royal Anthropological Institute of Great Britain and Ireland* 52:113-26.

Bynum, William F. 1975. "The Great Chain of Being after forty years: An appraisal." *History of Science* 13:1-28.

Calliste, Agnes. 1987. "Sleeping-car porters in Canada: An ethnically submerged split labour market." *Canadian Ethnic Studies* 19(1):1-20.

Corrigan, Philip and Derek Sayer. 1985. *The Great Arch: English State Formation as Cultural Revolution.* Oxford: Basil Blackwell.

Cose, Ellis. 1993. *The Rage of a Privileged Class.* New York: Harper Collins.

D'Alessio, Stewart J. and Lisa Stolzenberg. 1991. "Anti-semitism in America: The dynamics of prejudice." *Sociological Inquiry* 61:359-66.

Davis, Mike. 1993a. "Who killed Los Angeles? Part Two: The verdict is given." *New Left Review* 199:29-54.

_____. 1993b. "Who killed LA? A political autopsy," *New Left Review* 197:3-298.

Dunk, Thomas. 1991. *It's a Working Man's Town: Male Working-Class Culture in Northwestern Ontario.* Montreal: McGill-Queen's University Press.

_____. 1993. "Racism, regionalism, and common sense in Northwestern Ontario." In Chris Southcott, ed. *Perspectives from a Provincial Hinterland: Social Inequality in Northwestern Ontario*, pp.103-119. Halifax: Fernwood Books.

Durkheim, Emile. 1933. *The Division of Labour in Society.* New York: Macmillan.

Engels, Frederick. 1969 [1844]. *The Condition of the Working Class in England.* London: Granada.

Fields, Barbara Jeanne. 1990. "Slavery, race and ideology in the United States of America." *New Left Review* 181:95-118.

Filson, Glen. 1983. "Class and ethnic differences in Canadians' attitudes to native people's rights and immigration." *The Canadian Review of Sociology and Anthropology* 20(4):454-82.

Frankenberg, Ruth. 1993. *White Women, Race Matters: The Social Construction of Whiteness.* Minneapolis: University of Minnesota Press.

Geertz, Clifford. 1975. *The Interpretation of Cultures.* New York: Basic Books.

Gobineau, Arthur comte de. 1967. *The Inequality of Human Races.* New York: H. Fertig.

Greese, Gillian. 1984. "Immigration policies and the creation of an ethnically segmented working class in British Columbia, 1880-1923." *Alternate Routes* 7:1-34.

Hall, Catherine. 1992. *White, Male and Middle Class: Explorations in Feminism and History.* New York: Routledge.

Hall, Stuart. 1980. "Race, articulation and societies structured in dominance." In *Sociological Theories: Race and Colonialism*, pp.305-45. Paris: UNESCO.

Halle, David. 1984. *America's Working Man: Work, Home, and Politics among Blue-Collar Property Owners.* Chicago: University of Chicago Press.

Harris, Marvin. 1964. *Patterns of Race in the Americas.* New York: Walker.

Jackman, M.R. and M.J. Muha. 1984. "Education and intergroup attitudes: Moral enlightenment, superficial democratic commitment, or ideological refinement?" *American Sociological Review* 49:741-769.

Jacobson, Eleanor. 1974. *Bended Elbow: Kenora Ontario Talks Back.* Kenora: Central Publications.

Kuklick, Henrika. 1991. *The Savage Within: The Social History of British Anthropology, 1885-1945.* Cambridge: Cambridge University Press.

Li, Peter. 1988. *The Chinese in Canada*. Toronto: Oxford University Press.

Lipset, Seymour Martin. 1959. "Democracy and working-class authoritarianism." *American Sociological Review* 24:482-501.

Marx, Karl. 1976. *Capital, Volume One*. London: Penguin.

_____ and Friederich Engels. 1976. *The Communist Manifesto*. Harmondsworth: Penguin.

McClintock, Anne. 1995. *Imperial Leather: Race, Gender and Sexuality in the Colonial Context*. New York: Routledge.

Miles, Robert. 1989. *Racism*. London and New York: Routledge.

Parsons, F.G. 1921. "On the long barrow race and its relationship to the modern inhabitants of London." *Journal of the Royal Anthropological Institute of Great Britain and Ireland* 51:55-81.

Phizacklea, Annie and Robert Miles. 1979. "Working-class racist beliefs in the inner city." In Robert Miles and Annie Phizacklea, eds. *Racism and Political Action in Britain*, pp.93-123. London: Routledge.

Reich, Michael. 1986. "The political-economic effects of racism." In Richard D. Edwards, Michael Reich and Thomas E. Weisskopf, eds. *The Capitalist System*, pp.305-11. Englewood Cliffs, New Jersey: Prentice-Hall.

Reich, Wilhelm. 1970. *The Mass Psychology of Fascism*. New York: Farrar, Strauss and Giroux, Inc.

Roediger, David. 1991. *The Wages of Whiteness: Race and the Making of the American Working Class*. New York: Verso.

_____. 1994. *Towards the Abolition of Whiteness: Essays on Race, Politics, and Working Class History*. New York: Verso.

St. Onge, Nicole. 1989. "Race, class and marginality in a Manitoba Interlake Settlement 1850-1950." In Jesse Vorst et al., eds. *Race, Class, Gender: Bonds and Barriers. Socialist Studies* 5:116-32. Toronto: Between the Lines.

Saxton, Alexander. 1990. *The Rise and Fall of the White Republic: Class Politics and Mass Culture in Nineteenth-Century America*. New York: Verso.

Stedman Jones, Gareth. 1971. *Outcast London: A Study in the Relationship Between Classes in Victorian Society*. Oxford: Clarendon Press.

Stymeist, David. 1975. *Ethnics and Indians: Social Relations in a Northwestern Ontario*. Toronto: Peter Martin Associates.

Sumner, William Graham. 1952 [1883]. *What Social Classes Owe to Each Other*. Caldwell, Ohio: Caxton.

Syzmanski, A. 1976. "Racial discrimination and white gains." *American Sociological Review* 41:403-414.

Thompson, Edward P. 1968. *The Making of the English Working Class*. Harmondsworth: Penguin.

Valverde, Mariana. 1991. *The Age of Light, Soap, and Water: Moral Reform in English Canada, 1885-1925*. Toronto: McClelland and Stewart.

Ward, W. Peter. 1978. *White Canada Forever: Popular Attitudes and Public Policy Towards Orientals in British Columbia.*. Montreal; McGill-Queen's University Press.

Weber, Max. 1978. *Economy and Society, Volumes 1 and 2*. Berkeley: University of California Press.

Wolpe, Harold. 1976. "The 'White working class' in South Africa." *Economy and Society* 5:197-240.

Woodsworth, James S. 1909. *Strangers within Our Gates or Coming Canadians*. Toronto: The Missionary Society of the Methodist Church.

10

Neither "Ethnic Heroes" nor "Racial Villains": Inter-Minority Group Racism

Edite Noivo

"I used to be called a wop, macaroni, a *voleur de job*.... I was treated as an inferior, too hot-blooded and stupid, and people made racist jokes.... Of course I felt discriminated against," Nino recalls of his immigrant life in Canada thirty years ago. Minutes later, he says of recent immigrants: "These people are no good for this country, they don't like to work hard, they exploit the government, abuse our social system ... and they'll never change because it's in their culture, that's how they are." In depicting how discriminated White immigrants racialize other immigrants, this account raises important questions about the relationship between immigrant status, class, ethnicity and racism in Canada. Specifically, how are we to understand why previously racialized immigrants in Canada hold racist ideas about, and engage in racial discrimination against, more recent newcomers? Even though there is a paucity of conceptual tools to apprehend it, and even though it is often expressed in "foreign" languages and tends to go undetected (and hence unstopped), given Canada's multiethnic composition we can ill afford to overlook the problem of "ethnic minority racism."[1]

While inter-minority group racism remains largely undiscussed publicly, and unanalyzed sociologically in Canada, it has been recognized as an important issue in the United States. Racist prejudices of northern Europeans directed towards southern European immigrants, and the tensions between Afro-Americans and Euro-Americans were documented by Ross (1938) and other members of the Chicago School of sociology in the 1930s. More recently American historians have begun to analyze how racialized Irish immigrants in the Unites States in the nineteenth century were socially, politically and ideologically transformed into "White" Americans, and how they in turn participated in the racism of the wider society that was directed at African Americans (Roediger, 1991). Further-

---

[1] By "ethnic racism" I simply mean that which is manifested by ethnic group members, in contrast to racism expressed by individuals belonging to the dominant group(s). Likewise, "minority-group racism" refers to that expressed by minority members, in this case, by White European immigrants.

more, the riots that erupted in Los Angeles in 1992 in the aftermath of the verdict in the Rodney King civil rights case demonstrated that racism is not simply a Black-White phenomenon. While sociological interpretations of the riot vary, it is clear that the violence that occurred in Los Angeles in 1992 also involved Black youth physically assaulting and damaging the property of Korean and Latino Americans. Korean Americans were seen by some Black youth as "exploiters" of their community, because they owned corner grocery stores in ghetto areas and purportedly charged premium prices for everyday commodities; Latinos were seen, in part, as competitors in an already crowded low-wage job market. These diverse articulations of ethnic racism and discrimination need to be understood as reflecting the specific cultural background and structural position of minority groups and the material realities of inter-ethnic minority tensions specific to each historical and political context.

This chapter deals, then, with the issue of ethnic minority racism. At this point, since I have collected a rather limited amount of data, I consider my research to still be somewhat exploratory.[2] However, my criticisms of existing conceptual and theoretical positions are nonetheless informed by empirical materials whose analysis will inform this work. As such, this chapter focuses on the racialized attitudes and reactions of some "established" immigrants towards newcomers to Canada. It presents empirical material that challenges some of the underlying premises of the so-called "new racism" approach (which is also known as cultural racism), and attempts to resuscitate the analysis of the intricate relationship between immigration, racism and ethnic minority group status. Unlike most studies, which depict the mechanisms of "ethnicization, racialization and minoritization" as processes which minorities undergo at the hands of dominant groups, and not as schemes which those minorities also construct, negotiate and re-define in light of their own experiences, this chapter examines the contexts within which minority groups ethnicize and racialize each other and its meaning. Inter-ethnic minority racism is understood here in light of the view that racism takes on different forms and meanings depending on the historical context and lived experiences of those who articulate it (Satzewich, 1989). Therefore, I do not conceive of "White" immigrant racism as autonomous from local, national or internationally articulated racist ideologies and practices. I suggest that maintaining the racism of "invisible" minorities as invisible in the scientific literature and in the public arena is in itself a form of exclusion. In other words, the conceptual misrepresentation of cultural minorities as merely emulating the

---

2

Data were collected for my study on "Minority Group Racism" with the help of *Fonds CAFIR*, of the *Université de Montréal*, to whom I am grateful. I am also thankful to Tassos Moussas and Kathy D'Ovidio for the assistance with the interviews, to Christopher McAll and the reviewers for their useful comments, and in particular to Vic Satzewich for his interest and helpful suggestions. Of course, I alone am responsible for this paper.

racist beliefs and practices of the dominant group may in itself contain certain prejudices and patronizing assumptions.

Conceptual and Theoretical Issues

Over the years, the theoretical explanations of how and why immigrants are racialized by dominant groups have tended to be based on the assumption that there is a binary opposition between racists and those who are racialized. But one of the confounding paradoxes of minority group racism is that minority members voice their resentment over having been discriminated against and their own racist opinions about other immigrant groups almost simultaneously. In one moment, White European ethnics (henceforth Euroethnics) attribute their inferior social and ethno-cultural position to their immigrant status and express strong indignation at being racialized, and in another, they fragment the socially constructed categories of immigrant and ethnic into "benign" and "malign" (Steinberg, 1989). To assess such striking contradictions, and to deconstruct minority group racism, I draw on some key sociological concepts and approaches to the study of race and ethnic relations.

My approach to the analysis of inter-ethnic antagonism has been formed in the context of a critical engagement with the work of Stanley Lieberson (1980; Lieberson and Waters, 1988), debates about the definition of the terms *ethnicity*, *race* and *minority groups*, and recent theoretical approaches to the analysis of racism. In his theoretical and empirical studies of ethnic and racial groups in the United States, Lieberson (1980) addresses the impact of ethnic identification and group consciousness on social mobility and integration. In *A Piece of the Pie*, Lieberson argues that the biggest divide in American society is racial. While he recognizes that ethnicity was one basis of stratification of American society in the past, he stresses that ethnicity has not permanently prevented Whites from entering into mainstream American society or politics the way that racism has kept non-Whites in ghettos. His study shows that while White immigrant workers and American-born Blacks have historically competed for similar jobs and scarce resources, White minorities were exploited but still employed, whereas non-Whites were simply left out of the economy.

More recently, Lieberson and Waters (1988:264) have suggested that despite intra-White ethnic marriages in the United States, there are significant differences in inter-marriage rates between northern and southern European ethnic groups and African, Asian and Latino Americans. The divide, they say, is no longer between hyphenated and unhyphenated individuals; it is between the evolving racialized categories of Whites and non-Whites. In other words, the specification of one's European ancestry and heritage is being augmented by racial identities and identifiers, and group boundaries are beginning to be solidified around "race" and notions of common skin colour. In the United States, most southern European immigrants have come together around the perception of a shared "Whiteness." The important point about Lieberson and Waters' work for the Canadian context, which I discuss more fully later on, is that the shifting composition of Canadian immigration flows has an impact on the ethnic and racial identification of longer settled southern European immigrants. More than just developing a strong "Old World" ethnic identity or a consciousness of their being hyphenated Canadians, most also develop a reverence for their Whiteness, increasingly demarcate themselves from the category of immigrant and insist on differentiating between themselves and new immigrant ethnic groups in racial terms. In our expanding multiracial context, so-called Euroethnics are increasingly aware of how colour brings them closer to dominant members, and therefore may thus use their purported common colour to reinforce social and political identities and alliances with them.

The work of Lieberson and Waters (1988) is also valuable insofar as it points to a fundamental problem with the conceptualization of race and ethnic relations by reference to the terms *minority* and *majority group*. There are some possible grounds for trying to dissolve the distinction between race and ethnicity under the more general term minority group. In Canada, as in the United States, ethnic and racial groups admittedly often share basic structural positions and existential conditions. Their experiences are also both profoundly contextual and deeply interactive in that their formation and persistence are "intertwined with political and economic institutions, events and processes" (Ragin and Hein, 1993:255). Ethnicity and "race" are indeed both quasi-groups in the sense that members share feelings of belonging to a real or mythical common homeland and history. Since they usually also share similar material conditions and experiences, they tend to organize in order to attain certain common goals (Rex, 1986).

While some analysts seek to dissolve the basic distinction between ethnicity and "race" under the umbrella of minority group, some caution about their conflation is warranted.[3] The term minority group presents a much too static and simplistic picture of the nature of identity and inequality in capitalist societies. Ethnic and racial identities are not fixed and unchanging. Groups who at one time have been racialized and minoritized have been incorporated into the dominant group, or have been able to insert themselves as intermediaries between dominant and subordinate groups. Minority groups are not homogenous, and so lumping all socially marginalized groups into a singular conceptual category blurs important differences in people's experiences and social positions. For example, as ethnicity becomes "symbolic" (Gans, 1979) or "costless" (Waters, 1990), groups like Italians in the United States and Canada are able to enter into

---

3

I realize that there are as many problems with separating them as with taking them as equivalents. On this issue, see Rex, 1980. My own position is that undertaking one or the other depends on the issues, circumstances and contexts under study.

mainstream society (Alba, 1994). As such, ethnic groups are said to have cultures and behaviour patterns that are susceptible to change. Regardless of whether or not ethnic and racial minorities are also immigrants, racial groups are sometimes also seen as having an ethnicity. Nonetheless, ethnicity for racial groups tends to be downplayed, and so they are generally conceived as having immutable physical characteristics that are not subject to change. Unlike ethnic groups, then, racial groups are seen in popular consciousness to have a permanence that tends to extend beyond generations and changing social circumstances. In short, outstanding differences in socio-economic status, levels of discrimination and perceptions of group permanence proscribe lumping together highly distinct groups as minorities. Taken together these issues point to problems with the tendency to juxtapose ethnic and racial relations in terms of minority-majority group relations.

While Lieberson (1980) and Lieberson and Waters (1988) point to important changes in how European immigrants define their identity, and in patterns of ethnic and racial relations in the United States, they do not provide an adequate theoretical basis upon which to understand minority group racism. The third set of literature that informs this chapter, then, is that which focuses on the contemporary meaning of racism. Traditionally, racism has tended to be conceived solely in terms of dominant and subordinate group relations. This has in turn led to the view that racism is largely a White versus Black phenomenon, and that racism always involves unidirectional relationships of power and dominance.

This view is both historically and conceptually limited. Given that "race" is often constructed on the basis of a combination of presumed distinct and salient cultural traits and not only on physiognomic features (Banton, 1987), racism has at times also been directed at "White" immigrant workers (Miles, 1993) and others who are perceived not so much as biologically but rather culturally distinct and inferior (Anthias, 1990).

One of the terms that has been developed to try to capture this aspect of racism is the concept of *new racism*. In naming the so-called new racism and explaining it as "differentialist" or "culturalist," Taguieff (1987) and Balibar and Wallerstein (1988) point out that racism tends to be directed mostly at immigrants and their descendants, regardless of the colour of their skin. This, they describe, is largely because immigrants are generally perceived as holding identities and engaging in practices that are undesirable or incompatible with the dominant culture. According to theorists of the new racism perspective, racism now tends to entail the negative evaluation of cultural difference, and not necessarily the expression of ideas about the supposed biological inferiority and superiority of groups of people (Barker, 1981). Endorsing this perspective, Miles (1993:11) and others link new modalities of racism to immigration by claiming that it inserts "into the nation state a population that potentially may be defined as unacceptable."[4]

The contention that the new racism currently refers to anti-immigrant sentiments (Balibar, 1988; Miles, 1993; van Dijk, 1993) that aim to prevent and exclude individuals from entering state boundaries is theoretically sound. It is the case that core societies such as ours import workers from around the world whose cultures in turn may be regarded as inferior and as "colliding" with, or threatening, national traditions and practices. It also captures the historical racialization of so-called "White ethnics," such as Italian and Greek immigrants in Canada and the United States (Harney, 1993:29-74; Constantinides, 1983). But while the new racism approach emphasizes the continuity in the expressions of racism, and recognizes that White ethnic groups have historically been racialized and continue to be victimized by racism, it must also be recognized that White ethnics suffer significantly lower levels of discrimination than racially defined groups (Lieberson, 1980; Henry and Ginsberg, 1984). In North America, as elsewhere, the racialization of Euroethnics has been selective, transient and situational. Williams (1988) reminds us that the racialization of immigrants in core contexts changes with external factors. For example, Canadian perceptions of Italians altered when Italy became a relatively affluent society. Furthermore, the most victimized White ethnic minorities are immigrants and their first-generation descendants. Subsequent generations generally experience much less institutional or systemic racism (Harney, 1993).

Most importantly, however, few of these theorists of new racism recognize the racialization and ethnic discrimination articulated and practiced by White immigrants and ethnic minorities towards their "non-White" counterparts. In fact, this silence on racism among immigrants and ethnic groups appears to run through even the most innovate analyses of what Ali Rattansi (1994) calls "Western racisms, ethnicities and identities." Such an omission results from the tendency of the various theoretical paradigms to explain identity formation, group boundaries and the politics of exclusion strictly through such binary oppositions as minority-majority, or racists-racialized.

My critical review of Lieberson's work,[5] the definition of minority groups and literature on the new racism has led me to re-think identity formation and the formation of group boundaries in capitalist societies. More specifically, I question why certain pan-immigrant identities remain weak or non-existent, and why,

---

[4]
  But Miles (1994) still prefers "differentialist" to "new racism," mostly because, as he says, such racism has been preceded by the "old" type and thus both forms should be incorporated into one paradigm.

[5]
  The American and Canadian contexts being so different, not all of Lieberson's claims apply to Canada. Here, old and new working class immigrant groups generally meet in the labour market, and compete for scarce jobs in the unskilled and semi-skilled sectors. There is also a clear danger of extrapolating labour market relations to other areas of social life. Individuals are known to develop racist beliefs in one area and not in another. Or, as Wellman (1977) notes, many Whites do not oppose anti-discrimination measures at work but nevertheless want to keep their neighbourhoods "White."

historically, strong ethnic solidarities have included some "distinct" ethnicities and excluded others. I recognize that ethnic boundaries may shift and expand so as to accommodate an ethnic membership composed of distinct classes, regional cultures and political ideologies (Hannerz, 1974). Thus, I reasonably envisage that if immigrant and/or ethnic groups managed to forge a collective minority identity, or developed what Maffesoli (1996) calls a sense of "community of destiny" based on shared social and cultural locations, their "consciousness of kind" (Rex, 1986) would annul any pre-existing racist imagination. I base my assumption on the thesis that "consciousness of kind" does not stem only from subjective feelings of common ancestry, but is also a product of immigrant and/or ethnic experiences including a shared subordinate status (see also Ragin and Hein, 1993). But the problem, as this chapter seeks to demonstrate, is that existing racism prevents White and non-White immigrant minorities from coming together and developing that type of consciousness.

The idea that some immigrants develop a consciousness or identity as "immigrants" and others as "ethnics" is proposed by Hein (1991, 1994). Based on his work, one could say that the more recent, largely racialized immigrant groups tend to interpret their unfavourable immigrant conditions as stemming from racial discrimination and structural inequality. Most will likely develop a minority identity and ethnic consciousness. In contrast, established southern European groups have generally attributed their hardship and unequal standing to their immigrant status, and consequently develop instead an immigrant identity. Unlike those who link their problems to ethnic stratification and group closure, and therefore protest against discrimination, European immigrants are more likely to explain their social conditions as ensuing from their foreign status. Many see that their descendants, by acquiring linguistic skills and sufficient education, will move up the social ladder and integrate socially and economically into Canadian society. These immigrant groups also develop an ethnic identity, but it is largely based on language and other cultural differences, which, in their minds, accounts for their social underprivilege. Non-White immigrant groups on the other hand, perceive that they confront greater discrimination and so they are more susceptible to developing a racialized consciousness or engaging in anti-racist struggles. In such cases, European immigrants may even want to disassociate themselves from new immigrants' reactions, which further undermines intra-group unity and cooperation.

But identity formation and consciousness are never constructed in isolation. Nor are the relationships among racialized immigrants exempt from external influences. For example, Euroethnics' misconceptions about new immigrants abusing the welfare system or the presumed higher propensity of newcomers to engage in criminal behaviour are largely built on media representations of such populations. Underclasses also contribute to the fragmentation of "race" and ethnicity through their own racist convictions. Since racist beliefs permeate the class structures of many different societies, foreign-born White ethnic groups need not be seen as simply appropriating the racism of the elites of dominant groups in their new society. It is human subjects who migrate, and pre-existing racist ideas and ideologies may also be part of the cultural baggage that tags along with these migrating subjects. As such, certain White European immigrant workers may actually be racist before becoming immigrants and ethnic minorities in a new country. By interpreting the poor treatment they suffered from dominant members as due to their immigrant status and cultural differences, European immigrants are less likely to allow their own experiences to challenge their racist ideas.

In the remainder of this chapter, these theoretical and conceptual concerns are addressed by reference to the analysis of the historical racialization of southern European immigrants in post-Second World War Canada, and their present racialization of recent Third World immigrants to this country. My research focuses specifically on two groups of southern European immigrants in Quebec. It remains to be seen whether the results of my research may be generalized to include other previously racialized groups in the rest of Canada.

Historical Racialization of Greek and Italian Immigrants

With 174,530 Quebec residents reporting an Italian ethnicity and 49,890 defining themselves as Greeks in the 1991 census, these groups are two of the largest ethnic groups in the province. Because most arrived in Canada between 1951 and 1971, they can now be considered to be "established" immigrants. Considering their relatively low educational levels, their initial concentration in manual labour occupations and their possession of limited economic resources upon arrival in Canada, Italian and Greek Canadians are now described as two of Canada's immigrant success stories. An overall improvement in the material conditions of these immigrants may, however, blind us to past, and some current prejudice and discrimination faced by them.

The opposition of majority group Canadians to the arrival of southern and eastern European immigration is now well documented (Porter, 1965; Li, 1990). According to historians, "with each new wave of immigration, Canadians have reacted with anxiety or alarm; they have denounced the indiscriminate mixing of diverse peoples and the changing racial make-up of the country" (Iacovetta, 1992:104). Historians also argue that while the victims of scorn and concern change over time, new immigrants, regardless of their ethnic origin, tend to "take up the undesirable jobs and live in unfashionable districts previously occupied by earlier immigrants" (Iacovetta, 1992).

Some theorize this by suggesting that historically Canada had an ethnic and racial preference ladder, and argue that immigrants have been accepted in Canada in an descending order of value in which British, northern European and

White American and Australian immigrants are at the top, southern and eastern European immigrants in the middle, and so-called non-White immigrants at the bottom. Others contend that because majority groups (charter groups) control the political and economic structures of our society, they easily appropriate the most desirable jobs and leave the less-preferred ones to other ethnic groups. John Porter (1965) argued that the latter possessed an "entrance status," and described how it is embedded in the conviction that certain groups, in light of their perceived ethno-cultural and racial traits, are better suited for some tasks than others. As identified by the author of *The Vertical Mosaic*, in the aftermath of the Second World War, southern Europeans who came to Canada entered a society that was already highly stratified along the lines of class, ethnicity (and gender). Consequently, they faced certain barriers to occupational mobility, and experienced occupational segregation and discrimination upon arrival in Canada.

As Porter (1965), Harney (1993), Constantinides (1983) and others have documented, Italians and Greeks, much like other southern and eastern European groups entering Canada at that time, were assigned to the least desirable jobs in logging, construction, manufacturing and service occupations. As Harney (1993:54-55) remarked of Canadians at the time, many "condemned the importation of Italian labour on ethnic grounds but condoned it as an economic necessity." Harney goes on to describe how many Canadians in the 1950s and 1960s believed that there was "work for 'White' labour and work which required 'Black' labour. Italians, Macedonians, Greeks and Asians who did 'Black labour'—that is, work so dangerous, dirty, underpaid, unregulated [and] noxious that no northwest European immigrant or old stock Canadians would take it ... were seen as confirming their racial inferiority and low standards."[6]

Empirical studies documenting the discrimination endured by Italian and other southern European Canadians during that period describe the humiliation and insults they suffered at the hands of many longer-settled Canadians.[7] In many cases these immigrants were perceived as "disrupting the labour market and disturbing the economy." They were also accused of helping to "depress wages, lower workplace standards, and inflate the unemployment rolls" (Iacovetta, 1992:109). Southern Italians were particularly victimized in that they were regarded as "stocky and dark-skinned," thought to be too emotional and were believed to lack the inner discipline that was necessary to succeed in, and fit into, Canadian society. According to Harney, Iacovetta and Constantinides, Italian and Greek immigrants are quite conscious of having been racialized as new immi-

---

6

A further indication of their racialization by Anglo Canadians is contained in a newspaper headline which described a riot involving strikers in the following terms: "Black Italians implicated in rioting" (Harney, 1993:64).

7

Note that there is comparatively less historical analysis and sociological material on the racialization of Greek-Canadians.

grants, and many still feel that they are the objects of racism and ethnic prejudice.

Three decades after arriving, both groups remain overrepresented in the manual and lower non-manual occupations. However, an increasing number are becoming self-employed, and some are also becoming property owners and landlords. Their children and grandchildren have also begun to experience significant levels of upward mobility by entering into managerial jobs and the professions. Nonetheless, as those whom I interviewed sought to emphasize, "we arrived here with nothing, and so we worked twice as hard for half the pay of Canadians. We really slaved and saved all our money in order to buy the houses we now own. They're grounded on sacrifices." In fact, Jansen (1987:26) and others have remarked that Italians are *de facto* more likely to own than rent their homes, and that their home ownership rate is 16 percent higher than that of the Canadian population. This apparently applies to Greeks as well, since in Montreal, European immigrants are more likely to own their own homes (46%) than the Canadian-born population (23%).[8]

In light of widespread essentialist interpretations of patterns of home ownership, which tend to see it as a reflection of certain cultural values of southern Europeans, including the culturalist explanations given by the immigrants themselves, I found the respondent's comments on the link between ethnicity and rental ownership enlightening. "This building is more than a pile of bricks and wood," I heard from an unskilled Italian-Canadian restaurant worker, who currently rents out ten apartments. "It is the reward of my hard labour, and the evidence that I've managed to do something with my life," he adds proudly. The relationship between owning property and the immigrant condition was also illustrated by a Greek factory worker and duplex owner in these terms: "Owning property in a foreign country is very important ... the sense of power that gives.... I guess one becomes more Canadian." In short, southern European immigrants have struggled to establish roots in their new context in ways that give them meaning, psycho-social gratification and economic security. Having been racialized and remaining as potential victims of discrimination and prejudice, most have managed to secure average and in some cases above-average working-class living standards.

In the remainder of this chapter, I examine how their material conditions, their interpretation of their treatment by majority group Canadians during their early years in Canada and their pre-existing prejudices help to shape their current reactions to newly arriving non-White immigrants. This aspect of the chapter is based on my original research on Minority Group Racism in Housing conducted in Montreal in 1995. Using a snowball sampling technique, I interviewed Greek

---

8

    In *"Le logement et les communaute culturelles"* prepared by the *Conseil des Communautés culturelles et de l'Immigration*, Government of Quebec (1991:6).

and Italian landlords who have lived in Montreal for twenty-five years or more. All males, aged between forty-one and sixty-three, most worked in Canada in skilled and unskilled manual labour employment. When we met, a few had retired and a few had become self-employed. Their level of formal education ranges from four to six years of schooling, and their proficiency in the official languages varies considerably. Some must rely on family members to communicate with tenants, while others function in "broken" English or French or both. Landlords were selected across eight neighbourhoods within the island of Montreal. The type and size of their rental property varies substantially. Nearly half of the landlords I interviewed reside within the building that they rent out. All participants have, or have had, recent immigrants as tenants.

Contemporary Manifestations of Ethnic Racism

> European immigrants came here to work hard and helped build this nation. Look around, we added style, we built houses, we enriched the Canadian cuisine.... We are proud, respectful people and we adapted well. Now these Blacks, Latinos, Indo-Pakistanis and others like them, those people are unskilled, and right upon arrival they all want rights. Those people don't like to work, some steal, others defraud the government.... In their countries this was normal, so they're used to living that way. Though the Blacks are the worst, those others groups are also quite dirty and their food smells awful. I enter their houses, I know them well.

Such virulent racist remarks are disturbing insofar as they reflect a constellation of beliefs, stereotypes and attitudes that negatively evaluate the presence in Montreal of certain recent immigrant groups. But perhaps even more troubling is that the misconceptions, contempt, ethnocentrism and deeply ingrained racial stereotypes lead many Italians, Greeks and others to avoid social contact with these new immigrants. Moreover, as landlords, they admit to refusing housing to non-Whites and to treating them in discriminatory fashion. Like those Canadians who once opposed the immigration of southern Europeans, both groups are unabashedly critical of the Canadian state for "letting those people in." Their poignant Eurocentric and xenophobic attitudes lead them to repeatedly state that "whereas Europeans built this country, new immigrants from Haiti, Bangladesh, El Salvador, Pakistan, have nothing to offer Canada." Insisting that "new immigrants are lazy, drain the social welfare, do not adapt to North America and resort to crime and live off the government," the people I interviewed maintain that Blacks and Asians are invading the country and destroying their city and neighbourhoods. In this section I want to explore these inter-related themes more fully.

Ethnocentrism certainly seems to be common among Greek and Italian immigrants in many communities in North America. According to Harney (1988:3-4), Italian Americans claim that "there is no nationality that produced more great people than the Italians. The Italians have contributed more to civilization than many other people." Harney and others explain such pretences as "a defense against the helplessness in which Italians find themselves." Italian's aggressive ethnocentric assertions are thus accounted for in terms of the discomfort they feel about their historical location in North America and in terms of a defense mechanism stemming from their presumed ethnic inferiority complex. While Harney's explanation may be compelling, it does not ring true in my own research findings, which show no evidence of this presumed inferiority complex. In describing their humiliation whenever an employer tore apart their job application form in front of their face or when other workers called them *"voleurs de job"* (which is roughly translated as "job thieves"), they disclose both their past experiences and their present interpretations of discrimination. Their general opinion seems to be that

> we were *"maudits Italiens"* because we were hard workers. Although we didn't know how to speak well, we made more money than them [majority members] and soon started buying houses and driving nice cars. They were extremely jealous of our success.... And then, when employers praised immigrants, the others got jealous and this led to conflicts ... and some also picked on Italians and Greeks for speaking English instead of French.

The ease with which these immigrants reduce racism to jealousy of the dominant groups and to their own superior competitive abilities in the economic sphere is noticeable. In the United States, Vecoli (1988) identified similar perceptions among Italians who interpret their past discrimination to their hard work, and the resentment of dominant group members who recognized their keen ability to compete for work and rewards.

To pursue our White Euroethnic's portrayals of non-White minorities as fraudulent, exploitative and lazy, it is clear that their racist prejudices are not articulated in very subtle ways. Indeed, they are expressed in quite flagrant and blatant terms. Most were particularly infuriated over what they saw as new immigrants raising unemployment rates, causing violence and contributing to increasing crime. Clearly, in the analysis of their perceptions of new immigrants, there is no need to make a distinction between the so-called new racism and the old, biologically determinist forms of racism that are said to have all but disappeared from the post-War social landscape. There is a sense in which the racialized "others" are defined as both biologically and culturally inferior to both themselves and other Euro-Canadians.

In their demeaning views of other ethno-cultures, these Euroethnic minorities also demonstrate culturally specific styles of scapegoating. Regarding cultural forms of racism as equivalent to anti-immigrant sentiments (which is supposedly based on the fear that new ethno-cultural groups might threaten their own national culture) does not explain why these immigrants express racist ideas not only against racialized immigrants, but also towards the contexts from which they originate. I frequently heard Italians, Greeks and other southern Europeans in my interviews argue that, whereas they had already worked hard in their own country before emigrating to Canada, recent immigrants originate from countries with a slower pace of living and working, "where," they say, "corruption, law breaking, crime and violence" are the norm. Furthermore, none of my respondents voiced any opposition to the current immigration of central and eastern Europeans who have recently arrived in Canada. This suggests that the immigrant racism under study here needs to be understood, in part, as a wider form of European racism. It is an ideological residue of colonialism and racial and cultural supremacy that is re-constructed, re-contextualized and re-defined in North America in the context of their social contact and personal experience with recent non-White immigrants.

The fact that White immigrants articulate their racist prejudices more fiercely by constantly comparing what they perceive to be the experiences of recent immigrants with their own experiences and current circumstances also requires more comment. In general, comparisons stop short of recognizing that newcomers now face the same kinds of structural social and economic barriers that they met up with over thirty years ago after first arriving in this county. Nor do they take into account the remarkable differences in migration patterns or the family and community support which they enjoyed.[9] Instead, they emphatically see themselves, as historian Franca Iacovetta (1992) puts it, as "such hardworking people," while insisting that "new immigrants have no pride and no morals [and] skillfully exploit the welfare system." Such contentions have been explained by Wellman (1977) who argues that the belief that "if I can make it, anyone can" allows individuals to blame the victim and thereby discount structural causes of racism. Moreover, those convictions are also self-enhancing in that they make established immigrants feel good about their own economic achievements.

These immigrants' tentative comparisons of their ethno-cultural traits and early experiences in Canada with those of racialized "new" cultural minorities often stirs up an array of racist sentiments. In their eagerness to defend the idea that "old" and "new" immigrants are radically different kinds of human beings, respondents tended to complement their criticisms of newcomers with episodes from their daily lives. In explaining his decision to move from the multiethnic neighbourhood in Montreal in which he lived for over thirty years, a Greek factory worker reported the following:

> Waiting in line at the bank, in front of me, was this Indian guy dressed in his native clothes, barefoot, and smelling as they all do. Now, thirty years ago, one never saw a Greek man walking in the streets in traditional costumes. These people have no respect for others, no sense of decency. They've destroyed the neighbourhood.... White families, the working people like us, they're all moving to decent areas.... These new immigrants are filthy, and what can we do? They're like that, it's their cultures, they'll never change, they just don't want to live like us.

---

9   Despite my respondent's relative linguistic isolation and low education, they can hardly ignore the economic crises, structural unemployment and increasing poverty in Canada. Established immigrants also dismiss the fact that recent immigrants cannot or have not received the more "informal" support from members of their own community that they benefited from.

This comment is interesting for a number of reasons. It highlights the distinction made by Steinberg (1989) regarding malign and benign ethnicity. It also clearly demonstrates, as Lieberson and Waters (1988) found in the United States, that Europeans who were negatively racialized in the past emphasize their "White" identity. More importantly, however, this account also shows that some Euroethnic minorities strongly oppose public manifestations of minority cultures and ethnic identities that are different from their own. Their reports, which admittedly echo some of the same racist perceptions of dominant group members, also display their conviction that, whereas their ethno-culture is compatible with mainstream society, the racialized cultures of certain more recently arrived newcomers are not. Their representation of non-White cultures as inferior and as fixed and impermeable to dominant cultural practices, show the extent to which their views are disconnected from their own experiences as immigrants, from their collective concerns with the loss of their culture of origin and from their historical refusal to assimilate into mainstream cultures.[10]

Still in terms of their comparisons, the people I interviewed voiced a great deal of resentment against governments and mainstream society at large for what they regard as the more favourable treatment accorded to more recent immigrants. According to one respondent, governments "spend millions to support immigrants"; he also insisted on adding that they "come from poor, backward, war-torn countries that have nothing to offer us." This suggests that Italian and Greek immigrants in my research tend also to blame the Canadian and Quebec governments for granting resident status to certain groups. In their attacks, some contend that the new immigrants are less to blame "for taking advantage of the situation" and for "living off taxpayers' pockets" than are those who let them in to begin with. But as "foreigners" and minority group members themselves, the people I interviewed felt powerless to protest against such policies.

This is of course yet another illustration of how social relations between different immigrant groups are not entirely forged outside of state intervention and their relations with the dominant group. These established immigrants grieve over the "advantages" that new immigrants have, and insist that "recent immigrants benefit from policies and assistance from programs non-existent thirty years ago." Many angrily compare their lack of access to language instruction and public assistance when they arrived in Canada to what they perceive to be the overly generous assistance newcomers now receive from community groups and state agencies. Recalling the cruel conditions surrounding their own re-settlement, established immigrants are most angry over the lack of anti-racism and

---

10

  Many immigrants remark how their acculturation or "integration" into mainstream society is usually appraised as insufficient or superficial. Others echo the generalized assumption that by absorbing dominant cultural traits, Third World immigrants are seen as benefiting from or being emancipated and modernized by the dominant culture and mainstream practices. It hardly needs to be mentioned that such societal attitudes reflect racist assumptions about people from Third World countries.

anti-discrimination legislation and the relative absence of human rights protection when they needed it in Canada in the 1950s and 1960s, and the insensitivity that the dominant groups displayed towards linguistically and culturally isolated immigrants.

So far, we have looked at the attitudes of "old" towards "new" minority groups. I now want to briefly consider some of the practical manifestations of their racist convictions, namely their discriminatory behaviours. As members of the working class and self-employed entrepreneurs, they arguably have fewer opportunities to discriminate than dominant group members. However, as both homeowners and owners of rental property, one of the areas within which they have the opportunity to discriminate is in the area of housing.

First, although half of the landlords I interviewed reside near their racialized tenants, all of the former report having intentionally maintained social distance from the latter. As they acknowledge contact avoidance, some landlords admitted that "interaction with those people is limited to business transactions."

Second, my findings illustrate a considerable reluctance on the part of Italian and Greek landlords to rent their property to racialized new immigrants. Nearly everyone of the landlords interviewed admitted having employed strategies to deny housing to non-White immigrants.[11]

Some also admitted to having evicted Blacks, Hindus and Asians, not because these tenants breached the rental contract, but because these landlords perceived them as "troublemakers, noisy and dishonest."

Despite such attitudes, most of the landlords I met continue to rent out to non-White immigrants. The respondents' explanations of the apparent contradiction between not wanting to rent their property to so-called "troublemakers" but continuing to rent to them anyway are equally informative. Most deplore being "forced" to rent to non-White newcomers, which led me to ask how threatened they felt by anti-discrimination and human rights legislation in housing and the fear of public opprobrium. It turned out that their rationale in continuing to rent to new immigrants even when they did not want to was not at all linked to a fear of being dragged in front of a human rights tribunal, but rather to their economic standing and social location as immigrants and minorities. "Immigrants like us bought low-cost houses to rent out and make money.... Now, we need the rent payments for mortgage instalments ... so we are forced to rent to these people of colour. We can't afford vacancies ... and people like us prefer to live elsewhere" disclosed one landlord, reflecting the opinion of other interviewees. His account, which helps us understand how class, immigrant and minority status affect racist discrimination, points out how needy landlords cannot afford to act in as dis-

---

11   Their strategies are those regularly used by landlords at large. For a description see Quebec's *Commission des droits de la personne* (1989). However, as I have stated, all have at one time or another rented to non-White immigrants.

criminatory ways as they might wish. Another remarkable discrepancy is in their self-understanding of being racist and discriminatory towards other minorities. Some openly acknowledge being racist but immediately add that they "would never harm a Black person." Others, having themselves denied housing to non-White immigrants, later voiced that "it's against the law to discriminate ... and immigrants come here to live free from discrimination." Equally disturbing was the discourse of those who, after verbalizing blatantly racist comments, added, "but one can't say we're racist.... How could we, being immigrants ourselves, discriminate against other immigrants?"

Conclusion

Insofar as "old" and "new" immigrant minorities usually share a geophysical location, and co-reside in highly multiethnic neighbourhoods, they are likely to have a good deal of social contact. By sharing certain class and social locations in urban spaces, established and recent immigrant workers have many more opportunities to interact with each other at work and on the street than they might have with upper-class members of dominant groups. Ideally such contacts would generate greater tolerance, respect and understanding. Unfortunately, in the situation I examined they breed resentment, hostility and discrimination.

As understudied and underconceptualized as "ethnic minority racism" remains in academia, such racism seems no less brutal than so-called "mainstream racism." However limited, the material presented in this chapter attests to the fact that the racism articulated by "White" immigrants in Canada is inseparable from local practices, national contexts and international ideologies of "race" and racism. In partaking in the minoritization and racialization processes that victimize all Canadian minorities, the immigrants in this study re-articulate anti-immigrant sentiments of some national political parties, and reproduce many of the discriminatory practices of dominant group landlords. Yet their present social location as Canadian cultural minorities, along with their pre-migration experiences and their current identity as both southern European and White, all imprint upon their racism.

Empirical findings in the study of ethnic minority racism inform more than confirm the propositions of the "new racism" perspective. They question the widespread assumption that racism and the racialization of "others" are the exclusive domain of dominant group members. More specifically, this material challenges explanations of racism that necessarily link it to relations of power and dominance, and interpretations of racism that suggest that it is orchestrated by dominant groups in society. This is not to deny that there are power relations involved in landlord-tenant relationships, or that there is not a dominant racist ideology. However, the findings show that minority group members, who themselves feel *disempowered* by their immigrant and ethnic status and too materially hard-squeezed to be even more discriminatory, hold convictions which appear to have anteceded migration and have been nourished by their own inferiorization. In other words, inter-minority racism cannot be reduced to the Machiavelianism of Canadian elites who wish to hinder the formation of relations of inter-ethnic solidarity and class alliances.

In the end, the Italian and Greek Canadians of this study express their racism primarily as Whites. Some accentuate their "Whiteness" and instrumentally use it to re-construct new forms of identification with other white Euroethnic and/or dominant group members. But their immigrant experiences and minority status in Canada also impact on their identification as both White and southern European. In their position as objects of minoritization and racialization, they are unable to fully partake in White identity claims. In their position as agents of minoritization and racialization, they may take recourse and new pride in the recognition of the contributions made by their culture of origin to both Western civilization and Canadian culture. One discerns that the Italians and Greeks seek to distance themselves from newly established immigrants and minorities, both celebrate and refute the immigrant label, re-construct their ethnic identity and create new meanings for Eurocentricity.

It also seems that the ethnic minority racism discussed here needs to be linked to a wider European and international context insofar as the Italian and Greek landlords condemn non-European immigrants and cultures from their historical intolerance of racialized cultures. Their desire for non-White immigrants to assimilate to the supposedly superior "Canadian" culture, which they see as having originated not just in Britain and France but more generally in Europe in the first place, reflects both ethnocentrism and Eurocentrism. In an effort to come to terms with their racialized experiences and position after their arrival in Canada, several people I interviewed believed that they hardly needed to integrate into Canadian culture insofar as their cultures were similar to the two European cultures of the founding people of Canada. New immigrants, on the other hand, are seen to lack the "proper" ethnic character, or what Steinberg calls "benign" European ethnicity.

Besides questioning some fundamental premises of the "new racism" approach and the conventional juxtaposition of dominant-minority group relations, this chapter also challenges the common assumption of there being a singular face to racism in contemporary Canadian society. In other words, given the multiethnic composition of our society, race relations or racism can hardly be grasped unless ethno-cultural diversity is taken into account. For in Canada as elsewhere, racism is not homogenous. In this case, it speaks unofficial minority languages, has culturally distinct backgrounds and has manifestations which are rooted in distinct histories and sets of experience. We must therefore question monolithic notions of both racism and "White" identity. I began this study persuaded by the belief that the omission of ethnic minority racism in the current sociological climate was a form of exclusion. As I continue to probe and reflect on the meaning of ethnic minority racism, I am convinced that in the end there really is no binary opposition between "ethnic heroes" and "racial victims"; they are usually one and the same.

REFERENCES

Alba, Richard. 1985. *Italian Americans: Into the Twilight of Ethnicity.* Englewood Cliffs: Prentice Hall.

_____. 1994. "Identity and ethnicity among Italians and other Americans of European ancestry." In L. Tomasi, P. Gastaldo and T. Row, eds. *The Columbus People.* New York: Centre for Migration Studies.

Anthias, Floya. 1990. "Race and class revisited: Conceptualizing race and racisms." *Sociological Review* 38(1):19-42.

Balibar, Etienne. 1988. "Le 'racisme de classe'." In E. Balibar and I. Wallerstein, *Race, Nation, Classe: Les Identités Ambigues.* Paris: Editions La Découverte.

_____ and Immanuel Wallerstein. 1988. *Race, Nation, Classe: Les Identités Ambigues.* Paris: Editions La Découverte.

Banton, Michael. 1987. *Racial Theories.* London: Cambridge University Press.

Barker, Martin. 1981. *The New Racism: Conservatives and the Ideology of the Tribe.* London: Junction Books.

Commission des droits de la personne du Québec. 1989. *Une expérience de testing de la discrimination raciale dans le logement à Montréal.* Montréal: Direction de la recherche.

Constantinides, Stephanos. 1983. *Les grecs du Québec. Analyze historique et sociologique.* Québec: Le Métèque.

Gans, Herbet, 1979. "Symbolic ethnicity: The future of ethnic groups and cultures in America." *Ethnic and Racial Studies* 2(1):1-20.

Gouvernement du Québec. 1991. *Le logement et les communautés culturelles.* Montréal: Conseil des Communautés culturelles et de l'Immigration.

Hannerz, Ulf. 1974. "Ethnicity and opportunity in urban America." In A. Cohen, ed. *Urban Ethnicity.* London: Tavistock.

Harney, Robert. 1988. "Italian immigration and the frontiers of Western Civilization." In J. Potestion and A. Pucci, eds. *The Italian Immigrant Experience.* Toronto: Canadian Historical Association.

_____. 1993. In Nicholas Harney, ed. *From the Shores of Hardship: Italians in Canada. Essays by Robert Harney.* Welland, Ont.: Soleil.

Hein, Jeremy. 1991. "Do 'new immigrants' become 'new minorities?'." *Sociological Perspectives* 34:61-78.

_____. 1994. "From migrants to minority: Hmong refugees and the social construction of identity in the United States." *Sociological Inquiry* 64(3):281-306.

Henry, Frances and Effie Ginsberg. 1984. *Who Gets the Work?: A Test of Racial Discrimination in Employment.* Toronto: Urban Alliance on Race Relations and the Social Planning Council of Toronto.

Iacovetta, Franca. 1992. *Such Hardworking People: Italian Immigrants in Post-war Toronto.* Montreal and Kingston: McGill-Queen's University Press.

Jansen, Clifford. 1987. *Fact-book on Italians in Canada.* 2nd edition. Toronto: Institute for Social Research, York University.

Li, Peter, ed. 1990. *Race and Ethnic Relations in Canada.* Toronto: Oxford University Press.

Lieberson, Stanley. 1980. *A Piece of the Pie: Blacks and White Immigrants Since 1880.* Berkeley: University of California Press.

_____ and Mary Waters. 1988. *From Many Strands: Ethnic and Racial Groups in Contemporary America.* New York: Russel Sage Foundation.

Maffesoli, Michel. 1996. *The Time of the Tribes: The Decline of Individualism in Mass Society.* London: Sage.

Miles, Robert. 1993. *Racism After "Race Relations."* London: Routledge.

_____. 1994. "Explaining racism in contemporary Europe." In Ali Rattansi and Sally Westwood, eds. *Racism, Modernity and Identity on the Western Front.* Cambridge: Polity Press.

Porter, John. 1965. *The Vertical Mosaic.* Toronto: University of Toronto Press.

Ragin, Charles and Jeremy Hein. 1993. "The comparative studies of ethnicity: Methodological and conceptual issues." In J. Stanfield and R. Denis, eds. *Race and Ethnicity in Research Methods.* London: Sage.

Rattansi, Ali. 1994. "'Western' racisms, ethnicities and identities in a 'postmodern' frame." In Ali Rattansi and Sally Westwood, eds. *Racism, Modernity and Identity on the Western Front*. Cambridge: Polity Press.

Rex, John. 1986. *Race and Ethnicity*. Milton Keynes: Open University Press.

Roediger, David. 1991. *The Wages of Whiteness: Race and the Making of the American Working Class*. London: Verso.

Satzewich, Vic. 1989. "Racisms: The reactions to Chinese migrants in Canada at the turn of the century." *International Sociology* 4(3):311-327.

Steinberg, Stephen. 1989. *The Ethnic Myth: Race, Ethnicity and Class in America*, 2nd edition. London: Beacon Press.

Taguieff, P.A. 1987. *La Force du Préjugé: Essai sur le Racisme et ses Doubles*. Paris: La Découverte.

van Dijk, Teun. 1993. *Elite Discourses and Racism*. London: Sage.

Vecoli, Rudolph. 1988. "Italian-American ethnicity: Twilight or dawn." In J. Potestion and A. Pucci, eds. *The Italian Immigrant Experience*. Toronto: Canadian Historical Association.

Waters, Mary. 1990. *Ethnic Options: Choosing Identities in America*. Berkeley: University of California Press.

Wellman, David. 1977. *Portraits of White Racism*. Cambridge: Cambridge University Press.

11

The Reform Party of Canada: A Discourse on Race, Ethnicity and Equality

Della Kirkham

A series of dramatic events has transpired in recent Canadian politics. These include the failure to deal with Quebec's constitutional demands, ongoing attempts to define a new relationship with First Nations, and a continental free trade agreement that is being progressively extended to more and more countries. These events have taken place within the context of an uncertain economic climate, leading many to lose faith in the capacity of political leaders to guide Canada out of economic and political turmoil. In this context there has emerged a new voice on the Canadian political landscape. The Reform Party of Canada had its founding assembly in October 1987 and has increased in popularity to the point where it now occupies the status of official opposition in the federal House of Commons.

This chapter examines the Reform Party's discourse on racial and ethnic-related issues. There has been a significant interest in the party's position on issues of race and ethnicity. Since its inception, the party and its members have been dogged by allegations of their latent, if not overt, racism. While Reform officials have steadfastly maintained they are not advocating any hidden racist agenda, and have taken to the courts to try to stop such allegations, both the media and political opponents continue to suggest otherwise. However, to date, no systematic analysis of the party's race- and ethnic-related discourse has been undertaken. My purpose then, is to explore the discourse of the Reform Party as articulated in its position on immigration and multiculturalism. In so doing I have elected to ignore what appear to be blatantly racist sentiments articulated by individual members of the Reform Party. Such statements (and the internal party strife that ensued) have garnered widespread coverage in the popular press. I do not undertake to review that coverage here, but instead will concentrate on the more difficult conceptual task of analyzing policy and its implications for racial-ethnic equality in Canada.

Race and the New Right

To begin, we must situate the party's discourse within a wider context. The era of official multiculturalism in Canada began in 1971. Under the auspices of multicultural policy, people have been encouraged to live together in harmony without losing their cultural distinctiveness. This vision for Canada, proudly proclaimed by Prime Minister Pierre Trudeau, was to open a bold new frontier and set an example for the rest of the world. The vision set Canada's cultural mosaic apart from the American "melting pot" south of the border, and many Canadians have embraced this image wholeheartedly.

However, the reality has fallen short of the ideal. In fact, recent opinion polls suggest that, far from living up to the principle of racial and ethnic harmony, a growing number of Canadians express intolerance not only of identifiable minorities but towards the ideal of racial and ethnic diversity itself. By the beginning of the 1990s commentators were warning that the multicultural vision of the Canadian mosaic was "under seige."[1]

The growing hostility towards racial and ethnic diversity coincides with changing immigration patterns. Since 1983, immigration levels have increased dramatically,[2] and the countries from which immigrants come have also changed. In 1965, 83 percent of all immigrants to Canada came from Europe and the United States. By 1992, 21 percent arrived from these areas, while 64 percent came from Asia, Africa and the Middle East.[3]

The Reform Party articulates its particular views on race, and ethnic-related issues in this mix of attitudes, perceptions and changing immigration patterns. It also articulates its discourse within the context of the resurgent right and an associated new era of racialized politics. There has been a resurgence of right-wing politics in most Western capitalist states in the past two decades, and the rise of the Reform Party is a part of this wider trend. Thompson (1990) defines

---

[1]

Maclean's, July 10, 1989:14. A Gallup poll in July 1991 showed that 45 percent of all those surveyed favoured decreased immigration. This was the highest proportion of people in favour of a decrease since Gallup started polling on the subject in 1975, and was significantly higher than the 32 percent who favoured a decrease when questioned in 1990. More recently, results of a survey released in July 1994 found 53 percent of respondents believed that immigration levels were too high (Maclean's, July 25, 1994:16). A Decima Research poll released in December 1993 found that 3 out of every 4 Canadians reject the notion of cultural diversity and think racial and ethnic minorities should try harder to fit into mainstream society. The same survey found that 54 percent of respondents believed that current immigration policy allows "too many people of different races and cultures" into Canada; 57 percent said they sometimes held negative views of minority groups; 50 percent agreed with the statement, "I am sick and tired of some groups complaining about racism being directed at them; " and 41 percent said that "I'm sick and tired of ethnic minorities being given special treatment." Yet in spite of such findings, the survey also found that two-thirds of the respondents declared that one of the best things about Canada is its acceptance of people from all races and ethnic backgrounds (Ottawa Citizen, December 31, 1993:B1; Maclean's, December 27, 1993:42).

[2]

In 1983 the total number of immigrants into Canada was 81,157. The federal Conservatives elected in 1984 began a policy of increasing immigration levels. By 1987 the numbers were 152,098 and by 1991 the level had increased to 230,781 (Government of Canada, 1994a:4). This trend has not been reversed with the election of the Liberal government in 1993. The projected level of immigration for 1994 was 230,000 (Maclean's, November 14, 1994).

[3]

Government of Canada, 1994b.

the new right as a particular constellation of discursive propositions and policy prescriptions, and that political movement which provides its articulation. The movement, however, cannot be viewed as a homogenous discursive or political entity. Indeed, there are probably as many variants of the new right as there are new right authors, parties and movements. It becomes difficult, therefore, to pin down the precise characterization or elements to include under the rubric of the new right. I will use the term to refer to the combination of neo-liberal economic policy prescriptions and a form of authoritarian conservatism. The neo-liberal influence includes an emphasis on individual freedoms and liberties, a limited role for the state and a faith in unfettered market forces. The focus of authoritarian conservatism on the other hand is social order. Here, the primary concern is to uphold traditional authority and morality from what is regarded as the perils of cultural decline, the breakdown of law and order and the excesses of the liberal democratic state (Gordon and Klug, 1986).[4]

The rise of the new right that occurred in the 1970s represented, not merely a change in policy emphasis, but a comprehensive shift in the nature and direction of politics. Its objective was nothing less than the transformation of social and economic relations of modern society. While questions of economic management were central, issues such as the role of the state, the family, sexuality, race and national identity became politicized and contested (Gunn, 1989). What came to be the accepted role of governments—fostering the redistribution of resources in society, promoting egalitarianism, harmonizing various interests and guaranteeing basic provisions (such as housing, jobs, education, and health care)—suddenly came under attack (Krieger, 1986).

The new right, therefore, began to promote economic, political and social policies that sought to establish an alternative hegemonic project. The goals of this project include resuscitating the economic power of the advanced capitalist states, containing the demands and political visions of the various new social movements that emerged in the 1960s, the restoration of "governability" to democracy and re-constructing traditional cultural and social values (Omi and Winant, 1986). In other words, the new right opposes the more progressive legacies of the 1960s, which include expanded welfare, the politicization of race and gender issues around the civil rights and women's movements and the gains of organized labour (Helvacioglu, 1990).

As such, the ascendancy of the new right should be understood as a "politics of backlash." It is within this context that we must locate the rise of the Reform Party and, in turn, its race- and ethnic-related discourse. In both Britain and the United States, the resurgence of the right has brought with it a new era of

---

4

The tension that is inherent in this combination of neoliberalism and conservatism, including that which is evident within the Reform Party, is a complex issue and a topic worthy of its own pursuit. This particular line of inquiry, however, is out of the scope of this present analysis.

racialized politics. The work of Martin Barker, Michael Omi and Howard Winant offers some useful conceptual tools to aid in the examination of this aspect of Reform Party policy.

In *The New Racism*, Martin Barker argues that a new form of racist ideology emerged in the 1960s. Unlike previous manifestations, which had relied upon notions of innate biological superiority and inferiority, the "new racism" makes no such extremist claims. Instead, it is much more subtle and, when taken at face value, can be regarded as relatively innocent. Central to the new racism, Barker suggests, is a particular understanding of human nature and the notion of a shared way of life or culture. Proponents of the new racism hold that it is natural for those who share a common culture "to form a bounded community, a nation, aware of its difference from other nations" (Barker, 1981:2). Similarly, it is human nature to be wary of these differences and even antagonistic towards outsiders who are different and who come to be viewed as a threat to group identity. Recognizing that differences among groups, cultures or nations exist is not racist, so the argument goes, for normative evaluations about these differences are not given and certainly claims of innate superiority of one group over another are never made. Instead, those who espouse this new racist ideology argue that they are merely recognizing differences between peoples much as they would recognize differences between individuals and, as such, are not displaying any racist or prejudiced sentiments (Gordon and Klug, 1986).

Barker explores how the new racism found its clearest expression in Britain's new right and was used to mask racist politics, especially during the era of Thatcherism. For example, in a major speech given in 1978, opposition leader Margaret Thatcher said Britain was being "swamped" by immigrants with alien cultures and called on the Labour government to take a tougher stance on immigration. When she was attacked for inciting racism she countered by suggesting she was only giving voice to a natural reaction people had when immigration levels were set too high. She claimed, "People do feel swamped if streets they have lived in for the whole of their lives are really now quite, quite different" (quoted in Barker, 1981:1). Thatcher, her defenders argued, was not attaching any value judgments to these differences, so it was not racist to make such an observation. Racism implies judgments of innate superiority and inferiority, promotes hatred of people of colour, plays on irrational fears and encourages prejudice. Arguing for a more restrictive immigration policy and suggesting that people feel "swamped" by "alien" cultures is not racist, but is in fact a realistic and rational assessment of the problems that may be engendered by immigration. A tough stance on immigration, therefore, does not encourage hatred and prejudice but is based on the facts of Britain's economic and political situation and from the reactions of ordinary people. Barker's contention is that such discourse is not as benign as it may appear. It is in fact the articulation of a new ideology that is no less racist than the old-style arguments about the supposed biological inferiority of certain groups.

Like Barker's analysis of a new form of racist ideology and practice in Britain, Omi and Winant argue that the rise of the right in the United States brought with it a specific form of racialized politics. Indeed, they suggest that a central aspect of the American new right project was the attempt to *re-articulate* understandings of race and racial equality. The process of re-articulation is defined as "the practice of discursive reorganization or reinterpretation of ideological themes and interests such that these elements obtain new meanings or coherence" (Omi, 1987:16). In other words, re-articulation occurs as a result of the *disorganization* of the dominant ideology and of the *construction* of an alternative, oppositional framework (Omi and Winant, 1986).

A re-articulation of racial discourse occurred in the 1960s and again in the 1980s. During the sixties, racial identity and racial politics were radically transformed. In this period, racial and other minority movements achieved real reforms (albeit limited in scope) in their struggles for racial justice and equality. The civil rights movement re-articulated meanings of race and racial equality by making demands not merely for equality of *opportunity* but equality of *outcome* and for a recognition of group rights as opposed to individual rights. By the 1970s, however, these movements experienced a sharp decline while the economic, political and cultural crises of the period deepened. Within this context, a space opened up for an attack made by "counter-reformers," who sought to reinterpret the meaning of race—that is, to re-articulate understandings of race and racial equality in a conservative direction.

Issues of race and racial equality, then, had been dramatically revived by the 1980s, but this time in the form of a "backlash" to the political gains of the racial minority movements of the previous two decades. Omi and Winant argue that the new right is mobilized precisely in its desire to overturn these achievements, but in order to do so, it needs to advance a new racial politics. The new right accomplishes the re-articulation of the meaning of race through the use of "code words." Explicit racial discourse is abandoned in favour of that which appears to be race-neutral language. Nonetheless, this non-racial rhetoric is used to disguise racial issues. Omi and Winant (1986) have argued that this is a common strategy of the new right, for it enables its adherents to avoid blatantly racist political ideology and discourse while simultaneously capitalizing on resentment over a wide range of social issues, including immigration, multiculturalism and employment equity. Employing code words, therefore, allows the new right to mask the issue of race within a more politically safe terrain.

By examining the Reform Party's discourse on immigration and multicultural-ism, we can uncover its new right character and its attempt to re-articulate racial-ethnic understandings.[5] However, an examination of the new racism and the re-articulation of racial discourse is not without its methodological difficul-ties. It is very rare to find explicit statements that constitute uncontested evidence of racism in Reform Party policy. What a study of the re-articulation of racial discourse requires is a careful de-construction of the underlying subtext in order to uncover its racialized meaning(s). In so doing we can begin to understand the implications of the party's positions on both immigration and multiculturalism.

Reform's Immigration Policy: Economics and Border Control

Early in the party's history, its discourse on immigration displayed a some-what angry, combative and vitriolic tone. As the party evolved, a more tempered discourse emerged, but the essence of its position on immigration remains un-changed. Reform's critique is premised on what it deems to be the inadequacies of Canada's immigration policy. Specifically, two themes emerge in the party's discourse. First, immigration policy must be focused primarily on the economic needs of Canada. Reform believes this can only be accomplished by limiting Family Class entrants and increasing Independent Class levels.[6] Second is the call for tighter border controls to stem the flow of illegal immigrants. In other words, the party has consistently called for a much more restrictive immigration policy focusing on economic imperatives and border control. Implicit in its posi-tion is a de-legitimation of the other goals of immigration policy that have been pursued over the past decade. These objectives include meeting not only eco-nomic goals, but also social, humanitarian and demographic needs. The follow-ing discussion will demonstrate how these themes have been articulated in the party's discourse, and how they reveal its new right character with its underlying racial sub-text.

5

While Omi and Winant's work focuses exclusively on the re-articulation of race, I have extended their analysis to incorporate the re-articulation of race as well as ethnicity. There exists an ongoing debate in the literature about the relationship of ethnicity *vis-à-vis* race in the theoretical analyses of racist ideology (see, for instance, Anthias and Yuval-Davis, 1992). While I certainly do not attempt to resolve this debate, I do believe that understandings of racism should be broad enough to include that which is experienced by ethnic as well as racial minorities. That is, ethnically constituted differences (language, religion, dress, etc.) can become the basis of exclusionary practices that are undoubtedly racist in their imputation of immutable differences and their inequitable outcomes (Stasiulis, 1990). Obviously the manifestations of racial-ethnic oppression will vary considerably across time and space and should not be treated as similar instances of racist practice. However, its racist implications are felt regardless of whether those who experience them belong to a specific racial and/or ethnic categories. My examination of Reform's discourse will therefore highlight how the party attempts to re-articulate racial and ethnic (or racial-ethnic) understandings.

6

Under current policy, there are a three basic classes of immigrants. They include: *independent class* who enter under a point system on the basis of their skills and education; *family class* who come into the country under the family reunification program; and thirdly, *refugees*. The breakdown of immigration by class from 1981-1991 was: 34.9 percent independent class; 38.6 percent family class and 26.5 percent refugees (Government of Canada, 1993: 116). At the time of writing, no official statistics on immigration were available for the period after 1992. However, the Liberal government's *proposed* levels for 1994 were 45 percent independent class, 45 percent family class, and 10 percent refugees (Government of Canada, 1994b).

Beginning with the assumption that immigration policy does not adequately address the economic needs of Canada, Reform's original policy states:

Immigration should be essentially economic in nature.
Immigrants should possess the human capital necessary to adjust quickly and independently to the needs of Canadian society and the job market. Sponsorship privileges should be restricted to members of immediate families, that is, wives or husbands, minor dependent children and aged dependent parents. All others should apply for entry through the normal selective process.[7]

This statement clearly reveals a strong exception to the Family Class of immigration. Tom Flanagan, former party director of Policy, Strategy and Communications, has stated the following:

When you start a trend of having a lot of immigrants from a particular country, if you have a very lax family reunification system, that tends to amplify itself, because then they bring in their parents, their children, their brothers and sisters, and then the brothers and sisters bring in their children and in-laws, and so on—it keeps building. So, you get further and further away from evaluating each individual immigrant as a potential contributor to the economy.[8]

That the Independent Class of immigrants is not given more priority is seen as the manifestation of an immigration system rife with abuse. As one party official writes:

Immigrants are allowed to enter Canada under three basic categories, Independent immigrants, Family Class and Refugees. The highest priority is given to family members and refugees, emphasizing the humanitarian nature of the system. The needs of immigrants take precedence over the needs of the country. Inevitably, in a world where generosity is often equated with foolishness, there have been massive abuses. Adult, non-dependent family members including cousins, nieces and nephews are commonly sponsored by newly naturalized citizens and are exempt from the selection process faced by self-starters seeking admission as independent immigrants (Morrison, 1990a).[9]

The preoccupation with illegal immigration and the country's ability (or lack thereof) to control its own borders is evident in the following statement on refugee policy:

Genuine refugees should be welcomed.
Bogus refugees and other illegal entrants should be deported immediately, and any person who encourages or promotes such activities should be subject to severe penalties without exception. The Constitution may have to be amended to ensure that Parliament can ultimately control entry into Canada, and, in the interim, the "notwithstanding" provision of the Charter should be used to ensure this is the case.[10]

---

[7]
Reform Party of Canada, 1988a:23.

[8]
Author interview with Tom Flanagan, July 13, 1993.

[9]
In the past, Lee Morrison has served as a member of the party's executive council, and is now a Reform MP. Quotes attributed to him are from a number of editorial pieces Morrison wrote that the party submitted to various daily newspapers. The author gratefully acknowledges the Reform Party of Canada for granting access to such materials from the party's archives.

[10]
Reform Party of Canada, 1988a:23. The call to use the notwithstanding clause of the Charter is a reference to what is known as the "Singh decision"—a landmark Supreme Court ruling that has enabled a number of unsuccessful refugee claimants to use a Charter defense to avoid deportation. The decision has had a significant impact on the refugee determination system. The party's discourse on this particular issue is raised below.

The party's original policy on immigration, therefore, not only insisted that the demands of the Canadian labour market be the only legitimate goal of policy, but also fostered the perception that the Canadian government was not controlling its borders and was allowing an unchecked flood of illegal immigrants into the country. From the outset, party officials were aware that their position on immigration would be attacked and could leave Reform open to charges of racism. In an attempt to pre-empt such attacks, the party's original policy statement on immigration concludes:

> The Reform Party remains convinced that immigration has been, and can be again, a positive source of economic growth, cultural diversity, and social renewal. No criticism of the problems of immigration policy should be construed as a failure to recognize either the contributions that thousands of immigrants make each year to Canadian society or the good fortune of having a society that people desire to move to. Likewise, the vested interests of bad immigration policy should not be so quick to label Canadians "racist" for desiring positive changes and should be more humble and honest about their own motives.[11]

But in spite of the party's efforts to ward off criticism, its policy was indeed attacked for being racially motivated. Echoing Margaret Thatcher's concerns over being "swamped" by alien cultures, the party's original policy book stated that "immigration should not be based on race or creed, as it was in the past, nor should it be explicitly designed to radically or suddenly alter the ethnic makeup of Canada, as it increasingly seems to be."[12] This phrasing was attacked by both the media and politicians.[13] Party officials, however, insisted that the phrase was not designed with any racial overtones. Stephen Harper, one of the party's chief policy architects and up until recently a Reform member of parliament, suggested that the phrase was "all part of a statement saying that immigration policy should not have any racial or ethnic qualifications."[14]

As a result of such attacks, and as it redoubled its efforts to be taken seriously as a legitimate national political party, many Reform policies (including both immigration and multiculturalism) were re-worked and re-worded. With the change in rhetoric contained in the party's 1991 policy manual, a less angry discourse emerged that advocated an immigration policy which would be "balanced and positive" and "which rejected the use of racial criteria" (Manning, 1992:273). A reading of the party's revised policy statements demonstrates that much of the tone which left the impression of a corrupt system, prone to abuse,

---

11
    Reform Party of Canada, 1988a:24.

12
    Reform Party of Canada, 1988a:23.

13
    Examples of such attacks include that by Southam News columnist Christopher Young who accused the party of trying to institute a WASP Canada which would "freeze out the multi-hued, multi-tongued people who have enriched Canadian culture" (*Alberta Report*, April 29, 1991:15). Liberal MP Sheila Copps made a number of statements comparing the policies of Preston Manning to those of the former Ku Klux Klan gubernatorial candidate in Louisiana, David Duke (for example see *Vancouver Sun*, November 21, 1991:A4).

14
    Author interview with Stephen Harper, July 15, 1993.

was dropped. The party's "Green Book" exhibits this more tempered discourse by outlining the policy's objectives:

1. To be a non-racist, non-discriminatory policy based on Canada's economic needs.

2. To create a positive source of economic growth, cultural diversity and social renewal for Canada.

3. To remain responsive to humanitarian needs through a legitimate refugee policy which adequately deters false refugees.

4. To provide a policy which is consistent with and supportive of the other social and economic polices of the Reform Party.[15]

The party's sanitized immigration policy reads as follows[16]

A. The Reform Party supports an immigration policy that has as its focus Canada's economic needs and that welcomes genuine refugees. The Reform Party remains convinced that immigration has been, and can be again, a positive source of economic growth, cultural diversity and social renewal.

B. The Reform Party opposes any immigration policy based on race or creed.

C. The Reform Party supports an immigration policy which would be essentially economic in nature. Immigrants should possess the human capital necessary to adjust quickly and independently to the needs of Canadian society and the job market.

D. The Reform Party supports restricting sponsorship privileges to members of immediate families, that is, wives or husbands, minor dependent children, and aged dependent parents. All others should apply for entry through the normal selective process.

E. The Reform Party supports a policy accepting the settlement of genuine refugees who find their way to Canada. A genuine refugee is one who has a well-founded fear of persecution and qualifies under the strict requirements of the United Nations Convention.

F. The Reform Party supports a policy of immediate deportation of bogus refugees and other illegal entrants, and persons who encourage or promote such activities should be subject to severe penalties without exception. The Constitution may have to be amended to ensure that Parliament can ultimately control entry into Canada, and, in the interim, the "notwithstanding" provision of the Charter should be used to ensure that this is the case.

G. The Reform Party opposes the use of immigration policy to solve the crisis of the welfare state through forced growth population policy. The problem of the pension costs of an aging population is neither caused nor cured by immigration policy.

H. The Reform Party supports submitting all major changes to immigration, including sponsorship requirements and amnesties, to referendum.

While party officials steadfastly maintain that their policy does not have any racist overtones and assert that its emphasis on economic criteria would not bar non-White immigration, this may be, at best, a naive appraisal of Reform's

---

[15]
Reform Party of Canada, 1992d.
[16]
Reform Party of Canada, 1991:33-35.

position. An article in the party paper highlights Reform's call for an immigration policy that "is based on non-racial criteria—ie., on Canada's economic needs and *adjustment potential* of the immigrant" [emphasis added].[17] The party's current policy echoes this by emphasizing the need for immigrants to "possess the *human capital* necessary to *adjust quickly and independently* to the needs of Canadian society and the job market" [emphasis added].[18] Do phrases such as these imply that immigrants must be English-speaking? Does adjusting quickly and independently suggest that funding for language training programs will be cut? What cultural backgrounds are assumed to have the greatest or least potential for "adjustment"? These are issues the party simply fails to address.[19]

Focusing on the skills and education of immigrants also conveniently ignores the persistent difficulty with the issue of accreditation. Numerous studies show how educational training and job experience from the non-Western world is de-valued, and in many cases not even accepted as legitimate. Yet party documents on immigration show no recognition of this difficulty, nor do they suggest how a Reform Party immigration policy which emphasizes skills and training would address this issue.[20]

The party's call to increase the Independent Class of immigrants and restrict Family Class entrants is therefore not as innocuous as it first appears. In 1987, 43 percent of all Family Class immigrants were from Asia. By 1992, this figure had increased to 55 percent.[21] It is therefore possible to conclude that the party's policy would in effect bar much non-European immigration into Canada, in spite of Reform officials' protests otherwise. In this sense, the intent of the party's original statement which called for an end to immigration policy that is "explicitly designed to radically or suddenly alter the ethnic makeup of Canada" becomes more clear, notwithstanding Reform's attempts at damage control. Yet in focusing its policy on economic criteria—something that appears neutral, fair, and most important, non-racial—the party is able to mask the racialized sub-text and implications of its policy.

17

Reform Party of Canada, 1992e.

18

Reform Party of Canada, 1991:34.

19

One party document did offer the following: "The Reform Party recognizes the economic, social and cultural contributions that immigrants make to Canadian society and recognizes the need for the support they initially require to adjust to Canadian society" (Reform Party of Canada, 1992d). Yet it is not clear from this what commitment the party would have to language training programs.

20

Party official Dimitri Pantazopoulos did note the difficulty with accreditation (interview with author, July 14, 1993). However, his concern was not reflected by any other party officials interviewed, or in any other party documents obtained throughout my research. In addition, Pantazopoulos offered no indication of how the party would address the issue.

21

In comparison, in 1987 only 28 percent of family class immigrants came from Europe and the U.S.; 21 percent in 1992 (Government of Canada, 1994a, 1989).

This is also true of Reform's discourse on refugee policy. The party's policy statements emphasize the acceptance of only *genuine* refugees. Furthermore, Reform calls for the immediate deportation of *bogus* refugees and stiff penalties for those who aid their entry.[22] The preoccupation with border control or, more appropriately in its view, the *lack* of border control, is particularly evident in early Reform discourse:

> We cannot solve the problems of global overpopulation, starvation and political repression by trying to accommodate the dispossessed of the world. If we opened our doors wide to everyone who wished to come, the only predictable result would be our own economic and social collapse with no significant improvement of conditions in the countries from where the migrants came. Therefore, our immigration policies should be designed primarily in the national interest with priority given to Independent Immigrants—people whose skills, education, health and good character will enable them to make a positive contribution to our society and economy (Morrison, 1990a).

What is implicit in this message, then, is the perception that the immigrants we are currently allowing in are unskilled, unhealthy and lack "good character." This is due to our loss of border control, resulting in a flood of illegal immigrants and refugees. An article in the party paper describes immigration policy as a "deeply flawed policy, which is so full of loopholes that illegal immigrants and phony refugees are allowed to remain and work in Canada while many established Canadians must struggle for years to bring their loved ones into the country."[23] A common refrain in much of the party's literature is "Close the door to illegal immigration. Establish a long-term immigration plan sensitive to Canada's needs and public opinion."[24]

While the tone has become less vitriolic, the perception of an immigration system out of control is still a theme party officials perpetuate. This is particularly evident in Reform's discourse regarding what is known as the "Singh decision." In 1985, the Supreme Court of Canada ruled that the word "everyone" in the Charter of Rights and Freedoms should be interpreted to mean not only citizens or landed immigrants, but should include any individual who sets foot on Canadian soil. This means that the liberty and security of any individual in Canada, regardless of his or her citizenship status is protected under the Canadian constitution. The landmark ruling has allowed a number of refugee claimants to use a Charter defence to avoid deportation and remain in Canada. The Reform Party abhors this trend and has called for a constitutional amendment to reverse the Singh ruling. Failing that, they argue for the use of the notwithstanding clause to override "excessively liberal interpretations of the Charter."[25]

22
  See items "E" and "F" in note 16 above.
23
  Reform Party of Canada, 1988c.
24
  Reform Party of Canada, 1989. Also Reform Party of Canada, 1988b. A number of party pamphlets also reiterate this same theme.
25
  Author interview with Stephen Harper, July 15, 1993.

Party leader Preston Manning has often stated his concern over the "illegal trade in refugees." In a speech before the Metro Toronto Police Association, Manning told his audience that a Reform government would ensure illegal immigrants would not be permitted to hide behind the Charter to avoid deportation.[26] Clearly the unease over border control is a theme that continues to resonate in Reform discourse.

The implications of Reform's position on refugee policy is therefore obvious. The guidelines for allowing refugees into the country would be severely restricted. As Preston Manning has stated, "We don't think you can just throw open the doors and take unlimited numbers of refugees."[27] Another official asserts that many of those who claim refugee status are not really people escaping persecution anyway ("*genuine* refugees"), but are economic migrants posing as refugees ("*bogus* refugees").[28] And as Morrison stated above, Canada cannot be expected to accommodate the "dispossessed" of the world, and certainly holds no responsibility for them.

Omi (1987) argues that a restrictive immigration policy coupled with strict enforcement efforts to "regain control of our borders" is one of the new right's defining characteristics. From its inception, Reform has consistently articulated an immigration policy that focuses on economic imperatives and border control. Neither of these themes when taken at face value are explicitly racialized. However, Reform's discourse has an implicit racial sub-text.

As noted above, one of the goals of the new right is to re-articulate racial-ethnic understandings. One of the strategies it uses to accomplish this re-articulation is the use of "code words." This is clearly the strategy of Reform. The party is able to re-articulate racial meanings and understandings by using code words embedded in its policy on immigration. Party officials are able to assert that their position on immigration has no racial character by disguising its racialized assumptions and implications in non-racial rhetoric; that is, the emphasis on economic criteria and the need to control our borders. Yet, when the party's discourse is scrutinized, the message behind such phrases as "adjustment potential," "human capital," and "genuine" versus "bogus" refugees is rendered clear. While the party may wish us to believe this message is not anti-immigrant, that it views immigration as a "positive source of economic growth, cultural diversity and social renewal," it is clearly against particular kinds of immigrants—family members, refugees, and all those who cannot "adjust quickly and independently to the needs of Canadian society and the job market."[29]

26

    Globe and Mail, January 13, 1993:A6.

27

    Globe and Mail, July 15, 1991:A6.

28

    Author interview with Tom Flanagan, July 13, 1993. A party document reads: "The Reform Party believes in the legitimacy of a refugee immigration component. However, the refugee status is often used as a mechanism for expediency and exception to non-genuine refugees" (Reform Party of Canada, 1992d).

It is somewhat ironic, therefore, that the party continually insists that its immigration policy is quite progressive for its lack of racial character. Indeed, Stephen Harper asserts:

> The overall intent [of the policy] cannot be construed as racial. It is clearly race-neutral. One may disagree with the emphasis on economics, the emphasis on border control, the emphasis on narrow family classes, but none of those things are inherently racist. And certainly they are not overtly racist.[30]

Claiming its positions are race-neutral is a standard defense used by the new right (Omi and Winant, 1986). The Reform Party not only employs this strategy to defend its position on immigration, but its multicultural policy as well. Reform's discourse on multiculturalism represents the party's most sophisticated attempt at the re-articulation of racial-ethnic meanings. By insisting its position on multiculturalism is "colour blind," the party promotes its particular vision of equality as the best recipe for racial-ethnic harmony in Canada.

"Hyphenated Canadianism": The (Multicultural) Ties That Divide

Even more than immigration, the Reform Party sees multiculturalism as an inherently flawed public policy arising out of dubious political motives. Indeed, Reformers maintain multicultural programs are designed more to curry favour with ethnic groups than to achieve other goals, such as preserving cultural heritage. Multicultural legislation does not foster a Canadian identity, but only serves to pit different communities against one another as they compete for financial assistance. Political scientist Rais Khan, who was instrumental in developing the party's position on multiculturalism, suggests that "if Canadians are looking for cultural harmony, divisive multicultural legislation is not the way to go. The cultural mosaic is being threatened by the politicization of multiculturalism.... We are ghettoizing the mosaic by creating walls between people over the few dollars this policy of multiculturalism tends to provide."[31]

According to the Reform Party, therefore, multicultural policy acts as a divisive force on the Canadian landscape, for it leads to "hyphenated Canadianism." Party official Lee Morrison (1990b) writes:

> It is the Reform Party's position that the federal Department of Multiculturalism is a divisive agency that encourages ghettoization and wastes our tax dollars to do it.... Thanks to the official federal policy of multiculturalism, Canada is being divided as never before along racial, linguistic and cultural lines. We have Anglo-Canadians, French-Canadians, Native-Canadians, Chinese-Canadians and a host of other hyphenated nationalities, but apparently no plain, ordinary *Canadians*.

29
   Reform Party of Canada, 1991:34.
30
   Author interview with Stephen Harper, July 15, 1993.
31
   Quoted in Reform Party of Canada, 1992b. Reform officials cite Professor Khan as the party's chief author for their multicultural policy.

Party leader Preston Manning often returns to the theme of hyphenated Canadianism and, like Morrison, laments the lack of a "Canadian" identity.

> It's been said that the symbol of this country is no longer the Maple Leaf, the symbol of the new Canada is the hyphen. Its federal politicians insist on talking about English-Canadians, French-Canadians, aboriginal-Canadians, ethnic Canadians. No one talks much about Canadians, period. And it is becoming patently obvious, as it has in some other countries, that you cannot hold a country together with hyphens (Manning, 1990:3).

Criticisms such as these have become increasingly salient as ongoing constitutional crises and unrest in Aboriginal communities have led to growing fears about the balkanization of Canada (Stasiulis, 1991). As one Reform official stated, "most Canadians are genuinely concerned about the tendency that many Canadians have to identify their ultimate political interest in some racial, linguistic, or even regional groups, as opposed to seeing an ultimate political loyalty to the overall polity."[32]

Based on such criticisms and concerns, the party arrives at its own position. Its original policy statement called for the elimination of multicultural funding, upheld the right of all individuals or groups to preserve their cultural background as a matter of personal choice and called on the federal state to "promote, preserve and enhance national culture" and to encourage "ethnic cultures to integrate into the national culture."[33]

As with its original immigration policy, the party soon found that some of the rhetoric used in this policy left it open to criticism. In particular the call to encourage ethnic cultures to integrate into the "national culture" caused consternation in many quarters. When the policy was being attacked, Reformers were quick to point out the architect of their position was Rais Khan—a member of a visible minority community. Stephen Harper further defended the original policy by noting that "my interpretation as the policy officer was always that this was referring to a national political consciousness—getting away from multiculturalism as a fundamental basis for defining ourselves."[34]

Although Reform officials insisted the phrasing was not based on any odious motives, the party chose to drop it from subsequent policy statements. Notwithstanding its re-phrasing, the party's position on multiculturalism did not change. Reformers believe government-sponsored multiculturalism perpetuates ghettoization and ethnic segregation, creates "hyphenated Canadians" and sets immigrants apart from other Canadians. Their prescription involves getting Ottawa out of the business of preserving ethnic groups and cultures, and calls for the dismantling of the Department of Multiculturalism. According to Reform policy,

---

[32]
   Author interview with Stephen Harper, July 15, 1993.
[33]
   Reform Party of Canada, 1990:23.
[34]
   Author interview with Stephen Harper, July 15, 1993.

individuals or groups should be left to pursue their cultural heritage as they choose, without the aid of the federal government.

The re-worded policy that was included in the party's 1991 policy manual (Reform Party of Canada, 1991:35) reads as follows:

A. The Reform Party stands for the acceptance and integration of immigrants to Canada into the mainstream of Canadian life.

B. The Reform Party supports the principle that individuals or groups are free to preserve their cultural heritage using their own resources. The Party shall uphold their right to do so.

C. The Reform Party of Canada opposes the current concept of multiculturalism and hyphenated Canadianism pursued by the Government of Canada. We would end funding of the multiculturalism program and support the abolition of the Department of Multiculturalism.

Reform views multiculturalism as little more than the subsidization of ethnicity. In the party's official policy, there is no acknowledgement of multiculturalism as the philosophical ideal of cultural pluralism, yet this is an important aspect of Canada's multicultural policy. Fleras and Elliot summarize the goals of the Multicultural Act which came into effect July 21, 1988:

In seeking a balance between cultural distinctiveness and equality, the act specified the right of all to identify with the cultural heritage of choice, yet retain "full and equal participation ... in all aspects of Canadian society." In effect, the act sought to preserve, enhance, and incorporate cultural differences into the functioning of Canadian society, while ensuring equal access and full participation for all Canadians in the social, political, and economic spheres. It also focused on the eradication of racism and removal of discriminatory barriers as incompatible with Canada's commitment to human rights. Policy goals, in brief, focused equally on cultural maintenance and social integration within a framework of equal opportunity (1992:75-76).

Since the 1960s there has been a growing debate around issues of multiculturalism as both ethnic and racial minorities make demands for greater access to political, institutional and economic power. While the Reform Party's official policy on multiculturalism seems to ignore this larger debate, I argue that the party does indeed take a position *against* cultural pluralism and the vision of racial-ethnic equality it promotes. An examination of Reform's discourse on issues of equality, therefore, reveals the party's new right character and its attempt to re-articulate racial-ethnic meanings.

According to the party's position paper on multiculturalism, eliminating multicultural funding and dismantling the department are part of its larger concern with fiscal responsibility: "At a time when the federal debt is over \$400 billion and growing by more than \$30 billion a year, it is necessary to make some difficult decisions. In order to balance the budget, the Reform Party proposes a broad program of expenditure reductions, of which cuts to multiculturalism are only one aspect." However, the document further states that "even if the federal budget were in balance, we would not want to use public money to subsidize multiculturalism" (Flanagan and Pantazopoulos, 1992).

Reform's criticism of multiculturalism, then, is based on a desire to reduce the role of government in the lives of Canadians.[35] Rais Khan told Reform delegates at their annual convention that "the best system is one of minimalist state intervention in the protection of language, culture and heritage.[36] Stephen Harper explains the party's view as follows:

> Let me give you a difference in philosophy. On the one hand, the current federal government would say, we will have a Department of Multiculturalism to produce and promote group identity and to run tolerance or anti-racism programs. The Reform Party's approach would be to say get the government out of the business of culture—get politicians and bureaucrats out of the business of racial identity.[37]

Manning himself suggests that

> cultural development and preservation ought to be the responsibility of individuals, groups, and if necessary in certain cases (for example, in the case of Quebec and Canadian aboriginals), of provincial and local governments. The role of the federal government should be neutral towards culture just as it is towards religion (1992:317).

The party's appeal to remove government from matters of language, culture, race and ethnicity, however, is based on more than its desire to reduce spending. It implies a stance where these are matters of individual concern only, and should not be promoted in any fashion by the state. Tom Flanagan notes, "There is fairly wide [party] support for a 'melting pot' concept, in which *ethnicity is a purely private concern*, and the public sphere is simply Canadian period. What your ethnic background is [should] not have any political consequences" [emphasis added].[38]

What this ignores is the reality that, in many instances, one's racial-ethnic background *does* have political consequences. As I argued above, Reform appears to favour certain ethnicities and/or cultures over others in their immigration policy, especially given the concern about altering the ethnic make-up of Canada. But in asserting that ethnicity should be a private concern, Reform can disregard such political consequences that in turn reflect certain structural barriers to achieving racial-ethnic equality. In effect, the party is saying that it is inappropriate to seek public, political solutions to issues and problems that are essentially private in nature (Laycock, 1993).

In this way the party's discourse on multiculturalism reflects the new right attempt to discredit demands for a re-distributive or egalitarian social policy (Winant, 1990). This view makes certain assumptions about equality in society

---

35

Demands for less state intervention is a central theme for the Reform Party. As one party documents reads, "Eliminate unnecessary government intrusions into the daily lives of individuals and business. A function performed by the public or private-sector should be based on who can do the best job most cost-effectively" (Reform Party of Canada, 1993b).

36

Reform Party of Canada, 1992b.

37

Author interview with Stephen Harper, July 15, 1993.

38

Author interview with Tom Flanagan, July 13, 1993.

and, more importantly, whether it is proper for the state to address itself to issues of equality. Harper provides a glimpse of the party's position:

> The two [views of equality] that I think are most prevalent in our society are on the one hand, that government should pursue some kind of pattern of behaviour towards people that makes them more equal, or that government is prepared to provide different sets of rules and standards for people, for provinces, for groups, that would "enhance their equality." There's another view that people should be treated identically or equally regardless of the differences otherwise that they possess. More than any mainstream political party in Canada, the Reform Party subscribes to the second view.[39]

That Reform views state actions geared to address inequality as inappropriate is further reinforced in the following party document:

> It is a fundamental Canadian belief that all persons should have the right to equality of opportunity, and the right not to be discriminated against in the workplace or society at large. The Reform Party believes that women and men, disabled persons, and persons of all ethnic origins, contribute to the enhancement and productivity of Canadian society. *Reformers also believe that government intrusions into a society of free individuals which attempt to impose a result rather than enhance equality of opportunity are undesirable* [emphasis added].[40]

The Reform Party, therefore, reflects the new right objection to attempts made by the state to create conditions of equality and ameliorate social problems. While Stephen Harper did concede some role for the state in the promotion of tolerance and the elimination of racism, he further stipulated that the party's understanding of this role is fundamentally different than that which is conventionally understood: "The party sees the fundamental role of government ... as first and foremost to treat people identically. And it sees systematic and repeated violations of that philosophy as a central cause of intolerance in society and not as a solution. The party believes in this fairly categorically."[41] Like new right advocates, then, the party suggests that state attempts to create conditions of equality, such as affirmative action, have been disastrous. Not only have they failed in aiding "target populations," but they have called into question such inviolable principles as fairness and individual rights (Omi, 1987).

Reform shares this view. A party document claims that "equal employment opportunities for women, ethnic minorities and the disabled are best promoted by improving education, emphasizing individual achievement, and dismantling unfair systemic barriers to advancement." Although the party suggests an "ongoing review of employment practices to ensure they do not impose unfair barriers," it never states how institutions could be persuaded to stop engaging in discriminatory practices.[42]

---

[39]
Author interview with Stephen Harper, July 15, 1993.
[40]
Reform Party of Canada, 1992c.
[41]
Author interview with Stephen Harper, July 15, 1993.
[42]
Reform Party of Canada, 1992c.

So while the statement suggests Reform would promote equal employment opportunities, the party certainly does not endorse state-led employment equality programs. As Stephen Harper states,

> [Reform] would be absolutely opposed to affirmative action. The party does not believe in using the government as a tool of discrimination to achieve certain social objectives. It doesn't believe that that's an appropriate role for the government and it certainly doesn't believe in that kind of approach to people.[43]

This kind of approach is not only considered wrong-headed, but dangerous. The party often warns of the perils of defining the relationship between the citizenry and the state on the basis of race, language and culture. To do so "leads to a house divided against itself and divided along the most dangerous of lines."[44] Indeed, Manning (1993a) insists that

> Canada must be a country where race is not a factor in determining the relationship between the citizen and the state or any of its institutions. Race should not determine any citizen's constitutional status. It should not determine any individuals immigration status. It should not determine any individual's cultural status. It should not determine any individual's employment status. It should not determine the relationship between an individual and the police. And race should not determine any individual's political status.

Based on this sentiment, the party therefore claims that "if elected a Reform government will abolish the Department of Multiculturalism, and focus the activities of the federal government on enhancing the citizenship of all Canadians regardless of race, language, or culture."[45]

By promoting the equality of all individuals, then, the party justifies its whole argument against multiculturalism. In Reform's vision of Canada, "the politics of privilege and special status give way to the equality of all Canadians in federal law regardless of their race, culture, language, income, place of residence, or gender" (Manning, 1993b).

The egalitarian nature of this vision is a theme often promoted by the party. Manning writes about the discussions Reform has undertaken with "ordinary Canadians" about the kind of country in which they wish to live. He notes:

> The one descriptive word we hear mentioned most often in these types of discussions is "equality"—treat all Canadians equally in federal law and the constitution, regardless of their race, language, or culture, rather than treating some Canadians specially because of their race, language, or culture.[46]

In this way the party insists its own policies on immigration and multiculturalism (as well as the constitution) are race-neutral. According to Preston Manning, his party's positions "are specifically aimed at removing racial considerations and

---

[43] Author interview with Stephen Harper, July 15, 1993.

[44] Manning quoted in *Vancouver Sun*, February 15, 1991:A12.

[45] Reform Party of Canada, n.d.[a]. This statement was also added to the party's 1993 policy statement on multiculturalism (Reform Party of Canada, 1993a:6).

[46] Reform Party of Canada, 1992a.

criteria from these policy areas."[47] As such, he asserts that Reform advocates "a more racially-neutral, anti-racist position ... than any other federal party."[48]

The party therefore deflects charges or racism by insisting that its policies are "colour blind":

> The way to combat negative labelling is not to go about saying "No we are not racist, no we are not racist," but to constantly promote and affirm federal laws, positions, and policies that are neutral and colour-blind with respect to constitution or immigration or multiculturalism. And this will give the Canadian people a choice between the traditional parties that promote special status for some Canadians based on race, language, and culture, and the Reform position that federal law and the constitution should treat all Canadians equally regardless of race, language, and culture (Manning quoted in Sharpe and Braid, 1992:128).

Manning further suggests that "this colour-blind approach, abandoning ethnic criteria in defining relations between citizens and the state, is the only formula that will allow different racial groups to live together in peace in a pluralistic society" (Manning, 1992:295).

Reform's colour-blindness does not, however, support an ideal of cultural pluralism, but instead reinforces the structural barriers that perpetuate racial-ethnic inequality. Yet the party appears to escape such charges through its appeal to "equality." This represents the new right's most sophisticated attempt at re-articulation. In its promotion of an "egalitarian" society, racial-ethnic considerations no longer need be the concern of state policy. While past racial injustices are acknowledged, contemporary society is characterized as egalitarian. Recent history is seen as a period of enlightened progress where minorities have been, and continue to be, incorporated into social, political and economic life. Racial and/or ethnic considerations in the selection of leaders, hiring decisions and the distribution of goods and services in general, therefore, need never be entertained. When such considerations are made, the new right argues "special status" is bestowed to specific groups resulting in a new form of racial injustice (Omi and Winant,1986).

The concern about this new form of injustice is not only reflected in Reform's stance on employment equity, but is also evident when Preston Manning suggests that the pernicious nature of multicultural policy "promotes the philosophy that some Canadians are more equal than others."[49] Another party official suggests that current policy, in effect, *promotes* racism for it "divides people into ethnic blocs, and it's pretty easy to see what happens when you divide a country up into ethnic or religious blocs of people. We've seen it all over the world.... You're inviting racism and prejudice in one sense, even though they're trying to fight

---

[47] *Financial Post Daily*, June 13, 1991:46.

[48] Manning, quoted in *Canadian Business Life*, fall, 1992:17.

[49] *The Toronto Star*, June 13, 1991:A1.

it."[50] A party position paper on multiculturalism warns that "in a pluralistic society, the politicization of ethnicity leads through envy to discord and, at the extreme, even to violent conflict" (Flanagan and Pantazopoulos, 1992). The Reform Party, therefore, dismisses the goals of the Multicultural Act by claiming multicultural policy in fact *creates* injustice and inequality.

One of the most significant accomplishments of the new right has been its ability to re-articulate the meaning of racial-ethnic equality as a matter of individual rather than group concern (Omi and Winant, 1986). That is, racial-ethnic inequality and discrimination occur only at an individual level. As such there is no need for the recognition of group or collective rights. The only role for the state is to remove legal systems of discrimination and to treat all people equally (Omi and Winant, 1986).

This stance is reflected in Reform Party discourse. A party position paper on multiculturalism reads, "The elimination of official multiculturalism will save a significant, if not enormous, amount of taxpayers' money. Even more importantly, it will send a clear message that the Canadian polity is based on the rights of individual human beings, not on ethnic allegiances of group loyalties" (Flanagan and Pantazopoulos, 1992). Of central importance to the party is the absolute equality of all Canadians without reference to language, culture, race, religion or any other group characteristic. In Reform's world view, individual rights must be paramount. There is no room for group or collective rights, as any form of group recognition ("special status") will infringe on the rights of individuals (Sharpe and Braid, 1992).

The re-articulation of racial-ethnic equality as a matter of individual concern is informed by a firm belief in the equalizing effects of a free-market economy advocated by such neo-liberal economic theorists as Milton Friedmann. The "market relations" approach posits that the market itself, unhampered by an interventionist state, will eliminate racial discrimination. Friedmann argues that it is not in the economic interests of White employers and workers to oppose non-White employment opportunities, for such racist behaviour or "bad taste" mitigates against market rationality and the maximization of profits. These "racist tastes" are thus viewed as irrational responses on the part of White workers and employers that interfere with market rationality and the best economic outcomes (West, 1987). Of course, what this approach ignores is the very real power dynamics embodied in the market itself that impose structural barriers outside and above individual attitudes, however racist they may or may not be. There is no recognition here of the iniquitous conditions imposed by global inequities, colonialism, imperialism, slavery, indenture and so on that result in racial and/or ethnic disadvantage.

---

[50]
Author interview with Dimitri Pantazopoulos, July 14, 1993. At the time of our interview Mr. Pantazopoulos was the party's Manager of Policy.

The refusal to acknowledge the structural barriers to racial-ethnic equality is clearly evident in Reform Party discourse. The party's vision of Canada is one where citizens shed their hyphenated identities (which are fostered by a divisive multicultural policy) and everyone has equal opportunity. This opportunity is assured by the operation of a free market and the removal of any legal barriers by the state. However, there will be no state guarantee of equality of outcomes (Sharpe and Braid, 1992). Manning states this himself:

> Reformers support "equality of opportunity," not "equality of results." We believe that an open, free-market economy, combined with a genuinely democratic political system, offers the best possible chances for individuals to pursue their goals in life. It is true that not everyone starts from the same position, but these inequalities are not necessarily cumulative and inherited. A market economy, open society, and democratic polity are great engines for the destruction of privilege (Manning, 1992:314).

He further states his belief that no amount of affirmative action or special status will accomplish much, "unless members of that disadvantaged minority are affirming themselves by their own efforts to achieve a better life." The role of the government is to ensure that "the economy and society are truly open and competitive, and that the means of self-improvement are available to all." He offers Reform's prescription for dealing with inequality: "Diagnose the problem and devise specific measures to enable people to take greater control of their lives. Do not ghettoize society by putting people into legal categories of gender, race, ethnicity, language, or other characteristic" (Manning, 1992:315). In this sense, Reformers believe that, at best, individuals should only expect that they be free to compete. They should not assume that equality should be a part of the competition (Eisenstein, 1987). In promoting the equality of all individuals regardless of "race, language and culture," the party obscures racial and ethnic differences that are still the basis of discrimination.

The call to treat ethnicity as a purely private concern takes on new meaning when read in this light. It demonstrates the attempt to re-articulate racial-ethnic equality in terms of civil privatism—i.e., equality is strictly a matter of individual actions of striving, merit and deserved achievement (Winant, 1990). But in so doing, the Reform Party disregards the realities of racism and discrimination. Equality without impediments could be achieved through the hard work of enterprising individuals. However, what this assessment ignores is that, in the real world, there *are* impediments such as systemic and institutional racism. Treating race and ethnicity as a private concern, therefore, denies that the state should have any role in prohibiting individuals, groups or institutions from acting out their discriminatory tendencies in such a way as to deny equal opportunity. Where discrimination is *not* punished by the state, equality cannot be achieved as a result of individual merit and deserved achievement.

Reform's rejection of multicultural policy is therefore a rejection of the state recognition of cultural diversity, and especially the need for state action to ensure the full and equal participation of racial-ethnic minorities in social, political and economic spheres as the Multicultural Act advocates. In other words, the party's position on multiculturalism de-legitimizes the vision of cultural pluralism. Despite its protestations otherwise, we must therefore view the party's position on multiculturalism as an attempt to maintain the political and cultural arrangements that systematically place racial and ethnic minorities at a disadvantage, both social-structurally and culturally.

Conclusion

In the final analysis, the party's discourse on immigration and multiculturalism reveals an attempt to undo decades of progress on a number of initiatives that have sought to redress the structural inequalities in the distribution of power and resources, and foster greater racial-ethnic equality. This includes advances in employment equity, the formulation of multicultural policies that (albeit minimally) provide legitimacy for non-French, non-English groups, as well as a more liberalized immigration policy. In other words, the Reform Party would not lead us to a society that is based on the equality of all citizens, but would reinforce those conditions that continue to disadvantage racial-ethnic minorities in Canada.

To what extent has Reform been successful in promoting its agenda? In 1992, then-Minister of Employment and Immigration, Bernard Valcourt, announced proposed changes to Canada's Immigration Act. It was suggested that the shift in Tory policy was due, in part, to the influence of the Reform Party. Indeed, a cursory examination of the policy highlights many of the themes echoed by Reform. The emphasis is clearly on the Independent Class, while the number of people allowed to enter under the family reunification program has been restricted. The policy also makes some attempts to speed up the refugee determination system and provide more power to immigration officials.[51] Under the short-lived government of Conservative Kim Campbell, some of the responsibilities of Employment and Immigration Canada were shifted over to the newly created Ministry of Public Security. Although immigration advocates were quick to point out their concern over the link made between immigration and national security, this change was welcomed by those troubled with Canada's lack of border control.

While in power, the Campbell government also dismantled the Department of Multiculturalism and Citizenship—one of the original planks of Reform's multicultural policy. Although some of the department's programs were taken over by other ministries, their funding was dramatically reduced. It is important to note that, once in power, the Liberal government of Jean Chrétien elected not to undo any of the Conservative initiatives that were adopted in an effort to counter the growing support for the Reform Party.

---

[51] Government of Canada, 1992.

In some ways, the Liberals have even "out-reformed" the Reform Party. In 1994, Immigration Minister Sergio Marchi announced his government's desire to redirect the flow of immigrants and refugees away from the three major Canadian cities where most choose to settle. Leading up to its 1991 national assembly, the Reform Party's policy committee actually rejected a constituency resolution that would have encouraged immigrants to settle in rural areas. Officials rejected the proposal because they were concerned it would make the party sound too extreme. Three years later, Marchi stated, "The 60 percent plus of immigrants and refugees go to three cities—Toronto, Montreal, Vancouver—and each of those cities probably has 85 to 90 percent of all the immigrants in the country. What people are saying is, 'Hey, we've got to have a fairer distribution.'"[52] While I am not suggesting that the Reform Party has been the only influence on Tory and Liberal policies, it does seem clear that Reform's presence has been felt on the Canadian political landscape. Indeed, the party's biggest successes may not be measured tangibly through the ballot box, but to the degree that certain political discourses—such as Marchi's on immigration—have become legitimized. Prior to the arrival of the party, there was very little political debate about immigration or multiculturalism. These are all policy areas the party has taken head-on and, in so doing, has made them difficult for other political actors to ignore.

The Reform Party has in effect re-politicized issues that in recent times have remained uncontested at the level of party politics. For many years discussions about immigration and multiculturalism have fallen outside of what was considered legitimate political debate. The Tories, Liberals and New Democrats have all supported increased immigration levels as well as the consolidation of multicultural policy. The Reform Party enters the political arena and approaches these issues as if they were long-standing shibboleths that require dismantling. The degree to which the party succeeds in this project is a story that continues to unfold, and one that should be of interest to all Canadians.

REFERENCES

Anthias, Floya and Nira Yuval-Davis. 1992. *Racialized Boundaries: Race, Nation, Gender, Colour and Class and the Anti-racist Struggle*. London: Routledge.

Barker, Martin. 1983. *The New Racism: Conservatives and the Ideology of the Tribe*. London: Junction Books.

Boston, Thomas D. 1988. *Race, Class and Conservatism*. Boston: Unwin Hyman.

Eisenstein, Zillah. 1987. "Liberalism, feminism, and the reagan state: The neoconservative assault on (sexual) equality." In Ralph Miliband et al., eds. *Socialist Register*, pp.236-262. London: The Merlin Press.

Flanagan, Thomas E. and Dimitri Pantazopoulos. 1992. "The Reform Party's multicultural policy," Reform Party of Canada position paper.

Fleras, Augie and Jean Elliot. 1992. *Multiculturalism in Canada: The Challenge of Diversity*. Toronto: Nelson Canada.

52
Ottawa Citizen, July 9, 1994:A4.

Gordon, Paul and Francesca Klug. 1986. *New Right/New Racism*. Nottingham: Searchlight Publications.

Government of Canada. 1989. *Immigration Statistics 1987*. Ottawa: Citizenship and Immigration Canada.

_____. 1992. "Bill C-86: An act to amend the Immigration Act (Legislative Summary)." Ottawa: Department of Justice.

_____. 1993. *Canada Yearbook 1994*. Ottawa: Ministry of Industry, Science and Technology.

_____. 1994a. *Immigration Statistics 1992*. Ottawa: Citizenship and Immigration Canada.

_____. 1994b. "Canada and immigration: Facts and issues." Ottawa: Citizenship and Immigration Canada.

Gunn, Simon. 1989. *Revolution of the Right: Europe's New Conservatives*. London: Pluto Press.

Helvacioglu, Banu. 1990. "The state in the Reagan era: Capital, labour and more?" In Larry Haiven et al., eds. *Regulating Labour: The State, Neo-Conservatism and Industrial Relations*, pp.149-171. Toronto: Garamond Press.

Husbands, Christopher T. 1988. *Race and the Right in Contemporary Politics*. London: Pinter Publishers.

Krieger, Joel. 1986. *Reagan, Thatcher, and the Politics of Decline*. Cambridge: Polity Press.

Laycock, David. 1993. "Institutions and ideology in the Reform Party project." A paper presented at the annual meetings of the Canadian Political Science Association.

Levitas, Ruth. 1986. *The Ideology of the New Right*. Cambridge: Polity Press.

Manning, Preston. 1990. "Canada no longer works: we need a new Canada," *Canadian Speeches*, 4,7(Nov.):2-7.

_____. 1992. *The New Canada*. Toronto: Macmillan Canada.

_____. 1993a. "Achieving the equality of all Canadians and reducing the potential for racism in Canada." Address to the Jewish Civil Rights Educational Foundation (January 13).

_____. 1993b. "Reformer's guide to Parliament Hill." Address to a Reform Party rally, Ottawa (June 26).

Morrison, Lee. 1990a. "We need 'made for Canada' immigration policies." Calgary, AB: Reform Party of Canada Archives.

_____. 1990b. "A nation of hyphens." Calgary, AB: Reform Party of Canada Archives.

Omi, Michael. 1987. *We Shall Overturn: Race and the Contemporary American Right*. PhD Dissertation, University of California: Santa Cruz.

_____ and Howard Winant. 1986. *Racial Formation in the United States from the 1960s to the 1980s*. New York: Routledge.

Outlaw, Lucius. 1990. "Towards a critical theory of 'race.'" In D. Goldberg, ed. *Anatomy of Racism*, pp.58-82. Minneapolis: University of Minnesota Press.

Reform Party of Canada. 1988a. "Platform & statement of Principles."

_____. 1988b. *The Reformer* (September) 1(5):2.

_____. 1988c. "B.C. Reformers force immigration issue." *The Reformer* (May) 1(2):3.

_____. 1989. *The Reformer Special Alberta Senate election issue* (October) 3.

_____. 1990. "Principles and policies."

_____. 1991 ."Principles and policies: The blue book."

_____. 1992a. "Preston Manning talks about the New Canada" [pamphlet].

_____. 1992b. "Canadian multiculturalism: legislation is 'ghettoizing' cultural groups." *The Reformer* (August) 5(3):7.

_____. 1992c. "How would the Reform Party promote equal employment opportunities for all Canadians?" Caucus Issue Statement No. 39 (July 28), The Green Book.

_____. 1992d. "What is the Reform Party position on Immigration?" Caucus Issue Statement No. 25 (February 22), The Green Book.

_____. 1992e. "Does the Reform Party promote or tolerate racism?" *The Reformer* (January) 5(1):2.

_____. 1993a. "Blue sheet: Principles, policies & election platform."

_____. 1993b. "Stop digging! Reform Party proposals for eliminating the federal deficit." *Mini Reformer* (April) 1(3):2.

_____. n.d.[a] "Who are the Reformers?" [broadsheet]

_____. n.d.[b] "56 Reasons why you should support the Reform Party of Canada" [pamphlet].

Sharpe, Sydney and Don Braid. 1992. *Storming Babylon: Preston Manning and the Rise of the Reform Party*. Toronto: Key Porter Books.

Stasiulis, Daiva. 1990. "Theorizing connections: Gender, race, ethnicity, and class." In Peter S. Li, ed. *Race and Ethnic Relations in Canada*, pp.269-305. Toronto: Oxford University Press.

_____. 1991. "Symbolic representation and the numbers game: Tory policies on race." In Frances Abele, ed. *How Ottawa Spends, 1991/92: The Politics of Fragmentation*, pp.229-267. Ottawa: Carleton University Press.

Thompson, Grahame. 1990. *The Political Economy of the New Right*. London: Pinter Publishers.

West, Cornel. 1987. "Race and social theory: Towards a geneological materialist analysis." In Mike Davis et al., eds. *The Year Left 2: An American Socialist Yearbook*, pp.74-90. London: Verso.

Winant, Howard. 1990. "Postmodern racial politics in the United States: Difference and inequality." *Socialist Review* (Jan-Mar) 20(1):121-147.

MEDIA SOURCES

"Changing Tracks: The Liberal's new Immigration policy reflects a less charitable mood." *Maclean's*, November 14, 1994:76-77.

"A boon or bust? A new report says immigrants have forged ahead." *Maclean's,* July 25, 1994:16-17.

"Minister directs immigrants to fan out." *Ottawa Citizen*, July 9, 1994:A4.

"Liberals key on kicking out worst criminals." *Ottawa Citizen*, July 8, 1994:A4.

"Nine trends to watch in '94." *Ottawa Citizen*, December 31, 1993:B1.

"A nation of polite bigots?" *Maclean"s*, December 27, 1993:42-43.

"Reformers on the ropes: Preston Manning seeks to reverse his party's fortunes." *Maclean's*, August 9, 1993:14-15.

"Legal reform necessary, Manning says: proposals on parole, punishment a bid to capture law and order vote." *Globe and Mail*, January 13, 1993:A6.

"No pain, no gain: Preston Manning, leader of the Reform Party, says some of his changes might smart a little, but nothing compared to how we're hurting now." *Canadian Business Life*, (fall) 1992:14-17.

"Copps believes Reformers 'not aware' on race policy." *Vancouver Sun*, November 21, 1991:A4.

"Manning plays down immigration policy: Reform Party literature advocates harsher restrictions." *Globe and Mail*, July 15, 1991:A6.

"Reform party tries to shrug racist label." *Halifax Chronicle Herald*, June 24, 1991:A1, A2.

"Manning hits back at critics." *Financial Post Daily*, June 13, 1991:46.

"Manning criticizes multicultural funding." *The Toronto Star*, June 13, 1991:A1.

"The moderate Reform party: the media says the movement has shifted, its leadership say it hasn't." *Alberta Report*, April 29, 1991:15-17.

"Manning lays down the Reform party line." *Vancouver Sun*, February 15, 1991:A12.

"An angry racial backlash: an increasing number of Canadians no longer share the vision of a multicultural society." *Maclean's*, July 10, 1989:14-20.

12

Racism and Stereotyping of First Nations

J. Rick Ponting

Mention the word "racism" today and certain images come quickly to mind: angry mobs burning Indians in effigy during the Oka crisis of 1990 and the equally appalling images of other non-Natives throwing rocks and stones at Mohawk women, children, and elders fleeing Kahnawake across the Mercier bridge during that same crisis. Contrary to what the myth-makers would have us believe, these are not isolated incidents, for racism is pervasive in Canadian society.[1]

We Canadians have prided ourselves on our "tolerance" of diversity, since at least the middle of the twentieth century when American racial conflicts were boiling over in brutal violence perpetrated by the state, and perhaps as far back as the mid-nineteenth century when Canadians gave refuge to fugitive slaves. At times we have adopted an "holier than thou" orientation towards the United States. However, such smugness is quite ill-founded, for racism has been a long-standing feature of Canadian society. For instance, slavery was not abolished in Canada until the passing of the *Emancipation Act* by the British Parliament in 1833. Indeed, slavery was legal and practiced by Europeans in Canada since almost the first European settlement in New France.[2]

Racism in Canada has sometimes been expressed blatantly, such as in our immigration policy and practice prior to 1978. At other times, racism has often been covert and aversive, rather than overt and confrontational. That, however, is of no comfort to its victims, as illustrated by Blacks who say that they would prefer to live in the racism of the U.S. south rather than in Canada, because in the U.S. south a Black person at least knows where (s)he stands.

This chapter is excerpted from J. Rick Ponting and Jerilynn Kiely, "Disempowerment: 'Justice,' Racism, and Public Opinion," in *First Nations in Canada: Perspectives on Opportunity, Empowerment, and Self-determination*, edited by J. Rick Ponting (Whitby, Ont.: McGraw-Hill Ryerson, 1997) by permission of the author and the publisher.

[1] In this section, the term "Indian" will usually be used, both because that is in more widespread use among the non-Native population whose views are being discussed here, and because at the time of most of the empirical studies cited herein the term "Indian" was used by researchers addressing respondents in the field.

[2] Dickason (1992) also notes the practice of slavery by some First Nations during the early contact era.

Adapting the definition of sociologist Pierre van den Berghe (1967:11), we can say that, strictly speaking, racism is a set of beliefs about the alleged inferiority of individuals who are socially-defined as members of a certain group (a "race") which is distinguished by its physical characteristics. This set of beliefs is usually accompanied by an ideology, often religious, which involves values, assumptions, historical interpretations, and other claims which "justify" the treatment of individuals from that group as inferior. In particular, it is used to justify allocating those individuals to particular economic positions and excluding them from receiving certain economic rewards and political rights (Miles, 1989:3). Thus, the racial ideology rationalizes, legitimizes, and sustains patterns of inequality (Barrett, 1987:7).

Physical attributes are used to define social groups ("races") only insofar as those attributes are socially recognized as important because they are believed to be associated with other intellectual, moral, or behavioral characteristics (Li, 1990:5-6). Thus, "races" are social constructs, not objectively identifiable physical realities, for there is much genetic variation within so-called races that are superficially similar in physical appearance. Sociologically, the *racialization* process, whereby a category of such superficially similar people comes to be socially defined as a "race," is very important. The state often plays a pivotal role in this process, as it did with Aboriginal people through the *Indian Act* definitions of who is to be considered an Indian in law, and who is not.

Since the advent of the Black Power movement in the United States in the late 1960s, the term "racism" has come to take on a broader meaning than indicated above. Now, the term is also used to describe outcomes of the operation of institutions when those outcomes differ systematically for people of different "races," regardless of the intentions of the individuals staffing those institutions. This is known as "institutional racism" or "systemic racism," as discussed above. Even though the term "discrimination" would suffice, the term "racism" has also been used to describe the behavior of individuals who consciously engage in discrimination against members of other "races."

Thus, there is no consensus on the proper use of the terms "race" and "racism." Indeed, some social scientists, like Miles (1989:72), feel strongly that these terms should be "confined to the dustbin of analytically useless terms." Given the prominence of the terms in popular parlance, that is unlikely to happen. Furthermore, it is important that readers understand the essentially social nature of "races," the historical roots of racial discrimination in Canadian society, and the mechanisms by which discriminatory outcomes are perpetuated despite the intentions of the actors in the system. Only with such an understanding can realistic policy options be formulated.

Like the tap root of the common dandelion, racism's roots extend deep below the surface of Canadian society. They extend far back into our history, where they are intertwined with a very pronounced ethnocentrism (belief in the superiority of the culture of one's own group). In fact, since the time of first British contact with the Aboriginal people, Canadian legal traditions have assumed that Indians were too primitive to have a legal system that could be considered "civilized" and "worthy" of recognition by the British-based courts. The non-Christian Aboriginals were considered to be "pagans." It was assumed that they had no law, and English law was imposed. To this day, a similarly arrogant orientation can be found in court decisions on comprehensive land claims, as seen in the remarks of Mr. Justice McEachern of the British Columbia Supreme Court in his 1991 ruling on the Gitksan-Wet'suwet'en land claim:

> It is the law that Aboriginal rights exist at the pleasure of the Crown, and they may be extinguished whenever the intention of the Crown to do so is clear and plain.

First Nation lawyer and academic Leroy Little Bear (1986:257) describes the Canadian government's orientation down through history as a "Grundnorm approach," which is to say that the government takes actions which are inconsistent with Aboriginal, British, and international law, in the hope that it can "get away with it" in the courts and that the government's actions will, in the future, come to be held to be legal.

Contemporary racism in the employment market and the housing market, while prevalent, receives much less attention in the mass media than certain other, more sensationalistic manifestations of racism such as police behavior toward Aboriginal people and other racial minorities. Box 12-1 outlines the findings of Manitoba's Aboriginal Justice Inquiry which examined two cases where racism on the part of the police was directed toward Aboriginal people. Other examples are legion and include the case of Donald Marshall Jr., a Mi'kmaw from Nova Scotia who spent eleven years in jail for a murder he did not commit, and Wilson Nepoose, a Cree from Alberta who was convicted of murder after police withheld from the Crown Prosecutor evidence which further weakened what the Prosecutor described as "one of the weakest cases" he had ever taken to trial.

Racist organizations and others promoting intergroup intolerance have a long history in Canada. In the late twentieth century there emerged numerous small extremist organizations such as The Ku Klux Klan in British Columbia (see Sher, 1983), The Western Guard in Toronto, The Aryan Nation in Alberta, The Canadian Nazi Party, Campus AlterNative, and The White Canada Council. In his landmark study of the right wing in Canada, entitled *Is God a Racist?* Barrett (1987:357-360) lists sixty such organizations of the "radical right"—which he defines (p.9) as "those individuals who define themselves as racists, Fascists, and anti-Semites, and who are prepared to use violence to realize their objectives"— and another seventy less extremist organizations of the "fringe right," all of which have emerged just since the Second World War. He identified only 586

Box 12-1: Findings and Recommendations of the Manitoba Aboriginal Justice Inquiry

The justice system has failed Manitoba's Aboriginal people on a massive scale. However, it is not merely that the justice system has failed Aboriginal people; justice has also been denied to them. For more than a century the rights of Aboriginal people have been ignored and eroded. The result of this denial has been injustice of the most profound kind.... A significant part of the problem is the inherent biases of those with decision-making or discretionary authority in the justice system... [and] even the well-intentioned exercise of discretion can lead to inappropriate results because of cultural or value differences.... However one understands discrimination, it is clear that Aboriginal people have been subject to it. They clearly have been the victims of the openly hostile bigot and they also have been victims of discrimination that is unintended, but is rooted in policy and law..."

So said Associate Chief Justice A. C. Hamilton of Manitoba's Court of Queen's Bench (Family Division) and Associate Chief Judge Murray Sinclair of the Manitoba Provincial Court in the report of The Manitoba Aboriginal Justice Inquiry which they led. The Inquiry was established in 1988 after the shooting death of Indian leader J.J. Harper in a scuffle with a Winnipeg policeman and after allegations were made that The Pas residents had known for years the identity of the non-Indian murderers of an Indian teenager by the name of Betty Osborne, but had maintained a conspiracy of silence, and that the RCMP had been less than conscientious in their handling of the case because the victim was Aboriginal.

The judges concluded: "It is clear that Betty Osborne would not have been killed if she had not been Aboriginal." They asserted: "The murder of Betty Osborne clearly was motivated by racism.... It is not difficult to identify individual acts of racism associated with the Osborne case." While they noted that "[c]ertain specific acts that

occurred during the course of the investigation happened because of the discriminatory attitudes or prejudices of some of the police officers ..." they expressed their satisfaction that the over ten-year delay in building the prosecution's case and the RCMP role in contributing to the delay "were not attributable to racism on the part of the force or any individual within the force...". However, they did comment critically on the segregation of the white and Aboriginal populations in The Pas, and did condemn the justice system for systematically excluding Aboriginal people from juries in northern Manitoba.

The Inquiry's investigation into the J.J. Harper incident found racism from start to finish. Harper was stopped by Winnipeg Police Constable Robert Cross while Harper was walking down the street. The judges concluded that the original decision by Constable Cross to approach Mr. Harper, ostensibly in connection with a car theft, was unnecessary and racially motivated. "He stopped the first Aboriginal person he saw, even though that person was a poor match for the description in other respects and a suspect had already been caught," the judges said.

Hamilton and Sinclair found that racism and negligence were central factors in the killing of Harper and in the hasty exoneration of Cross. They added: "We can say, with some assurance, that the confrontation did not occur in the manner which was accepted as fact by the Firearms Board of Inquiry, the police chief, and Judge Enns at the Inquest.... [T]he effort to protect Cross and to shift the blame to Harper took precedence. This effort precluded any objective determination of the facts.... We have been left with the impression that an 'official version' of what happened was developed. We are satisfied that version is inaccurate... It is our conclusion that the City of Winnipeg Police Department did not search actively or aggressively for the truth about the death of J.J. Harper. Their investigation was, at best inadequate. At worst, its primary objective seems to have been to exonerate Const. Robert Cross and to vindicate the Winnipeg Police Department.... We conclude that racism exists within the Winnipeg Police Department and that it was expressed openly the night that Harper was killed."

The judges found that police "collaborated in preparing their notes" and that a number of police officers were "less than truthful" in their notetaking and their testimony about Harper's death.

The judges label Canada's treatment of Aboriginal people an "international disgrace." After offering the legal opinion that

the existence of Aboriginal rights in the *Constitution Act, 1982* includes the right to self-government, they recommended the establishment within Canada of a separate Native justice system with it is own criminal, civil, and family laws and its own courts which would have "clear and paramount" authority. Among other things, they also recommended that the courts, the National Parole Board, jails, and police departments vigorously pursue affirmative action plans for the hiring of more Natives.

Source: *Globe and Mail*, August 30, 1991.

members of radical right organizations in Canada, but is "confident" that thousands more like-minded individuals exist here.

Barrett (1987:327) concludes that there is an overarching dimension which knits together all of the issues on which the radical right focuses—namely, the presumed decay of Western Christian civilization. This is a concern that is reinforced in the writing of some avowedly right-wing columnists in the mainstream print media. For instance, in criticizing certain children's movies produced by the Disney studios, including *Pocahontas*,[3] one such columnist[4] took particular exception to what he saw as the movie's denial of human beings' place atop the created order (see Genesis I:28). To him, such denial is clearly anti-Western.

Sociologists use the term "ethnocentrism" to refer to a belief in the superiority of one's own culture. Such highly ethnocentric ideologues as certain right wing columnists, whose opinions can be fully compatible with the underlying angst of White supremacists, do have the ability to achieve widespread dissemination of their views through the increasingly right-leaning popular media of late twentieth-century Canada. That dissemination, backed and defended by the considerable financial muscle of corporate media giants, operates subtly and cumulatively over time to undermine respect for diversity in Canadian society.

3
    For First Nation persons' critical views on the Disney movie *Pocahontas*, see the following website: http://indy4.fdl.cc.mn.us/~isk/poca/pocahont.html.

4
    For legal reasons, greater specificity is not possible here.

Systemic Racism

Systemic, or institutionalized, racism was defined above. It involves the situation which exists when the norms of an institution are predicated upon assumptions of racial equality that are not met in the society. As Anderson and Frideres (1981) note, systemic racism emerges initially from individuals' racist beliefs, but once created it survives independently of individual racism by virtue of being entrenched in the laws, customs, and practices of the society or organization. Crucial to an understanding of systemic racism is the notion of the web of institutional interdependencies. The web of institutional interdependencies involves racial controls and differentiation in one institutional sector, such as the real estate market, fitting together to feed into or reinforce distinctions in other institutional sectors, such as schools and the labor market (Baron, 1969). Thus, it is highly significant that, in a survey done by their own trade association, 92 percent of all personnel officers surveyed admitted to racial discrimination in hiring or promotion.[5] Significantly, a 1992 survey of persons who graduated from universities and community colleges in 1990 found that Aboriginal graduates from community colleges had a significantly higher unemployment rate than the total community college graduating class (22% vs. 13%).[6] When racism is so pronounced in such a pivotal institution as the labour market, its effects will be felt across a broad range of other spheres of daily life. For instance, a First Nation individual refused a job that is appropriate to his/her level of training and education will be excluded thereby from certain urban real estate markets. That, in turn, will probably determine the school which his/her children attend and the probability that they will graduate from university, which, of course, affects their job prospects. Thus, Canadians will often be relieved of having to make an explicitly racist choice (e.g., against those children) because it is made for them earlier in a chain of institutional linkages.

Cultural Racism

On a daily basis in society, the hegemony (dominance) of the dominant group's culture is expressed through various acts of omission or commission that redound to the detriment of those of other culture. When that dominant group is relatively homogeneous in terms of "race," the imposition of its cultural norms and standards on people of other "races," to their systematic detriment, can be called cultural racism. Perhaps the most unmitigated form of cultural racism in Canadian society

---

5

CBC news, March 30, 1988.

6

Aboriginal graduates earned virtually the same as other graduates in 1992 and among university graduates their employment situation was about the same as for the university graduating class as a whole. See Wannell and Caron (1994).

was the effort by governments and missionaries to "civilize" the Aboriginal people, especially in the infamous church-run residential schools.

Schools are a particularly important forum where cultural racism is manifested. For example, requiring excessive qualifications, such as a Ph.D., for the position of director of a Native Studies program in a university, might preclude most of the very candidates (Natives) who can best relate to Native students.

Furthermore, the officially prescribed school curriculum regularly gives short shrift to the vital economic, social, and cultural contributions which racial minorities have made to Canadian nation-building. Hence, the educational experience for students from those minorities is often quite alienating and their rate of dropping out or of transferring to vocational streams can become quite high.

The mass media are another central institution which imposes a culturally racist model of Canadian society. This is noteworthy in news, advertising, programming, commentary, and other content. Henry and Tator (1985:327) submit that "the media create a distorted image of society in which only those with white skin are seen as participating in mainstream activities." Consider, for instance, the absence of an Aboriginal reporter from the CBC television news program "The National," such that Aboriginal issues are routinely reported from non-Aboriginal perspectives.

Assessment of Canadian Racism

We Canadians can no longer afford to indulge ourselves in the myth that Canadian society is relatively free of racism. We have seen that racism is structured into the major institutions of society. and that Aboriginals and members of some other visible minorities, subordinated because of their physical appearance, are reaching the limits of their patience with the larger society. Inter-racial violence is becoming more common and racial tensions are mounting to alarmingly high levels, especially in the cities and among First Nation peoples. People are getting killed because of racism in Canada. Moderate Aboriginal leaders, like Georges Erasmus, warn that more violence will come if Canadian authorities do not deal sincerely and productively with existing moderate Aboriginal leaders.

The tragedies of Oka, of Betty Osborne, of J.J. Harper and others are profound. Yet, there are other facets of racism that, together, are also taking an alarming toll on Canadian society. First, racism hinders economic competitiveness, because the most qualified workers are often being denied the job, simply because they are not white. Secondly, the legitimacy of the existing political institutions (the political regime) is being called into question due to the inability of those institutions to make much tangible progress toward eradicating racism. A new and growing problem of national unity is emerging as First Nations withdraw whatever legitimacy they had attached to the political community itself. That is, their experience with having been excluded from the mainstream of Canadian society for racial reasons has left many Aboriginal people to think of themselves first and foremost as Aboriginal people, rather than as Canadians. With that orientation, they see themselves as having little stake in the status quo in Canada. As a result, they feel little compunction about engaging in obstructionist strategies and tactics, even on matters of the utmost importance to the power elite in Canadian society, as illustrated by Elijah Harper's obstruction of the Meech Lake Accord and the James Bay Crees' obstruction of the James Bay II project. Furthermore, issues of racism in Canada are increasingly being drawn into the international arena where the impact is to seriously embarrass Canada and to undermine Canada's influence abroad.

Stereotypes Held by Individuals in the Dominant Society

Discussions of negative stereotypes can be unpleasant both for authors and for members of the stereotyped group. While not wishing to give offence, we also do not wish to stick our head in the sand and pretend that there is no stereotyping problem in Canadian society. Hence, we tackle this problem below and include in our treatment a consideration of the effects of stereotypes (including positive ones) upon members of the stereotyped group.

Perhaps because of social desirability bias and the relatively low salience of First Nations to non-Native Canadians, studies of stereotyping of "Indians" yield different results when different methodologies or different phraseologies are employed.[7] Therefore, one must be cautious in making generalizations.

Mackie's (1974) study, conducted during the period 1968-70 in Edmonton, found that respondents' views of "Indians" emphasized laziness (30%), poverty (29%), lack of education (29%), oppression by others (20%), lack of cleanliness (28%), excessive consumption of alcohol (21%), and lack of ambition (15%).

In a 1976 national survey of 1,832 residents of Canada, Ponting and Gibbins (1980:72-75) found Canadians to have very low levels of knowledge about "Indians" and related matters. To questions about the "main differences between Indians and non-Indians" and "the main problems facing Canadian Indians today," only a minority (smaller than in Mackie's sample) responded in ways that clearly indicated that they held very negative views of Indians. Indians were seen as lacking motivation (21%), overly dependent on government handouts (18%), facing serious problems· with the use of alcohol (12%), and being factionalized (2%). A larger proportion of the Canadian mass public gave responses indicative of a view of Indians as facing problems that are not of Indians' own creation, such as discrimination and prejudice (39%), lack of economic opportunities (26%), and an obstructionist government (12%). Significantly, regional variation in stereotyping was pronounced. For instance, only 12% of respondents from

---

7
    For instance, using the approach of giving half her sample an open-ended question format and the other half a different format (the so-called "semantic differential"), Mackie obtained quite different results. Another example is from the 1976 national survey. There, alcoholism was cited by only 4% of respondents on a question asking about the main differences between Indians and non-Indians in Canada, but by 12% on that survey's next question which asked about "the main problems faced by Canadian Indians today".

Atlantic Canada, but 32% from the Prairies, perceived Indians to be charac-terized by what might be called "personality deficiencies," such as lack of moti-vation. The prevalence of the "alcoholism" stereotype varied from a high of 28% on the Prairies, to a low of 1% in Quebec.

The "Indian-as-victim" stereotype continued to have currency into the 1980s, although it was still not prominent in the minds of Canadians. For instance, a 1983 "law and justice" national survey found that among the 40% of respondents who felt that "the police in Canada are unfair to some individuals or groups in society," 29% (or only about 9% of the entire sample) cited Natives when asked "Which particular groups of Canadians do you feel the police do not treat fairly?" (Ponting, 1986:51-52). Such views, probably became slightly more widespread as a result of the public inquiries into such sensationalistic cases as the above-mentioned ones of Donald Marshall Jr., Betty Osborne, and J.J. Har-per. Yet, it is reasonable to hypothesize that the greater degree of Indian political and tactical assertiveness during the late 1980s and the 1990s would work in the opposite direction, so as to reduce the proportion of the population holding the victim stereotype. In Ponting's 1986 national survey of 1834 Canadian residents, the fact that the notion of Indians as "a bunch of complainers" was rejected overwhelmingly (57% to 23%) by respondents, could be interpreted as suggest-ing that most Canadians regard Indian protest as justifiable action to step out of the victim role. However, in our thinking we should not exaggerate the effects of mass media coverage, for research shows that a surprisingly large proportion of Canadians simply pays no attention to such media coverage unless the events are sensationalized or affect them personally, as in the Oka and Kahnawake confron-tations.

The 1986 survey offers other insight into how widespread the stereotype of Indians as victims or powerless people is. Early in the questionnaire, respondents were asked how much power and influence Aboriginal people tend to have on the federal government. The response options and percent choosing each one were: "none" (14%), "a little" (59%), "much" (13%), and "very much" (8%)"[8] The data suggest that the stereotype of Indian powerlessness does exist, but is by no means dominant, and is multi-faceted.

The survey also found evidence of the stereotype of Indians as "helpless." Again, though, this was a minority view held by only 18% of respondents,[9] if we take as our indicator a question which asked whether the federal government or

---

[8]

    The distribution on a corresponding question pertaining to power and influence on the respondent's own provincial government was virtually identical (Ponting, 1987c:31) With regard to the federal government, Aboriginal people are widely perceived to have much less power and influence than the French, much more power and influence than Ukrainians, and roughly as much as, or even slightly more than, Jewish people.

[9]

    However, over a third of the sample straddled the fence on this question and another sixth of the sample was classified as "don't know". Twenty-nine percent responded that adequately funded Native governments would perform more capably than the federal government. (Ponting, 1988a:18).

adequately funded Native governments would perform more capably in meeting Natives' needs. However, Canadians in every region exhibit a widespread lack of confidence in Indians' competence in handling money. By an overwhelming margin (57% vs. 10%) respondents expressed the opinion that the federal government can do a better job of managing natural resources revenues than can Indian bands.[10] Similarly, evidence of the "incompetent Indian" stereotype can be found perhaps in responses to a 1988 national survey in which a near majority (48%) of respondents preferred to have the federal department of fisheries manage the fishery in rivers that pass through Indian reserves, while only 39% favoured Indian management (Ponting, 1988b:96-97, 102).

Thomas Dunk conducted participant observation research which yielded important insights that go beyond what survey research is likely to detect. In the male working-class culture of Thunder Bay, Ontario, where he conducted his research during the mid-1980s, various stereotypes of Indians prevailed. Among his subjects ("the Boys"), "the Indian" was both the object of derision and the object of envy. Included among the stereotypical images of Indians were: the noble savage; the victim; the backward simpleton; the uncivilized, immoral, lawless, degenerate; the promiscuous "squaw"; and the pampered, dependent welfare bum who exploits taxpayers' generosity without reciprocating (Dunk, 1991:113-14). Although some of these elements have a positive tinge at the margins —for instance, the "Indian-as-victim" stereotype confers a measure of social equality with Dunk's subjects—most cast "the Indian" as a social inferior. The negative stereotypes were employed as a symbol through which Dunk's subjects not only *established their own moral worth*, but also their difference from the perceived dominant power bloc of southern Ontario, city-dwelling, liberal, gullible intellectuals (Dunk, 1991:102-3, 118). That is, the stereotypical "Indian" is perceived by Dunk's subjects not merely as an inferior "other" against whom local Whites define themselves (a symbol of what Whites are not). As recipient of state largesse in the form of "special privilege" believed to be conferred by the dominant power wielders in southern Ontario, "the Indian," for Dunk's subjects, is also a symbol of the domination of local Whites by that external White power bloc. As Dunk (1991:103) notes, "The least powerful segment (that is, Indians) of local society has come to represent local White powerlessness." Furthermore, Dunk (1991:131) notes, "For the Boys, what one thinks about Indians is a sign of what side one is on in the struggle to assert one's own moral and intellectual worth."

10

A further fifth of the sample expressed the view that the best job could be done by bands and the federal government working jointly to manage the resource revenues. The distribution of respondents in Saskatchewan (75% vs. 6%), Alberta (63% vs. 7%), and Vancouver (77% vs. 13%) was particularly skewed in favour of the federal government's money managing abilities over Indians.' (Ponting, 1988a:19, 65) In contrast, in 1987 another national survey done by Decima Research Ltd. found Canadians to be about evenly divided on the following statement: "Aboriginal peoples have been dependent upon the federal government for so long, they aren't competent to run their own affairs" (Decima Research Ltd., 1987:47).

The Impact of Stereotypes on First Nation Individuals

Stereotypes about "Indians" were once prominent in school textbooks (McDermid and Pratt, 1971) and in Hollywood movies. Although school boards and Hollywood directors are more enlightened about stereotypes and their detrimental impact upon the stereotyped group and have changed somewhat the content of the material they disseminate, old stereotypes die slowly. Change is particularly slow when inter-group contact which provides disconfirming evidence of the stereotype is not frequent and on-going. In Canada, the geographical segregation of Indian reserves militates against such contact. So does the situation of some highly visible urban First Nation individuals—namely, job discrimination and other forms of racism; culture shock, alienation, and escapist behaviour; jurisdictional disputes between different levels of government which leave many desperately needy persons without the services which they require; etc. Hence, stereotypes persist, although any given stereotype will not necessarily be held by a majority of the dominant population.

Even though stereotypes are often false or contain only a kernel of truth, where they persist great harm is done to Native people, especially to their identity. Furthermore, even stereotypes which are no longer part of popular culture still exert a debilitating influence on subsequent generations of Native people. This occurs both through remarks in which dominant group members unwittingly incorporate stereotypical phrases in the presence of Natives and through the negative self-concepts which Native parents have come to hold. For instance, First Nation parents going through childhood in the 1950s were exposed to numerous "cowboy and Indian" movies which portrayed "Indians" in terms of various negative stereotypes, such as that of "the blood-thirsty, wagon-burning, scalping, uncivilized, wild Indian savage." Not only did First Nation viewers fail to recognize themselves in that portrayal, but many actually came to feel ashamed of who they are (Matthews, 1991:2)[11] Some who lack a positive self-identity engage in behaviour which embarrasses, abuses, or endangers their children, thereby depriving the children of positive parental role models and diminishing their children's own sense of self-worth.

The stereotype of "the drunken Indian" is particularly problematic. As Matthews (1991:7) and one of her interviewees observe:

MATTHEWS: Lots of Indians have no problem with booze [but] all Indians have to face the drunken Indian stereotype. Lyle Longclaws knows the double standard it sets up.

LONGCLAWS: If you were a Caucasian and in that kind of state, you were having a great time. But, if you were an Indian in that kind of state, then you were dirty, drunk, and lazy, possibly violent, and then of course they bring in the police and the police as a third-party institution has a certain image towards you as well, and the next thing you know you could spend some time in jail and have this stigma attached to you, etc.

11

The remarks referenced under the rubric "(Matthews, 1991)" are actually from a variety of Aboriginal speakers featured on this two-hour radio program prepared by Maureen Matthews and produced by Bernie Lucht.

Matthews goes on to point out that stereotypes can become self-fulfilling prophecies. That is, some First Nation individuals, feeling that they have a certain degree of licence to imbibe to excess because it is expected of them by non-Natives, give themselves permission to conform to the stereotype. Misko-Kisikawihkwe (Janice Acoose/Red Sky Woman) makes the point in another way. In a critique of stereotypical images of First Nation people in contemporary literature, she points out (Acoose, 1995:75) that in W.P. Kinsella's 1977 novel *Dance Me Outside*, Little Margaret Wolfchild's brutal murder and its aftermath presage the real-life case of Helen Betty Osborne a few years later. In addition, some First Nation students, especially in non-Native schools, have succumbed to the "dumb Indian" stereotype and dropped out of school. Among the many reasons for the high drop-out/push-out rates of First Nation students is that teachers and non-Native students, themselves influenced by the "dumb Indian" stereotype, sometimes make First Nation students feel that they do not belong in school. As Matthews (1991:10) says:

> Belonging is so important in high school and if the thing you belong to, Indianness, is skewed by the dumb Indian stereotype, you haven't much left to hang on to.

Unfortunately, this "buying into" the notion that Aboriginal people should not be in school is a destructive, disempowering behaviour. Not only does it deprive Natives of the positive identity that can come from academic achievement and the employment rewards which that can bring; it also can leave Natives feeling dependent and feeling that one's well-being is someone else's responsibility (P. Doxtator in Matthews, 1991:10). However, as Matthews notes, the more non-Natives intervene to "help," the more powerless Natives become. The stereotypes of "Indians" as helpless and as victim are thereby reinforced. Matthews (1991:10) poignantly summarizes the effects of these stereotypes:

> Lyle Longclaws told me about his Indian classmates at high school. There were thirteen of them, really bright, tough kids. Every one of those kids tried to kill themselves at some point during high school. Four of them succeeded. Of the nine who survived, six are drunks, living pathetic lives on skid row. We place an almost unbearable burden on Indian people when we look at them and see the dumb Indian stereotype instead.

Conversely, the "noble Indian" stereotype, allows non-Natives to think about pretend "Indians" whom non-Natives have conjured up in their imagination and entertainment media. Some First Nation people strenuously object to this image as being just as racist as the "helpless Indian" image, for they see it as implying that First Nation people acquiesce in their plight with dignity. Insofar as First Nation individuals believe that First Nation people are supposed to acquiesce, this image is disempowering and, ironically, can thereby contribute to a negative self-image. Similarly, even the seemingly positive "Indian princess" image is disempowering, for as Cherokee ethnologist Rayna Green notes (in Matthews, 1991:19):

> Once you put on the princess costume, once you become their darling, then it's difficult to be the warrior that you need to be.... You can't ever take off the princess outfit.

Thus, the stereotype of "the Indian princess" "contributes to the exclusion of most First Nation women from front-line positions in politics, the modern-day battlefield.

Also devastating in its impact on First Nation individuals is the stereotype of "the squaw," with its strong connotations of promiscuity. Matthews' (1991:20-21) interviewees capture vividly the experience of living in the face of this stereotype. Excerpts from their accounts follow:

> KATHY MALLET: Squaw? I remember being called that word and I just kind of froze You know, it's like somebody shot you; that's how I felt—like a bullet went right through me.

> WOMAN 2: A lot of Native men think.... that Native women are easy ... and they think they're easier than the White woman, you know?"

> CONNIE FYFE: [T]he image that ... I deal with constantly is, I'm either a very erotic and exotic little animal [the Indian princess], or I'm not ...I either have this little pedestal that non-Native people put me on or I'm being kicked off of it.

> WINOWNA STEVENSON: So what you have happening from the first contact is this stereotypical notion that Native women have fewer sexual morals, for example, than European women. It's an unspoken stereotype, but every Native woman I know who's ever walked on a street alone has suffered from that kind of stereotyping. I'll give you an example. My daughter was eleven. Her and I went into Woolworth's one day, and some middle-aged non-Native man came along and offered us fifty bucks for five minutes of our time. And I am a mother and I have my kid with me and it's really humiliating and it's really hurtful, and it causes a lot of anger. So that kind of stereotype ... follows every Native woman around that I know. And that's one of the big uglies.

The damage to one's sense of self esteem can be profound. For instance, simply because they look Aboriginal, these women felt ugly. They reported great difficulty expunging such thoughts from their minds. The difficulty is compounded by the fact that many First Nation men internalize the standards and stereotypes of the non-Native culture, such that in their eyes, marrying a Caucasian woman marks a First Nation man as being more successful than does marrying a Native woman. Thus, First Nation women are denigrated by both cultures and many come to feel frustrated in their attempts at being whole persons. That feeling of being truncated, of not being fully developed, can be especially serious for those who have been taught the holistic Aboriginal world view.

Even positive stereotypes can have negative consequences. The examples of "the noble Indian" and "the Indian princess" have already been cited in this regard. Other examples are the stereotype of First Nation people as being highly spiritual and as being good environmental stewards. Those First Nation individuals who cannot measure up to these stereotypes are left feeling inadequate and perhaps guilty about being "not Indian enough."

Thus, as Matthews (1992:11, 17) notes, non-Natives' stereotypes of First Nation people change the way the latter think about themselves. First Nation individuals are now compelled to rebuild their identity in response to stereotypes and shame, instead of memory and legend.

Stereotypes have other consequences beyond those for a person's identity. For instance, as already discussed, police stereotypes of First Nation people as prone to criminality lead to police harassment of innocent citizens, occasionally with fatal results that also perpetuate the "Indian-as-victim" image. Another example is to be found in the extremely complex Oka crisis of 1990 where media personnel's stereotypes, combined with television's penchant for simplification, led to the framing of the events in the simplistic terms of "the Indian warrior" image (Matthews, 1991:4).

We must not lose sight of the fact that First Nation individuals' adoption of Whites' stereotyped views is processed through certain filters. As Braroe (1975, quoted in Dunk, 1991:130) observed in a small prairie town, "[E]ach group acts in ways that project this image of inferiority onto the other, though largely ignorant of the result of their actions. There is a sort of negative division of symbolic labour: the attainment of a morally defensible self for both Indian and White occurs at the expense of the other...".

The reader will recall that Dunk found that stereotypes of First Nation people, as held by working-class men in northwestern Ontario, came to symbolize for those men both regional alienation and what they, as Whites, are not. These are heavy symbolic burdens for First Nation people to bear. One consequence is that they get blamed for a wide variety of deviant behaviour (e.g., vandalism) that occurs in or near the city (Dunk, 1991:107-109). It also results in Whites avoiding First Nation individuals and places where the latter are to be found. Furthermore, negative sanctions are brought to bear against those Whites who violate these norms. Out of all this can come segregation, discriminatory behaviour against First Nation people, mutual alienation, and low feelings of self esteem among First Nation individuals.

Public Opinion[12]

Sometimes Aboriginal leaders are quite prepared to disregard Canadian public opinion, but at other times they are quite attentive to it. Regardless of Native leaders' orientation, non-Native politicians are concerned about, and in their creation of opportunities for First Nations, are somewhat constrained by, public opinion in the Canadian mass public. Indeed, the federal government commis-

12

The 1986 national survey reported in this section was conducted with the aid of a Sabbatical Leave Fellowship from the Social Sciences and Humanities Research Council of Canada (SSHRCC) and with funding from SSHRCC (Research Grants Division), the Multiculturalism Directorate of the Federal Department of the Secretary of State (Canadian Ethnic Studies Research Programme), The University of Calgary and the sale of reports issuing from the study. Data for the 1976 study reported in this section were collected under a generous grant from the Donner Canadian Foundation. The Angus Reid Group conducted the 1994 study reported here. The authors express their sincere appreciation to these supporters of the projects and to the respondents, research assistants, and other support staff members without whose assistance the projects would not have been possible. Data collection in 1976 and 1986 was done under contract by Complan Research Associates Ltd. and Decima Research Ltd., respectively. Percentages cited in this section do not sum to 100% because "Don't Know; No Response" is usually not reported here. In the 1994 survey, the "Don't Know; No Response" category was remarkably constant at about 15% of the sample.

sions expensive polling to keep its finger on the pulse of non-Aboriginal public opinion on Aboriginal issues. The mass media have also taken up the interest and commission polls on the topic themselves.

The first national survey on Aboriginal issues was conducted by Ponting and Gibbins in 1976. With few exceptions, such as significant deterioration of support for First Nations in Quebec and British Columbia, the findings from that comprehensive survey still hold true today, as evidenced by the findings from Ponting's detailed, ten-year follow-up national study and an even more detailed 1994 national survey kindly provided to the authors by The Angus Reid Group.

In this part of the chapter we shall discuss the main themes which emerge from those studies. In order to retain focus on the "big picture" and to avoid getting bogged down in detail, we usually report percentages only parenthetically, if at all. Similarly, readers are referred elsewhere (Ponting and Gibbins, 1980:71-72; Ponting, 1987a:A1-A7) for the methodological details of the surveys. Suffice it to say here that in all three surveys the samples were large (over 1800) and the 1976 and 1986 surveys were conducted using face-to-face interviews in respondents' homes in the official language of the respondents' choice, while the 1994 survey differed by using telephone interviews. All three surveys were conducted by reputable polling firms.

Little Knowledge, Low Priority

Canadians know very little about Aboriginal affairs. In part, that is because we tend to pay little attention to most Aboriginal matters in the mass media and attach a low priority to Aboriginal issues, except when Aboriginal issues touch close to home by involving personal inconvenience or threat to our livelihood. The evidence of this widespread ignorance is overwhelming, as measured by such indicators as not knowing the meaning of the term "Aboriginal people," not being aware of the existence of the Indian Act, not being aware of the existence of Aboriginal rights in the constitution, and over-estimating by a factor of at least two the proportion which Native people constitute in the total Canadian population. By means of a complicated analysis, it was concluded that around 15% of Canadians are almost totally oblivious to Aboriginal matters in this country.

Opposition to Special Status

With the exception of a select few situations, such as First Nations' special relationship with the land, Canadians manifest a pronounced tendency to reject what they view as "special status" for Natives. Later in this chapter this is shown in the curve in Figure 12-1, which plots the distribution of the sample on two indexes, one of which is the Index of Support for Special Status for Natives, in the 1986 survey. A respondent's score on this index is his or her average score on four items dealing with special institutional arrangements for Natives. As with most of the indexes reported in this chapter this one comprises statements with which respondents are asked to indicate their degree of agreement or disagreement, on a scale ranging from "strongly agree" to "strongly disagree."[13]

In Figure 12-1 we shall observe that most respondents fall at the unsupportive end of the scale measuring support for special status for Natives. In 1986 even stronger opposition to special status was found in most questions which explicitly use the word "special." For instance, in 1986 when respondents were given two statements—one of which described special institutional arrangements for Natives and one of which did not—and were asked to choose the one that comes closer to their views, it was repeatedly found that almost two-thirds of respondents opted for the statement that denied special status to Natives. One concrete example of this involved the two statements: "For crimes committed by Indians on Indian reserves, there should be special courts with Indian judges" (only 27% chose this); and "Crimes committed by Indians on Indian reserves should be handled in the same way as crimes committed elsewhere" (65% chose this). By 1994, there was some softening of this antagonism to special status[14] and the issue had become less clearcut. Some ambivalence had entered Canadians' minds. On some questions, Canadians were still more antagonistic than supportive.[15] On other questions, though, there was more support than antagonism.[16] Our interpretation of this discrepancy is that it is an indication of Canadians' opinions on Aboriginal issues being rather inchoate. Although opinions on Aboriginal issues are not exactly formless, because Aboriginal issues are so peripheral to most Canadians we should expect a less consistently structured set of opinions on Aboriginal issues than on some other issues such as the environment or national unity.

13
The statements in the 1986 Index of Support for Special Status for Natives are shown below, and are followed by the percent of the sample agreeing (strongly or moderately) and then the percent disagreeing (strongly or moderately) with each one:
If Parliament and the elected leaders of the Native people agreed that some Canadian laws would not apply in Native communities, it would be all right with me (38% vs. 44%);
Native schools should not have to follow provincial guidelines on what is taught (22% vs. 67%);
Native governments should have powers equivalent to those of provincial governments (31% vs. 51%); and Native governments should be responsible to elected Native politicians, rather than to Parliament, for the federal government money they receive (28% vs. 44%).

14
Given a choice of the RCMP having the "responsibility to enforce the law on Aboriginal land reserves regardless of what the band leaders might want" and the RCMP "respect[[ing] the wishes of the band leaders and leaving law enforcement up to the members of the reserve," a majority (56% of the 1994 sample) chose the former and only 25% chose the latter option.

15
For instance, given the statement "It just isn't right for Natives to have special rights that other Canadians don't have," 41% of the 1994 sample agreed and 34% disagreed. (QI1G) Similarly, in that same survey 51% agreed with the statement (QI10) "Aboriginal Canadians who eventually have self-government on their own land base should no longer have any special status or rights," while only half as many (26%) disagreed.

16
For instance, almost half (46%) of the 1994 sample agreed that "Aboriginals should have certain formally recognized rights such as these [exemption from certain taxes, special hunting and fishing rights]," while only 37% disagreed (QG1B).

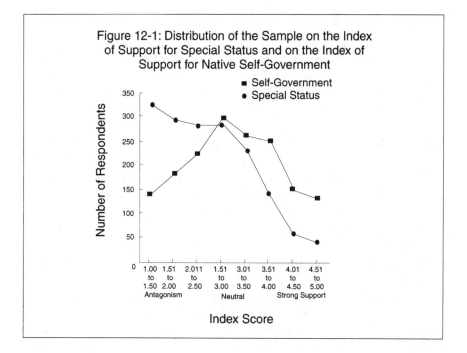

Figure 12-1: Distribution of the Sample on the Index of Support for Special Status and on the Index of Support for Native Self-Government

Such opposition to "special status" as does exist is probably rooted both in the longstanding opposition of many Canadians outside Quebec to special status in Confederation for Quebec, and in a norm of equality which is widely held among Canadians.

Obviously, Canadians' orientation to "special status" for First Nations could have important implications for the degree of self-determination which is attainable under the federal government's "self-government" legislation. The division of public opinion on this is captured nicely by a 1994 question (L1) pertaining to "self-government for Canada's Aboriginal peoples that is, both status and non-status Indians, the Métis and the Inuit." The remainder of the question and the equal division of respondents across the three response options, is shown below:

> Which of the following three broad statements best describes how you feel about Aboriginal self-government, or the right of Aboriginals to govern themselves:
>
> - Aboriginal peoples in Canada have an historic, existing, inherent right to self-government. (29%)
> - The federal and provincial governments should allow Aboriginal peoples to govern themselves. (27%)
> - Aboriginal peoples have no more right to self-government than other ethnic groups in Canada. (28%)

We pursue these issues of rights and self-government in more detail below.

Support for Self-Government and Aboriginal Rights

Paradoxically, antagonism toward special status co-exists with a support for Native self-government and even for recognition of the inherent right to self-government as an existing Aboriginal or treaty right. For many Canadians self-government is less a manifestation of special status than a basic democratic right of self-determination. This interpretation is suggested by the fact that in Figure 12-1 the curve representing the distribution of the sample on an Index of Support for Native Self-government[17] exhibits a markedly different shape than the curve for the Index of Support for Special Status for Natives. The curve depicting support for Native self-government is akin to the famous bell-shaped curve and the average score is slightly to the supportive side of the mid-point of the scale. The curve for support for special status is highly skewed.

Surprisingly, even when the notion of the inherent right to self-government was linked with the Charlottetown Accord defeated in the 1992 nation-wide referendum a small majority of the 1994 sample favoured its recognition as an Aboriginal and treaty right.

The degree of autonomy of First Nation governments from provincial governments is of pivotal importance in defining the fundamental character of First Nation governments. Replacing non-Native bureaucrats with brown-faced bureaucrats who administer essentially the same provincial policies is not self-determination, by any stretch of the imagination. Yet, that is precisely what a substantial majority (akin to the 1986 survey's two-thirds disapproving of special status) of the 1994 respondents preferred when given the option between two statements, as follows:

> Aboriginals could develop and run their own programs in [such areas as health, education and child welfare] without the province having any authority. (19%)

versus

> Aboriginals could manage the programs in these areas but they would still be subject to provincial laws and standards. (65%)

Canadians' views of the capability of Aboriginal governments are improving.[18] When asked in 1994 "how much confidence you have ... in terms of the

---

17
  The Index of Support for Native Self-government is made up of four items. A respondent's index score is his or her average score across the four items. The items are listed below, and are followed by the percentage of the sample agreeing (strongly or moderately) and then the percentage of the sample disagreeing (strongly or moderately):
  — It is important to the future well-being of Canadian society that the aspirations of Native people
      for self-government are met (42% vs. 33%);
  — Those provincial premiers who oppose putting the right to Native self-government in the constitution
      are harming Native people (38% vs. 34%);
  — Most Native leaders who call for self-government for Native people are more interested in promoting
      their own personal career that in helping Native people (30% vs. 41%); and
  — The constitution of Canada should specifically recognize the right of Indians to self-government
      (41% vs 40%).
18
  In 1986, 30% of respondents thought that, if Native governments were adequately funded, they would be more capable than the federal government in meeting Natives' needs, while 18% thought the federal government

role they might play in working towards some solutions to Aboriginal peoples' concerns," the chiefs of large bands garnered majority support, as did national Aboriginal organizations.[19] Also, there is plurality support for the eventual dismantling of the Department of Indian Affairs and strong majority support for the Manitoba approach of transferring DIAND responsibilities to Aboriginal control as "a model for moving towards Aboriginal self-government across the country." However, indications are that on the matter of the representivity of Aboriginal leaders, by 1994 the skeptics had closed the gap on the believers, such that the population had come to be evenly divided.[20]

General Sympathy

To some extent, the above support for Native self-government and Native rights is a reflection of a more general positive orientation toward, or attitudinal support for, Natives. This might be called "sympathy," if that word can be stripped of connotations of condescension. Overall, the Canadian population in both 1976 and 1986 tended to be more sympathetic than antagonistic toward Natives. This observation is based on respondents' scores on composite indexes of several questions in each survey.[21] In 1986 two separate indexes were used. Only about 10-15% of Canadians were *consistently* antagonistic (strongly or mildly) toward Natives across both scales. Twice as many were *consistently* supportive. On both indexes, as on the 1976 index the average score for the sample was well above the mid-point of the scale. Further evidence of a generalized sympathy comes from other questions not included in any of the indexes. For instance, in 1986 a majority (57%) disagreed with the statement, "Indians are a bunch of complainers" (only 23% agreed), and a large majority (71%) dis-

---

would be more capable, and 37% thought that they would be equally capable. In 1994, a large plurality (46%) was of the opinion that "if Aboriginal self-government becomes a reality the overall standard of living and living conditions of Canada's Aboriginal peoples, let's say 10 years down the road" will improve, whereas 19% thought it would stay the same and 18% thought it would get worse. Eighteen percent did not express an opinion. The stability of the "anti-Aboriginal" opinion (at 18%) over the eight years is noteworthy.

19

The question also asked 1994 respondents how much confidence they have in each of several other players. The full results are as follows, with the numbers in parentheses representing "a lot of confidence," "a fair amount of confidence," "not much confidence," and "no confidence at all," respectively: Chiefs of large Indian bands (9%, 45%, 19%, and 9%); Your provincial government (6%, 43%, 24%, and 10%); the federal government (8%, 45%, 23%, and 8%); Canada's justice system (10%, 43%, 23%, and 8%); the federal Department of Indian and Northern Affairs (5%, 42%, 26%, and 7%); Ovide Mercredi, leader of the Assembly of First Nations (15%, 40%, 14%, and 8%); Ron Irwin, the federal minster of Indian and Northern Affairs (4%, 36%, 18%, and 7%); The Royal Commission on Aboriginal Peoples (7%, 40%, 19%, and 7%); and National Aboriginal organizations (9%, 50%, 15%, and 5%).

20

In 1986, in response to the statement "Most Native leaders who call for self-government for Native people are more interested in promoting their own personal career than in helping Native people," 30% agreed (anti-Native) and 41% disagreed (pro-Native). The 1994 survey asked: "Now, thinking about Canada's Aboriginal leadership as a whole, based on your own impressions, do you think they represent the views and concerns of: all, most, some, or only a few of the Aboriginal people in this country?" The responses were: 4% for "all"; 38% for "most"; 29% for "some"; and 13% for "only a few."

21

See Ponting and Gibbins (1980:84-85) and Ponting (1987c:B11-B12) for the items comprising these indexes and for the distribution of the samples on those items.

agreed with the statement "The more I hear and see about Indians in the news media, the less respect I have for them" (only 13% agreed).

However, there has been a deterioration in support for Native people over the almost two decades covered by the surveys. For instance, in 1976 an overwhelming majority (72%) agreed with the statement "Indians deserve to be a lot better off economically than they are now." By 1986, only a plurality agreed (48% vs. 29% disagreeing). The question was not asked on the 1994 survey, but it was a smaller plurality that took the pro-Aboriginal stance in response to the following somewhat similar statement: "Most of the problems of Aboriginal people are brought on by themselves" (40% disagreed; 31% agreed). Yet, on another question that might carry moral overtones to respondents who adhere to the Protestant work ethic, a solid majority of the 1994 sample agreed (57%, vs. 15% who disagreed) with the statement "Aboriginal people are hard-working and industrious, and capable of earning their way if given a chance."

The deterioration in support for Native people can be seen in Table 12-1 below. There we observe that in Canada as a whole, the victimization stereotype of Indians/Aboriginals lost about half of its adherents (as a percentage of the total population) between 1976 and 1994, while the alcohol and drug-abuse stereotype almost doubled in prevalence during that period, to the point of reaching parity with the victimization view. Note that in 1976, British Columbia was right at the national average level of sympathy for Natives, but a decade later it was well below the national average. Quebec offers another example. For instance, whereas a majority of Quebecers, perhaps expressing a shared sense of deprivation as an ethnic minority in Canada, viewed Indians as victims of racism or discrimination in 1976, by 1994 only one-fifth did. The view that alcohol or drugs was the main problem facing Indians was scarcely detectable in Quebec in 1976, but eighteen years later it was not only held by a large minority of Quebecers, but was notably more prevalent in Quebec than the view of Aboriginal people as victims of racism and discrimination.

Sensitivity to Natives' Special Relationship to the Land

Respondents exhibited a generally supportive opinion for Natives on matters related to land and land-use conflicts. Two examples from among several available in the 1986 survey are:

- a (slight) majority of Canadians agreed (versus one-third who disagreed) with the statement: "Where Natives' use of land conflicts with natural resource development, Native use should be given priority";
- a near majority disagreed (48%, vs. 37% agreeing) that giving Native people special hunting rights "just isn't fair".[22]

---

[22] In a 1988 national follow-up study, when the question was reworded to deal with special fishing rights, rather than special hunting rights, the results were virtually identical.

Table 12-1: Regional Variation in Public Opinion on Aboriginal Issues

Item or Statement	Cda.	Atl.	Mont.	Rest of Que.	Toronto	Rest of Ontario	Man.	Sask.	Alberta	Van.	Rest of B.C.
Mean Score on Index of:											
Sympathy for Natives, 1976*	3.31	3.10	3.56		3.25		3.15	2.90	3.00	3.30	
Sympathy for Natives, 1986*	3.22	3.12	3.17	3.31	3.47	3.30	3.13	2.96	3.13	3.09	2.97
Sympathy for Indians, 1986*	3.29	3.09	3.24	3.45	3.48	3.38	3.39	2.91	3.08	3.04	3.04
Support for Special Status for Native People, 1986*	2.56	2.38	21.5	2.96	3.25	2.96	2.44	2.14	2.07	2.11	2.07
1994 Statement											
It just isn't right for Natives to have special rights that other Canadians don't have.											
% agreeing	41	47	57	30	24		53	55	47	41	41
% disagreeing	34	36	32	66	30		37	34	36	46	46
1994 Question											
Generally speaking, do you think Canada's Aboriginal people are being reasonable or unreasonable in terms of their current land claims?											
Reasonable (%)	38	34	30		32		55	53	50	49	
Unreasonable (%)	41	45	66		21		41	43	38	46	
Main (1976) / Most Serious (1994) Problem Facing Indians (1976) / Canada's Aboriginal People (1994) Today?											
% citing racism or discrimination											
1976	39	27	51		36			31		44	
1994	21	20	20		18		23	28	22	24	
% citing alcohol or drugs											
1976	12	7	1		13			28		12	
1994	23	25	30		17		29	21	29	13	

* Denotes possible range is 1.0 to 5.0, where 5.0 is most sympathetic.

On a 1994 question a plurality agreed (44%, vs. 29% disagreeing) with the statement: "Aboriginals have a special relationship to the land and can be trusted as better caretakers of the environment."

Inconsistency of Opinion

No person's ideology is totally consistent in its internal logic. On matters of such low salience to the mass public as Aboriginal issues, we expect to find significant inconsistencies. The survey results conform to our expectations. Box 12-2 presents several examples from 1994 survey questions which address some key issues. The phraseology in Box 12-2 remains as true as possible to that in the interview questionnaire. The inconsistencies in Box 12-2, if inconsistencies are what they are, stand as important qualifiers on some of the observations above concerning support for Aboriginal rights and self-government.

Opposition to Tactical Assertiveness

Canadians tend not to be accepting of any escalation of First Nations' protest tactics beyond a rather tame level. Protest was a major focus of the 1976 survey (Ponting and Gibbins, 1981) and the 1994 survey also included several questions on the topic. The results are broadly similar over the two decades. In 1976, the use of the courts and of protest marches received majority approval, as did "requesting that a royal commission be formed to study Indians' problems." The majority disapproved of the more assertive, tactics of barricading roads or railroads crossing Indian reserves, and threatening violence. Even boycotting private businesses elicited strong disapproval ratings.

In 1994, among five tactics listed, the only one for which approvers outnumbered disapprovers was the blockading of natural resource extraction on land claimed by Aboriginals.[23] A "peaceful blockade of a major highway to press for speedier action on land claims" met with resounding disapproval as did the strategy of unilaterally asserting sovereignty.[24] Even making a formal complaint to the United Nations was approved by only a little more than a third of the sample (37% vs. 45% disapproving). Similarly, only one-third approved of delaying completion of a resource mega-project.

Regional Variation

To this point, discussion of public opinion has been couched in terms of Canada as a whole. That, however, obscures important variations from one re-

---

[23]

The item was phrased as follows: "blocking resource companies from taking natural resources such as timber and minerals from lands claimed by Aboriginals." Approval was given by 41.6% of the 1994 respondents, while 41.2% disapproved.

[24]

The item read: "Indian bands establishing gaming houses and other gambling facilities on their reserve lands without the approval of other governments"; 70% disapproved; 15% approved.

BOX 12-2: Inconsistencies in Public Opinion on Aboriginal Issues, 1994

Pro-Aboriginal Opinion	*Anti-Aboriginal Opinion*

Aboriginal Rights

• A majority supports the federal government acting as though the inherent right of self-government is an existing Aboriginal and treaty right; and	• A majority agrees that Aboriginal people's special status and rights should cease when they eventually have self-government on their own land base.
• A plurality is of the opinion that Aboriginal Canadians should have formally recognized rights such as exemption from certain taxes or special hunting and fishing rights.	• A plurality opposes, as unfair, special Native rights that other Canadians do not have.

Health, Education and Child Welfare

• Concerning jurisdiction on Aboriginal lands, for each of these three areas at least a plurality was of the opinion that Aboriginal peoples should have either significant powers like a province or full independence or sovereignty, rather than mere municipal type powers or "very little authority".	• For the same three areas, a majority of respondents opted for Aboriginals merely managing their own programs while being subject to provincial laws and standards, rather than running their own programs without the province having any authority.

Land and Resources

• A majority agreed that having a land base with resource rights is essential if Aboriginals are to improve their situation.	• A plurality was of the opinion that Aboriginal Canadians should have only minority control or no control over oil and gas on Native reserve lands, rather than 100% control or majority control.
	• A majority favoured extinguishing Aboriginal ownership of land when land claim settlements provide financial compensation for loss of use of the land in the past, rather than Aboriginals receiving compensation and retaining ownership of the land.

Policing

• Concerning jurisdiction on Aboriginal lands, for policing/law enforcement a plurality was of the opinion that Aboriginal peoples should have either significant powers like a province or full independence or sovereignty rather than mere municipal-type powers or "very little authority".	• Responding to an hypothetical situation wherein the leaders on a particular reserve insisted that the members of the reserve would handle law enforcement and that the RCMP should stay off the reserve, a majority of respondents was of the opinion that the RCMP has a responsibility to enforce the law on "Aboriginal land reserves" regardless of what the band leaders might want, rather than thinking that the RCMP should respect the wishes of the band leaders and leave law enforcement up to the members of the reserve.

Data Source: Angus Reid Group Ltd.

gion of the country to another. Those regional variations take on considerable practical significance when one remembers that many of the reforms sought by First Nations require the approval of provincial governments. In some provinces, notably Saskatchewan and now Quebec, support for Aboriginal people is clearly rather low, while in Ontario support is comparatively high. Table 12-1 provides examples from the three surveys. Note how Quebecers stand out as thinking Aboriginal people are being unreasonable in their land claims and how a high proportion of them, along with Manitobans and Albertans, view alcohol or drugs as the most serious problem or issue facing Aboriginal people in Canada. Conversely, alcohol and drugs rank as only the seventh most serious Aboriginal problem in British Columbians' world view. All four western provinces also stand apart from the rest of Canada in thinking that Aboriginal people are being reasonable in their land claims.

Table 12-2 depicts regional variation in answers to the open-ended question asking respondents to name the Aboriginal issue or problem which they think is most serious. In numerous ways, this table reveals that Canadians in different regions have a very different picture of Aboriginal matters. For instance, "Integration into society" is most commonly identified by Quebecers as the most serious Aboriginal issue or problem, whereas, at the other extreme, it ranks ninth in importance in Saskatchewan. Ontarians and British Columbians rank education as the most serious Aboriginal issue or problem, whereas in Quebec it ranks seventh. Prairie residents stand apart as being more likely to see self-government as a more serious issue than do residents of other provinces. Regional subcultures are reflected in other ways, too. For instance, Alberta, with its frontier ideology's emphasis on self-reliance and "rugged individualism," has a notably higher proportion of respondents citing "lack of initiative or motivation" than do the Atlantic provinces and Quebec, where structural barriers to personal success are more widely recognized and acknowledged.

Regional variation is also pronounced on other measures not shown in Table 12-1 or 12-2. For instance, the proportion of the public which is oblivious to Native issues is much larger in Quebec than in the other provinces. In addition, familiarity with Native matters tends to be regionally-specific. To the extent that Canadians are familiar with Native matters at all, that familiarity is usually confined to matters in their own region. The 1986 survey found that even on issues that are clearly of national applicability, such as Aboriginal rights in the constitution or the 1985 amendments to the Indian Act to remove sex discrimination, regional variation emerges in respondents' degree of familiarity.

Causes of Hostility

The 1986 national survey offers some important insights into the causes of hostility toward government policies designed to help Aboriginal people. Using

Table 12-2: Most Serious Aboriginal Issue or Problem, by Province, 1994

Problem	Canada Rank	Canada %	Atlantic Rank	Atlantic %	Quebec Rank	Quebec %	Ontario Rank	Ontario %	Manitoba Rank	Manitoba %	Sask. Rank	Sask. %	Alberta Rank	Alberta %	B.C. Rank	B.C. %
Alcohol/Drugs	1	23.2	2	24.8	2	29.9	5	17.4	2	28.6	5	20.6	1	28.6	7	13.4
Integration in Society	2	22.4	6	14.4	1	38.2	6	16.6	6	14.2	9	8.3	5	18.0	6	15.6
Racism/Discrimination	3	20.8	3	20.4	3	19.6	3	18.4	3	23.3	2	27.7	2.5	21.8	1.5	24.0
Unemployment/Jobs	4	20.2	1	31.2	5	13.7	2	20.4	1	29.4	1	30.5	4	21.3	4	19.8
Education	5	18.9	5	15.1	7	12.6	1	24.6	5	16.3	3	24.1	6	17.7	1.5	24.1
Land Claims	6	16.3	10	10.0	4	16.9	4	17.6	8	10.5	8	8.8	7	13.4	3	23.1
Self-Government	7	14.8	7	14.1	8.3	10.8	7	14.0	4	20.5	4	21.0	2.5	21.7	5	16.3
Culture/Traditions	8	12.7	4	15.3	6	13.2	8	13.8	10.5	9.8	10	8.0	8	10.6	8	12.0
Poverty	9	10.1	8	11.6	8.3	10.8	9	8.4	10.5	9.9	6	12.6	9	9.3	9.5	11.1
Dependency on Gov't/ Want Everything for Nothing/Too Much Gov't Funding/Handouts	10	8.6	9	10.3	8.3	10.8	12	4.7	7	11.4	12	3.7	11	7.8	9.5	11.1
People Don't Understand Them	11	5.5	11	8.9	11	4.9	10	7.5	13	4.2	13	2.8	13	2.6	12	4.3
Lack of Initiative or Motivation	12.5	4.3	--	0.0	12	2.3	11	5.4	12	7.1	7	11.1	10	8.9	13	2.6
Low Self-esteem/ Self-worth/Self-respect	12.5	4.3	12	3.7	13	1.2	13	3.3	9	10.2	11	7.2	12	7.4	11	8.2
Valid Cases	**1493**		**139**		**451**		**395**		**66**		**66**		**160**		**209**	

Source: Angus Reid Group Ltd.

advanced statistical techniques, Langford and Ponting (1992) determined that ethnocentrism is a minor to negligible determinant of hostility. Instead, economic conservatism (the "free enterprise" belief that government should minimize its role in economic relations), prejudice, and perceptions of conflicting group interests[25] as between Aboriginals and themselves are key determinants of respondents' policy preferences. Furthermore, there is an important *interaction effect* between prejudice and perceived group conflict. That is, to take an hypothetical example, if a British Columbia logger has a low level of prejudice toward Natives, her perception that Native land claims threaten her livelihood from logging would have little impact on her support for Native self-government or on her support for special status for Natives. However, for another logger in whom the level of prejudice against Natives is high, that same perception that his livelihood is threatened by Native land claims will produce a dramatically lower level of support for both Native self-government and special status for Natives.

It is also possible to analyze these relationships from the opposite side. In doing so, we found that prejudice has very little impact on the dependent variables (support for Native self-government; support for special status for Natives) when the level of perceived group conflict is low. However, when perceived group conflict is high, prejudice again becomes an important determinant of Canadians' policy preferences toward Aboriginal people.

Our findings suggests the utility of distinguishing between two types of prejudice: dormant and activated. Prejudice against a group is dormant when it is unattached to any sense of conflict with that outgroup. Dormant prejudice has minimal effects on policy preferences vis-à-vis that outgroup. On the other hand, prejudice against a group is activated when it is linked to a perception of contemporary conflict with the outgroup. Such activated prejudice has important effects on policy preferences.

Regardless of whether prejudice is dormant, activated, or absent, economic conservatism was found statistically to produce antagonism toward Aboriginals and their preferred policies. Aboriginal people and their supporters might despair at that finding, in light of the contemporary influence of economic conservatism and in light of the fact that substantial state financial participation will be necessary to overcome the effects of past and present racism, as the final report of the Royal Commission on Aboriginal Peoples asserted.

Conclusion

The forces of disempowerment of First Nation people in Canadian society are formidable. Chapter 5 enumerated them [*Editor's note:* see Chapter 5 of original

---

[25] Perceptions of conflicting group interests were measured in terms of such dimensions as the belief that Natives already receive excessive financial assistance from government, and the belief that Natives already exercise considerable power and influence with the federal or provincial government.

text] and provided relevant background information. In this chapter we have seen the racism of Canadian society come to the fore. It takes especially potent forms in the so-called "criminal justice" system a system in which the basic precepts (e.g., deterrence, retribution, guilt, police, adversarial justice) are foreign to many Aboriginal cultures and have failed Aboriginal people profoundly. First Nation persons' experience with the "justice" system tend to be highly unsatisfactory and detrimental, marred as they are by systemic discrimination, cultural racism, and sometimes the personal prejudices of agents of that system. To date, indigenization efforts have, in effect, tinkered at the margin. The results, as measured by incarceration statistics, remain appalling. This constellation of factors led the Royal Commission on Aboriginal Peoples to recommend urgently the creation of a separate system of Native justice. However, because public opinion in the Canadian mass public is not conducive to such reforms, it is highly questionable whether the spirit of those recommendations will ever be implemented in institutional reforms to create a more pluralistic and more effective Canadian justice system.

Although public opinion has softened slightly over the years on the issue of "special status" for First Nations, debilitating stereotypes remain alive in a significant minority of the non-Native population. In its broader contours, public opinion is no longer the ally that it was when social scientists first began monitoring it over two decades ago. Canadians have a low tolerance for precisely the kinds of protest strategies and tactics that create leverage for otherwise disempowered peoples. Aboriginal peoples have had to resort to those strategies and tactics and have paid the price in a deteriorating level of support from non Natives. Furthermore, the very assertiveness that Aboriginal peoples are finding necessary to attain concrete results is likely to bring Aboriginals into competition with private and commercial interests in the larger society. Non-Natives' perception of such competition as a threat is associated with opposition to government policies favoured by Aboriginal leaders.

Non-Native politicians might seek to discount non-Native public opinion on Aboriginal issues as uninformed, uninterested, and inconsistent. It is all three of those things. However, there are limits to how far politicians in office are willing to go when, as was the case in Canada in the mid-1990s, the courts are wavering, political opponents are seeking to reap political gain from government's policies toward Natives, financial costs increase relentlessly, and the recommended reforms veer off at a one hindered and eighty degree angle from the increased level of accountability that the mass public seeks from the state.

Violence-prone right-wing extremist organizations do exist in Canada, but they have little influence and, Carnie Nerland notwithstanding,[26] their main focus

---

[26] A member of The Aryan Nation in Saskatchewan, Nerland was convicted of manslaughter for shooting a Native man (Leo LaChance) who had mistakenly wandered into Nerland's gunshop.

has not been on Aboriginal people. Of more concern should be the more influential right-wing ideologues. Their ethnocentric, anti-statist, pro-individual rights, radical egalitarian, fiscal retrenchment philosophy is profoundly antithetical to First Nations' needs. The probability is that they will inject partisan politics into Aboriginal issues such that Aboriginal people, lacking electoral clout will again be buffeted by political forces that are largely beyond their ability to control. A real danger is that the political atmosphere created by right-wing ideologues will lead the state to offer either mere incremental, tokenistic change, which would exacerbate the problems of distrust of government, or conversely, to offer in desperation some drastic "solution" of radical equality. Neither approach offers true justice in the sense of arrangements that permit the survival and well-being of Indians as Indians (Boldt, 1993:57).

The author expresses his appreciation to Jerilynn Kiely for her research assistance with the public opinion data in this chapter.

REFERENCES

Acoose, Janice (Misko-Kisikawihkwe [Red Sky Woman]) *Iskwewak—KaH' Ki Yaw Ni Wahkomakanak; Neither Indian, Princess nor Easy Squaws.* Toronto: Women's Press, 1995.

Anderson, Allan B. and James S. Frideres. 1981. *Ethnicity in Canada: Theoretical Perspectives.* Scarborough, ON.: Butterworth.

Assembly of First Nations. 1993. "Reclaiming our nationhood, strengthening our heritage." *Brief to the Royal Commission on Aboriginal Peoples prepared under the Intervenor Participation Program.* Ottawa.

Baron, Harold M. 1969. "The web of urban racism." In Louis L. Knowles and Kenneth Prewitt, eds. *Institutional Racism, in America,* pp.134-76. Englewood Cliffs, N.J.: Prentice Hall.

Barrett, Stanley R. 1987. *Is God A Racist? The Right Wing in Canada.* Toronto: University of Toronto Press.

Boldt, Menno. 1993. *Surviving as Indians. The Challenge of Self-Government.* Toronto: University of Toronto Press.

Braroe, Niels W. 1975. *Indian and White: Self Image and Interaction in Canadian Community.* Stanford, California: Stanford University Press.

Brodeur, Jean-Paul. 1991 *Justice for the Cree: Policing and Alternative Dispute Resolution.* Grand Council of the Crees of Quebec.

Canadian Centre for Justice Statistics. Adult Correctional Services in Canada. Ottawa: Statistics Canada.

Cawsey, Hon, Mr. Justice Robert A. 1991. *Justice on Trial: Report of the task Force on the Criminal Justice System and Its Impact on the Indian and Métis people of Alberta.* Edmonton: Queen's Printer.

Decima Research Limited. 1987. *A Study of Canadian Attitudes Toward Aboriginal Self-Government.* Toronto.

Dene Tha'Band of Assumption. 1990. "Submission to the task force on the criminal justice system and its impact on the Indian and Métis People of Alberta." June 12.

Dickason, Olive P. 1992. *Canada's First Nations: A History of Founding Peoples from Earliest Times.* Toronto: McClelland and Stewart.

Dunk, Thomas. 1991. *It's A Working Man's Town: Male Working Class Culture in Northwestern Ontario.* Montreal and Kingston: McGill-Queen's University Press.

Elizabeth Fry Society of Calgary. 1990. "Submissions of the Elizabeth Fry Society of Calgary regarding the task force on the criminal justice system and its impact on the Indian and Métis People of Alberta." Calgary.

Getty, Ian A.L. and Antoine S. Lussier, eds. 1983. *As Long as the Sun Shines and Water Flows: A Reader in Canadian Native Studies.* Vancouver: University of British Columbia Press.

Hamilton, Mr. Justice A.C. and Judge Murray Sinclair. 1991. *Report of the Aboriginal Justice Inquiry of Manitoba.* Winnipeg: Queen's Printer.

Henry, Frances and Carl Tator. 1985. "Racism in Canada: Social myths and strategies for change." In Rita Bien-venue and Jay Goldstein, eds. *Ethnicity and Ethnic Relations in Canada*, 2nd Edition. Scarborough, Ont.: Butterworth.

Jackson, Michael. 1988. *Locking Up Natives in Canada*. Report of the Canadian Bar Association Committee on Imprisonment and Release. Reprinted in U.B.C. *Law Review XXIII (1989)*.

Langford, Tom and J. Rick Ponting. 1992. "Canadians' responses to Aboriginal issues: The role of prejudice, perceived group conflict, and economic conservatism." *Canadian Review of Sociology and Anthropology* XXIX(2):140-166.

LaPrairie, Carol. 1988. "Native criminal justice programs: An overview." Unpublished.

_____ et al. 1996. *Examining Aboriginal Corrections in Canada*. Ottawa: Solicitor General of Canada (Supply and Services Canada Cat. No.JS5-1/14-1996E).

Li, Peter S., ed. 1990. *Race and Ethnic Relations in Canada*. Don Mills, Ont: Oxford University Press.

Little Bear, Leroy. 1086. "Aboriginal rights and the Canadian 'grundnorm'." In J. Rick Ponting, ed. *Arduous Journey: Canadian Indiens and Decolonization*, pp.243-259. Toronto: McClelland & Stewart/Oxford.

Long, David Alan and Olive P. Dickason. 1996. *Visions of the Heart: Canadian Aboriginal Issues*. Toronto: Harcourt Brace.

Matthews, Maureen. 1991. "Isinamowin: The White Man's Indian." CBC IDEAS Transcripts #9237, Toronto: Canadian Broadcasting Corporation.

McCaskill, Don. 1983. "Native people and the justice system." In Ian A.L. Getty and Antoine S. Lussier, eds. *As Long as the Sun Shines and Water Flows*, pp.288-298. Vancouver: University of British Press.

McDiarmid, Garnet and David Pratt. 1971. *Teaching Prejudice: A Content of Social Textbooks Authorized for Use in Ontario*. Toronto: Ontario Institute for Studies in Education.

Miles, Robert. 1989. *Racism*. London: Routledge.

Misko-Kisikawihkwe (Acoose, Janice [Red Sky Woman]). 1995. *Iskewak-Kah' Ki Yaw Ni Wahkomakanok: Neither Indian Princess nor Easy Squaws*. Toronto: Women's Press.

Monture-Angus, Patricia. 1996. "Lessons in decolonization: Aboriginal overrepresentation in Canadian criminal justice." In David A. Long and Olive P. Dickason, eds. *Visions of the Heart*, pp.335-354. Toronto: Harcourt Brace.

Ponting, J. Rick and Roger Gibbins. 1980. *Out of Irrelevance: A Socio-Political Introduction to Indian Affairs in Canada*. Scarborough, Ont.: Butterworth.

_____. 1981. "The reactions of English Canadians and French Quebecois to Native Indian protest." *Canadian Review of Sociology and Anthropology* XVIII(2):222-238.

Ponting, J. Rick. 1986. *Arduous Journey*. Toronto: McClelland & Stewart.

_____. 1987a. *Profiles of Public Opinion on Canadian Natives and Native Issues. Module 1: Constitutional Issues*. Calgary, Alberta: Research Report #87-01, Research Unit for Public Policy Studies, The University of Calgary.

_____. 1987b. *Profiles of Public Opinion on Canadian Natives and Native Issues. Module 2: Special Status and Self-government*. Calgary, Alberta: Research Report #87-02, Research Unit for Public Policy Studies, The University of Calgary.

_____. 1987c. *Profiles of Public Opinion on Canadian Natives and Native Issues. Module 3: Knowledge, Perceptions, and Sympathy*. Calgary, Alberta: Research Report #87-03, Research Unit for Public Policy Studies, The University of Calgary.

_____. 1988a. *Profiles of Public Opinion on Canadian Natives and Native Issues. Module 4: Native People, Finances, and Services*. Calgary, Alberta: Research Report #88-01, Research Unit for Public Policy Studies, The University of Calgary.

_____. 1988b. *Profiles of Public Opinion on Canadian Natives and Native Issues. Module 5: Land, Land Claims, and Treaties*. Calgary, Alberta: Research Report #88-02, Research Unit for Public Policy Studies, The University of Calgary.

Quigley, Tom. 1994. "Some issues in sentencing of Aboriginal offenders." In R. Gosse, J. Youngblood Henderson and R. Carler, comps. *Continuing Poundmaker and Riel's Quest: Presentation Made at a Conference on Aboriginal Peoples and Justice*, pp.269-300. Saskatoon: Purich Publishing.

Rolf, Mr. Justice C.H. 1991. *Policing in Relation to the Blood Tribe*. Lethbridge, Alberta.: Commission of Inquiry.

Ross, Rupert. 1992. *Dancing with a Ghost: Exploring Indian Reality*. Markham, Ont.: Octopus Publishing.

Royal Commission on Aboriginal People (RCAP). 1996. *Bridging the Cultural Divide: A Report on Aboriginal People and Criminal Justice in Canada*. Ottawa: Supply and Services Canada.

Sher, Julian. 1983. *White Hoods: Canada's Ku Klux Klan*. Vancouver: New Star Books.

Sinclair, Mr. Justice Murray. 1994. "Aboriginal peoples, justice, and the law." In R. Gosse, J. Youngblood Hender-son and R. Carter, comps. *Continuing Poundmaker and Riel's Quest: Presentation Made at a Conference on Aboriginal Peoples and Justice*, pp.173-184. Saskatoon: Purich Publishing.

Turpel, Mary Ellen. 1993. "On the question of adapting the Canadian criminal justice system for Aboriginal peoples: Don't fence me in." In Royal Commission on Aboriginal Peoples, *Aboriginal People and the Justice System: Report of the National Round Table on Aboriginal Justice Issues*. Ottawa: Supply and Service Canada.

van den Berghe, Pierce. 1967. *Race and Racism: A Comparative Perspective*. New York: Wiley & Sons.

Wannell, Ted and Nathalie Caron. 1994. "The class of 1990: Visible minorities, Aboriginal peoples, and persons with activity limitations." *Statistics Canada Daily*, October 4.

13

The Politics of Educational Change: Taking Anti-Racism Education Seriously

George J. Sefa Dei

The challenge of establishing inter- and intra-group sociability and transnational civility in a "postmodern age" is not simply to learn to live peacefully with one another. More importantly, it is to begin to share power, social resources and wealth among and within groups. In a pluralistic society, apart from power differences among social groups, there exists a constellation of conflicting, contradictory and competing social, economic and political interests. Such interests are regulated by structural ideological forces of society to ensure the prevalence of hegemonic interests of the most dominant groups. A manifestation of this tension can be seen in the contradiction between a national democratic ideal and gross social inequities. The anti-racism project is about more than managing a diversity of interests. It is about creating a non-hierarchal social order where all diverse and competing interests are balanced equitably with the common good.

In this chapter, I present a historical and contextualized definition of racism, and situate that definition within a political project of anti-racism education that empowers stakeholders and challenges structural inequalities and White dominance. Since it is impossible to imagine anti-racism without the concepts of race and racialization, I discuss the place of race as a pernicious if unstable social category that flows between biologically and culturally based criteria. This requires that anti-racism education resist White hegemony by integrating multiple forms of oppression. Critical anti-racism education seeks to rupture racist projects in schools, and question White dominance and pathologized views of marginalized groups that result in the production and reproduction of racialized practices. In an environment of resistance, teachers, administrators and students critically discuss race and oppression, and link theory to lived experience. This resistance must include exposing the links between policies, pedagogies and curricula, which may lead to a transformative education inclusive of the cultural knowledges of youth, parents and communities. Working against transformation

of the hegemony are the economic realities of fiscal uncertainty and globalization of capital. At both the community level and in national popular discourse,
"back to basics" rhetoric often excludes analysis of the reproduction of the
dominance through the hidden curriculum, while the interests of global capital
encourages competition between unionized (often White, male and in the north)
and marginalized workers (often female, non-White and in the south). The discussion of racism and inter-locking of other social oppressions is not seen as
salient in the mainstream discussions of capital and employment. Therefore,
anti-racist education must incorporate domestic and interactional foci.

I offer a paradigm of anti-racism education that has implications beyond the
confines of the school system. I take a broader view of anti-racism and education
that includes addressing the questions and challenges associated with educational
transformation and social change. I see myself implicated in the discussion and I
do not intend to pontificate from a position of a dogmatic observer. While I make
particular reference to schools, I would hope that readers will make the necessary
connections with other institutional and educational settings in which they are
located.

Defining and Understanding Anti-Racism

Anti-racism education is an action-oriented educational strategy to deal with
the problems of racism and the intersections of other forms of social oppression.
The anti-racism discourse is an academic discourse as well as a political practice.
Like all discourses (public and academic), anti-racism is not "politically innocent." The educational practice of teaching and learning requires a clear position-
ing of one's politics, as well as an explication of a political project. In fact, the
"act" of education means precipitously launching a political project. For as Apple (1991:vii) points out, academic discourses take place within "a shifting and
dynamic social context in which the existence of multiple sets of power are
inevitable."

The anti-racism discourse began in Britain and later emerged in Canada,
Australia and the United States. Among the early scholarly works that influenced
and shaped the development of the anti-racism dialogue are: Mullard (1980,
1985); Brandt (1986); Troyna (1987); Troyna and Williams (1986); Gilroy
(1982); Cohen (1988/9); Bains and Cohen (1988); Jeffcoate (1984); Nixon
(1984); and Carby (1982) [see also Reed, 1994]. In Canada, the pioneering
works of Abella (1984), Thomas (1984) and Lee (1985) laid the groundwork for
anti-racism education as a serious academic and political project with the initial
objective of transforming schooling and education.

Li (1990:3) contests the scientific and cultural assumptions about race and
ethnicity that exist within the "popular notion that Canada is a multi-ethnic and
multicultural society." He reviews the history of elite, popular and political dis-

course and argues that race and ethnicity have been mechanically interpreted in the dominant discourse. In this process, culture is used to "make the other" (Abu-Lughod, 1991:162). Thus, cultural differences "make" ethnicity as phenotypical differences "make" race. The logical conclusion of "making" leads one to believe that individual cultural ignorance and racial intolerance are the root causes of conflicted identities and inequalities. Following such assumptions, the resources of government and popular discourse (especially the education and media) support "managing race and ethnic relations" (Li, 1990:14-15) at the expense of working towards equal opportunities and outcomes for all Canadians.

If White individuals, groups and institutions do not perceive how they have perpetrated, and continue to perpetrate, inequality in the educational system and in larger society, then they will not relinquish their "innocence" to affect reparations (see Razack, 1992:5). It is marginalized youth, family and communities who suffer the consequences of this "innocence" when the White majority refuses to be accountable for the racialized inequalities in *its* own system. It is the marginalized youth, family and community who experience the statistics behind the overrepresentation of Black youths as "drop-outs," who feel that the teaching and administrative staff of the school *"will not look like us,"* and who must deal with the diminished expectations of youth achievement implicit in the White teacher's pathologization of the Black family (see Dei, Mazzuca, McIsaac and Zine, 1997). Consequently, the impetus for anti-racism change came from local community political struggles asking the state to live up to the democratic ideals of citizenship, social justice, equity and fairness.

Fundamental to anti-racism analysis are the concepts of equity, social justice and educational democracy. Understanding the principles of equity and justice is key to harmonious co-existence in a highly structured, differentiated and professedly democratic society. At both the theoretical and practical levels, the concepts of "justice," "equity" and "democracy" are not only value-laden but also subject to different interpretations depending on racial, ethnic, class, gender and sexual positionalities. Our subject positions generate distinct versions of what, for example, social justice means or ought to look like. Equity is still a contested notion, in terms of what it means, as well as how, when, and what form it should take. Similarly, the meaning of democracy is contested and extended beyond politics to sexual, gender and economic issues.

For the anti-racism worker, the task is not merely to contest social meanings; anti-racism work also involves the development and use of shared assumptions. For example, in anti-racism work, social justice and equity are defined in terms of how a society treats the most disadvantaged or least privileged in its midst. Historical antecedents may serve as adequate political, cultural and social referents in the struggle for social justice and equity. Undoubtedly, the redressing of historical and contemporary structural inequalities is bound to create resentment and the perception of injustice among dominant groups. Historically subordinated groups will struggle among themselves for a voice and identity. Tensions are bound to arise in the struggle for justice in a climate of intense diversity and "celebrated difference." The test of anti-racism politics is to deal with these emerging challenges.

Rather than focusing only on theoretical questions of interpretation and meaning at the cost of interrogating the constructed basis of social systems, the anti-racism project examines social and political structures and contexts influencing the distribution of valued goods in society. One such "social good" is education, broadly defined to include the production, interrogation and dissemination of knowledge for self- and collective improvement and human problem solving. This understanding is in many ways antithetical to the view that the main purpose of education is to "get a job." The examination of social and political contexts for the production, procurement and utilization of education calls for interrogating entrenched patterns of domination and marginality in schools that create unequal outcomes for students. We must remember that schools produce social inequality, and are not simple "reflections" of larger social processes (McCarthy, 1988, 1990).

Anti-racism educational praxis can accomplish educational transformation and social change if it empowers individuals and groups to find ways to actualize their individual and collective abilities and strengths. Empowerment here entails the unravelling of structural constraints that hinder or mitigate against individual and collective advancement of minority population groups in White-dominated society. The powerful social forces and structures that regulate the material conditions within which all members of society satisfy their needs, dreams and aspirations should therefore be critically examined. This means that the issues of race and social difference cannot be formulated in narrow, inter-personal terms, but rather in their broader, structural sense. This is the academic and political objective of anti-racism education in the site of schooling and education in the Euro-American context.

The anti-racism challenge has provided a critique of dominant hegemonic discourse about race relations and multiculturalism in White-dominated societies in the following six ways: (1) anti-racism workers and educators challenge conventional discourse and praxis of race relations that simply imply "let us all get along" without any serious interrogation of the power dimensions embedded in social relations and education (for example, classroom teaching); (2) the discourse exposes the need to recognize institutionalized power and its discretionary use to establish dominance and unearned privilege in society; (3) anti-racism critiques the valorization of diversity and the failure to consider seriously the pointed notion of "difference" (for example, how difference is named, recognized, interpreted, acted upon in social/race relations); (4) the discourse offers a model to interrogate the failure to see difference as a site of power imbalance and to deal with the intersection of oppressions, as well as the relational aspects of difference; (5) the traditional emphasis within multicultural education on "culture" is problematized; and (6) while not negating the relevance of the concept of "culture," politicized notions of race, culture and history are relevant for a progressive politics of transformative change in schools and other institutional settings.

Today, anti-racism education has become the study of relations of power and domination within and beyond the school systems. The anti-racism educational struggle is a call for political commitment and action geared towards educational transformation and social change on the part of educators and community workers. Anti-racism education challenges the de-personalization of minority students in the school system and ruptures the institutional processes that disengage some students while engaging others. Anti-racism seeks to subvert the institutional processes that reproduce the dominance and normalcy of "Whiteness" and White culture in the schools and in society. "Whiteness" has historically bestowed unquestioned privilege and power. Members of the dominant group disproportionately occupy positions of influence and authority. While authority and power are not necessarily coterminous, it has nevertheless been possible for authority to translate to power and privilege. Anti-racism questions the discretionary use of authority to serve exclusive and narrow interests.

The Idea of Race in Anti-Racism

Current thinking on anti-racism recognizes both the centrality of race in human lives and the multiple and shifting meanings of the concept. Anti-racism sees race identification as a fundamental organizing principle and tool which profoundly mediates the concrete realities of our lives in conjunction with other socially constructed, and empirically significant, locations of gender, sexuality, ability and class. Social scientists recognize the importance of de-essentializing the race concept (see Gillborn, 1995a, b). Race is not a homogenous or one dimensional category. It is possible for individuals to both identify as, and/or be perceived as, belonging to more than one race (see also Train, 1995). Race is also understood as a material and ideological signification of difference (Omi and Winant, 1993; Miles, 1989). It is a social construct with changing meanings that are historically specific (Goldberg, 1993). I define race as a social relational category defined by socially selected physical characteristics (see also Wilson, 1973). While race is without scientific validity, its powerful social effects are recognized and lived. The material consequences of race signification are severe and are evident in everyday practices of society. Race classification is a potent act or weapon in the distribution of rewards, privileges, penalties and punishment in a highly stratified, racialized society. Racism is a practice of social deceit, manipulation and division in society. We cannot deny its existence.

Furthermore, the connection between an understanding of the concept of race and the practice of racism should also be recognized. I am reminded by a request from a graduate student that I become a member of a doctoral thesis committee. The student would not use the term "race" in discussions because "it is meaningless." In fact, according to the student, "there is only one race and that is the human race." Such academic misreading that denies the materiality and social potency of the race notion is not uncommon in the academy. Interestingly, I have seen some respected scholarly colleagues enclose race in quotation marks. All social concepts lack scientific validity. Terms like gender, race and class are concepts that society has chosen to engage in conversations and practices. They are socially constructed categories whose meanings are historically specific and change in different political and cultural contexts. They are contested notions and yet it is race that appears in quotation marks. Why? Just because race is an unstable category does not mean that the term lacks social application. Moreover, numerous other terms used in academic discourses are rooted in false scientific and biological explanations and/or interpretations, yet many terms never appear in quotation marks.[1]

Historical and emerging usages point to the fact that skin-colour racism is only one of many forms of race and racialized practices. The recognition of new and multiple forms of racisms should not, however, deny the saliency of skin-colour racism. We cannot use relativism as a tool to obscure the specificity of skin-colour racism. Inequalities constructed by skin-colour racism are not easily negated or transformed. In fact, as Fumia (1995) also argues, there is a difference between those who can transcend their ethnicity through social integration and assimilation and those who "remain disadvantaged because of their race" (Fumia, 1995:13; see also Walcott, 1990). For in the discourses of racism one cannot avoid the wrath of oppressive practices which continue to signify skin colour as racial difference. The powerful social and material effects of skin-colour racism are glaring even in a postmodern context.

Currently, new culturalist forms of racism are practiced in the name of religion, culture, class, economics and language (Miles, 1989). We have also witnessed a new populist politics that scapegoats "difference" and racializes "others." Culturalist forms of racisms do not rely on preeminence of perceiving phenotypical differences among people. Today we can speak of race without mentioning the word (Gilroy, 1992:53; see also Banton, 1970:28). The coded language of "welfare mothers," "pushy immigrants" and "inner-city" have be-

---

1   The rational for enclosing race in quotation marks appears to assume that there is a biological reality that must be kept separate from an alternate meaning, much as writers who use quotations to demonstrate their dramatic appropriation of an otherwise understood term. I argue that such usage denies the important social meanings and political consequences of allowing race to be singled out as proof of the incomprehensibility of oppression.

come the popular refrain for those whose racialized discourses have the intent of blaming and punishing people. Racial meanings are easily inferred from powerfully coded words, as well as in the emerging definitions of citizenship and nationhood. Language has become a powerful marker of racial discrimination just as gendered cultural assumptions have increasingly assumed racist undertones.

Apart from anti-Black, anti-Asian, anti-immigrant racisms, different and complex processes of racialization have emerged which utilize powerful ideologies and political practices to identify certain populations by reference to perceived biological and cultural unity. These populations are thought and spoken about in racialized terms, using language, biology and religious criteria (see also Reed, 1994). One can cite the rise of neo-Nazism and fascism, and the public discourse and treatment of Muslims in Europe and North America.

The consequences of the new culturalist, as well as de-politicized, approaches to race are manifold. The new racialized discourses appear in subtle ways to reproduce and sustain hegemonic ideologies. The "new" forms also make it easy for people to openly express hostility without admitting that their actions are profoundly discriminatory. It also makes it difficult to organize against structural racism. In fact, I see Goldberg's (1993) reference to "consumer-directed discrimination" to be in many ways connected with the power of an emerging populist politics of race-baiting. It is not just that race policies today are driven by public opinion. As Rockhill (1995) has observed in a different context, there is open refusal to even explore the possibilities of a new society where anti-racism work and analysis is featured more seriously in everyday social practices in schools, workplaces and other organizational settings. The unwillingness of many academics and administrators in universities and colleges to link the theory of anti-racism to equitable hiring practices is remarkable. Actions become stalled by a defensive posture that insists that anti-racist education must not interfere with the Euro-male dominated "canon." Avouched "liberal" academics join with their conservative colleagues in maintaining the dominant curriculum and the "old boys" network of instructors who will reproduce that curriculum. In the rare cases where racialized professors are hired, the same academics who disavowed such a departure will consider their critics to be neutralized and their institutions' quota filled. In such a climate, the restrictive structure of domination within the academy scarcely needs to be interrogated. Instead of attracting a diverse student body by re-designing courses, broadening subject areas and reforming pedagogy, institutions tend to "control" enrolment through minor adjustments in restrictive tuition and admission policies, thereby attracting students who are already trained to reproduce White supremist institutions, and who are willing to continue to do so.

The contemporary challenge of anti-racism education is how to foreground race in the understanding of the intersections of social difference. Elsewhere I have discussed how race can and must be understood in relation to gender, class and sexuality (see Dei, 1996). There are obvious dangers in the reification of race as the only category of oppression. Fortunately, there is a growing understanding that racism and other forms of oppression need to be fought together, not separately. To change power relations in society requires the removal of every bit of oppression in human lives. Oppression may be separate and distinct in their origins but nevertheless do demonstrate remarkable commonalities in their practices. As Train (1995) also argues, social identities overlap and therefore ought not to be separated. Oppression is experienced as a *whole* and must therefore be fought as such. Identities constitute markers of difference between and among individuals and social groups. All identities are relational, restrictive, socially and situationally constructed, and are products of human agency. Identities are continually invented and re-invented through self- and group consciousness in response to historical and prevailing individual and collective circumstances. The problems of hyperlocality and de-localization means that identity today is elusive and contradictory (see Said, 1993; Bhabha, 1994).

While anti-racism education recognizes the multifaceted aspects of social differences and individual identities, it does not seek to equate the varied forms of oppression. As a political, practical and academic project of educational change and social transformation, anti-racism knowledge is anchored in an understanding of how a "politics of identity" can transcend the boundaries of race, class, gender and sexuality to bring people together to work for social change.

An integrative approach to anti-racism education should explore how racism intersects with other forms of social difference and oppression (class, sexual, gender and sexuality) in a race-centred analysis. Such understanding is key to a progressive politics for social change. Additionally, the anti-racism educational project resists White hegemony in its myriad forms (e.g., colonial, capitalist and neo-colonial). According to Giroux (1981), hegemony operates in the attempts by the dominant group to use its control over the resources of the state (education, media, telecommunication, military power) to establish its view of the world as inclusive and universal.

Anti-Racism in the Schools

In this section, I discuss the challenge of educational transformation in schools. The concern is over how schools continually transmit social inequality along the lines of social difference, as well as their failure to acknowledge the connections between questions about identity, culture, experience and knowledge. Schools are being called upon to deal with erasures in texts and discourses, appropriation of cultural knowledge and the lack of transparency in the processes of delivering education. A critical anti-racism educational approach that challenges exclusionary practices within schooling and education will ensure that academic excellence is accessible and equitable to all groups. It also moves beyond acknowledging the material conditions that structure societal inequality to questioning White power and privilege and its accompanying rationale for dominance in the schooling and education process.[2] And, it questions the marginalization of certain voices in society and the de-legitimation of the knowledge and experience of subordinate groups in the educational system.

The anti-racism approach also questions pathological explanations of "family," "home environment," and "culture" as sources of the "problems" that minority youths face in the schools. Such explanations divert attention from a critical analysis of the institutional structures within which the delivery of education takes place. For example, the "cultural deficit" paradigm ascribes academic underachievement to students' cultures, family and home backgrounds. It is argued that marginalized off-school cultures do not provide the requisite values, norms, ideas, attitudes and motivations needed to promote academic success. No attempt is made to conceptually distinguish roles and responsibilities of parents and families in their children's education from the attribution of causes of educational failure. There is inadequate critical examination of the complex circumstances and material-political conditions that create students' "failure" and "success." Furthermore, there is no interrogation of what has conventionally counted as success and failure and what is specified as the "family." In Canadian contexts, how can cultural differences be the problem for African-Canadian students' academic underachievement when many of the youths were born and grew up in Canada?

An anti-racism discursive framework to understanding the processes of public schooling in Canada questions the role of the educational system in producing and reproducing racial, gender, sexual and class-based inequalities in society. It also acknowledges the pedagogic need to confront the challenge of diversity and difference in Canadian society, and the urgency to create an educational system that is more inclusive and capable of responding to minority concerns about public schooling. Anti-racism calls on educators to question the racialized practices of schools that erase peoples histories in the curriculum and classroom pedagogies.

An anti-racist political project that challenges definitions of what valid and legitimate knowledge is, and how such knowledge should be produced and distributed both nationally and globally, is opposed to established hegemonic social, economic, and political interests and forces. The public school system, as a

---

2

  While there are obvious ethnic, class, gender and sexual difference that inform location in the privileged structures of society, the use of "White power and privilege" is intended to emphasize the dominance of "Whiteness" in a racialized society.

state-sanctioned institutional structure, has historically served the material, political, and ideological interests of the state and the capitalist social formation.
The school prepares students to become productive workers in a pre-set position
in society according to racial and other social locations. The school serves to
limit the expectations and choices of marginalized students while equipping the
dominant group to normalize and reproduce inequalities (Dei, 1997). Hence,
while anti-racism starts with the critical examination of the daily practices of
individual and collective lives, it is recognized that there are larger and broader
macro-systems that structure social lives and practices.

There are issues worthy of note as educators engage in an anti-racism political
practice of educational transformation in schools. For example, we should be
able to deal with the tensions, paradoxes and contradictions of talking about race
and social oppression in our classrooms. Rather than deny racism and social
oppression, we can talk about how we are individually and collectively implicated in its reproduction and eradication. Sleeter (1993:161) has raised a poignant question that should be on the minds of all educators: What does it mean to
construct an interpretation of race that denies it? Similarly, what does it mean
when, as educators, we claim to be "colour blind"? Educators must be aware of
the dangers of treating racism as if it were a recent phenomenon, or as something
that can easily be eradicated by bringing it to the attention of Whites (Firchuk,
1994). It is embedded in the institutional structures of society and must be
acknowledged and confronted. We start by asking everyone to recognize and take
responsibility for the acts of racism, classism, sexism and homophobia, and to
challenge ourselves to transform the self, the classroom and other educational
settings.

Educators cannot unproblematically subject racist viewpoints to "rational academic debate." As Sullivan (1995) points out, this academic practice can have
"the effect of legitimating an otherwise wholly illegitimate and/or unsubstantiated viewpoint" (p.12). Conversely, racism cannot be seen as strictly a theoretical
discourse. In fact, asking students to prove the accuracy or "truth" of their
experiences of racism can have the effect of subjecting those who have been
victims of racist abuse to further victimization (see also Tatum, 1992).

An anti-racism struggle for educational transformation allows social theory
and theoretical abstractions to speak to the actual lived realities and conditions of
the oppressed human subject. As critical educators, our theories and academic
scholarship have to be accountable (see also Moghissi, 1995) by speaking to the
materiality of human existence. For the anti-racism worker, a distinction between
theory and politics can be only problematic. Theory and political practice are
inseparable. Theory is about knowledge production while practice is about "practical politics." Rather than reify theory, the anti-racism worker must ground
theory in actual political practice. Social justice activism is more than theorizing

about change. It is about engaging in political practice informed by a theory of social change at the same time as the theory itself is refined by political practice. This is anti-racism praxis.

While one cannot expect schools to solve all social ills, schools (and particularly teachers) can influence students to the extent of questioning the status quo. As teachers, we can teach what we practice and also practice what we teach. Learning and teaching in the schools can proceed by acknowledging experience and practice as the contextual basis of knowledge. Such knowledge can inform the politics of educational transformation in the schools. In fact, a key consideration in the pursuit of anti-racism political organizing for educational and social change is theorizing the personal and the political. A theoretical understanding of the personal is, in fact, a prerequisite for effective political action. Understanding the trajectories of individual and group experiences may point to significant lessons about alternative forms of social and political resistance to a myriad of oppressive human conditions. It is necessary for anti-racism workers to critically theorize both individual and collective historical and contemporary experiences in order to provide a methodology of social change (see also Butler and Scott, 1992; Scott, 1991; Pierson, 1991 in other contexts).

Theorizing the personal and the collective starts with a critical interrogation of voice and experience. The voice that claims authority, based on experience or birth, must be problematized without necessarily denying individual agency. Self-criticism is crucial to anti-racism politics. As Scott (1992) argued, experience should not be a source of truth or the "origin of knowledge." Experience cannot be taken for granted. While we may seek to understand experience and practice as a contextual basis of knowledge and political action, it must be noted that experience itself requires an explanation.

hooks (1994) elaborated on the importance of personal experience and how the telling of such experience can help "transgress" the boundaries of intellectual exploitation, appropriation and misrepresentation in education. Personal experience by itself is not enough to provide a complete account of social oppression. There are problems in claiming an "authority of experience" without recognizing how power relations shape processes of knowledge creation or construction. Personal experiences are lived through social relations of power.

Educators also have to provide alternative meanings and interpretations of the "political" to our students. Educators can unpack the notion of "political" through a review of all forms of education and scholarship (progressive and reactionary) as serving defined interests. In order to understand how and what knowledge gets produced and validated, anti-racism educators should assist students to see through the tropes of domination and social power. We engage social issues with a set of ideological assumptions about the nature and functioning of society. Such assumptions also help us interpret society. Knowledge is positional and reflects human interests. Our personal journeys reflect how we see the world (see Banks, 1995) and how, as individuals, we structure and engage in pedagogical and communicative practices (see also Sleeter, 1995). This is the context for the "political" in the sense of how educators and students can, and do, produce, interrogate and disseminate knowledge about ourselves.

Educators can avoid essentialist interpretations of the nature of human relations by pointing to questions of social difference, as well as the dialectical relationship among social and political structures, history and culture. It is important for educators to understand and teach history as a totality of a people's lived experiences. Histories can be critically interrogated without necessarily being de-valued, negated or misrepresented. Specific historical events happen in larger political-economic contexts, and anti-racism educators can challenge a narration of cultural history de-contextualized from broader questions of political economy. Just as there are no discrete cultures, history cannot be insulated from developments around it.

Other problems of misrepresentation of cultural histories exist which the anti-racism educator may address. An example can be found in current writings and discursive practices that periodize peoples' histories in what Ahmad (1995) calls the "triadic terms of pre-colonial, colonial and post-colonial" (pp.6-7). This pedagogic and communicative practice "privileges as primary the role of colonialism as the principle of structuration in that history, so that all that came before colonialism becomes its own prehistory and whatever comes after can only be lived as infinite aftermath" (Ahmad, 1995:7).

Educators can spearhead the challenge to broaden conventional and restrictive definitions of "merit" and "meritocracy." Education should challenge the focus on individual achievement and responsibility which negates how structural forces and processes may hinder the realization of individual aspirations and dreams. Transformative learning is preparing youth to overcome structural barriers rather than an outright denial of their existence. Educators can teach about the power of individual agency and how it is linked with the collective power of the social group to bring about change.

Educational strategies to transform schools must be geared to the "deep curriculum," that is, both the "official" and "hidden" curriculum, as well as the intersection of school cultures, environments and the organizational life of schools. Educational transformation requires a "disruption" of standard knowledge, classroom practices and instructional materials. Diversity is acknowledged and addressed not because of local community pressure, but because educators recognize the importance of educating about the diversity of events and ideas that have shaped, and continue to shape, human growth and development.

Educators can imagine and create new ways for the development of "inclusive schooling"; situations where schools become "working communities" in which notions of community and social responsibility are valued and rewarded. Schools as "working communities" means that authorities value the individuality of their students, as well as the connection between individuals and a larger collective. All academic practices are connected to a global consciousness. The idea of schools as working communities also means that schools teach the values of human co-existence, group unity, mutual respect, collective work and responsibility. The educator genuinely and unequivocally values the experiences of every member of the school system. Education proceeds on the understanding that every person in school has something to offer and that the diverse viewpoints, experiences and perspectives of all should be heard. In fact, education of youth can only be truly transformative if it taps the cultural knowledge of parents, guardians and community workers. In order to address the challenges of anti-racism education, the active recruitment, retention and promotion of minority staff and teachers among the school administrative staff and faculty is essential. This will help address questions of representation of actual physical bodies, students' identification with the school and the question of power-sharing, especially since many students see teachers as occupying positions of power and influence in schools.

But successful and transformative education also means that school curricula are taught from a perspective that reflects a conscious and determined attempt to centre individual and group experiences and cultures in students' learning. Classroom pedagogy and instruction could find alternative ways to deal effectively with race and/or ethnic, class, gender and sexual bias, omission and negation in curriculum and texts. Educators can deal with the marginality of social difference in schooling by stressing the racial, ethnic and gender implications of knowledge and academic texts. Classroom teachings can be culturally, politically and economically relevant to the students' lived experiences. Educators can pay particular attention to the spiritual and psychological aspects of teaching so as to promote the social and emotional growth of students.

Conclusion

A major challenge for anti-racism education is that it must work within the confines of the very system and structures that anti-racism opposes. There is always the danger of the anti-racism project being co-opted to serve the needs of industrial capital. The business world's desire to address equity issues is not always driven by a nagging imperative to see justice done. Material motives and incentives (for example, the maximization of profits) are at the core. The interests of capital do not necessarily serve the public good as its primary goal is to improve productivity, an aim which is readily addressed through programs of cultural sensitivity and managing cultural diversity without addressing systemic racism. Corporate and government strategies to avoid admission of culpability are gaining prominence among tight fiscal constraints and massive public and private sector lay-offs. In a shrinking job market, the dominant group's "divide and rule" policies are overshadowed by concerns of survival.

In fact, one question that often crops up in discussions about educational change is: where is the money going to come from in order to effect all the changes? Some rearranging of educational and social priorities may be in order. In many cases, what is really being discussed is the need for a political commitment on the part of "leaders" to follow through on moral imperatives and convictions. Admittedly, to talk about anti-racism organizational change in the schools in a neo-conservative political climate may be akin to swimming against the current. The social agenda for anti-racism and equity in schools, workplaces and other organizational settings is threatened given the recent radical electoral shift to the xenophobic right as represented by the 1994 congressional elections in the United States and the victories of the Conservative government in Alberta and Ontario. In such a political climate, and given fiscal constraints, racial intolerance becomes the hallmark of many thought processes opposed to any rupturing of the status quo. For right-wing ideologues intent on discrediting anti-racism, this is about the "perfect time."

Admittedly, we live in a time of great uncertainty. The pressures and challenges of sharing wealth and power are more profound now than ever before. Economic, political and cultural changes in the world have brought forth unprecedented changes in the way we live together, and share space and material resources. The effects of a globalized hegemony of Western industrial capital on modern societies is astounding. I refer in particular to the global presence of capital in all available geographical spaces, or what Ahmad (1995) aptly sees as a globalized marketplace, resulting from the penetration of imperialist capital into every global space. Current global economic restructuring processes have intensified human misery and economic deprivation among and between social groups, communities and nation states. Therefore, new critical approaches to anti-racism studies must theorize social change beyond the boundaries of race, nations and communities.

The transnationalization of capital has been accompanied by mass population movements, as well as information flow across nations and territories. The process of global knowledge production is being controlled by Euro-American industrial capital. Similarly, Euro-American political and economic hegemony is continually reproduced through the use of Western capital and resources (education, mass media, wealth) to establish a Eurocentric view of the world as inclusive and universal (see also Giroux, 1981). It presents a challenge to adopt a domestic, as well as an internationalistic, posture to anti-racism education and politics.

REFERENCES

Abella, R. 1984. *Equality Now: Report of the Special Committee on Visible Minorities in Canadian Society.* Ottawa: Queen's Printer.

Abu-Lughod, L. 1991. "Writing against culture." In Richard Fox, ed. *Recapturing Anthropology*, pp.137-62. Santa Fe, NM: School of American Research Press.

Ahmad, Aijaz. 1995. "The politics of literary post-coloniality." *Race and Class* 36(3):1-20.

Apple, Michael. 1986. *Teachers and Texts: A Political Economy of Class and Gender Relations in Education.* New York: Routledge.

_____. 1991. "Series editor's introduction." In Patti Lather, ed. *Getting Smart: Feminist Research and Pedagogy With/In the Postmodern*, pp.vii-xi. New York: Routledge.

Bains, H. and P. Cohen (eds.). 1988. *Multi-racist Britain.* London: MacMillan.

Banks, James. 1995. Presentation at the symposium on "Teaching Culturally Different Students: Political Assumptions of the Educational Research." Annual Meeting of the American Educational Research Association. San Francisco, April 18-22.

Banton, Michael. 1970. "The concept of racism." In S. Zubaida, ed. *Race and Racialism.* London: Tavistock.

Bhabha, Homi. 1994. *The Location of Culture.* London & New York: Routledge.

Brandt, Geoffrey. 1986. *The Realization of Anti-Racist Teaching.* Lewes: Falmer Press.

Butler, Judith and Joan Scott (eds.). 1992. *Feminists Theorize the Political.* London: Routledge.

Carby, Hazel. 1982. "Schooling for Babylon." In Paul Gilroy/Centre for Contemporary Cultural Studies, ed. *The Empire Strikes Back*, pp.183-211. London: Hutchison.

Cohen, Philip. 1988/89. *Tackling Common Sense Racism. Cultural Studies Project Annual Report.* London.

Dei, G.J.S. 1996. *Anti-Racism Education: Theory and Practice.* Halifax: Fernwood Publishing.

_____. 1997. "Race and the production of identity in the schooling experiences of African-Canadian youth." *Discourse* 18(2):241-257.

_____, J. Mazzuca, E. McIsaac and J. Zine. 1997. *Reconstructing "Dropout:" A Critical Ethnography of the Dynamics of Black Students' Disengagement from School.* Toronto: University of Toronto Press.

Firchuk, Beverley. 1994. Personal Communication, Toronto.

Fumia, Doreen. 1995. "Identifying sites of anti-racism education: Everyday lived experiences seen as the micro-politics of institutionalized racialized practices." Unpublished paper, Department of Sociology in Education, Ontario Institute for Studies in Education, of the University of Toronto, Toronto.

Gillborn, David. 1995a. "Racism, modernity and schooling: New directions in anti-racist theory and practice." Paper read at the American Educational Research Association, San Francisco, April 18-22.

_____. 1995b. *Racism and Anti-racism in Real Schools.* Philadelphia: Open University Press.

Gilroy, Paul (and Centre for Contemporary Cultural Studies). 1982. *The Empire Strikes Back: Race and Racism in 70s Britain.* London: Hutchison.

_____. 1992. "The end of anti-racism." In James Donald and Ali Rattansi, eds. *"Race" Culture and Difference*, pp.49-61. Newbury Park, CA: Sage Publications.

Giroux, Henry. 1981. *Ideology and Culture and the Process of Schooling.* Philadelphia: Temple University Press.

Goldberg, David T. 1993. *Racist Culture.* Oxford: Blackwell.

hooks, Bell. 1994. *Teaching to Transgress: Education as the Practice of Freedom.* New York: Routledge.

Jeffcoate, R. 1984. "Ideologies and multicultural education." In M. Craft, ed. *Education and Cultural Pluralism.* Lewes: Falmer Press.

Lee, Enid. 1985. *Letters to Marcia: A Teacher's Guide to Anti-Racist Education*, pp.5-12; 35-56. Toronto: Cross-Cultural Communication Centre.

Li, P.S. 1990. "Race and ethnicity." In P.S. Li, ed. *Race and Ethnic Relations in Canada*, pp.3-17. Toronto: Oxford University Press.

McCarthy, Cameron. 1988. "Rethinking liberal and radical perspectives on racial inequality in schooling: Making the case for nonsynchrony." *Harvard Educational Review* 58(3):265-279.

_____. 1990. *Race and Curriculum: Social Inequality and the Theory and Politics of Difference in Contemporary Research on Schooling.* Basingstoke: Falmer Press.

Miles, Robert. 1989. *Racism.* London: Tavistock.

Moghissi, Haideh. 1995. "Anti-racist feminism: Sisterhood without white gloves." Paper read at the Learned Societies Meeting of the Canadian Sociology and Anthropology Association, Université du Québec, Montréal, June 5-7.

Mullard, Chris. 1980. *Racism in Society and Schools: History and Policy.* London Centre for Multicultural Education.

_____. 1985. *Race, Power and Resistance.* London: Centre for Multicultural Education.

Nixon, J. 1984. "Multicultural education as a curriculum category." *New Community* 12:22-30.

Omi, Michael and Howard Winant. 1993. "On the theoretical concept of race." In Cameron McCarthy and Warren Crichlow, eds. *Race, Identity, and Representation in Education,* pp.3-10. New York: Routledge.

Pierson, Ruth. 1991. "Experience, difference, dominance and voice in the writing of Canadian women's history." In Karen Offen, Ruth Pierson and Jane Randall, eds. *Writing Women's History: International Perspectives*, pp.79-106. Bloomington, IN: Indiana University Press.

Razack, R. 1992. "Collective rights and women: The cold game of equality staring." *The Journal of Human Justice* 4(1):1-11.

_____. 1994. "What is to be gained by looking white people in the eye? Culture, race, and gender in cases of sexual violence." *Signs: Journal of Women in Culture and Society* 9(4):894-923.

Reed, Carole-Ann. 1994. "The omission of anti-semitism in Anti-Racism." *Canadian Women Studies* 14(2):68-71.

Rockhill, Kathleen. 1995. "Memo to adult education research committee." Ontario Institute for Studies in Education, of the University of Toronto, Toronto, Ontario.

Said, Edward. 1993. *Culture and Imperialism.* New York: Alfred A. Knopf.

Scott, Joan W. 1991. "The evidence of experience." *Critical Inquiry* 17(3):773-797.

_____. 1992. "Experience." In J. Butler and J. Scott, eds. *Feminists Theorize the Political*, pp 22-40. London: Routledge.

Sleeter, Christine. 1993. "How white teachers construct race." In Cameron McCarthy and Warren Crichlow, eds. *Race, Identity and Representation in Education*, pp.157-171. New York: Routledge.

_____. 1995. Presentation at the symposium on: "Teaching Culturally Different Students: Political Assumptions of the Educational Research." Annual Meeting of the American Educational Research Association, San Francisco, April 18-22.

Sullivan, Ann. 1995. "Realizing successful integrative anti-racist education." Unpublished paper, Department of Sociology in Education, Ontario Institute for Studies in Education, of the University of Toronto, Toronto.

Tatum, Beverley. 1992. "Talking about race, learning about racism: The application of racial identity development theory in the classroom. *Harvard Educational Review* 62(1):1-24.

Thomas, Barb. 1984. "Principles of anti-racist education." *Currents* 2(2):20-24. Toronto: Urban Alliance on Race Relations.

Train, Kelly. 1995. "De-homogenizing 'Jewish women': Essentialism and exclusion within Jewish feminist thought." Unpublished M.A. Thesis, Department of Education, University of Toronto, Toronto.

Troyna, Barry. 1987 (ed). *Racial Inequality in Education.* London: Tavistock.

_____ and J. Williams. 1986. *Racism, Education and the State.* London: Croom Helm.

Walcott, Rinaldo. 1990. "Theorizing anti-racist education." *Western Canadian Anthropologist* 7(2):109-20.

Wilson, Williams. 1973. *Power, Racism and Privilege.* New York: Free Press.

NOTE: I acknowledge the assistance of I. Marcia James and Andrew Thornton of the Department of Sociology and Equity Studies in Education, Ontario Institute for Studies in Education of the University of Toronto (OISE/UT) in commenting on early drafts of the paper. I am also grateful to Olga Williams for proofreading the manuscript and to the reviewers of the manuscript for their unattributed comments.

14

Anti-Racism and the Organized Labour Movement

Tania Das Gupta

This chapter is an analysis of some of the obstacles and contradictions associated with anti-racism in the organized labour movement. What makes anti-racism work truly challenging in unions is that it has to address the many dimensions of racism simultaneously, including attitudinal, systemic, individual-behavioral and cultural. Moreover, not only does racism have to be addressed within work sites, but also within unions themselves. Unions are also marked by a contradictory position within the capitalist political economy; they contest employers and managers as collective bargaining agents, yet seem to share common class concerns with employers when it comes to union staffing issues.

Issues of race and gender in the organized labour movement are underresearched and underdocumented (Ng, 1995; Leah, 1993). Writing this chapter was, therefore, a challenge. As a long-time activist and educator in the area of anti-racism as it relates to unorganized workers of colour, most of the interviewees were personally known to me, and they readily agreed to share their experiences. They were in fact eager to tell their stories. In the summer of 1995, a number of activists from the organized labour movement in Ontario, mostly based in Toronto, were approached in order to gather information on the state of anti-racism work at both policy and practical levels. My initial interview was with June Veacock, Human Rights Director at the Ontario Federation of Labour (OFL), who also suggested a first set of potential interviewees. Thereafter, other names were suggested by those with whom I spoke. In-depth interviews[1] were conducted with nine individuals, all of whom are or have been involved directly in anti-racism work within their unions. Four of the interviewees were Black women, three were South Asian men and two were White, one man and one woman. They represented unions such as the United Steelworkers (US), the

---

[1] I would like to acknowledge the assistance of Carol Duncan in conducting most of these interviews, summarizing them and in some instances transcribing the tapes. People interviewed were the following: June Veacock (OFL), Nick Decarlo, Susan Spratt and Hassan Yusuf (CAW), Beverley Johnson and Yvonne Bobb (OPSEU), Harminder Magon and Carmen Henry (CUPE), Mohamed Baksh (USW) and Barb Thomas (Doris Marshall Institute).

Canadian Union of Public Employees (CUPE), the Canadian Autoworkers (CAW) and the Ontario Public Service Employees Union (OPSEU). In addition, I interviewed a former community worker, a White woman, who has a history of doing collaborative work with union activists on anti-racism. Interviewees were extremely forthcoming and candidly shared their experiences and expertise.

I begin with a brief history of racism in the organized labour movement, followed by a description of the rise of anti-racism within unions. I then present excerpts from the interviews to highlight challenges and problems that are encountered in organizing around anti-racism.

Racism in the Organized Labour Movement

As far as anti-racism is concerned, the history of the organized labour movement in Canada has travelled over some bumpy terrain. Before the 1940s, the movement was openly racist, building its membership base on the exclusion of people of colour and women. Ward (1978) argues that, at the turn of the century, White Canadians were imbued within a racist culture. Anti-Asian sentiments and activities were given an organizational base, in part, by the labour movement that included the Knights of Labour, the Vancouver Trades and Labour Council, the Victoria Trades and Labour Council, the British Columbia Fishermen's Association and the Dominion Trades and Labour Congress.[2] In this context, the state enacted immigration and labour policies which systematically segregated most Asians and other people of colour into working-class, chiefly manual, occupations. Earlier in Canadian history, people of African heritage were brought over as slaves or came as refugees from slavery and war in the United States and were likewise streamed into manual and service-related jobs. This was systemic racism in its most institutionalized form, since the government sustained policies and practices which adversely affected people of colour. Ideologies invoked to justify such state practices were orientalism, anti-Black racism and other forms of racism that had developed earlier in the context of colonialism, neo-colonialism and slavery. These ideologies provided a justification for the de-humanization, exploitation and violation of people of colour simply on the basis of their physical difference from Europeans. Fixed ideas (stereotypes) and negative judgments (prejudices) about the so-called inferiority of people of colour continued to prevail long after slavery was abolished and colonialism was on the wane.

Despite Ward's (1978) ahistorical and uncontextualized analysis, his work remains useful given the paucity of research on racism and unions in the early years of Canadian history. Labour unions were instrumental in spearheading racist organizations like the Anti-Chinese Union, the Asiatic Exclusion League

---

[2] Ward's analysis of white racism remains problematic because he assumes racism as a psychological and cultural phenomenon, unconnected to the political economy at the time which was characterized as an emergent industrial capitalist nation-state with a dire need for cheap labour.

and the White Canada Association. They engaged in a range of activities including rioting and physically attacking Asian immigrants in British Columbia, lobbying Canadian politicians to stop Asian immigration and to restrict the rights of Asian immigrants who were living on Canadian soil. They helped create a sense of racist hysteria within communities at large. Canadian workers and their unions clearly identified workers of colour as threats to their economic life, and they endeavoured to marginalize them using racist ideas from the past. The polite, democratic[3] racism of the state was complementary to the open hostility of popular racism. Being denied various citizenship rights by the government, Chinese workers were vulnerable to exploitation by White employers and by Chinese contractors. Employers clearly took advantage of them by paying low wages. While it seemed that employers were supportive of Asian immigration, their preference was only premised on their ability to exploit them as cheap labour, and their racism was openly expressed when they switched their preference to White workers when they could no longer pay lower wages to Chinese workers. The payment of lower wages to Asian workers was premised on ideas about the inherent inferiority of Asian labourers that emanated from colonialism.

Calliste (1987) has analyzed Black sleeping car porters in Canada, their experiences of exclusion, their differential wages compared to White porters, and their efforts to organize. White unions, in this context, allied with employers to perpetuate systemic racism. The Canadian Brotherhood of Railway Employees (CBRE) is a case in point. Calliste writes that until the mid-1940s, Black men were exclusively hired as porters on Canadian railroads, except for the Grand Trunk Railway (GTR), which also hired them as waiters and cooks. However, the GTR was taken over by Canadian National Railways (CNR) in 1926 at which point Black waiters were replaced by Whites. Therefore, portering was a significant occupation for Black men in the late 1800s and most of the 1900s. However, the CBRE was for Whites only prior to 1919. In that year, the Order of Sleeping Car Porters, formed by Canadian Black porters in 1918, pressured the CBRE for integration. The Order was accepted as an auxiliary organization. However, the CBRE racially separated their members into two units (I and II) with the latter made up of low-paid Black porters and cooks from former GTR cars. The former were higher-paid White conductors, inspectors and stewards. Promotions could only occur within their own unit. This segregation ended in 1964.

Unions allying with employers to disadvantage another group of workers is reminiscent of craftsmen who tried to maintain their bargaining edge by restricting their own numbers. In the case of the White porters in Canada, their fear of

---

[3]
The concept of "democratic" racism has been advanced by Frances Henry, Carol Tator, Winston Mattis and Tim Rees in *The Colour of Democracy: Racism in Canadian Society* (Toronto: Harcourt Brace, 1995). They argue that Canada has a form of racism which is subtle and polite because it coexists with liberal democratic notions such as freedom of expression and equality. The latter notions will often be invoked to marginalize people of colour and anti-racism efforts.

competition and efforts to increase their bargaining strength became racialized[4] as the group of workers they excluded in the process were Black. This exclusion and differential treatment of Black porters was based, in part, on a belief about the inherent inferiority of Black peoples reminiscent of slavery. Thus, racist attitudes in the form of stereotypes and prejudices helped sustain systemic and individual acts of racism, such as the differential payments and treatment by White employers of Black, Asian and White workers.

Instead of including Black and Asian workers as members of their unions and thereby protecting them under general collective agreements, White workers selected to exclude and de-humanize them. Creese (1991) shows that Chinese workers earned one-half to one-quarter less than their unskilled White counterparts and such differential wages were written into union agreements. Other campaigns by White union members included demands such as replacing Chinese workers with White workers, ending "oriental" employment in mines and excluding Japanese workers from the fisheries by restricting and eventually eliminating their licenses. Exclusion and devaluation of Chinese labour was based on racist assumptions about their inherent inferiority. It also entailed scapegoating them for the low wages earned by White workers.

In the absence of support from the organized labour movement, Asian and Black workers formed their own unions and associations, and engaged in strikes (Creese, 1991; Ward, 1978) and other forms of resistance (Calliste, 1987). Chinese workers struck for higher wages, to shorten working hours, to end discrimination, to support licensing rights and against the contracting system (Creese, 1991). Japanese fishermen formed the Amalgamated Association of Japanese Fishermen, which in 1926 contested the House of Commons Standing Committee on Fisheries which proposed a reduction in licenses issued to Japanese fishermen by 10 percent a year with the aim of eventually eliminating them altogether (Ward, 1978:122). The case was held up by the Supreme Court of Canada. The government, however, found other indirect ways of accomplishing its objective such as enforcing restrictions through orders in council.

Creese (1991) argues that between the end of the First World War and the Depression, radical unions with socialist aspirations such as the OBU (One Big Union) and the Workers' Unity League (WUL) actively recruited and involved Chinese workers. Most of these unions were, however, short-lived. The WUL had Chinese workers on union executives and strike committees. It appears that class unity based on advanced levels of class consciousness and socialist aspirations had been achieved and that racial divisions had been bridged as a result of that consciousness. Many Chinese workers took part in sympathy strikes during

---

4

Racialization is a concept used to describe a process by which an individual becomes seen as a member of a "race," keeping in mind that this process is a social and cultural one. Similarly, one could argue that there was a simultaneous process of gendering porters as all accounts point to them being overwhelmingly male.

the 1919 Winnipeg General Strike. In 1917, joint strikes were organized by the White Shingle Weavers' Union and the Chinese Canadian Labour Union. Although Canadian unions remained exclusionary, joint industrial action increased. Employers, though, tried their best to break up these early solidarity movements by replacing striking Chinese workers with White workers at a higher rate of pay, or by refusing to re-hire striking Chinese workers where their White counterparts had been (Creese, 1991:42). Solidarity between White workers and workers of colour signified to employers an end to their ability to maintain a "cheap" pool of immigrant labour. Their ability to do that was premised on divide and rule and the associated disempowerment of all workers, but particularly those of colour.

Anti-Racism in Trade Unions

Ward (1978) argues that, by the 1920s, trade unions were no longer major mouthpieces of the racist, exclusionary movement to keep Canada white, although elements still lingered within it. Perhaps racism in the labour movement began to resemble the polite and systemic racism exemplified by state institutions and employers. In its 1931 convention in Vancouver, the Trades and Labour Congress dropped its exclusionist position and supported the call for extending the vote to all native-born Canadians, including people of colour. The Cooperative Commonwealth Federation (CCF), formed in 1933, led a movement towards greater inclusion of Asian Canadians. In later years, members of the organized labour movement, particularly African Canadian and Jewish members, became actively involved in the campaign for human rights legislation in Canada.

The Jewish Labour Committee (founded in 1935) waged a tireless campaign to fight racism and bring in legislation against human rights violations. The National Committee on Human Rights within the Canadian Labour Congress argued that discrimination and prejudice were threats to the union ideals of "brotherhood and equality."[5] Labour committees for human rights were established in cities such as Winnipeg, Toronto, Montreal and Vancouver to assist local members to work against discrimination, particularly in areas outside the scope of collective bargaining. These committees investigated and documented cases of discrimination in employment, housing and in services. To fight systemic racism, they also contested attitudinal racism. Therefore, along with Black and Asian organizations, these labour committees conducted public education and organized for the enactment of human rights legislation provincially and federally. As Hill (1977) shows, they continued to push for improvements and for proper implementation even after laws were enacted.

---

[5] Note the sexist phrasing.

Internal education and conferences were also organized to help address racism at work. Labour human rights committees supported those who suffered discrimination on the job or in the community, pressed for laws and negotiated anti-discrimination clauses in collective agreements. Local "fair practices committees" were established to deal with racism in the workplace.

Aided by the Fair Employment Practices Act of 1953, the Brotherhood of Sleeping Car Porters (BSCP), the Canadian Brotherhood of Railway Transport and General Workers (CBRT) and the Toronto Labour Committee for Human Rights won promotional rights for Black porters to become conductors and other supervisors between 1955 and 1961. However, some lost their seniority as a result of these promotions, which acted as a disincentive for promotions. The Order of Railway Conductors, which was White, resisted opening their union to Black membership (Calliste, 1987). Moreover, the unions concerned never accepted responsibility for perpetuating earlier racist employment practices that excluded Blacks, for segregating its members racially by maintaining two separate units and for restricting seniority and promotional rights between these two units. It focused only on the racism of employers, just as the employers blamed it all on the unions. Porters in the CBRT who won to maintain their seniority rights did so as a result of a local's charge of racism against their union. Calliste (1987) shows that the combining of seniority lists between units I and II was approved to "avoid embarrassment."

By the 1960s, when human rights legislation had been passed and commissions set up, some of these labour-based human rights committees became inactive. Hill (1977) argues that unions became more involved in the rights of women, the elderly and people with disabilities. Ng (1995) writes that the call for economic equality for women in later years did not take into account the particular experiences of immigrant women and women of colour. This indicated a narrow form of feminism which personified "women" as White and thus not taking into account the particular experiences of non-dominant women, including women of colour, who generally experience multiple oppressions simultaneously. Anti-racism became more a preoccupation of "minority groups and religious organizations." In most instances, these latter organizations did not connect with feminism until the 1970s when a number of women of colour and immigrant women's organizations developed.[6]

While it still focused on human rights, anti-racism was no longer a concern of the organized labour movement. Anti-racism continued, however, to be a major concern of people of colour in the community.

---

[6] See Tania Das Gupta, *Learning From Our History: Community Development By Immigrant Women in Ontario, 1958-86* (Toronto: Cross Cultural Communication Centre, 1986).

One of the community groups that was doing anti-racist work from the 1970s was the Cross Cultural Communication Centre (CCCC) in Toronto, an educational resource centre which also produced programs on issues of racism, immigration and immigrant settlement. The Centre was approached by the Humber College Labour Studies Centre to develop a ten-week course on anti-racism. Workers at the centre began talking to labour activists about how this course might be designed. *Combating Racism in the Workplace: A Course for Workers* came out of the process, an early example of collaboration between the labour movement and a community organization.

The Ontario Federation of Labour (OFL) launched its official campaign in 1981 with its slogan "Racism Hurts Everyone" (Leah, 1991, 1993). Posters, leaflets and television commercials were used for public education. An anti-racism coordinator was hired for one-year. In 1984, the coordinator initiated a one-week "Train the Trainer" program for activists within various affiliated unions, many of whom were activists of colour. This resulted in the development of a core of anti-racist union activists who could initiate similar work in their own unions and locals.

Staff from the CCCC worked closely with the Ontario Federation of Labour (OFL) on the "Racism Hurts Everyone" campaign. This involved facilitating discussions about combating racism and developing support materials. The OFL anti-racism coordinator and the CCCC staff person travelled around the province doing anti-racist work. They wrote eight fact sheets on racism for the OFL and also documented a number of cases of racism based on stories people told them.

In 1983, the OFL became the first provincial labour body to allocate affirmative action seats for women and later on an additional position for people of colour on its Executive (Ng, 1995). Influenced by the OFL's campaign, the Canadian Labour Congress (CLC) developed a standing proposal in 1984 to include a non-discrimination clause in collective agreements. The "plight of Indians, Inuit and Métis of Canada" was also recognized.

Much to the disappointment of anti-racist activists, the one-year contract of the Anti-Racism Coordinator of the OFL was not renewed. It was a blow to anti-racist activists within and outside the union movement. It illustrated that anti-racism work was still seen as a peripheral activity by labour organizations and therefore a low priority. Moreover, Ng (1995) suggests that the "Racism Hurts Everyone" campaign was politically misguided, marginalized to one segment of the movement (to people of colour activists) and served more as window dressing rather than being integrated into all the activities of the organization. The core group of anti-racist activists were never fully utilized in their unions, nor did union leaders receive any education in anti-racism.

In 1986, a group called the Ontario Coalition of Black Trade Unionists (OCBTU) was initiated by union activists of colour, most of whom had been involved in anti-racist work inside unions as well as in their own communities.[7] Its objective was to educate and raise the profile of Black workers in Ontario by providing them with an "independent voice" and by "enabling them to have a stronger presence within the trade union movement." The term "Black" was used in a political sense and included South Asians, Chinese, people of African origin and others who defined themselves as Black. Other OCBTU goals were to provide resources to Black workers seeking leadership positions in their unions, organize educationals and develop a telephone line to counsel workers who experienced racial discrimination (OCBTU Newsletter, 1987-88).

As a result of pressures from the community as well as from within the labour movement, a new and permanent position was created within the OFL to maintain and coordinate its anti-racist work. This position still exists. A variety of forums, conferences and workshops on anti-racism which included people of colour were organized by the OFL throughout the latter part of the 1980s. The OFL later reverted to encouraging its affiliates to conduct anti-racist training since its own efforts in this area had not attracted much participation. A document released at the 1986 annual convention (November 24-27, 1986) entitled "Racism and Discrimination" urged affiliated unions to look at their methods of hiring for possible biases against members of colour, to establish human rights committees, to negotiate no-discrimination clauses into collective agreements, to provide anti-racism training to stewards, to not tolerate racial harassment and to translate collective agreements where there were large numbers of non-English-speaking members. The document also urged the OFL to work with the Ontario New Democratic Party (NDP) to make racism and discrimination election issues.

Urged on by women activists of colour within the labour movement and in the community, there is also some recognition of the need to link issues of racism and sexism. In 1987, the OFL's Human Rights Committee and the Women's Committee jointly wrote a "Statement on Equal Action in Employment." At its 1991 convention, the OFL released a paper on "Challenging Harassment," which was adopted by its membership. At this same convention, the Human Rights and Women's Committees organized a forum called "Making Employment Equity Happen" (Leah, 1993).

At the 1990 Convention of the CLC in Montreal, a person of colour ran for election to the Executive Committee and was almost elected. A Task Force on Structure came back in 1992 with a recommendation that one seat be designated for people of colour. Members of colour wanted two seats, one for a woman and one for a man. The latter was achieved. Such victories have been hard fought for and have never been taken for granted.

---

[7] The author's mother, Madhu Das Gupta, was a founding member of the OCBTU.

In the 1990s, the OFL has focused more on employment equity. In September 1994, the provincial NDP government brought into force the Employment Equity Act to improve unequal conditions faced by the designated groups and to require employers to take proactive measures to achieve equity in the workplace. The OFL was represented when Bill 79 was drafted, as well as when its associated regulations were formulated. The Act required employers and bargaining agents to be jointly responsible for the implementation of employment equity. This required both parties to be involved in informing employees, conducting work force surveys, reviewing employment policies and practices and developing employment equity plans. It also included initiating educational and communication strategies as well as setting goals and program evaluation. Since 1993, the OFL has been involved in training staff representatives and building local leadership related to employment equity in nine Ontario cities. It has focused on explaining what employment equity is, why it is needed, areas of joint responsibility and issues of racism and sexism. It has also held "train the trainers" workshops in the area of employment equity. With the assistance of Cornish Advocates, Barristers and Solicitors, the OFL published a *Trade Union Guide To Carrying Out Joint Responsibilities Under the Employment Equity Act, 1993 and Its Regulations* (1994). The Guide mentions that in addition to the OFL, a number of unions, such as CUPE, OPSEU, USW and CAW, have already prepared materials related to employment equity.

The NDP was defeated in the 1995 provincial election and the Progressive Conservatives (PC) were elected on an anti-equity platform. One of the first actions of the new government was to scrap the Employment Equity Act and its associated infrastructure. This was a devastating setback to anti-racism work everywhere in Ontario, including the organized labour movement.

Given this general background, the next section will analyze some of the current issues that were discussed by those unionists interviewed for this chapter. Even though they talked about their struggles in the context of Ontario, the issues identified are by no means unique to that province.

Factors Giving Rise to Anti-Racism in Unions

To begin with, the general political environment and anti-racist organizing in the community were seen as precursors of anti-racism work in the early 1980s. Nick DeCarlo of CAW said:

> In the 70s and '80s, various social issues became integrated in the labour movement.... Activists did this.... The leadership was forced to deal with these issues.... In the late '70s there were police shootings.... There were campaigns around that ... which had significant impact ... increased awareness.... There were protest movements—W5 campaign and the Wei Fu Support Committee. These organized public and union support... (August 15, 1995).

The Wei Fu case, which involved a security officer with the Ontario Government Protection Service, had a big impact on sparking anti-racism awareness within the labour movement. Mr. Fu, an OPSEU member, lodged a complaint against his supervisor for sustaining racial harassment against him. Subsequently, a Support Committee developed, which included both OPSEU and community members, representing, among others, Toronto's Chinese community and anti-racist organizations. The Support Committee held public rallies and demonstrations against racism and managed to gain considerable public attention. Unfortunately, Fu's complaint was dismissed by a Board of Inquiry of the Ontario Human Rights Commission in 1984. Winnie Ng (1995), one of the leaders of the Support Committee for Wei Fu, confirms that the impetus for anti-racism in the labour movement came from community events in 1979 and 1980.

Members of colour also pushed for anti-racist work and helped put the issue onto union agendas. CUPE's national anti-racism coordinator, Harminder Magon, recalls:

> At the 1987 convention in Quebec City, a Black sister got up and spoke on the lack of response on racism.... Everybody surprised at that.... Every microphone was occupied by a visible minority to relate a personal experience. A national call went out—an emergency meeting was called.... (August 22, 1995).

Racist incidents within unions also created the impetus to take action against racism. Hassan Yusuf, anti-racism coordinator of CAW since 1992, reports:

> The president of a local was in a party—drunk—referred to a member as _____ [racial slur]. Insistence that local president should quit. [I] met with the president and urged him to apologize.... Lengthy fight on how to resolve it.... Union has a policy against racism, yet issue continued for over one year.... No one took responsibility.... Six months later I was approached to take on the anti-racism coordinator's role (August 24, 1995).

Anti-Racism a Priority for Unions?

Most interviewees indicated that anti-racism was a high priority of their unions. One issue that was emphasized repeatedly is the strong support of their union leadership, while overwhelmingly White, for this kind of work. This is indicated by the extension of human and financial resources to advance this work, public statements made by the leadership to condemn racial and sexual harassment and to implement affirmative action measures in union structures and activities. This support of anti-racism work by union leadership reflects the years of advocacy by activists of colour in and outside the labour movement, and which continues today. The leadership is also faced with a membership that consists of an increasing proportion of people of colour.

There is a recognition by unions that racism harms the labour movement. Baksh, past Anti-Racism Coordinator of USW says: "It[racism] affects the integrity of the bargaining unit, it affects the membership itself.... and people who are targets of racism tend to isolate themselves and do not and cannot participate in the whole body of the union" (August 11, 1995).

At the 1989 National Policy Conference of the United Steelworkers (U.S.), a "Policy to Prevent Racial and Sexual Harassment in the Workplace" was adopted. A booklet describing the policy mentions that the union has appointed Sexual and Racial Harassment Complaints Counselors to help deal with incidents of harassment in the workplace. These counselors help local unions to deal with incidents, hold workshops and distribute information. Moreover, in its "harassment policy," the union emphasizes that all its activities should be provided in a harassment free environment, that any violations will be taken seriously and acted upon. "A substantiated complaint will result in the removal of the harasser from the event" (U.S. Harassment Policy).

CUPE has a contract compliance program according to which any company that has a contract with it worth more than $20,000 has to abide with equality principles. This has been a successful program. In terms of employment equity, CUPE has recently completed a work force review and is now scrutinizing policies and practices.

All CAW officers have to take an oath "to promote a harassment and discrimination-free environment and work to ensure the human rights of all members are respected" (CAW, Article 36, Installation Ceremony).

Organizing with/for Members of Colour

Yusuf, of CAW, explained that his priority has been to work with members of colour:

> Get workers of colour to understand the union—raise their consciousness about union structure, policy—to become involved in the politics of the union—also fight for change—fight for leadership—if they become conscious, can take leadership—can make substantive changes in the union.... (August 24,1995).

To this end, he has helped organize a number of activities, including a workers of colour development program held twice a year and a workers of colour conference held for the first time in 1996 and which will now be held annually. The latter brought together 140 delegates from across the country. One of the demands that surfaced from this process was to establish a human rights department within CAW with a full-time coordinator. At the time of the interview, CAW was in a process of further clarifying the issues, structure of work and responsibilities of this new department. The establishment of this department is an indication of more recognition and support of human rights work within the union which has developed as a result of work done by members of colour. Caucuses of colour in locals also facilitate this collective process.

Magon of CUPE reports that from the beginning anti-racist initiatives within the union involved the grass-roots. He is the support staff person to a national organization within CUPE called the National Working Committee on Racism, Discrimination and Employment Equity, also known as the Rainbow Committee. Members play a key role at the provincial level, meeting at least once a year. Carmen Henry, a CUPE staff representative in Toronto, also reported that there is a Racial Minority and Aboriginal Peoples' Caucus in Toronto.

OPSEU members have been active in the establishment of the Ontario Public Service Network for Racial Minorities, an organization that brings together people of colour within the bargaining unit as well as from management. There is a recognition that the issue of racism hurts people of colour no matter which side of the collective bargaining process they are on. Its major focus has been on employment equity, particularly when the NDP formed the government.

Education around Employment Equity and Resistance against It

Employment equity has been a major priority for the organized labour movement. A variety of activities have made up this work, including the writing of course curricula, the development of audio-visual resources and course and workshop delivery to members and management. Efforts to reach the membership on the issue of employment equity is impressive. Early in 1995, for example, the CAW launched a campaign to educate locals. The coordinator of this campaign, Spratt, said, "95 percent of CAW had the training done within 6 months.... This included about 4,000 workers.... It gave us the opportunity to talk about human rights.... We used local union discussion leaders.... Rank and file people were trained to do educationals" (August 25, 1995).

The 1995 Conservative bill to eradicate the Employment Equity Act in Ontario was entitled "An Act To Repeal Job Quotas And To Restore Merit-Based Employment Practices." The Conservative government was able to mobilize support by playing on certain misconceptions and fears about employment equity. Having described employment equity as a "quota system," it then invoked the liberal-democratic value of meritocracy to further define it as "non-merit-based" and thus unfair and undemocratic. According to interviewees, many White workers expressed their fears around employment equity in union educationals. This is how it was described by unionists interviewed: "discrimination against White workers," "seniority," "reverse discrimination"—they bought what was in the paper ... lots of racist comments.... " (Spratt, August 25, 1995).

Workers' ambivalence to human rights in general and to anti-racism in particular were also mentioned by some: "They want to be progressive and fair, but are also afraid. More scared of what will happen to their "White Boy." They all thought that women should work but in gender-stereotyped vocations" (Spratt, August 25, 1995).

Resistance to employment equity was analyzed by activists in the following ways: "Reaction is negative because of insecurity and right wing backlash. In-

stead of being against banks and corporations, we're mad at people of colour...."
(Spratt, August 25, 1995).

One instance of resistance to anti-racist practice from some White workers inside CUPE is illustrated by an incident where a White member objected to the racial representation in a CUPE poster called "Break the Barriers." One of her objections was that there was no "White face" on the poster. Another example of resistance to anti-racist initiatives was expressed by a member in the *Local 4900 Newsletter* (June 30, 1995). In a column called "Sound Off" he talks about the NDP creating "Employment equity law and matching useless bureaucracy, to handle the most sexist and racist legislature this country has ever seen...." (p.8).

Resistance to employment equity and anti-racism programs is also expressed in indirect and subtle forms, described as "refined resistance" by Henry et al. (1995:280). The following discussion highlights some of these forms of resistance in unions.

Employment Equity within Unions

Most unions have developed statements on affirmative action for union executive boards, committees and locals. However, unions have a long way to go when it comes to the representation of people of colour on its leadership structures. Given the expressions of racism from some White members cited earlier, it is not surprising that the representation of people of colour within union leadership ranges from tokenistic, segregated to non-existent. The following are some expressions of this:

> It is an ongoing struggle... need more workers of colour, women and people with disabilities.... White women have done a lot but not the kind of work we would like to see. They deal more with membership, but not in collective bargaining.... They [White women] organized earlier, in the 1970s.... (Spratt, August 25, 1995).

Moreover, efforts to diversify union leadership are often met with lack of support. In talking about representation on the CUPE National Executive Board (NEB), Magon says: "The biggest challenge is representation on the national executive board—need one position for visible minority and one for Aboriginal community.... Right now, there is one Black sister out of fourteen" (August 22, 1995).

CUPE's Rainbow Committee recommended two designated positions of colour on the NEB by 1995, including one for an Aboriginal person. Just prior to the National Convention, some members felt that this recommendation did not have much support among the membership. At its subsequent National Convention, the proposal for two designated positions on the Executive Board was defeated for failure to get two-thirds majority. In speaking against the proposal, there were some, including members of colour, who felt that affirmative action was tokenism and that they have to rely on "merit." The question was called and unfortunately the speakers of colour at the microphones were prevented from speaking.

Magon of CUPE reports: "Speakers were stunned at the microphones—people felt stunned, hurt and pain—some people wanted to leave the Convention. It took 3-4 days of caucuses and meetings to heal the pain...." (December 19, 1995).

Due to strong advocacy by the Racial Minority and Aboriginal Caucuses at the Convention, CUPE's NEB accepted a proposal to have one Aboriginal member and one person of colour make direct representations to the NEB. These two representatives would be elected by the Caucuses and therefore be accountable to them. This example also illustrates structural rigidity—the maintenance and preservation of traditional structural arrangements[8]—at the cost of diversity in representation. Special bodies and advisory committees will be set rather than change the basic structure to accommodate anti-racist aspirations.

Magon recalls that a great deal of negotiation and behind-the-scenes work had to be accomplished to achieve the unity needed to present a proposal to the NEB on behalf of the Racial Minority and Aboriginal Caucuses. Members from Ontario are resented for being "leaders" in the anti-racism field because of having the largest proportion of people of colour and for being the only province which has a Caucus of its own for people of colour and for Aboriginal peoples. Some were unclear whether the Caucus members from Ontario were representing the province or anti-racist issues. Eventually, it was recognized that all the Caucus members had the same objective and that there was a need to "put our differences aside.... They started to see the colonization in our own caucus" (Magon, December 19, 1995).

Bev Johnson, now the Human Rights Officer of OPSEU, recalls that she was hired in 1990 to activate and monitor local human rights initiatives. A Race Relations and Minority Rights Committee of from ten to twelve people representing regions, sectors and equity-seeking groups was involved, as well as an advisory body for the OPSEU president, a person of colour, to develop policy in these areas. Conferences were organized across the province with regard to fighting discrimination in the workplace. Non-union people had been brought in as speakers. One outcome was the establishment of seven regional human rights committees, some of which subsequently organized local conferences. However, Johnson says that many members wanted to see an elected committee at the workplace rather than the non-elected Race Relations and Minority Rights Committee. She suggests that this was another subtle way to undermine anti-racist work in the union.

The particular struggles of women of colour is generally recognized by unionists. They said:

> We talked about women of colour. They face two barriers, being women and their race—more at a disadvantage—more of a challenge. They have to deal with White men

---

[8]
Henry, et al., *Colour of Democracy*, p.292.

and men of colour struggling against racism. Women of colour were very militant and outspoken.... (Spratt, August 25,1995).

Needed facilitators for the [anti-racism] courses—hand-picked eighteen instructors across country—all people of colour and aboriginal members—always maintained gender balance—very little women of colour involvement in unions.... (Magon, August 22, 1995).

The general resistance to furthering employment equity within unions is documented in Ng's study, particularly at provincial and local levels. She talks about her apparent disqualification from a Labour Studies Coordinator's position because of having "the least seniority" (Ng, 1995:59), even though she had worked there previously for ten years. She was further informed that, had it been an equity position, she would have been hired. There is some evidence to suggest that most people of colour among union staff are segregated into equity-related positions. Such tokenistic gestures also indicate reluctance to open up these organizations to a more balanced representation. Johnson says: "[People of colour] are not in the meat and potatoes of the union... same thing with grievances... not too many staff reps of colour in all unions...." (Oct. 17, 1996).

Ng (1995) discusses the resistance that people of colour face in their role as instructors. This issue was discussed with particular reference to English in the Workplace (EWP) instructors in Toronto and Ng's personal experience with recruiting people of colour in these positions. She describes the resistance that came not only from White workers but also from some workers of colour who had internalized a stereotype of a "good English teacher" as someone who is White and one who has "no accent."

Henry et al. (1995) also refer to the treatment of people of colour who are "change agents" as particular examples of subtle resistance. The negative labeling faced by them is not faced by their White counterparts. Ng (1995) highlights the pressures of co-optation on people of colour who gain leadership positions within unions. Isolation, threats of being excluded and general alienation from White members are subtle ways in which members of colour are made ineffective in leadership. Johnson of OPSEU shared that people of colour in executive positions are often not provided with adequate resources and become ineffective and unaccountable to the membership in the long run. She observes that "optics are good, but it doesn't work. On paper we're progressing. In actual fact, you get removed, you can't go to the Convention or are taken off a committee" (Oct. 17, 1996).

Yvonne Bobb, an activist from OPSEU, talks in a similar vein about her personal experience as a Black woman advocating for equity and social justice. She notes that "it still remains an uphill struggle." She lost an election because she advocated for employment equity. She was labelled as a "racist" for advocating on behalf of people of colour. She felt that a bitter campaign was carried out against her because of her speaking out against racism (Sept. 12, 1995), and was

unable to get support from many so-called progressive people. She feels dissatis-
fied with her experience in the union and feels that there is systemic racism in it.

Tackling Harassment in the Workplace

Interviewees reported that many collective agreements contain anti-harassment and anti-discrimination clauses. A landmark victory for CUPE was the case
of Local 1 at Ontario Hydro where a Workplace Harassment Policy was developed that includes women, people of colour, people with disabilities, First Nations and gays and lesbians. According to the Policy, employees have the right to
"leave work without loss of pay in an atmosphere of harassment." Some CUPE
divisions have also adopted anti-harassment policies.

It is now USW policy to negotiate the union's anti-harassment provisions into
collective agreements. However, unionists also maintain that a great deal of
education and awareness-raising needs to be done among employers as well as
within unions to develop the willingness, skills and knowledge to combat harassment. When incidents of harassment happen, often the local executive members
are not equipped to deal with them since training is still mostly voluntary:

> When I was involved in local, I had a racist incident happen to me. I pointed out to local
> executive that it was racist. They were not equipped to deal with it.... We negotiated in
> training around sexual and racial harassment.... There was resistance to training and
> problem of availability of people.... (Henry, August 2, 1995).

> Your rep doesn't have a clue about racism. They [the harassed member] go to June
> [Veacock], she gets lots of calls. Some try but are not adequately equipped to deal with
> these issues. Sometimes when people really wake up to the issue, the issue is a real
> mess, it costs more to the victim.... (Johnson, Oct. 17, 1996).

It appears that training to implement anti-harassment policies within workplaces
and in unions is inadequate. This weakens their effectiveness. In light of this
shortcoming, union commitment to fighting harassment has to be questioned.
Inadequate training has been cited as another example of subtle resistance to
anti-racism by Henry et al. (1995), since it makes policy and program objectives
unachievable.

Dealing with Racism of White Workers

Some educational strategies used by anti-racist unionists to deal with worker
racism can be instructive to all educators and practitioners. The following are
some experiences:

> ... want to hear them and want to talk to them. Sometimes takes 2-3 hours.... Give them
> stats, root it in economics, reality for designated groups. In the process of doing work
> force surveys, we can see that women and people of colour are increasing, but still are
> dominated by White males.... (Spratt, August 25, 1995).

> I was in this little town called_____. Then the discussion start talking about unemploy-
> ment and immigration and immigrants take away jobs and one guy got up and says
> "What's the unemployment rate in Toronto?" I can't remember the figure—10 or 11
> percent. And the guy says "And do you know the unemployment rate up here?" And at

that time it was 16 or 17 percent. "Do we have any person of colour here? Why is it higher? So do immigrants take away jobs?" All of a sudden, the lights went on, you know.... (Baksh, August 11, 1995).

The involvement of designated group members as instructors also helps to reach White worker participants. The sharing of the former's personal experiences of discrimination were very effective in consciousness raising. However, such a process is controversial. Many people of colour say that the objectification of their own oppression and suffering for the benefit of White peoples' education is both objectionable and unacceptable.

On the objection to the racial representation in the "Breaking the Barriers" poster, Harminder Magon, CUPE Anti-Racism Coordinator, replies that "the faces reflected on the poster are the ones who are often marginalized, prejudiced.... Our poster shows the faces of people who have been excluded because of institutionalized racism, power imbalance.... Media has both a responsibility and, indeed, an obligation to project an accurate image of our demographic make-up. Instead it mostly reflects the stereotypes...." (March 20, 1995). In other words, progressive organizations have to take a proactive stand to challenge hegemonic ideologies rather than simply mirror them.

CUPE has piloted courses on "Combating Workplace Racism" and "Cross Cultural Awareness" led by its Anti-Racism Coordinator and its Education Department, and has trained rank-and-file members from diverse backgrounds to deliver them. There has also been a review process to identify biases in all its educational materials.

Partially funded by the now-defunct Ontario Anti-Racism Secretariat, in 1991 the USW launched a consultative process in Ontario with the assistance of members of the now-defunct DMI, a social justice organization that did educational consultation based in Toronto. The objective was to develop an anti-racist educational module and train eighteen activist workplace facilitators. Three modules were developed, ranging from one to three hours in length. The challenge was to convince employers to approve of holding these educational sessions in the workplace and to assign paid time to them. After two years, about 35,000 USW members attended these sessions across the province. These sessions were also open to management staff. As a consequence of these sessions, the union was able to assist employers to develop anti-harassment policies, educate employers about the USW's anti-harassment policy and establish joint committees to deal with workplace harassment. Baksh (1995) reports that in some companies, newly hired employees would be trained in anti-racism through these union-organized sessions. According to Baksh, some of the company management recognized the benefits of the training, albeit from their own particular point of view. Baksh says, "It's an initial cost for them to pay for those employees to be there to participate... but they saw it on a long-term basis, that it's better for them, it's

more productive, it increases productivity, efficiency and it avoids problems...."
(August 11, 1995).

Management's perspective on training seems to contradict a political economy approach, which would view racism as being beneficial for employers by keeping the work force divided and by depressing wages. While this view still has validity, capitalists today face many new contradictions due to worker resistance as well as changed labour processes. In many workplaces, Fordism and scientific management have been replaced by worker teams and Quality of Work Life (QWL) strategies to enhance productivity. Animosities among workers on the basis of ascribed features may militate against such approaches. Thus, racism in the workplace may contribute to greater costs to management through lost productivity, low morale and motivation and conflicts between workers. Given this perspective, anti-racist educationals may in fact contribute to a team-building exercise for management.

From a union perspective, however, the main point of the educational sessions is to combat racism and hence strengthen the bargaining unit against management. The support of anti-racist educationals by management and unions alike may be motivated by different reasons emanating from their conflicting class interest and in fact may represent a contested terrain. Perhaps in recognition of this fundamental conflict, Yusuf of CAW offers a word of caution on joint union-management educational programs: "Negotiate time for human rights education in the workplace provided union has control over curriculum. If there is 'joint ownership' with employers, the end result will be different—'class analysis' is missing" (August 24, 1995).

Seniority: A Thorny Issue

As far as employment equity is concerned, unions and outside communities have sometimes clashed on the issue of seniority. Spratt of CAW said, "It was very painful. Seniority is a barrier. [Community groups were saying] people should be promoted irrespective of seniority. For trade unions, this is a difficult thing to accept.... It helped to separate the groups. We were told that we are trying to maintain the status quo—trying to put trade unionism before feminism...." (August 25, 1995).

Employment equity has sometimes been used as a tool to divide workers in the workplace and to undermine the union. Barb Thomas, formerly with DMI, said that she recently did some work with a Toronto organization where management had been taking leadership on anti-racism issues. The union and the management came together for the first time in a workshop. A power struggle emerged over racism. The unionists looked extremely racist. Thomas suggests that the dichotomies of racist/pro-union and anti-racist/anti-union needs to be critically examined (October 19, 1995).

Reaction to Harris Government

Disappointment and frustration were expressed when asked about the impact of the Conservative government in Ontario. One said, "I wish we had more time.... Depressing to know that Tories are in. We could have trained every workplace in Ontario. I am angry with the Harris government...." (Spratt, August 25, 1995).

Interviewees were committed to continuing their work on employment equity despite government opposition. Their strategy will consist of negotiating employment equity principles into the collective agreement which is something that many have done over many years. For example, the CAW had negotiated such a clause with the Big Three auto companies prior to the passing of the Employment Equity Act in Ontario. Interviewees said:

> About 20% of companies want to continue with the joint training sessions.... Have to continue with education around equity. We have to negotiate language to push employers (Spratt, August 25,1995)

> We'll bargain it into contracts—want to continue discussion with employers. Set a few targets, spend some time and money and use it as a model (Baksh, August 11, 1995).

A news release (July 27, 1995) from CUPE said that the Metro Toronto Separate School Board, Barrie Public Library, Community Living Algoma, Ontario Hydro and most universities want to continue their negotiations around employment equity plans.

The Ontario Public Service Network for Racial Minorities, which is made up of people of colour, both in OPSEU and in management, is continuing to function despite being de-funded by the Conservative government. According to its chairperson, Yvonne Bobb, the Network is reviewing its position regarding advocacy under the current government. She is optimistic and feels that the time has come to be outspoken about racism.

Conclusion

Three years have gone by since we interviewed the activists whose voices are reflected here. Details of people and programs within unions may have changed; however, the anti-racist challenges highlighted here still remain.

Interviews with union activists reveal that their work around employment equity and anti-racism is fraught with contradictions. All spoke about public support of human rights and anti-racism by union leadership, strong statements against racial harassment and sophisticated efforts to conduct a variety of anti-racist educational programs. The ability of organized labour to reach thousands of workers in a relatively short period of time through their organizational channels is empowering and gives hope that it will "really have some impact." At the same time, some talked about the systemic obstacles, lack of representation of people of colour in leadership positions, personal harassment and burnout. Some unionists of colour remain pessimistic about achieving employment equity within their unions. The election of a Conservative government in Ontario has been a major setback to their work, increasing job losses, harassment and injuries. The anti-equity rhetoric of the government has promoted a general environment where open expressions of racism and other forms of discrimination have once again become an everyday reality. Yet, interviewees remain committed to their anti-racism work, if not for themselves, then for their children.

As mentioned at the beginning of the chapter, racism is a multidimensional and complex phenomenon that makes it truly difficult to counteract. There seems to be less of an understanding of how racism specifically disempowers people of colour and how White members are privileged just because of having "white skin." Such an understanding is not captured by the statement "Racism Hurts Everyone." It does hurt everyone in the long run, but it also privileges White people daily. People of colour within and outside the labour movement have historically had to organize autonomously using their own community base rather than relying on "mainstream," predominantly White institutions and movements. The formation of the Ontario Coalition of Black Trade Unionists on November 15, 1996 is an example of that. This was the first Canadian chapter of the American-based Coalition of Black Trade Unionists (CBTU). The CBTU was established twenty-five years ago and there are over forty chapters in the United States.

REFERENCES

Calliste, Agnes. 1987. "Sleeping car porters in Canada: An ethnically submerged split labour market." *Canadian Ethnic Studies* XIX(1).

Canadian Auto Workers (CAW). "Article 36: Installation Ceremony."

Canadian Union of Public Employees, Local 4900. Newsletter, Volume II, Edition 9, Summer Issue, June 30, 1995.

Creese, Gillian. 1991. "Organizing against racism in the workplace: Chinese workers in Vancouver before the Second World War." In Ormond McKague, ed. *Racism in Canada*. Saskatoon: Fifth House Publishers.

CUPE News Release. "Union and employers still committed to employment equity," July 27, 1995.

Henry, Frances, Carol Tator, Winston Mattis and Tim Rees. 1995. *The Colour of Democracy: Racism in Canadian Society*. Toronto: Harcourt Brace.

Hill, Dan. 1977. *Human Rights in Canada: A Focus on Racism*. Canadian Labour Congress.

Leah, Ronnie. 1991. "Linking the struggles: Racism, sexism and the union movement." In Jesse Vorst et al., eds. *Race, Class, Gender: Bonds and Barriers*. Toronto: Garamond.

_____. 1993. "Black women speak out: Racism and unions." In Linda Briskin and Patricia McDermott, eds. *Women Challenging Unions*. Toronto: University of Toronto Press.

Ng, Winnie Wun Wun. 1995. *In the Margins: Challenging Racism in the Labour Movement*. University of Toronto, Master's Thesis.

Ontario Coalition of Black Trade Unionists (OCBTU). Newsletter, 1987-88.

Ontario Federation of Labour (OFL). 1994. *Racism and Discrimination: Trade Union Guide to Carrying Out Joint Responsibility under the Employment Equity Act, 1993 and its Regulations*.

United Steelworkers Harassment Policy.

Ward, Peter. 1978. *White Canada Forever: Popular Attitudes and Public Policy Towards Orientals in British Columbia*. Montreal: McGill Queen's Press.

15

Race and Racism: Strategies of Resistance

Anton Allahar

Throughout history, when faced with the seemingly most inescapable situations of inequality and domination, human beings have proven to be remarkably innovative. Whether dealing with such diverse phenomena as slavery, concentration camps, prisons or even abject poverty, the spirit of creativity and resilience has enabled humans to offer numerous forms of resistance to their social entrapment. This paper focuses on one example of such entrapment, racism, and examines three strategies of resistance that have been employed to deal with it in the Canadian context. My basic contention, however, is that most social conflicts based on race, ethnicity and nationalism are more fruitfully understood as rooted in class or politico-economic pursuits. This is not to deny that non-class identities are real to those who hold them, but rather to suggest that such identities are to be situated in a broader context of differential economic and political power.

"Race" Is Real?

Given the growing ethnic plurality of modern societies, and the fact that ethno-racial identity markers are still widely adhered to in virtually all the advanced industrial nations, social theorists must begin to revise their ideas around class. Such theorists must now take into account those who increasingly understand their social and economic situations as ethnically or racially conditioned, and whose political actions are informed by such understandings. Examples may be seen in the 1992 Los Angeles race riots in the United States, ethnic cleansing in Bosnia, Serbia and Croatia, the bloody battles between the Hutus and Tutsis in Rwanda, Burundi and Zaire, Kurdish genocide in Iraq, Arab-Jewish atrocities in the Middle East, the Basque struggles in Spain and the ongoing disputes between the French and the English which threaten to divide Canada. In addition, we might also mention the related disputes surrounding the ever-present claims to nationhood being registered by Aboriginal populations in countries such as Australia, Canada and the United States.

The persistence of conflicts based on race and ethnic (primordial) identities today is seen in large measure (though not entirely) to follow from the inherent contradictions of three related sources. First, there is the large-scale international migration of peoples from more traditional cultures and societies to the so-called more developed societies, where culture is highly secularized, and where the values of liberalism, individualism and achievement have been constitutionally enshrined.

The second source of conflict relates to the fact that constitutions *formally* embrace the ideas of social justice and equality, which implies that social, economic and political opportunities are free and open to all individual citizens. But in actuality, because those notions of freedom, equality and justice are ideological, and because ethnic and racial privilege abound in those societies, competition, confrontation and resistance are likely to result (Nagel and Olzak 1982; Nagel 1984).

A third source of conflict concerns the international post-Cold War conjuncture, which began with the breaking down of the Berlin Wall and the dismantling of the Soviet Union, where "there were about 130 officially recognized nationalities" (Williams 1994:50). The removal of travel restrictions and the ensuing flood of refugees from the former socialist bloc to the West has been accompanied by widespread ethno-national conflicts. Thus, in a world which sees "ethnic groups as emerging transnational actors" (Stack 1981:17-45), ethno-racial identities are adding new dimensions to the older, pre-existing conflicts that are now so rife around the globe. In the process, class considerations appear increasingly to have been relegated to a secondary position in explaining such conflicts. But this is not without consequence, for while race might be experienced as *real* by any number of social actors, when dealing with capitalist societies one must remember that capital has no race, ethnicity, colour, nationality or gender. This does not mean, however, that the ideologies of race, ethnicity, nationalism and gender will not be manipulated by capital to enhance the rate of exploitation of labour.

Race, Ethnicity, and Resistance: Operational Definitions

Before providing operational definitions of some key terms that are used in this study, it is important to note that those who might offer resistance to racism do not necessarily have a critical understanding of the phenomenon, nor have they necessarily developed an alternative vision of the society in question. Thus, their resistance must not automatically be presumed to be carefully tailored to address or eliminate the practice of racism. For in the minds of social actors there is not likely to be broad agreement on the many sources, consequences and remedies of racism.

If we begin with *race,* the first step is to separate biological from social definitions. In biological terms, race refers to the categorization of the human population on the basis of certain hereditary characteristics such as blood type, genetic makeup, and phenotype or physical appearance. Since a person from one genetic group can inter-breed with a person from another, such categorizations, and their combinations, offer infinite possibilities, which might be biologically interesting. Where problems arise, though, is with those socio-biologists who seek to argue that biological differences can explain social differences or social inequalities (Herrnstein and Murray 1994; Rushton 1995).

The non-biological conception of race, on the other hand, stresses the idea of social construction, and argues that although the term has no biological utility, it continues to serve political and economic interests because most people believe it to be real (Allahar 1993:52; Miles 1981:71). Thus, the politics of race begins where the biological and social conceptions of it intersect. As long as there are those who want to justify social practices by resorting to biological claims, disagreement and conflict will be commonplace. In other words, when jobs, housing, education, marriage partners and other social amenities are distributed along racial (biological) lines, human beings will never agree. Those who are denied or disenfranchised will always find ways of resisting.

In this context, those who insist that races are real will usually have a political agenda according to which social contrivances such as poverty, intelligence, powerlessness or even class privilege are cast as *natural*, thus seeking to remove responsibility for them entirely from the realm of social interaction. But as Steven Rose asks in relation to the easy invoking of "human nature" to explain away social disadvantage, "What is this mysterious, looming abstraction which seemingly lies at the core of any piece of human conduct, any type of social relation?" (1979:278). The answer is clear: it is an attempt to legitimize a socially produced situation of fundamental disadvantage by giving to it the veneer of a natural, biological, inflexible fact.

Racism occurs when racial categorizations are informed by negative meanings and when those meanings relegate people to subordinate positions in a system of hierarchical social rankings. For along with its ideological message, racism is the practice of including and excluding individuals and groups from participating fully in the social economy on the basis of imputed racial similarities or differences, and their denial of access to certain services and resources on these same bases. Through labelling, some are consigned to supposedly inferior races, thereby raising the questions of power and legitimacy: Some are able to label others and have those labels stick, which is an intrinsic aspect of racism.

If races or racial groups are supposed to speak to the biological aspects of human populations, *ethnic groups* speak to the socio-cultural composition of those populations. Depending on the social climate in which they exist, ethnic groups in multiethnic societies will face differing degrees of pressure to assimilate or conform to the dominant culture. In those cases where they resemble the

dominant group culturally, that pressure is not likely to be perceived or interpreted negatively; conversely, in those cases where ethnic groups have less in
common with the dominant group(s) or culture, pressure to assimilate is likely to
be resisted. Since groups, ethnic or otherwise, have a tendency towards self-pres-
ervation, in instances where such pressure appears to threaten the survival of the
group, one can expect that the resistance will be even greater.

Resistance in this context is defined as any action, whether physical, verbal or
psychological, and whether individual or collective, that seeks to undo the negative consequences of being categorized for racial reasons. Thus, unlike those
approaches which seek to portray the victims of racial and other types of oppression as unwitting pawns and passive recipients of the dominant ideology and
practice, this paper will seek to understand some ways in which the concept of
race can be used or manipulated to resist or mollify the deleterious consequences
of racism. Resistance will be seen as a political act intimately tied to the wider
cultural forces that frame it.

Strategies of Resistance

In the remainder of this chapter, I identify and discuss three different strategies of resistance that tend to be reformist and conservative. They are not revolutionary in that they do not see the problem of racism as rooted in the economic
practices of capitalism (Bonacich, 1980). As a consequence, each presumes that
racism can be eliminated without a fundamental alteration of the social and
economic institutions of capitalist society. Nevertheless, in the minds of those
associated with each of the strategies identified, their resistance is meaningful
and yields important psychological gains to them.

The first of these strategies, which is not usually thought of as resistance, can
be termed multiculturalism. As a means of resistance, multiculturalism involves a
strategic retreat, whereby instead of seeking acceptance and integration into the
majority group, the members of a given minority group will reject the dominant
group's culture and value system in favour of a retreat into their *original* culture
and value system. This strategy, which is known in the sociological literature as
accommodation, concerns the creation of imagined communities and primordial
attachments to them, and pursues the development of separate or culturally parallel institutions such as small businesses, schools, churches and community centres. Recognizing the existence of racism in the society at large, and their
inability to do anything immediately or in the short-run to change it, supporters
of multiculturalism are caught in something of a bind. In a country such as
Canada, for example, economic opportunities are likely greater than in their
native countries and what they are in effect saying is: (1) they like their cultures
of origin, (2) they want, in some measure and to the extent that it is possible, to
retain them in their new land, and (3) they want peaceful co-existence with the

dominant, host culture. Where it works, however, multiculturalism is a very effective form of resistance to racism.

If multiculturalism and accommodation serve to characterize one strategy for resisting racism, a second identifiable strategy is known as *assimilation*. The politics of assimilation speaks to the acceptance by the minority ethnic group of the culture and values of the dominant group and the attempt to "pass" into the latter. This strategy is no less ideological than accommodation, although it may be characterized as the path of least resistance. It does, however, fit the above definition and is resistance nonetheless. In contemporary Canadian society assimilation is best exemplified by those members of minority groups who reject multicultural policies, whether they result from the demands of other organized minority groups, or from those in authority who see such policies as a means of paying what they call official lip service to equality among the diverse, competing ethnic segments of the society.

When it deals with minority ethnic groups that are visibly different from an entrenched, racist majority, assimilation amounts to a form of naïveté or denial, which, albeit fated to be ineffective, is an attempt at the personal and subjective levels to soften (resist) the harshness of racism.

Unlike the calculated strategies of accommodation and assimilation, which involve either a strategic retreat or active self-deception, the third approach to understanding resistance to racism is the most commonly thought-of strategy of resistance: violent, physical engagement of the (racist) aggressor. The violence, however, is not always clearly planned and coordinated; nor does it always have a clearly articulated vision of an alternative social order. Indeed, it is often a spontaneous form of violence that sparks other pockets of resistance and develops into a situation that the authorities are unable to contain or control. In the de-colonization of Algeria, Fanon described this as the period "when the niggers beat each other up, and the police and magistrates do not know which way to turn when faced with the astonishing waves of crime" (1963:52).

The three approaches have two features in common: (1) they address the question of resistance to racism, albeit in different forms, and (2) none advances an understanding of racism as a systemic feature of capitalist society. Thus, though descriptively interesting, none of them seeks theoretically to link racism with the dominant class and economic structures of exploitation under capitalism. As a consequence they tend to be ideologically conservative and reformist by assuming that racism can be defeated without drastically changing the system (capitalism) which nurtures it.

Multiculturalism as Strategic Retreat

Since "Canada invented multiculturalism as a national policy in 1971" (Hawkins, 1991:217), most Canadians are at least superficially familiar with the term. Indeed, as the 1992 *Canadian Ethnic Studies Bulletin* reports, "77% [of a sample of Canadians] believe multiculturalism will enrich Canada's culture," while "73% agree that multiculturalism will ensure that people from various cultural backgrounds will have a sense of belonging to Canada [and will] provide greater equality of opportunity for all groups" (1992:3). A survey done in 1977 showed that 61 percent of Canadians agreed that "Canada may not be perfect but the Canadian Way has brought us about as close as human beings can get to a perfect society" (Driedger, 1989:328).

This notwithstanding, the above-mentioned *Canadian Ethnic Studies Bulletin* also reports that among Canadians "66% think that discrimination against non-Whites is a problem" and on the whole: "Canadians feel less comfortable with people whose origins are Indo-Pakistani, Sikh, West Indian Blacks, Arabs, Moslems than they do with persons of other origins" (1992:3). It is not common, however, for Canadians to see multiculturalism as a strategy for resisting racism, since the nation as a whole could be said to be in denial about the existence of racism, preferring to point fingers south of the border to the United States for examples of this scourge. Indeed, on the question of tolerance for racial and ethno-cultural diversity nationally and internationally, Canadians tend to have a rosy understanding of themselves as enlightened, progressive and non-racist. And the political embrace of multicultural policies is seen as evidence of such tolerance and understanding.

In recent years, Canada has become a racially and ethno-culturally diverse country. However, this diversity has not been entirely welcome by traditional (Anglo-European) communities and interests, particularly those who see multiculturalism as synonymous with equality. For a variety of reasons having to do with identity and security (including occupational, residential, racial and ethno-cultural), traditional groups in society feel threatened and react defensively, using the various means at their disposal (economic, political, legal, socio-cultural) to resist the new "intrusions," especially those whose physical appearances and ways of life differ most from theirs. Facing political pressures and demands from the greater urban and industrial centres, such as Toronto, Montreal, Vancouver and Edmonton, where new immigrants have tended to settle in largest numbers, and recognizing the vital economic contributions that immigrants make to the entire society and economy, governments in the 1960s began to draft and implement multicultural policies and programs across the country.

These, nevertheless, have not exactly been enthusiastically greeted by those who are privileged and who see in multiculturalism a threat to their traditional, unquestioned "right" to dominate. But this is understandable in a society with Anglo-European traditions and where institutions of dominance are in place. After all, this is a society where reserves were created to contain the Aboriginal population, where, at the time of the First World War, some 8,000 Ukrainian-Canadians were labelled "enemy aliens" and interned without due process in twenty-four camps across Canada (Malarek, 1987:11) and where, in 1914, Canadian authorities prevented the landing of a freighter with four hundred would-be Indian immigrants on board (Fleras and Elliott, 1992:56). This is also the same country in which Italian and German citizens and residents, and over 22,000 Japanese-Canadians, were placed in prison camps during the Second World War. During the late 1920s, Canada's official immigration policy made a clear distinction between "preferred" and "non-preferred" immigrants and countries from which immigrants were welcome (Corbett, 1957:52-54; Hawkins, 1991:27; Malarek, 1987:11). As late as 1947 a prime minister (William Lyon Mackenzie King) was unequivocal, racist and patronizing in his ruling out of Asians and Orientals as acceptable immigrants:

> It was clearly recognized with regard to immigration from India to Canada, that the native of India is not a person suited to this country, that, accustomed as many of them are to the conditions of a tropical climate, and possessing manners and customs so unlike those of our own people, their inability to readily adapt themselves to surroundings entirely different could not do other than entail an amount of privation and suffering which render a discontinuance of such immigration more desirable in the interests of the Indians themselves (quoted in Hawkins, 1991:18).

And,

> The people of Canada do not wish to make a fundamental alteration in the character of their population through mass immigration. The government is therefore opposed to large scale immigration from the Orient, which would certainly give rise to social and economic problems.... (quoted in Hawkins, 1972:93).

Recognizing the fact of ethnic diversity in Canada, various levels of government have opted to develop and implement policies of multiculturalism with a view to minimizing the potential for ethnic conflict. These policies were designed to address the potentially serious political fall-out for a society, economy and labour force that has been historically fractured along racial and ethnic lines. Public participation in such culturally diverse and colourful spectacles as Caribana, Panorama and Caravan create a climate (if not an illusion) of political acceptance that, in the minds of minority ethnic individuals, symbolizes a way of combatting the cultural alienation, exclusion and even rejection that they face in wider social interactions outside of their communities. Such public celebrations and festivals empower them, if only momentarily, and foster a sense of pride in their cultural traditions that they are eager to impress upon other Canadians.

But multiculturalism is not consumed by minority groups alone. In the calculations of politicians, the celebration of multicultural and ethnic diversity serves as an effective mechanism of social control. Multiculturalism does seek to promote a sense of tolerance and understanding among all Canadians, but along with the superficial pomp and celebratory aspects of multicultural policies and programs, there are other gains—they distract citizens from the entrenched inequalities in the wider society; they are great for business (tourism, commercial retailers, hotels, restaurants, the transportation industry and so on); and they confirm for most Canadians the idea that Canada is an open and accepting mosaic of all peoples and cultures regardless of colour, creed or national origin. Ethnic diversity is portrayed as highly compatible with national unity, and political speeches, which always make reference to the rich fabric of Canadian society, can be counted on to depict that fabric in terms of an intricate ethno-cultural tapestry.

As a means of resisting racism, then, multiculturalism has a triple function for the minority individual and community: (1) it enhances their self-esteem and cultivates a favourable predisposition to the society and its institutions; (2) through exposure it promotes greater understanding of difference in the minds of others, thus reducing tension and the possibility of conflict; and (3) it holds out the promise of equality to members of ethnic minorities both new and old.

For most immigrants of colour and members of ethnic minority groups, it is clear that Canada's central social, political and economic institutions are dominated by "White" people, particularly those of Anglo-Saxon, western European and Jewish descent (Reitz, 1990; Reza Nakhaie, 1995; Driedger, 1996). In superficial, colour terms, then, power resides in "White" hands and this fact is not lost on the members of ethnic minority groups. Thus, even in those cases where multiculturalism only pays lip service to socio-cultural equality, the powerless are eager to embrace it, for they see in it a means of resisting the more subtle forms of systemic racism that have traditionally excluded them from full participation in society. To them the "White" power structure is formidable and any (even minor) concessions to equality it grants are to be taken very seriously. As a modern, Western, liberal society caught up in the age of political correctness, therefore, Canada publicly and officially holds out to all its citizens the promise of equality; those who have been traditionally less equal take the promise to heart.

A key difficulty with multiculturalism and its strategy of accommodation, though, is that it leaves intact the traditional structures and institutions of domination that have been in place in this country while seeking to encourage the building of other parallel structures and institutions that are unable to compete on an equal footing with the traditional ones. It thus gives ideological legitimacy to the latter by creating an atmosphere of equality while serving simultaneously to distract potential political criticism of the wider system. Thus, immigrant and other minorities proudly proclaim their roots and delight in the possibility of retaining them while simultaneously professing loyalty to Canada: "Ethnic minorities possess the option of secondary identification with a preferred cultural tradition so long as this does not interfere with core institutional values, the laws of the land, or the rights of individuals" (Fleras and Elliott, 1992:57). Viewed in this light, multiculturalism offers the best of both worlds to ethnic minority communities and immigrants whose physical and cultural attributes differ significantly from the dominant, ethno-cultural norm. And when made into law, multicultural policies are very effective tools for resisting racism. Politically, however, proponents of such policies are essentially reformists and see the overall socio-political system, particularly as it deals with ethnic and racial minorities, as basically legitimate, though in need of some minor tinkering or adjusting.

Assimilation as Resistance

If the accommodation that is pursued by multiculturalism represents one form of resisting racism, then the promise held out by the notion of assimilation can surely be considered as another. It stands to reason that newcomers to a society and culture will desire as smooth a process of adaptation and inclusion as possible. And where there is prejudice and discrimination against such adaptation and inclusion, the newcomers can be expected to offer different forms and degrees of resistance. They will seek to minimize them by "melting" or blending into the dominant institutions as quickly as possible. This implies a process of becoming "invisible" to the prejudiced members of the host society who would seek to discriminate against them; and where it works, assimilation is an effective form of resistance to racism. The questions, then, are how, where, and for whom does it work?

According to the classic formulations of Robert E. Park (1950) and Milton Gordon (1964), the various stages leading to assimilation are not inevitable. For a variety of reasons a specific group may voluntarily or involuntarily remain at a given stage. The principal stages identified by Park and Gordon speak largely to groups that are not phenotypically different from the mainstream. Thus, there is cultural assimilation (acculturation), which sees the subordinate group gradually taking on the cultural traits (language, music, food, eating habits, politics and so on) of the dominant group. Next is structural assimilation, which speaks to the increased participation of members of the new minority group in the *secondary* economic and political institutions of the dominant group: recreational sites, public transport, retail shopping, political gatherings and places of work. Finally, as admission into *primary* group relations (friendship and intimacy) becomes regularized, inter-marriage or biological assimilation (amalgamation) results. In successive generations, as cultural differences evaporate and a new ethno-racial phenotype emerges as the norm, old patterns and practices of racism become anachronistic.

Accompanying these three macro-structural processes of assimilation is a fourth, micro-interactive process known as psychological assimilation. This speaks mainly to first-generation immigrants, particularly those who are phenotypically different from the majority. Acknowledging their powerlessness to combat the forces of prejudice and discrimination in the new society, and unable to do much by way of changing their physical appearance, members of visible minority groups resort to a psychological form of resistance premised on self-deception. With psychological assimilation

> members of an ethnic group undergo a change in self-identity. To the extent that individuals feel themselves part of the larger society rather than an ethnic group, they are psychologically assimilated. As psychological assimilation proceeds, people tend to identify themselves decreasingly in ethnic terms (Marger, 1994:120).

Psychological assimilation focuses on the individual and differs depending on the parties to be assimilated and the norms to which they are seeking assimilation. To the extent that culture, national origin and race are seen as connected, assimilation to a racist or xenophobic society will be far more difficult for those who are visibly different. In other words, the option of using assimilation as a strategy to resist racism will be more problematic for the latter. In Canada, for example, where "White," Anglo-Saxon phenotypes and Judeo-Christian beliefs and practices are dominant, those immigrants who most closely approximate this norm, even if they are not English-speaking, will understandably have less difficulty assimilating by the second or third generation. For assimilation is both a matter of degree and a process of "melting" or disappearing into the dominant social institutions and cultural and value systems. As subsequent generations acquire the language and accent of the dominant society, German, Italian, Polish, Ukranian and Greek immigrants are *free to choose* to leave their ethnic roots behind.

On the other hand, where colour and other related phenotypical features are associated with culture and national origin, for example, among East Indians, Orientals, and Africans, the challenge of assimilation is much greater. They are *not as free to choose* assimilation as a means for resisting racism. As we know, Black people have been in Canada and the United States for hundreds of years; longer in fact than many other immigrant groups that have since melted into the fabric of these societies and lost their hyphenated identities.

> Canada is not a pluralist heaven where diversity is celebrated and minorities integrated as full and equal participants. By the same token, American life does not conform to its cliché, either. Reality, it seems, lies somewhere in between these visionary—and *illusory*—ideals (Fleras and Elliott, 1992:66; my emphasis).

Illusion, then, is a key aspect of psychological assimilation when it comes to dealing with visibly different minorities; but that illusion is nonetheless real in the minds of those seeking acceptance and assimilation. However, regardless of how much an individual may convince him- or herself that he or she is an unidentifiable part of the larger society, that he or she is not "an ethnic," the final decision to admit lies with the wider society.

> Prejudice on the part of a dominant group may prevent the granting of full membership in a society to members of minority groups, even though the latter think of themselves only in terms of the larger society (Yinger, 1981:253).

A clear example of this in the Canadian context can be garnered from an examination of Neil Bissoondath's (1994) *Selling Illusions: The Cult of Multiculturalism in Canada*, in which the author, an Indo-Trinidadian, goes to great lengths to deny his ethnic heritage, acknowledges that he is ashamed of it, despises it and desires nothing more than to be accepted as "a Canadian." Bissoondath writes that, "after half a lifetime away from the island [Trinidad], I have no emotional attachment left, and my interest in its events is no different from my interest in events in China or Russia or Botswana" (*Ibid.*:25). Home for Bissoondath is Canada:

> When I feel myself in need of comfort, security, familiarity, it is this country [Canada]— its air, its sounds, its smells, the textures of its light—that I long for. It is here, everywhere, that I find the comforts of home (*Ibid.*).

The major obstacle to his full acceptance is multiculturalism, which, together with its advocacy of quota systems and equity policies in occupational, educational and other spheres, he finds personally embarrassing:

> I can think of few things more demeaning to me than to be offered an advantage because of my skin colour.... No matter what I have struggled to achieve.... I am still, even with the best of intentions, being viewed racially—and that is offensive to me (*Ibid.*:95).

Clearly the problem here is that Bissoondath confuses equity and fairness with unfairness. He is adamant that "a multicultural society can ill afford the use of past discrimination as justification for future recrimination" (*Ibid.*:186-87), preferring instead to see the world from the individual point of view with no regard for the fact that some people may face social-structural impediments to "success." Because he made it, all others should be able to do the same; and those who do not have only themselves to blame! What he refuses to acknowledge, however, is the fact that quota systems and equity programs are not meant to reward incompetence or "to hire people of visible minorities who have no talent, but to control the mainstream's tendency to exclude members of visible minorities regardless of their talent" (Davetian, 1994:136).

In ideological terms, therefore, Bissoondath's is a limited and distorted understanding of multiculturalism according to which he is cast as a hapless victim in need of hand-outs. Thus construed, multiculturalism draws undue attention to his clear differences and causes him constantly to have to apologize for those things of which he is ashamed:

> Multiculturalism ... has heightened our differences rather than diminished them; it has preached tolerance rather than encouraging acceptance; and it is leading us into a divisiveness so entrenched that we face a future of multiple solitudes with no central notion to bind us (Bissoondath, 1994:192).

Bissoondath's solution to the problem is to abolish multiculturalism in favour of the self-deception of being considered assimilated. Thus, "Don't call me ethnic!" was the apt headline that appeared in the October 1994 issue of *Saturday Night*, which featured pre-publication excerpts of his book. Though generally ignored by intellectuals, the book has been popularly received in non-academic circles by politicians, media commentators and other lay observers who wish to deny that theirs is a racist society and who are grateful whenever a "person of colour" (Bissoondath's self-description, 1994:5) joins the chorus of voices denouncing those who would seek to label Canada in that way.

To situate Bissoondath's response to multiculturalism, it is useful to see him as one who is seeking psychological assimilation, which is evidenced by his emphasis on the individual, non-structural aspects of the assimilative process. His frustration, however, comes from the fact that psychological assimilation is a two-way process whereby (1) one identifies with the new society and (2) the latter is accepting. As a "person of colour" in a racist society, though, he may just be fooling himself into thinking that the wider society sees beyond his ethno-racial features and their imputed meanings and accepts him for who he is. But as Marger correctly points out, "Visibility is, of course, critical here. Those with salient marks of ethnic identity—skin colour in particular—are unable to fully achieve out group recognition as 'nonethnics'" (Marger, 1994:121).

Bissoondath's passionate desire to become accepted by the "White" mainstream is premised upon a denial of the racism in the society at large, and points to the way in which assimilation might be used by some to mollify or resist the deleterious consequences of that racism. Thus, he seeks to dismiss racism in Canada as a thing of the past: "Nasty things happened years ago in Canada. But that is a Canada that no longer exists. The world is no longer what it was" (1977:166). Exactly what the Canada of today is, however, and how it came about, is never specified.

It may be said, then, that Bissoondath is correct to talk about "selling illusions," but what he needs to acknowledge is that in his economic market place he is both seller and buyer. Thus, in the very last paragraph of his book he reveals his unrealistic yearning for "[a] nation of cultural hybrids, where every individual is unique, every individual distinct. And every individual is Canadian, undiluted and undivided" (1994:224).

Clearly, there are those for whom assimilation can serve effectively to counter or resist racism in later generations, but there are also those for whom this strategy is likely to be inefficacious; it is not a practical option. Politically speaking, if the strategy of multicultural accommodation is said to be ideologically reformist, assimilation must be seen as ideologically conservative. Indeed, Bissoondath says it best when he notes that "revolutionary change is illusory.... True and lasting change, then, cannot be imposed; it must come slowly, growing with experience, from within" (1994:187).

Resistance through Violence: The Colonial Context

> Leave this Europe where they are never done talking of Man, yet murder men everywhere they find them, at the corner of every one of their own streets, in all the corners of the globe (Fanon, 1963:311).

Mobilization against injustice, actual or perceived, can assume many forms that are more or less confrontational. It can range all the way from symbolic gestures proclaiming that "Black is Beautiful," to participation in peaceful protests or demonstrations such as the "Million Man March," to civil disobedience and legal public challenges or to covert terrorism and armed engagement of the oppressor. The actual form taken will depend on the specific situation at hand, the resources available to the oppressed and the means at the disposal of the oppressor to retaliate. This section addresses that which is most commonly thought of as resistance, whether to racism or any other institutional form of oppression: direct confrontation leading to the use of violence.

Nowhere is the injustice leading to violence more evident than in a colonial system on the eve of collapse. When in full force, however, the forms of resistance to the racism of colonialism are more subtle. In the case of the New World, resistance involved slaves engaging in what Gordon Lewis termed "covert protest," and a whole range of behaviours short of escape and rebellion: "everything from feigned ignorance, malingering, sabotage, slowed-down work habits, suicide, and poisoning of masters, on to the endless invention of attitudes that reflected a general war of psychological tensions and stresses between both sides in the master-slave relationship" (Lewis, 1983:175). Realizing the futility of attacking the system in a head-on manner, most slaves devised coping mechanisms to survive on a daily basis:

> They lied; they played dumb; they deliberately, yet defiantly, slowed their movements and thus reduced their work output. They perfected circumlocution as a fine art.... They developed repression of their feelings and "playing it cool" as defence mechanisms against the system.... The slave also learned to release his frustration and misery into humour and laughter—often at himself, sometimes at his fellow slaves. For him laughter became a safety valve (Hiro, 1991:22).

But we know that colonialism did not come to an end with the abolition of slavery; nor did the racism and violence it inspired. As perhaps the most complete form of institutional racism, colonial domination produces a sense of rage in the colonial subject that explodes when the colonial masters are about to exit the colony. This is poignantly captured in Franz Fanon's *The Wretched of the Earth* and Albert Memmi's *The Colonizer and the Colonized*, which deal with the case of Algeria and the struggles of the Algerian people to free themselves from French colonial tutelage. But as Jean-Paul Sartre (1965:xxv) has noted, rather than viewing colonialism as a "situation," it is better understood as a "system"; thus, useful generalizations can be made from the Algerian case when seeking to describe other cases where de-colonization had to come to terms with racism and violence.

It should be emphasized from the outset, however, that the racism which embraced "the loathsome idea derived from Western culture that the black man is impervious to logic and the sciences" (Sartre, 1965:162) was not the goal of colonialism. Rather, it was one of the methods of domination employed by the colonizer to give ideological legitimacy to the system. Racism was also premised upon the imputed subhuman qualities and features of the colonial subject: "Racism is ingrained in actions, institutions, and in the nature of the colonialist methods of production and exchange. Since the native is subhuman, the Declaration of Human Rights does not apply to him.... (Sartre 1965:xxiv). Therefore, whether the African slave, the Indian indentured servant, the Chinese "coolie," or the captured indigenous inhabitant of the colony, the colonial subject was seen as "the other," and was invested with all the negative attributes that represented the opposite of the colonizer: sexual immorality, savagery, Godlessness and evil. As Fanon writes, "The native is declared insensitive to ethics; he represents not only the absence of values, but also the negation of values. He is, let us dare to admit, the enemy of values and in this sense he is the absolute evil" (1963:41).

For Fanon, de-colonization is of necessity a violent process. Its point of departure is the violence visited on the colonial subject by the colonizer. In the early phase of the struggle for freedom, as the rage builds, the colonized is unable to lash out against the oppressor and directs his anger at his fellows. As the struggle builds, however, when the colonized native "finds out that the settler's skin is not of any more value than a native's skin.... This discovery shakes the world in a very necessary manner" (1963:45). This is when the violent resistance of the colonized begins to strike fear in the hearts of the colonizer. The former come to realize that their freedom is impossible so long as colonialism and racism remain intact. Thus, Sartre minces no words when he sums up the native's options: "In the first days of the revolt you must kill: to shoot down a European is to kill two birds with one stone, to destroy an oppressor and the man he oppresses at the same time: there remain a dead man and a free man" (1963:22).

In Fanon's assessment, colonialism and violence are synonymous. No process built on the forceful removal of tens of millions of people from their homelands, their enslavement and compulsion to perform forced labour without pay and their denial of human and civil rights can seriously pretend to be anti-violent. No process that is premised on invasion, plunder and theft of previously inhabited countries that were supposedly "discovered" by Europeans, that perpetrated the virtual extermination of their indigenous inhabitants and claimed it was being done in the name of God and civilization can legitimately expect that the victims will acquiesce forever. Resistance was as certain as the lash of the master's whip. For in the process of colonial expansion, when savage nobles met noble savages, the latter were initially made to know their place. But as the internal contradictions of colonial capitalism mounted, as the resentment of the colonized grew and the forces of de-colonization began to take shape, no one could realistically expect the process to be non-violent.

For colonialism is fascism, and like colonialism, fascism is violence. As Memmi tells us, "there is no doubt in the minds of those who have lived through it that colonialism is one variety of fascism" (1965:62-63). "It is violence in its natural state," Fanon writes, "and will only yield when confronted with greater violence" (1963:61). Thus, as the violence of colonialization confronts the counter-violence of de-colonization, few are left unscarred. In the minds of the former colonized, the resistance symbolized by their counter-violence is frenzied and energizing: "At the level of individuals, violence is a cleansing force. It frees the native from his inferiority complex and from his despair and inaction; it makes him fearless and restores his self-respect" (Fanon, 1963:94).

In this context we can cite the struggles for ethno-cultural autonomy among the French Canadians, particularly those of Québec, who claim to be colonized by English Canada and who are determined to break free of their colonial shackles. To this end, in the early 1970s the country was plunged into a state of emergency as wanton violence erupted on the streets of Montreal, bombs exploded in public places, the Québec labour minister (Pierre LaPorte) was murdered and a British diplomat (James Cross) was kidnapped and held for several days. The *Front de Libération du Québec* (FLQ) took responsibility for the violence and issued a Manifesto outlining the philosophy of the movement, its major goals and demands. But what is interesting is that, while the FLQ called for an end to Anglo-Saxon capitalism, it did not call for the abolition of capitalism *per se*; nor did it mention anything about socialism. It is as though the authors of the Manifesto were thinking in ethno-linguistic terms and supposing that somehow French-speaking capitalists would be kinder to French-speaking workers than English-speaking capitalists. The reformist content is unmistakable as could be gathered from the actual text of the Manifesto.[1]

Conclusion

It was stated in the introduction that the central aims of this chapter were to examine a number of different strategies of resistance to racism that have been essayed by minorities in Canada, and to reaffirm the underlying importance of class in all conflicts that have to do with race and ethnicity. As far as the first is concerned, I made the case for seeing the social processes of accommodation, assimilation and violence as strategies of resistance. And while the first two are not commonly viewed as resistance, my contention is that, from the point of view of the powerless, they are indeed. In the minds of some minority individuals and groups, multicultural policies are to be pursued precisely because they afford

---

[1] See Appendix to this chapter.

those minorities some legal and practical space for manoeuvre in an otherwise hostile environment. They promise accommodation, and to have such policies in place is to have defences against discrimination. It is therefore not unreasonable to see why minority communities and organizations would be ardent supporters of multiculturalism and the idea of "separate but equal."

Assimilation, on the other hand, might also be viewed as a defence against discrimination. Indeed, there are many minority individuals and groups who would prefer this strategy for combatting discrimination. But while the solution offered by multiculturalism is more short term, assimilation is a longer-term process. Nevertheless it argues that the best defence is a good offence; if you can't beat them, join them! Thus, instead of developing separate or parallel institutions as the multicultural policy of hyphenated identities suggests, the objective of assimilation is to have everyone attend integrated schools and live in integrated neighbourhoods, to encourage the development of generic political parties that address issues of mutual concern to all citizens and to promote nationalist and/or provincial allegiances over ties of loyalty to ones' countries of origin.

In time, such practices will lead to both biological and cultural assimilation. Like multiculturalism, therefore, it is not difficult to see why some minority individuals and groups might prefer to embrace assimilation. And while some degree of assimilation will automatically take place with the passage of time, it is possible to hasten the process by consciously and deliberately pursuing policies that do not single out minorities for undue attention, but enable them instead to blend in with the majority. And although it is not conventionally thought of in this way, the politics of assimilation that are aimed at the de-segregation of schools, workplaces, neighbourhoods, recreational organizations and so on, as well as those who lobby for such things as employment and pay equity, are easily equated with the politics of resistance.

Finally, I discussed the question of violence as the most commonly considered strategy of resistance to almost any situation of inequality or domination. Here the general case of colonial peoples was highlighted and explicit reference was made to those Québécois who claim that French Canada is an internal colony of English Canada and who, as a result, see themselves as suffering the same fate suffered by colonized people elsewhere. Arguing that colonialism is, among other things, a system of institutionalized racism which provokes violence, attention was drawn to the early 1970s in Québec and the violence-inspired FLQ movement that sought to resist the violence of colonialism and the racism on which it is built.

In each of the three forms of resistance discussed, I suggested that strategies of resistance are not necessarily or automatically radical and revolutionary. Indeed, the above cases were depicted as conservative and reformist in that they did not go to the root of the problem and link it to the political interests and economic structures that are served by racism and discrimination. And this is where the second aim of the present paper is addressed: the class aspects of ethno-racial domination.

In the debate over the role of race versus class, and which of these is more salient in informing political consciousness and opposition in capitalist society, the lines of demarcation are clearly drawn. On the one hand, there are those such as Robert Miles who refuse to give legitimacy to the concept of race by even treating it as a meaningful category. And on this basis he criticises those who "have, perversely, prolonged the life of an idea that should be explicitly and consistently confined to the dustbin of analytically useless terms" (Miles, 1989:72). Miles, therefore, favours a stricter class approach to analyzing social inequality under capitalism, and is thus in agreement with Peter Li, who argues that all other forms of inequality are basically derived from class: "This is the way race and ethnicity should be understood under the capitalist system" (Li, 1988:48).

But this is only one part of the debate. On the other hand, Paul Gilroy feels that "'race' must be retained as an analytic category not because it corresponds to any biological or epistemological absolutes, but because it refers investigation to the power that collective identities acquire by means of their roots in tradition" (Gilroy 1987:247). In other words, even if primordial membership in a race is a purely imaginary phenomenon, even if race consciousness is false consciousness, and even if races are social constructs and not biological realities, so long as people in power continue to treat them as real, they will have real consequences for all involved (Allahar, 1993; 1994).

It seems, then, that the most fruitful approach to the intellectual stand-off is to recall the words of C.L.R. James (quoted in Gilroy, 1987:15), who is committed to the class position, but in dealing with capitalism and imperialism cautions us as follows:

> The race question is subsidiary to the class question in politics, and to think of imperialism in terms of race is disastrous. But to neglect the racial factor as merely incidental is an error only less grave than to make it fundamental.

Theoretically speaking, then, class is fundamental to the critical understanding of resistance against social inequality under capitalism; but unlike the orthodox Marxist position which holds that race consciousness is merely epiphenomenal or a matter of "false consciousness," neo-Marxists correctly leave the door open to the possibility that the class struggle can be advanced by embracing the race struggle (or even the gender struggle) at strategic moments.

The point is summed up by Gilroy when he says that "racism does not, of course, move tidily and unchanged through time and history. It assumes new forms and articulates new antagonisms in different situations" (1987:11). This is a call for empirical research to inform theoretical insight, for different forms of oppression demand different strategies of resistance. But under capitalism, and especially in those cases where oppression is perceived as being based on race and racism, we must be mindful that "the interiorization of 'race' within the class struggle" (Wolpe, 1986:111) offers a broader, and hence possibly more viable, base for resistance. There are, however, no automatic or mechanical guarantees, for we are dealing here with a question of process. Thus, resistance, whether spontaneous or planned, is a two-way street; and each oppositional act of resistance can expect to produce or provoke counter-resistance by the establishment.

> Apparent breakthroughs often turn out to be momentary and fleeting, victories somewhat hollow, concessions gestural and reforms less consequential than they at first appear, with advance subsequently turning into retreat (Ben-Tovim et al., 1986:146).

Clearly, then, the strategy is not to surrender to the forces of racism in Canada or elsewhere, but to prepare oneself better for the challenges of resistance. And this implies more study of, and research into, the various available strategies (retreatist, reformist, violence, class revolution) that correspond to the empirical conditions at hand, and the efficacy of each. One must not be deluded into thinking that a mere tinkering with surface manifestations of such a deep-rooted social problem will rid society of racism.

APPENDIX: The FLQ Manifesto

The *Front de Libération du Québec* is not the Messiah nor a modern day Robin Hood. It is a group of Quebec workers who are committed to do everything they can for the people of Quebec to take their destiny into their own hands.

The *Front de Libération du Québec* wants the total independence of the Quebeckers brought together in a free society, purged forever of its band of voracious sharks, the big bosses who dish out patronage and their servants, who have made Québec into their private preserve of "cheap labour" and of unscrupulous exploitation .... what is called democracy in Québec is and always has been nothing but the victory of the election riggers .... Consequently we wash our hands of the British parliamentary system; the *Front de Libération du Québec* will never let itself be distracted by the electoral crumbs that the Anglo-Saxon capitalists toss into the Québec barnyard every four years. Many Quebeckers have realized the truth and are ready to take action .... We have had our fill of taxes which Ottawa's man in Québec wants to hand out to the English-speaking bosses to give them "incentive" to speak French, to negotiate in French. Repeat after me: "Cheap labour is main d'oeuvre a bon marché."

Working people in the factories, in mines and in the forests; working people in the service industries, teachers, students and unemployed: Take what belongs to you, your labour, your determination and your freedom. And you, the workers at General Electric, you make the factories run; you alone are capable of producing, without you, General Electric is nothing!

Working people of Québec, begin today to take back what belongs to you; take yourselves what is yours. You alone know your factories, your machines, your hotels, your universities, your unions, do not wait for a miracle organization.

Make your revolution yourselves in your neighbourhoods, in your workplaces .... You alone are capable of building a free society.

We are Québec workers and we will go to the end ... we want, with all the people, to replace this slave society with a free society, functioning of itself and for itself, a society open to the world.

Our struggle can only be victorious. Not for long can one hold in misery and scorn, a people once awakened.

Long live Free Québec!

Long live our comrades the political prisoners! Long live the Québec Revolution!

Long live the *Front de Libération du Québec*!

REFERENCES

Allahar, Anton L. 1993. "When black first became worth less." *International Journal of Comparative Sociology* XXXIV (1-2):39-55.

_____. 1994. "More than an oxymoron: The social construction of primordial attachment," *Canadian Ethnic Studies* XXVI (3):18-33.

Ben-Tovim, Gideon, John Gabriel, Ian Law and Kathleen Stredder. 1986. "A political analysis of local struggles for racial equality." In John Rex and David Mason, eds. *Theories of Race and Ethnic Relations*. Cambridge: Cambridge University Press.

Bissoondath, Neil. 1994. *Selling Illusions: The Cult of Multiculturalism in Canada*. Toronto: Penguin Books.

Bonacich, Edna. 1980. "Class approaches to ethnicity and race." *Insurgent Sociologist* 10(2):9-23.

Canadian Ethnic Studies Association Bulletin. 1992. Vol. X1X, No.2.

Corbett, David C. 1957. *Canada's Immigration Policy: A Critique*. Toronto: University of Toronto Press.

Davetian, Benet. 1994. "Out of the melting pot and into the fire." *Canadian Ethnic Studies* XXVI(3):135-140.

Driedger, Leo. 1989. *The Ethnic Factor: Identity in Diversity*. Toronto: McGraw-Hill Ryerson.

_____. 1996. *Multi-Ethnic Canada: Identities and Inequalities*. Toronto: Oxford University Press.

Fanon, Frantz. 1963. *The Wretched of the Earth*. New York: Grove Press Inc.

Fleras, Augie and Jean Leonard Elliott. 1992. *Multiculturalism in Canada: the Challenge of Diversity*. Scarborough, Ontario: Nelson.

Gilroy, Paul. 1987. *There Ain't no Black in the Union Jack: The Cultural Politics of Race and Nation*. London: Hutchinson.

Gordon, Milton. 1964. *Assimilation in American Life: The Role of Race, Religion and National Origins*. New York: Oxford University Press.

Hawkins, Freda. 1972. *Canada and Immigration: Public Policy and Public Concern*. Montreal: McGill-Queen's University press.

_____. 1991. *Critical Years in Immigration: Canada and Australia Compared*, 2nd Edition. Montreal: McGill-Queen's University Press.

Herrnstein, Richard and Charles A. Murray. 1994. *The Bell Curve: Intelligence and the Class Structure in American Life*. New York: The Free Press.

Hiro, Dilip. 1991. *Black British White British: A History of Race Relations in Britain*. London: Grafton Books.

Lewis, Gordon K. 1983. *Main Currents in Caribbean Thought*. Baltimore: The Johns Hopkins University Press.

Li, Peter. 1988. *Ethnic Inequality in a Class Society*. Toronto: Thompson Educational.

Malarek, Victor. 1987. *Haven's Gate: Canada's Immigration Fiasco*. Toronto: Macmillan of Canada.

Marger, Martin. 1994. *Race and Ethnic Relations: American and Global Perspectives*, 3rd Edition. Belmont, California: Wadsworth Publishing.

Memmi, Albert. 1965. *The Colonizer and the Colonized*. Boston: Beacon Press.

Miles, Robert. 1989. *Racism*. London: Routledge.

Nagel, Joane. 1984. "The ethnic revolution: The emergence of ethnic nationalism in modern states." *Sociology and Social Research* 68(4):417-434.

_____ and Susan Olzak. 1982. "Ethnic mobilization in new and old states: An extension of the competition model." *Social Problems* 30(2):127-143.

Park, Robert E. 1950. *Race and Culture*. Glencoe, Ill.: Free Press.

Reitz, Jeffrey G. 1990. "Ethnic concentrations in labour markets and their implications for ethnic inequality." In Raymond Breton et al. *Ethnic Identity and Equality: Varieties of Experience in a Canadian City*, pp.146-195. Toronto: University of Toronto Press.

Reza Nakhaie, M. 1995. "Ownership and management position of Canadian ethnic groups in 1973 and 1989." *Canadian Journal of Sociology* 20(2):167-192.

Rose, Steven. 1979. "It's only human nature: The sociobiologist's fairyland." *Race and Class* XX(3):277-87.

Rushton, J. Philippe. 1995. *Race, Evolution and Behaviour: A Lifehistory Perspective*. New Brunswick, N.J.: Transaction Publishers.

Sartre, Jean-Paul. 1963. "Preface" to *The Wretched of the Earth* (Franz Fanon). New York: Grove Press Inc.

_____. 1965. "Introduction" to *The Colonizer and the Colonized* (Albert Memmi). Boston: Beacon Press.

Stack, John F. Jr. 1981. "Ethnic groups as emerging transnational actors." In John F. Stack Jr., ed. *Ethnic Identities in a Transnational World*, pp.17-45. Westport, Connecticut: Greenwood Press.

Williams, Robin M. Jr. 1994. "The sociology of ethnic conflicts: Comparative international perspectives." *Annual Review of Sociology* 20:49-79.

Wolpe, Harold. 1986. "Class concepts, class struggle and racism." In John Rex and David Mason, eds. *Theories of Race and Ethnic Relations*. Cambridge: Cambridge University Press.

Yinger, J. Milton. 1981. "Toward a theory of assimilation and dissimilation." *Ethnic and Racial Studies* 4:249-64.